HISTORIC CYPRUS

"Cyprus . . . a land famous in all ages. The rosy realm of Venus, the romantic kingdom of the Crusaders."

LORD BEACONSFIELD

Historic Cyprus

A GUIDE TO ITS TOWNS & VILLAGES
MONASTERIES & CASTLES

Rupert Gunnis

The **Orage** Press

First published in 1936

This edition published 2014 by the Orage Press
16A Heaton Road
Mitcham
Surrey
CR4 2BU
England

ISBN: 978-09544523-9-1

The **Orage** Press

PREFACE

THIS volume has taken three years to write—most pleasant years, which have enabled me to know even better the Cypriots, both Greek and Turk, without whose help this book could never have been written; for I have made, as far as I am aware, the first and only complete survey of every village and monastery, church or mosque in Cyprus. And this task could never have been accomplished if it had not been for the willing help and assistance of the Cypriote peasant, who would frequently go miles out of his way to guide me to some ancient building; and the occasions were few and far between when my time was wasted; indeed, I can only recall one such occasion, in the Paphos district, when an enthusiastic shepherd dragged me several miles to see "ancient writing in curious letters", which turned out to be not so much an inscription in the Cypriote syllabary as a flat stone covered with scratches from a plough passing over it.

It is possible with truth to say of Cyprus, as the author of *Les Iles Méditerranéenes* once wrote: "Cyprus, a little world in itself . . . no wild beasts or reptiles disturb the solitude. The water is sweet and cool, the wine is nectar, and the food plain but good; above all, I know that my grave will be respected and that kind hands will close my eyes."

I shall feel myself more than sufficiently rewarded if this book induces any who may read it to visit the most *gemütlich* and yet one of the most unknown of all the Colonies of England. This Cinderella of Empire has a richer and more varied history, and more of interest and beauty than many of the larger and better known Dependencies of our Empire.

It would be superfluous to enumerate the long list of books and authors I have consulted, but I must especially mention Professor R. M. Dawkins, who has allowed me to make such generous use of his edition and translation of the *Chronicle of Makhairas*. I have also quoted largely from *Excerpta Cypria*, by the late C. D. Cobham, the most valuable contribution yet made to the history of Cyprus, and to a less extent from *The Church of Cyprus* by the Rev. John Hackett, and *The Historic Monuments of Cyprus* by G. Jeffery, who dedicated the greater part of his life to the antiquities of Cyprus.

To Professor David Talbot-Rice and Mr. B. J. O'Brien I owe an especial debt for their kindness in reading the proofs throughout; and I must record my indebtedness to them both for their criticism and their valuable suggestions and corrections.

It was from Sir Ronald Storrs and Sir George Hill that I derived my first impulse to write this book. I must mention Mr. W. H. Buckler, to whom I am in debt for help with the churches of Asinou and Galata. Also Mr. Stanley Casson, of New College, Oxford, and Miss Joan du Plat Taylor for help with the chapter on the Palace of Vouni.

I should like to take this opportunity of thanking Lieutenant-Colonel A. E. Gallagher, late Chief Commandant of the Police, and Mr. W. C. C. King, the present Chief of Police, and all other ranks of that force who have helped in innumerable ways, by giving me shelter in village police stations, guiding me to deserted and forgotten churches, bringing ladders so that I could climb some wall to read a worn inscription, and on more occasions than one assisting in its translation.

Nor must I forget those members of my own household especially my chauffeur Yanni, who accompanied me to practically every village, helped me to clean icons, found the keys of churches, which were only too frequently in the pockets of a villager working in some field far distant from the church; also Alexis and Salahi, who collected village legends, walked with me, sometimes twenty miles a day, to isolated villages and deserted chapels, and assisted in endless other ways to smooth my path during those years in which I visited the 670 villages and 1,800 churches and chapels of Cyprus.

I am much indebted to Mr. Godwin Austin, Mr. Mace, and Mr. Sergides of the Land Registration Office in Nicosia for preparing the plans of the towns used in the book. Also to the British Museum and Professor Gjerstad for the plans of Kouklia and Vouni respectively. Finally, to Mr. Mangoian, of Nicosia, for most of the illustrations.

In conclusion, I would wish to warn any reader into whose hands this book may fall that it is intended first and last as a guide-book, to be read in small doses and not in a single draught; and to that same reader I would apologize for the inconsistencies, of which I am only too well aware, in the spelling of place- and other names. There are more ways than one of transliterating Greek words into English characters, and I am conscious of not always having employed the same way. I have, however, aimed at spelling the names of places in my text in the same way as they are spelt in the map at the end of the book.

GRID REFERENCE MAP OF CYPRUS

Based on Rupert Gunnis's 1947 'Sketch Map of Cyprus'

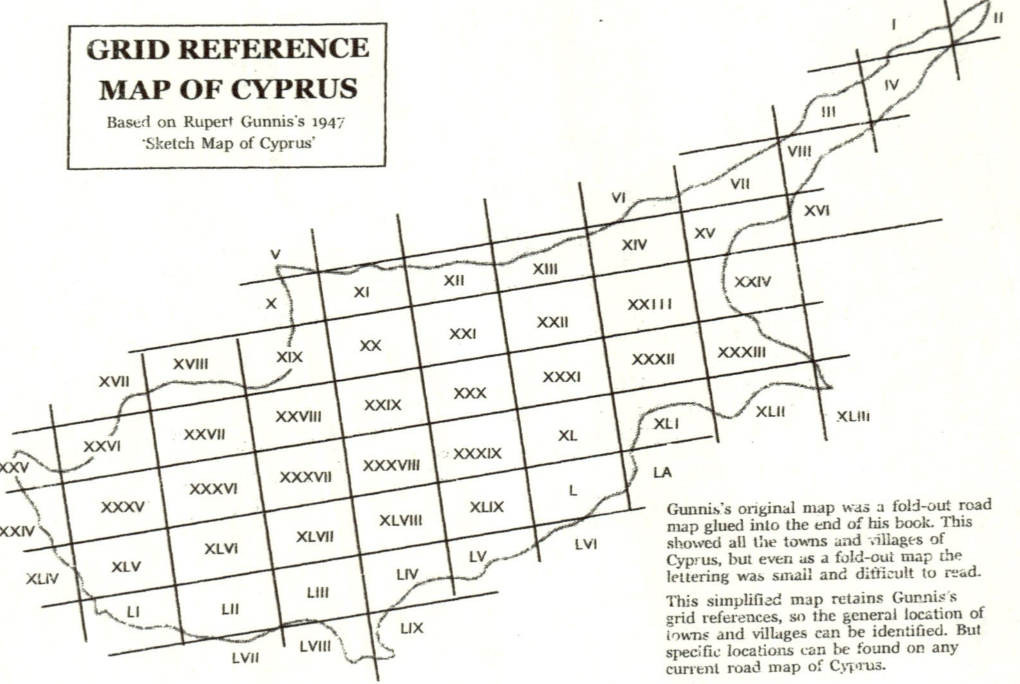

Gunnis's original map was a fold-out road map glued into the end of his book. This showed all the towns and villages of Cyprus, but even as a fold-out map the lettering was small and difficult to read.

This simplified map retains Gunnis's grid references, so the general location of towns and villages can be identified. But specific locations can be found on any current road map of Cyprus.

CONTENTS

HISTORIC CYPRUS

ICONS AND THE GREEK CHURCH

THE place occupied by the icon in the art of the Orthodox Church is far more important from a religious point of view than that of the religious picture in the West, for it is wellnigh impossible to conceive of an Eastern church without its icons, whereas a Western one would but be denuded of its ornament were all pictures or paintings removed from it. In very early times there were but a few icons in each church, and these depicted either the Christ, the Virgin and Child, or certain particular and more important saints. But later the choice of the saints shown on icons became much wider, and by the fourteenth century it became customary not only to depict scenes as well as figures, but also to increase considerably the number of icons in each church. At first the scenes were restricted to either the ten or the twelve major "feasts" or events of the New Testament, the Annunciation, the Nativity, the Presentation in the Temple, the Baptism, the Transfiguration, the Raising of Lazarus, the Entry into Jerusalem, the Crucifixion, the Resurrection (Descent into Limbo), the Ascension, Pentecost, and the Assumption of the Virgin. But as time went on other scenes, certain apocryphal events, or numerous local and often obscure saints were added to the repertory, so that by the sixteenth century the number of figures and subjects was enormous. In all larger and more central places also the erection of an elaborate wooden screen or iconostasis, taking the place of the Western rood-screen between the sanctuary and the main body of the church, had become usual. This was entirely covered with icons, arranged in tiers of different heights one above the other. Icons were in addition treasured in every house. Some of the figures and scenes on these were universal over the whole Orthodox world; others were peculiar to special regions. Thus icons with views of particular monasteries, which were so common in

Russia in the sixteenth and seventeenth centuries, were practically unknown elsewhere, while such figures as local Bishops or heroes were depicted on icons of their own town or region only; St. Mammas, for instance, is hardly ever seen outside Cyprus (Plate faces).

The study of icons from the artistic and stylistic point of view is still very much in its infancy, and it is really only in Russia that much serious work has been done in this sphere. As regards the early periods it is not only made especially difficult owing to the natural scarcity of material —a few small panels from the Monastery of St. Catherine on Mount Sinai, some of which are now preserved at Kiev, are the most important—but also owing to the fact that practically nothing has come down to us of the work which can definitely be assigned to Constantinople, the capital and main artistic centre of the world from the fourth to the thirteenth century. Even at a rather later date Constantinopolitan work is very scarce, and as Mr. Berenson has said, we are wellnigh in the position that we would be in had we to study the paintings of the French Impressionists without having available any of the works produced in Paris by the leaders of the movement. One work, however, which is certainly to be assigned to Constantinople and which belongs to the eleventh century, has survived, namely, the icon known as our Lady of Vladimir, in the Tretiakov Gallery at Moscow. It is universally recognized as one of the world's finest religious pictures.

From the thirteenth and following centuries there are a few more works that can be assigned to Constantinople, most of which are preserved in the Hermitage at Leningrad and the Museum of Fine Art or the Tretiakov Gallery at Moscow, though a particularly fine example in the Benaki Museum at Athens, a Transfiguration, may be noted, while in the Byzantine Museum in the same town there are a number of icons from Salonica which are in the fine, polished, and wholly excellent manner of the capital. It would seem that after the twelfth century or thereabouts quite a considerable amount of material was exported from Constantinople, that in the thirteenth century Constantinopolitan painters migrated and worked elsewhere, mainly as a result of the Latin occupation of the city in 1204, and that in the fourteenth century provincial painters were in the habit of going to the capital and studying there. In any case, icons of the thirteenth and fourteenth centuries preserved in various distant parts of the Orthodox world show the fully polished manner of the capital, and among these not the least important is a tall panel in the Church of the Chrysolaniotissa at Nicosia, dated in 1356, and bearing Christ the Pantocrator, the Archangels Gabriel and Michael, two lay figures, and the portrait of a Princess. A fine Ascension in Ayios Cassianos at Nicosia also shows the manner of Constantinople, though it is to be attributed to a Cypriote painter.

With the fourteenth and fifteenth centuries a number of local schools grew up in various parts of the Orthodox world, the most important of which outside Russia was that known as the Cretan. Among the most characteristic schools of the sixteenth century are those of Cyprus, where a main stem, with various subgroups, is to be distinguished. To study the subdivisions in detail is beyond our purpose here; suffice it to say that a very great number of its products are icons of an *ex-voto* character, and that we see included in them the kneeling figures of lay "donors". Such donors are seldom met with on icons of the rest of the Orthodox world; they belong to a Western conception, and find their way to Cyprus mainly as the result of Latin influence, which was exercised all through the Lusignan period. Other icons are more truly Byzantine in that these figures are absent, and alongside them we see also a number of panels which are essentially to be regarded as the result of Western influence, and which are closely akin to certain duogento paintings of Italy.

As a result of this Latin influence Cyprus presents an extremely interesting complex as regards the development of its art, and a great deal of important material is preserved there. The value of this is enhanced by the fact that a large number of the icons are dated by inscriptions, and in the rather chaotic state of our knowledge such concrete factors are of more than local importance, for they serve as guides in a study of material outside the island. In an art wherein the importance of what may be termed "the handed down model" was extreme, and where a surprising conservatism reigned, such guides are especially useful, since it is usually almost impossible to determine at all exactly the date of an icon on stylistic or iconographical grounds alone.

The great conservatism is one of the features that is most striking about icons, and to those of us brought up in the Western tradition they are apt at first to appear monotonous, if not actually incompetent and unpleasing. After the fifteenth century, it is true, a great deal of uninspired hack-work was produced, but before that date many of the panels are outstanding, and even after it quite a few of them are fit to take their place in any museum or gallery. Their sameness is purely superficial, and the picture-lover, who is persevering enough to look into them seriously, will, in the long run, not be disappointed.[1]

[1] For a study of icon-painting as a whole, see Wulff and Alpatov, *Denkmäler der Ikonenmalerei*, Leipzig, 1925. Russian icons can be studied in the West in the excellent works of Kondakov, *The Russian Icon*, translated and edited by E. H. Minns, or in Muratov's *Icone Russe*. A monograph on the *Icons of Cyprus*, edited by D. Talbot Rice, will be published in the series *Courtauld Institute Publications on Near Eastern Art* in the near future.

I

HISTORY OF CYPRUS

1. INTRODUCTORY

The singular interest of the history of Cyprus is primarily due to its geographical position. There is no country whose fortunes have been more varied, or which has reflected more faithfully the ebb and flow of races. It has been the meeting-place of Aryan and Semite, of West and East, of Egypt and Asia, of Christian and Moslem. Possessed in turn by great monarchies of the East, by Greeks, Arabs, Crusaders, Turks, and Christians, it has been in the forefront of every racial and religious struggle until, finally, after a transitional period, during which it was occupied by a Christian Power of the West, while paying tribute, as in the earliest times, to an Eastern master, it has been numbered amongst the possessions of the British Crown.

2. THE NEOLITHIC (STONE) AGE

Of the Paleolithic period in Cyprus, or the earliest traces of man, nothing is known.

The earliest settlements so far found belong to the Neolithic (or new Stone) Age. They are numerous on the south and north coast, usually being situated near a spring. Only two have been found on the plain, near Kythrea.

The huts were round with loose stone foundations and earth floors; the upper parts of wattle and mud. As each hut collapsed or was destroyed, another was built upon its ruins, resulting in some cases in as many as nine layers superimposed one upon another.

Within the huts were open hearths, and near them have been found the remains of cooking vessels of carefully made and painted pottery. Stone and flint weapons, steatite ornaments and idols were scattered about the floors, with the remains of animal bones and stags' antlers.

Burials were found in one or two places, sometimes within, sometimes just outside the huts: the skeletons were placed in a contracted position, in narrow pits. Nothing was buried with them.

The civilization of these people appears to be a fairly advanced one; they were a sturdy race, rather short in stature, who occupied the island before *c.* 3000 B.C.. Their connections with the Bronze Age people are not yet evident, and their settlements are not found in close proximity.

The pottery, exhibited in the Cyprus Museum, is of good quality, and of a type not found in the neighbouring countries. The settlements were first discovered in 1933, and much yet remains to be done in tracing the origin of these people and their cultural relations.

3. THE BRONZE AGE

With the succeeding Bronze Age, however, the light of knowledge begins to dawn. This Age, which began some time before 3000 B.C. and ended about 1000 B.C., is here of peculiar importance, since Cyprus was herself one of the chief early sources of the metal. Whatever may have been the origin of her own name—a disputed point—there is no doubt whatever that she gave it to the metal which we know as copper, and that her mines were worked from very early times, as they still are. The sources of our information are to be found in the discoveries made by modern scientific excavation. It is impossible to compute the losses to knowledge incurred, in times before the British Occupation, through the hasty and unscientific methods of the past. Earlier excavators have, in fact, often been no better than tomb-robbers; and it is not too much to say that a site dug at haphazard is a site lost to science. The unscientific excavator is rewarded by a greater or lesser haul of objects, but can give no clear account of the exact place and order in which they were found. Yet upon this depends their true value as datable evidence of the past, since among the most interesting finds are naturally those of objects imported from abroad, which can be dated in the light of facts already established elsewhere.

Various settlement sites and a considerable number of tombs belonging to this period have been identified and explored. They provide clear evidence of a large population with an art and culture distinct from those of Egypt, Syria, and the neighbouring mainland of Cilicia. We are able to distinguish three stages in the culture of this Age:

(i) *The Early Bronze Age*, in which tools and weapons contain only 2–3 per cent of tin, and are therefore of copper rather than true bronze. The types found are common to those of neighbouring countries; and we may observe two characteristics notable throughout the whole course of Cypriote art, namely, a certain lack of originality and a slowness both in accepting and also in discarding foreign innovations—an insular people, in fact. The pottery of this period is rough hand-made stuff, and ornamented with simple patterns.

(ii) *The Middle Bronze Age* (2500–2000 B.C.), in which implements are made of copper hardened to true bronze, and foreign imports occur with increasing frequency, e.g. blue glazed beads from Egypt and cylindrical Asiatic seals. To this period, or later, may be assigned the Biblical references to the Kittim or Chittim, a name preserved to us in that of the town of Citium (modern Larnaca).

(iii) *The Late Bronze Age* (2000–1000 B.C.), in which Greek colonists from the Aegean introduce the culture and industries of the so-called "Mycenaean" Age, which is well known to us through the Homeric poems and further illustrated by the magnificent discoveries made in the palace of Minos in Crete. Pottery is now manufactured on the wheel; decorative designs are free and naturalistic; and artists use the richest materials, such as gold, ivory, enamels, and glass.

It is now that Cyprus makes its first—and characteristic—appearance in history, figuring in Egyptian records as having been conquered by Thothmes III about 1500 B.C. Towards the close of the period (about the eleventh century B.C.) both the Egyptian power and the Aegean sea-power declined, and Cyprus appears to have been left in isolation to face the Iron Age, which was a period here, as elsewhere, of obscurity and relapse.

At this point it may be well to attempt to form some mental picture, however slight, of the inhabitants. They seem to have been composed of an indigenous race with a strong admixture of colonists from Greece and, most probably, a number of Phoenician trading settlers from the neighbouring coast of Syria. Of their numbers, the date is far too early to allow us to speak with any sort of precision. One of the most learned authorities (Professor Oberhummer), in a discussion on the probable population in Graeco-Roman times, following the method of working back from the known to the unknown, observes that the earliest *certain* figures we have are the Venetian statistical reports of the fifteenth century A.D., which mention 150,000 (but this was after a long period of mingled vicissitude and luxury, neither of which is a favourable factor). For the prosperous and peaceful Graeco-Roman age he considers that the usual estimate of 500,000 is too high, and is of opinion that the facts do not warrant a higher estimate than 300,000. For the similarly prosperous period of the Late Bronze Age we might, perhaps, though it is the merest guess, take 200,000 as a possibility, followed by a very marked decline to perhaps half that number for the Iron Age. They were, in any case, a rich and cultured people, speaking a language tinged with the dialects of Greece, from which their colonists came; and though they knew the Greek alphabet, they wrote mainly in a mysterious syllabic system akin to the hitherto undeciphered Cretan script. In matters of religion their gods were those of Olympus, whom they tended to identify ever more closely with those of their Phoenician neighbours, giving especial honour to Aphrodite, the goddess of love (the Astarte of the Phoenicians), whose principal shrine was at Paphos.

4. THE IRON AGE (1000 B.C.)

The introduction of iron as a material for tools and weapons, which may be dated at about 1000 B.C., seems to have taken place under much the same conditions as in other parts of the ancient world. It was, above all, sudden and accompanied by serious economic, and probably also political, changes. A high civilization relapses at once into comparative barbarism. Gold, and even silver, become rare, and foreign imports are scarce. Decorative art again relapses to crude geometrical patterns, as the lingering Mycenaean tradition comes into contact with Oriental influences from the Syrian coast. The long duel between East and West has begun.

5. GRAECO-ORIENTAL PERIOD

Although we have as yet no clear proof of Semitic activity in Cyprus until the last years of the eighth century B.C., it seems certain that the ubiquitous Phoenician traders, who went as far as Cornwall for their tin, had from very early times settlements in the island which was so near their native coasts of Tyre and Sidon. Their main centres appear to have been Citium (Larnaca) and Idalium (Dali). At the date above mentioned we find that Sargon II of Assyria received the submission of seven kings (i.e. petty princes) of Cyprus; and a little later (668 B.C.) the Assyrian expedition against Egypt was joined by ten such kings, one of whom at least bore a recognizably Phoenician name.

In this period three distinct foreign influences can be traced, namely, from Egypt, Assyria, and the Aegean. Of these the first two gradually recede in favour of the third. Thus, on the failure of the Assyrian expedition, the island was conquered by Egypt and held until 525 B.C., when it was voluntarily surrendered to the rising power of Persia under Cambyses. In 500 B.C. the Greek cities, faring ill under the Persian rule, joined the great Ionic Revolt, in which it is to be noted that the Phoenician strongholds of Citium and Amathus stood firm to their Oriental master. The revolt was soon put down, and in 480 B.C. we find Cyprus (whose timber had long been a matter for imperial competition) supplying 150 ships to the great expedition of Xerxes against Greece. On the ensuing triumph of the Greek arms there followed a series of attempts on the part of the allied Greek "Delian Confederacy" to "liberate" Cyprus. These were, however, foiled by the steadfastness of the Phoenician party: but eventually a local Greek prince in the person of Evagoras of Salamis (410 B.C.) succeeded, by an adroit combination of diplomacy and force exercised during a long and successful reign, in securing for his country a position of practical independence which decided for good and all the question of the predominance of Greek culture. When, therefore, in 333 B.C., Alexander of Macedon finally shattered the Persian power at the Battle of the Issus, Cyprus welcomed him with open arms, and supplied him with timber for his ships at the siege of Tyre.

6. RULE OF THE PTOLEMIES (294–258 B.C.)

On the death of Alexander (323 B.C.), during the squabbles which followed amongst his generals, covetous of the spoils of empire, there were several rapid changes of sovereignty before Cyprus fell to the share of the Greek Ptolemy I of Egypt. Of this period there is but little to tell save that the island was administered by viceroys, and was regarded as one of the most valuable possessions of the Egyptian Crown. The same bareness is observable in the field of art. It seems as though the Cypriots, in spite of having been linked so long by the closest bonds of trade and relationship to the glories of the Hellenic world, were still incapable of profiting by those models. Though not without famous men of their own, such as Zeno the founder of the Stoic philosophy, they were in fact a by-word for their over-precious luxury.[1]

7. ROMAN PERIOD (58 B.C.–A.D. 395)

It was not likely that so rich a jewel as Cyprus would for long be allowed to tempt the rising power and appetites

[1] Illustrated by a story from *Athenaeus* (VI, 257): "A certain King of Neo-Paphos, when dining, was kept cool by doves hovering round him. To allure them he was anointed with Tyrian oil made from a fruit greatly relished by the doves, the odour of which they knew well. As they approached to settle on his head, attendants warded them off, and the constant flutter of their wings produced the necessary effect of cooling."

of Rome. Accordingly in 58 B.C. the Romans, who had in fact made large unsecured loans to the reigning Ptolemy, appeared in force and annexed the island on two grounds: firstly, that they were its heirs under the will of the last legitimate Ptolemy; and, secondly, that the inhabitants had connived in piracy. The booty was immense, and the Roman treasury was enriched not only by a large revenue but by a capital sum approaching in value to £2,000,000 sterling. The new province was at first joined to that of Cilicia, and during this time was administered by Cicero. Julius Caesar then presented it to Ptolemy and Arsinoe of Egypt, after which Antony gave it to Cleopatra. On their defeat at the Battle of Actium in 31 B.C. it became an "imperial" (i.e. a military) province under Augustus, who feared the "Eastern danger". In 22 B.C., however, it was transferred to the Senate and became a "civil" province administered by proconsuls, the capital being transferred from the ancient Salamis to Paphos, the centre of the worship of Aphrodite. Here, as everywhere, the Romans paid great attention to road-making, and encircled the main part of the island with a road running from Salamis in the east diagonally to Kyrenia in the north, and from there roughly following the west and south coasts round, and so back to Salamis; in addition to which there were doubtless other roads in the interior.

8. RISE OF CHRISTIANITY

In view of its nearness to the Holy Land, it is hardly surprising that Cyprus was one of the first places to be converted to Christianity. Moreover, the ground was prepared by the populous settlements of Jews who were already established in the island as the result of disturbances in Palestine. These were amongst the first to be converted by the Christians who fled from the mainland in the persecution that followed the martyrdom of St. Stephen. Barnabas himself was a Jew of Cyprus, and, in A.D. 46, together with John Mark, he accompanied St. Paul on his first journey to Cyprus, where they converted the Roman proconsul, Sergius Paulus. To Cyprus, therefore, belongs the honour of being the first country to be ruled by a Christian governor. Barnabas revisited Cyprus twice, and finally suffered martyrdom in his native town of Salamis. Christianity rapidly increased in the island at the expense of paganism, which was perhaps the more vulnerable as being stained, in its devotion to the Paphian Venus, with the grosser forms of mere nature-worship.

9. JEWISH REVOLT (A.D. 117)

The only other event in this period that calls for remark here was the general Jewish revolt against the Roman power, which was marked in Cyprus by a formidable massacre before it was suppressed with merciless severity by the future emperor, Hadrian. The historian affirms that no less than 240,000 persons lost their lives in this affair, but the number is almost certainly exaggerated. All Jews were then expelled from the island by a decree of the Senate, and it is said that for several centuries afterwards any Jew found in Cyprus, even though merely shipwrecked, was immediately put to death. Indeed, as late as the middle of the last century, a ship carrying Rumanian emigrants was wrecked on the coast of Cyprus, and when the unfortunate passengers tried to struggle ashore through the surf the villagers shot at them with guns and rifles, believing them to be Jews.

10. BYZANTINE PERIOD (A.D. 395–1191)

Cyprus continued under the administration of Rome until A.D. 395, when the sons of Theodosius the Great, Honorius, and Arcadius divided what was left of the tottering empire and settled down, the one among the salt-marshes of Ravenna and the other in Byzantium, to resist the attacks of their northern enemies, the Goths, Vandals, and Huns. Cyprus fell naturally to the share of Byzantium, and was at first governed by an official called *Consularis*, who was appointed from Antioch. The capital was transferred from Paphos to Salamis, then known as Constantia. For more than two centuries the island was safe from attack and enjoyed considerable prosperity. At the beginning of the seventh century, however, a new danger appeared from the East, where the meteoric rise of the Mohammedan religion in less than a hundred years spread fire and sword from Spain to the frontiers of India. The Eastern empire was soon involved in a death-struggle. More, it seems, by luck than anything else it survived the first and most fiery onslaughts of fanaticism, after which Arab activity degenerated into an affair of persistent raiding. To such incursions Cyprus, as an outpost of empire, was of course peculiarly exposed; and according to the historian Stephen de Lusignan it suffered from no less than twenty-four Arab invasions. The first of these took place in 632, when Abu Bekr, father-in-law and successor to Mohammed, obtained temporary possession of Citium (Larnaca); another, led by Mu'âwiya, the first Ommayad Khalif, owes its interest to the fact that the wife of a companion of the Prophet, the Lady Umm Harâm, took part in it, was killed at Larnaca by a fall from her mule, and was buried in the Tekkè by the Larnaca Salt Lake, now one of the most revered of Moslem shrines. Among other distinguished Arab invaders was Harun-al-Rashid, the Abbasid Khalif of Baghdad, the Caliph of the *Arabian Nights* (*c.* 800). Finally the emperor, Nikephoros Phocas (963–969), expelled the Arabs from Asia Minor, and even from part of Syria, and thus freed the island from these periodic catastrophes. The following two hundred years were a time of peace, only interrupted by insignificant risings on the part of two Byzantine governors.

The next rising, however, which took place towards the end of the Byzantine period, was of the greatest importance, being destined to tear Cyprus away for ever from that empire. It was led by a certain Isaac Comnenos, who was a cadet of the distinguished dynasty of that name then reigning in Byzantium. He held the position of Imperial Governor of Tarsus in Cilicia, and suddenly (1184) appeared in Cyprus with forged imperial letters purporting to appoint him governor of the island. He proceeded to establish himself with all the violence and brutality which seem to have characterized the less reputable members of his family, and having done so assumed the proud title of

"Emperor". Cyprus was already groaning beneath his oppression when, in 1191, he had the misfortune to fall foul of Richard I of England, Cœur de Lion, who was on his way to Palestine on the Third Crusade.

II. RICHARD CŒUR DE LION AND THE TEMPLARS (1191–1192)

Richard, who had spent the winter at Messina, was accompanied by his sister Joanna, Queen Dowager of Sicily, and his betrothed wife, Berengaria of Navarre. On the voyage from Sicily to Acre the fleet was scattered by a succession of storms. Richard's ship was blown into the Gulf of Adalia, while that containing the two Queens was driven towards Cyprus and anchored off Limassol. Whereupon the Emperor Isaac was so misguided as to endeavour by menaces to induce them to land, and this in spite of the fact that he was related to Joanna by his own marriage to a sister of the King of Sicily, William the Good. The royal ladies were in great embarrassment when, fortunately, Richard arrived and promptly demanded of the Emperor, who had also plundered some of his vessels which had been wrecked on the coast, an explanation of his treatment of these and of two defenceless women. Isaac was defiant, and Richard landed in force and took Limassol, where he proceeded to celebrate his marriage with Berengaria, who was there crowned Queen of England. The Emperor meanwhile had fled, first to Nicosia and thence to Famagusta. On the breakdown of certain negotiations for peace, Richard, with the assistance of Guy de Lusignan, who by right of his wife had become King of Jerusalem, and who in the interval had arrived in the island, gave chase to his enemy. Guy captured the castles of Kyrenia, St. Hilarion, and Buffavento, and finally Isaac emerged from his retreat at Kantara and surrendered to Richard at Cape St. Andrew. The latter handed him over to the Hospitallers, who confined him in their castle of Margat, near Tripoli in Syria; and here the only Emperor of Cyprus perished in 1194. Richard, having made himself master of the island, appointed Richard Camville and Robert of Turnham to govern it as justices and sheriffs on the English model, and then proceeded to Acre. Here he found that the Crusade demanded all his men, and more money than he possessed; he therefore sold his new conquest to the Knights Templar for 100,000 byzants,[1] of which 40,000 were to be paid at once, and the remainder by instalments.

The Templars[2] soon found their new burden a heavy one; the war with Saladin was already absorbing all their energies in Syria, and the small garrison which they were able to maintain in Cyprus could barely cope with an unruly Greek population almost constantly in a state of revolt. Accordingly, in May 1192, they begged Richard to resume the island on the same terms as he had sold it; but Richard, who was not prepared to restore the 40,000 byzants, induced Guy de Lusignan to acquire the island as some compensation for the loss of his kingdom of Jerusalem, the shadowy sovereignty over which had been transferred to Richard's nephew, Henry of Champagne. The Templars withdrew to Syria, and in 1291, on the capture of Acre by the Saracens, returned to Cyprus, but no longer of course as its rulers.

12. CYPRUS UNDER THE LUSIGNANS (1192–1489)

The three hundred years during which the kings and queens of the House of Lusignan held sway over Cyprus constituted undoubtedly the most brilliant epoch in its history. It was, however, entirely a foreign, i.e. a Latin, brilliance: of the fortunes and aspirations of the local inhabitants we hear nothing. Reduced to the position of mere vassals of the new dominant caste, they doubtless regretted the "home-rule" government of Byzantium; and they must have viewed with apprehension the arrival of these Crusaders who had long lost their pure enthusiasm for the Holy Places, and were entirely bent on carving out for themselves some portion of the kingdoms of this world.

[1] The byzant is usually regarded as equivalent to about £3 (gold) at the present day.

[2] This, and most of the following paragraph, is quoted textually from the *Handbook of Cyprus*, by Storrs and O'Brien, London, 1930.

Among all the kingdoms so carved out, that of Cyprus was the fairest, the richest, and the most durable. Its remarkable achievements in every domain of human activity gave it an importance among the nations of Europe wholly out of proportion to its small size and population. Its constitution was the model of that of the mediaeval feudal state; its laws, as embodied in the *Assizes of Jerusalem*, a pattern of mediaeval jurisprudence. In the abbey of Bellapaise, in the cathedrals of Nicosia and Famagusta, and in the castles of St. Hilarion, Buffavento, and Kantara, it could boast rarely beautiful examples of mediaeval architecture; its men of letters, Philippe de Novare, Guillaume de Machaut, Philippe de Mézières, occupy no undistinguished place in the realm of literature. In King Peter I it possessed perhaps the greatest knight-errant the world has ever seen; in his Order of the Sword the most perfect expression of chivalrous ideals. To kings of Cyprus such widely different writers as St. Thomas Aquinas and Boccaccio dedicated works; the wealth and luxury of its citizens, especially in the fourteenth century, evoked the amazement of all Western visitors. The rich merchants of Famagusta were wont, we are told, to give their daughters, on their marriage, "jewels more precious than those of the Queen of France". There is, on the other hand, no doubt that all this grandeur and luxury, of which we hear and can still see so much, was accompanied by a great deal of poverty and oppression. One contemporary epigram may perhaps best convey to us the atmosphere of the period: "The overweening pride of France, the effeminacy of Syria, and the smooth wiliness of Greece, how clearly they stand out on this one island!"

Guy de Lusignan, who died in 1194, contented himself with the title of Seigneur of Cyprus. He was indeed already a king, having been crowned at Jerusalem, which he had then lost to the Saracens at the disastrous battle of Hittin (1187). His brother and successor, Amaury, obtained the right to a royal crown from the emperor, Henry VI. The energies of these earlier Lusignans were absorbed in fruitless attempts to enforce their claims to the throne of

Jerusalem, of which they continued to bear the royal title, though only ruling such dominions as the Franks retained in Syria up to the fall of Acre (1291).

By a curious interplay of cause and effect, the worse the Crusaders fared in Syria the more they prospered in Cyprus, since each new Saracen victory on the mainland strengthened with new refugees the dominant caste on the island, which acquired the further distinction of being the outpost of Christendom. Within a century from the flight of the Europeans from Acre, Famagusta had become the "emporium of the East" with a very important international trade, which flourished in spite of papal protests against commerce with the infidels.

In spiritual matters also the Latins were not long in making their presence felt in the island. The Orthodox Church was to a large extent dispossessed of its property and subordinated, gradually but firmly, to a Latin Church. Finally, in 1260, Pope Alexander IV issued the famous *Bulla Cypria*, whereby the Latin Archbishop was made the supreme ecclesiastical chief of Latins and Orthodox alike. The Orthodox bishops were reduced to the position of dependants of the corresponding Latin bishops, and at their installation were obliged to take an oath of obedience to them and to the Holy See. This position was maintained until the arrival of the Turks, who revived the Orthodox Church for political purposes of their own.

The Lusignan power reached its zenith in the middle of the fourteenth century, at about which time successful expeditions were made against many towns on the coasts of Asia Minor and Egypt, usually in co-operation with the Hospitallers and the Knights of Rhodes. The leader of these undertakings was King Peter I (1359–1369), who twice went round the Courts of Europe to collect subsidies of men and money; and in whom, it has been said, the characteristics of the idealist and the filibuster were equally blended. Under his successor, Peter II (1369–1382), the fortunes of Cyprus began to wane. The first mishap arose at his coronation. It was the custom of the Lusignan sovereigns to be crowned in Nicosia as kings of Cyprus and in Famagusta as kings of Jerusalem; and at the latter ceremony the consuls of Genoa and Venice had the privilege of leading the King's horse, one on either side. On this occasion a dispute as to precedence arose between them. In the fight which followed mortal blows were exchanged, and the King sided with the Venetians. Upon this the Genoese Republic sent a fleet to avenge her dead. The island was mercilessly ravaged, and Famagusta was captured and held by the Genoese till 1464. Thus the best port in the island passed into foreign hands.

Further misfortunes followed in 1417, when a raid on the coast of Egypt provoked the vengeance of the Egyptian Sultan. Limassol was sacked, and King Janus was defeated at Khirokitia and carried off captive to Egypt, whence he was only allowed to return on payment of an enormous ransom and an annual tribute. Continued outbreaks of plague, prolonged droughts and attacks of locusts further increased the damage suffered during this period.

The final ruin was brought about by James, an illegitimate son of the royal house and Archbishop-elect of Nicosia. He did not hesitate to invoke the aid of the Sultan of Egypt in order to deprive his sister Charlotte, the rightful queen, of her throne.[1] He managed to retake Famagusta from the Genoese, but then made a fatal marriage by accepting from Venice the hand of Catherine Cornaro, the daughter of a Venetian noble (1471). He died two years later, poisoned, it is said, by order of the Venetian Government; and from that time Catherine was a mere cat's-paw in the hand of Venice. In 1488, in consequence of a war with the Turks, Venice determined to take full possession of the island as a valuable naval and military station; and in 1489 Catherine was forced to abdicate her rights at a solemn ceremony in the cathedral of Nicosia. Thus ended the power of the house of Lusignan.

[1] From Charlotte, by her marriage to Louis of Savoy, the present Royal House of Italy derives its claim to be considered as the heir of the Lusignans.

13. VENETIAN OCCUPATION (1489–1571)

The Lusignans, though doubtless oppressors, had at least done their best to look after their possessions. The Venetians, on the other hand, regarded Cyprus primarily as a military post. They built magnificent fortifications at Nicosia, Famagusta, and elsewhere, and for the rest contented themselves with drawing from the island as large a revenue as its impoverished state could supply. Their Governor, the "Captain of Cyprus", who resided at Famagusta, had large civil powers as well as the command of all troops in the island, and the duty of inspecting the fortresses. With the exception of one incident in 1546—when there was an abortive rising of the inhabitants—the history of Venetian rule is a mere chronicle of decay. Drought, floods, locusts, and earthquakes added to the distress caused by misgovernment; trade languished; manufactures practically ceased, and all who could afford to do so emigrated, thinking even the rule of the Turk preferable to that of the great Republic.

If, however, the Venetians did little for Cyprus, they at least defended it well against the Turks. Of the immediate cause of the Turkish attack there are two accounts. The first, and official, account is that the Sultan, Selim II, simply claimed the island as his own on the ground that the tribute paid to him implied the recognition of his sovereignty. As regards this tribute, it will be remembered that it had been first exacted by the Sultan of Egypt from the later Lusignans. The Venetians had continued to pay it, at first to Egypt, and later, on the conquest of that country by Selim I in 1517, direct to the Porte.

The other, and more picturesque, account—which is, however, well founded in history—is that Selim II, deservedly known as Selim the "Sot", was devoted to the strong wine of Cyprus, and determined to become master of an island that produced so delicious a vintage. In any case, he did flagrantly violate his treaty with Venice on the specious grounds that a Mohammedan sovereign might disregard any treaty in order to recover from the infidels territory that had once belonged to Islam—as Cyprus had belonged to the Arabs.[1]

On July 1, 1570, the Turkish forces landed at Limassol, which surrendered at once. Three weeks later Nicosia was taken, and 20,000 of its inhabitants were put to the sword. Siege was then laid to Famagusta, which capitulated after a resistance of ten months, prolonged in the vain hope of receiving help from Venice. The terms of surrender were not respected, and the massacre of Nicosia was repeated. Peculiarly atrocious—even in that age of atrocity—was the treatment meted out to the gallant Captain of Cyprus, Marco Antonio Bragadino. After being subjected to the most excruciating public tortures, which he bore with great fortitude, he was flayed alive and his skin was stuffed with straw and sent to Constantinople. There it remained until, some years later, it was redeemed for a great price and laid in its present resting-place in the Church of SS. Giovanni e Paolo at Venice.

The fall of Famagusta marked the end of Venetian resistance in Cyprus; and in spite of the naval victory won by the Christian alliance at Lepanto later in the same year (1571), Venice was compelled to sue for peace. In 1573 a treaty was signed, by which it was agreed that the Sultan should retain Cyprus and that the expenses of his expedition should be refunded to him.

14. TURKISH RULE (1571–1878)

The Turkish conquest was welcomed by many of the Cypriote peasantry, who had groaned under the harsh tyranny of Venice. The serfdom of the feudal age disappeared; a certain measure of autonomy was granted to the Christian population; the Latin priests were expelled and the Greek Orthodox Church restored. This latter reform was originally due to the desire of the central Government to devise some primary check on its extortionate and not always submissive local officials. In later

[1] The wine eventually killed him; a bottle, drained at a draught, leading to a fatal slip on the marble floor of his bath.

times the Church developed so great an influence on temporal affairs that the Turks became alarmed and, in 1821, arrested and executed without any evidence the Archbishop and all the leading personages of the Orthodox communion on a charge of conspiring with the insurgents in Greece, then struggling for their independence.

The Turkish administration showed the same characteristics here as in other parts of their empire, viz. an increasing material decay combined with a mild and negligent rule, varied by outbursts of great severity. Thus by the middle of the seventeenth century the adult male population was reduced to only 25,000. In 1838 the island benefited by the general reforms introduced by the liberal Sultan, Mahmud II, when many of the abuses from which it had suffered, including the farming of taxes, were abolished. In 1839 the Pashas, who had administered the island under the supervision of the Grand Vizier, were replaced by Kaimakams (Deputy-Governors), who governed with the assistance of a Council on which the local communities were represented. Under this system a measure of prosperity began to return; and, on the whole, the condition of the people compared favourably with that of other Christian subjects of Turkey when, by the Anglo-Turkish Convention of June 4, 1878, the island was handed over by the Porte to be administered by Great Britain.

15. BRITISH ADMINISTRATION

This convention arose from the rivalry then existing between England and Russia. It was a defensive alliance guaranteeing the Asiatic possessions of the Sultan against Russian encroachment. In return for this protection, and in order that England might be able to make necessary provision for executing her engagement, Cyprus was assigned to be occupied and administered by her. It was further provided that the Sultan should receive an annual sum equivalent to the excess of revenue over expenditure, calculated upon the average of the previous five years.

A High Commissioner, with all the powers usually conferred upon a Colonial Governor, was at once appointed.

He governed the island with the assistance of an elective Legislative Council.[1]

On November 5, 1914, when the entry of Turkey into the Great War automatically annulled the Convention, Cyprus was annexed to the British Crown, and, on March 10, 1925, was given the status and name of a Colony, the office of High Commissioner being replaced by that of Governor.

[1] Abolished after the riots of 1931.

II

THE ARRANGEMENT OF AN ORTHODOX CHURCH

ALL churches in Cyprus stand due east and west, with the altar at the east, from the original tendency to turn towards the rising sun because the essence of God is light. The church is entered from the west through the narthex or porch, though this feature is sometimes omitted or becomes a cloister on one or more sides of the building. The nave has a pulpit on the north wall, often approached by a movable step-ladder or steps cut in a thickness of the wall. Stalls or seats are ranged round the walls, and the throne of the Bishop, usually having a carved wooden canopy, and with an icon of St. Barnabas let into the back, is placed against the south wall. At the west end of the nave is the gynaiconitis or gallery for women and children, while in the centre of the nave stands the proskenetarion or icon-table on which the icon of the day is placed.

The most distinguishing feature of the Orthodox Church is the iconostasis or screen dividing the sanctuary from the choir and congregation, and usually raised one or more steps above the floor of the nave. The iconostasis has three doors: the central one being called "the Holy, Royal, or Beautiful Door". In front of this is the step for the solea or platform, on which the priest stands when administering the Communion or addressing the people. Frequently the iconostasis is returned against the north and south walls of the church, in order to find the space for large icons, the patron saint of the church being commonly placed on the south wall and St. George on the north wall. Within the iconostasis stands the Holy Table, with, on the south side, the vestry and, on the north, the altar of prothesis, usually a niche in the wall, where the elements are placed and prepared before consecration. The Holy Table may be of any material, but seems usually to consist of a wooden framework supported on stone columns; in one or two village churches cippi from Roman tombs take the place of these columns. An iron or wooden railing runs round the back of the altar, which is more often than not covered with the baldachino supported on wooden or stone columns. On the altar itself are kept the Gospel, the Cross, and the pyxis or box in which part of the consecrated elements are preserved for visiting the sick. Around the altar and on the walls hang the vestments and robes of the priests.

Upon the iconostasis of a Greek church always hang the sacred icons or pictures. In the place of honour on the south side of the Holy Door is the figure of the Redeemer. On the north side is the Madonna, whom the Greek Church holds in deep veneration, without allotting her any precise part in the scheme of salvation or protection of the Church. The other icons which are always placed in positions of honour and near the Saviour and Virgin are St. John the Baptist, St. John the Evangelist, the Archangel Michael, and the Saint to whom the church is dedicated; but there is no hard-and-fast rule as to their exact position, though the Archangel more often than not forms the upper panel of the northern of the three doors of the iconostasis.

The Greek Church admits the use of pictures to instruct the ignorant, and to assist the devotion of others by those sensible representations; nor do they herein think themselves guilty of any breach of the second commandment, as to the manner of worship, not only because they say these pictures are used merely as remembrances of the saints, to whom their respect is directed, but because the design of Moses, according to them, in prohibiting the making and worshipping graven images, was merely to prohibit worshipping the idols of the Gentiles, which the Gentiles believed to be gods, whereas they admit no graven images, but pictures only, upon which the name of the saint represented must always be inscribed.[1]

In the olden times great veneration was paid to icons, as Master Anthonie Jenkinson, who visited an Orthodox

[1] Augustus Hare, *Russia*, p. 24.

church in 1557, tells us that "All their churches are full of images, unto which the people, when they assemble, doe bowe and knocke their heads, so that some will have knobbes upon their foreheads with knocking as great as egges".[1]

It must be remembered that nearly all village churches are kept locked and visitors must be prepared for the almost inevitable wait while the priest or the verger, or whoever has the key, is found.

In the description of the villages I have not mentioned the exact positions in the church of the icons I have described, for they are not infrequently changed, and when a new one is presented the old icon is relegated to the women's gallery, or to the apse behind the iconostasis.

Visitors must also remember that no woman is allowed to pass behind the iconostasis, but the village priest is nearly always delighted to bring an icon into the body of the church, where the light is far better, and where it can be examined at leisure.

[1] *Travels to Court of Russia.*

III

NICOSIA

THE capital of the island and the seat of the Governor and the Orthodox Archbishop lies in the middle of the plain of the Messaoria, and on the right bank of the River Pedias, here flowing to the north. Nicosia does not appear as a capital until as late as the Lusignan dynasty, but that there has been a city here from remote times is proved by the vast number of ancient tombs, dating from the Early Bronze Age (3000 B.C.) down to the Roman period, surrounding the place. Many of the tombs lie beneath the houses of the modern suburb of Ayii Omoloyitades. On the site of the present Nicosia may have been the city of Ledra, the foundation of which was attributed to Lefcon, son of Ptolemy Soter (280 B.C.).

The earliest reliable reference to Nicosia is made by Wilbrand, Count of Oldenburg, who visited Cyprus in 1211.[1]

> Passing on we reached Cossia (Nicosia) [he writes]. This is the King's capital city, situated almost in the middle of the plain; it has no fortifications. A strong castle has just now been built in it. It has inhabitants without number, all very rich, whose houses in their interior adornment and paintings closely resemble the houses of Antioch. In this city is the seat of the archbishop. Also the court and palace of the king, where I first saw an ostrich. This city is five miles from Schernea (Kyrenia).

The wealth mentioned by the Count of Oldenburg must have quickly increased, for Dante Alighieri, in a mystical passage of the *Paradiso*,[2] refers to the luxury and gluttony of Nicosia under Henry II (1285–1310).

[1] C. D. Cobham, *Excerpta Cypria*, Cambridge, 1908, p. 13.
[2] XIX, 145–8.

In earnest of that day, e'en now are heard
Wailings and groans in Famagosta's streets
And Nicosia's, grudging at their beast,
Who keepeth even footing with the rest.

Benvenuto da Imola, the commentator of Dante, explains this passage as follows:

And truly he does not separate himself and keep himself apart from the bestial living of others, nay rather o'ertops and exceeds with his Cypriot subjects all rulers and peoples of the kingdoms of Christendom in superfluity of luxury, gluttony, effeminacy, and every kind of pleasure. But to be at pains to describe the kinds of feasts, their sumptuousness, variety, and superfluities, would be tiresome to tell, and tedious to write, and harmful to hear.[1]

The kings of Cyprus received many important visitors, among them St. Louis of France on his way to the Fourth Crusade, who established himself in Nicosia with King Henry and the nobles of the Court while his army was camped at the port of Limassol. Here, too, his wife, Queen Margarette, recovered her health after the danger and stress of the voyage from France. But their son the Dauphin died, and was buried in St. Dominic in Nicosia.

Things went on peaceably with the Lusignans, and Ludolf, priest of the Church of Suchen in Westphalia, gives a vivid account of the carefree life of the King and his Court in about 1340.[2]

There is another great city in Cyprus called Nycosia. It is the capital of the island, and lies under the mountains in a fine open plain with an excellent climate. In this city, by reason of its well-tempered air and healthfulness, the king of Cyprus and all the bishops and prelates of his realm, the princes and nobles and barons and knights, chiefly live, and daily engage in spear-play and tourneys, and especially in hunting. There are in Cyprus wild rams[3] which are not found in other parts of the world. But they are caught with leopards, in no other way can they be taken. And in Cyprus the princes, nobles, barons and

[1] *Excerpta Cypria*, p. 15.
[2] Ibid., p. 20.
[3] The mouflon, of which there are still a few in the hills of Cyprus.

knights are the richest in the world. For one who has a revenue of three thousand florins is no more accounted of there than if he had an income of three marks. But they spend all on the chase. I knew a certain Count of Japhe (Hughes d'Ibelin, Comte de Jaffa et d'Ascalon) who has more than five hundred hounds, and every two dogs have their own servant to guard and bathe and anoint them, for so must dogs be tended there. A certain nobleman has ten or eleven falconers with special pay and allowances. I knew several nobles and knights in Cyprus who could keep and feed two hundred armed men at a less cost than their huntsmen and falconers. For when they go to the chase they live sometimes for a whole month in their tents among the forests and mountains, straying from place to place, hunting with their dogs and hawks, and sleeping in their tents, in the fields and woods, carrying all their food and necessaries on camels and beasts of burden. You must know that in Cyprus all the princes, nobles, barons and knights are the noblest, best, and richest in the world. They live there now with their children, but they used to live in the land of Syria, and the noble city of Acon, but when that land and city were lost they fled to Cyprus, and there have remained until the present day.

These pleasant times lasted for another fifty years or so until, with the dawn of the fifteenth century, the glories of Nicosia began to fade. In 1426 the Mamluks landed at Limassol and defeated the royal troops under King Janus at the Battle of Khirokitia, taking the king himself a prisoner. With none to oppose them they marched on Nicosia, pillaging and burning to their hearts' content.

They took their men to the king's most marvellous palace, and pillaged all they could and set fire to it; and also at the back of the factory. There is no man who can say how great and how beautiful this place was. You may see how big it was: it contained four churches for the servants and for the people who were there. And they carried off all the plunder.

And on Friday they pillaged the houses and the churches of God and the monasteries, and they robbed the Christians of much substance and also pillaged the church of the Great Cross.[1]

The Venetian military occupation caused almost irre-

[1] Leontios Makhairas, *Chronicle*, p. 673 (ed. R. M. Dawkins: Clarendon Press).

parable damage to the capital, for at the end of the fifteenth century Nicosia had as many as 250 churches and some 50,000 inhabitants, a mixed crowd of Latins, chiefly Italians and French, Greeks, Maronites, Armenians, Copts, Nestorians, Jacobites, Abyssinians, and Georgians, while the circuit of the city extended for seven miles, so scattered were its buildings and so numerous its gardens and squares.

In 1567 it was realized that the day when the Turk would attack the city was not far distant, and that, with the limited troops at their disposal, it would be impossible for the inhabitants to guard and defend the great length of straggling walls. Therefore, in 1565, the Seigniory despatched Ascanio Savorgnano, the Venetian engineer, to report on fortifications. His report was not encouraging.[1] "I am of the opinion that, even though it were in other respects suitable, the Most Serene Republic would be ill advised to fortify it, and this for many reasons apart from reasons of State, as to which I am not competent to speak."

However, two years later the present fortifications were begun under the superintendence of Francesco Barbaro from Savorgnano's designs, and their form when completed was very much as we see them to-day. The original mediaeval walls were pulled down and the old circumference reduced by three miles. Everything outside the new circumvallation was destroyed or blown up so that a free field of fire would be left for the artillery mounted on the walls. In this general destruction nothing was spared; churches and palaces alike perished in the general demolition irrespective of their interest or beauty.

The most grievous loss to history was the monastery and royal château of St. Domenico, the Campo Sancto of Cyprus, wherein the bodies of many of the rulers of the House of Lusignan lay buried. The material from its destruction proved to be of the greatest use during the siege, numbers of its beams being used in the construction of fortifications and for carriages for the guns.

The long-expected storm burst at last. In 1570 the siege of Nicosia was begun by Mustafa Pasha, the commander

[1] Translation of an MS. of Savorgnano by H. C. Luke, Malta, 1932, p.25.

of a large Turkish army, sent against it by Sultan Selim II. Although the garrison consisted of only 10,000 men of different nationalities, the Turks spent seven weeks in reducing the city, and it was not till after several desperate assaults that they were able to gain an entry.

As it was, without labour or peril the Turks scaled the walls of the Costanzo bastion, crushed the wearied defenders, and dashed wildly into the inmost shelters, while the Count di Rocas was too late to put spirits into his troops, already disordered and flying. He fell by a musket ball, and with him were lost all steadiness, all judgment: the host ran blindly, each man seeking in his own house a treacherous shelter. Pietro Pisani, a Councillor, and Bernardino Pollani, Captain of the Salines, came up, but their presence made little impression on the confused and flying troops. The first was trodden down and killed, the other retreated with a large following into the city, and for a long time held his own against the terrible charges of the invaders. But the Turks were masters of the Costanzo bastion, and pressing on to seize the rest, made terrible havoc, showing no mercy to those who threw down their arms and begged for life, and hacking down the soldiers, and so passed to the square where the citizens held out with a courage and fierceness equal to that of their assailants. At last the Pasha of Aleppo, who had entered the city by the Tripoli bastion, brought up thence three cannon, and with repeated shots drove the crowd, disordered and maimed, into the courtyard of the palace. Thither had retreated many distinguished persons, among whom were the Lieutenant and Bishop Contarini. The Pasha despatched to the Lieutenant a Cypriot monk who had fallen into his hands, summoning the citizens to treat. To save their lives they agreed to yield, and by the Pasha's orders laid down their arms, but the doors were scarcely opened when the Turks sprang with their weapons upon the defenceless crowd, and butchered them all, the chiefs, the bishop, and every fugitive.

Such was the lamentable end of the wretched citizens, such the tragic fate of Nicosia, a city famed as a fortress, glorying in its buildings, and widely known for its riches. Its happy position, its pleasant climate, the gifts showered on it by Nature, the added charms of art, had given it a place among the fairest, strongest, and most renowned cities of Europe.[1]

---

[1] Diedo, *Excerpta Cypria*, p. 95.

It was said that 20,000 Christians were killed in the street fighting which followed. Calepio, who was himself present at the siege and was taken prisoner, gives a ghastly description of the horrors of September 8th:

And now indeed that terrible roar of artillery and musketry ceased to thunder in our ears; but the change was a sad and mournful one, for on every side we heard nothing but the ceaseless wailing of poor women parted from their husbands, the shrieks of children torn from their mothers' arms, the sighs of the wretched fathers which mounted to the very heavens, the cries of maidens and lads who saw themselves separated from their parents, one driven this way, another that, in irremediable division. All had their hands behind them, they were pushed and hurried with blows from sticks and sword hilts, many had an arm lopped off, or a skull cleft open. Any man or woman who resisted was killed. The victors kept cutting off the heads of old women; many of them as they marched along to prove their swords split open the heads of men who had already surrendered. Did a prisoner try to escape, he was caught up and his legs cut off, and as long as any life was left in him every janissary who passed had a cut at him.

Among the slain were Lodovico Podocatoro, and Lucretia Calepia, my mother, whose head they cut off on her serving maid's lap. They tore infants in swaddling clothes from their mothers' breasts, dashed some down on the ground, others by the feet against a wall: of whom I could baptize only one. To be brief, this sack lasted three days. Churches were desecrated, altars stripped, sacred pictures burnt, tombs torn open, and those who took refuge in the churches slain. One piece of savagery I saw, that wherever the Turks met swine they drove them off with darts and swordcuts, so that we saw a human body along with that of a pig. As they themselves owned, they enriched themselves to such an extent that never since the sack of Constantinople had they won so vast a treasure, as well of things sacred as those of common use.

The Countess of Tripoli, without stirring from her house or seeing the Pasha, gave herself up with all her family. She set before her door her coaches and carts, and part of her three hundred soldiers, telling the besiegers that they were Mustafa's prisoners. He accepted her lavish promises and rich gifts, but kept after all little or no faith with her, and her household met perhaps the hardest fate of all. He sent Hector Podocatoro her brother from his tent to Nicosia to be tended by doctors, and had his head cut off on the road. The rest of these prisoners, with the Countess' treasures, were put on a lighter, nor is it known where they are: some say they were drowned.[1]

Few of the Italian officers or the Cypriote nobles escaped the general holocaust. There is still extant a list showing how grievous was the loss to the "nobili del Gran Consiglio" of Venice and the native aristocracy of Cyprus. In the siege of Famagusta and Nicosia perished:

Nicola Dandolo, Lieutenant of the Realm and Vice-Proveditor.
Pietro Pisani, Councillor.
Antonio Pasqualigo, Chamberlain.
Vicenzo Malipiero, Vice-Captain of Paffo.
The Grand-Chancellor; and his brother Almorone, Master of the Ordnance.
Count de Ruchas, Coadjutor of the Realm and General of the Cypriot cavalry.
Count de Tripoli, General of artillery.
Thomas, Viscount of Nicosia.
Hector Podocatoro.
Francesco Maria de Nores.
Count Alberto Scotto.
Gabriel de Bergamo.
Giovan Batista de San Coluban.
Calo da Rimini.
Count Sigismondo da Casoldo.
Captain Piero, Count of Mont' Alberto.
Count Giacomo della Corbara.
The little Count of Triviso.

The Turks when they captured Cyprus were peculiarly bitter against members of the Roman Catholic faith, and especially persecuted them. Therefore such members of the Latin aristocracy as escaped—for the mass of the people were of the Orthodox Church—found it expedient to change their names and their religion, and were gradually absorbed into the Greek Cypriote peasantry. Where, now, is Nores? Where d'Ibelin? Where Giblet? Gone in name, perhaps, but not in blood; somewhere still run these

[1] *Excerpta Cypria*, p. 140.

noble strains; diluted and thin they may be, but they are there. The peasant in the village, the policeman in Nicosia, the fisherboy at Paphos, or the priest in the Carpass may, if they but knew it, have bluer blood in their veins than half the aristocracy of Europe, and could boast, perhaps, quarterings that a Howard or a Sackville might envy.

And of the royal blood itself? The great house of Plantagenet is said to have ended in an illiterate farm hand. The end of the proud house of Lusignan is as sad. For three hundred years kings and queens, their sons had mated with the ruling houses of Europe, while of the daughters five had worn crowns, others had married members of the royal families of Majorca, Naples, Savoy, and Portugal.

The last descendant of all this glory and wealth of blood and heraldry is said to have been a poor little shrunken old lady, a Miss Eliza de Lusignan, who was a governess in Ceylon in the middle of the last century. She died at a villa in Lower Edmonton, and with her death the last thin flickering flame was extinguished. Thus ended in a London suburb the Most Noble House of Lusignan, Kings of Cyprus, Jerusalem, and Armenia.

The three hundred years of Turkish occupation were, on the whole, uneventful. In 1741 Nicosia was damaged by an earthquake, and one of the minarets of St. Sofia Cathedral fell to the ground.

In 1764 Chil Osman, one of the worst of all the Turkish governors, was appointed by the Porte to Cyprus. He exacted huge sums from the unhappy peasantry by the cruellest means. Soon after he arrived in Nicosia he sent for the Archbishop and informed him that every Christian householder must pay forty-seven piastres. Such a heavy tax was unheard of, and even the harshest of governors had never demanded half the sum. The Archbishop was horrified and begged for a more lenient order, but the Governor was adamant and refused to reduce the tax.

In despair the Archbishop called together the Synod, and it was decided to send a messenger to Constantinople to implore the Sultan himself to intervene.

The Sultan listened and sent an imperial edict forbidding

the Governor to impose the tax, and stated that this order should be read in public.

The Governor was furious, and vowed to be avenged on the Archbishop. October 25th was the day appointed for the reading of the document, and on that day all the leading Greek citizens of Nicosia assembled in the Governor's Palace. The Archimandrite Cyprianos gives an eye-witness's account of this meeting:

> The Governor began in a reproachful tone to ask the Archbishop what harm he had done the rayah, that the Archbishop should accuse him to the Porte. Paisios replied, "God forbid, we came with tears to implore mercy on the poor rayah, but we never accused you." He had hardly spoken these words, when the floor on the side on which we Greeks stood, for I was among them, suddenly and utterly collapsed, and we were hurled into a black gulf, bishops and attendants, Greeks and Turks, with other victims, and the beams of the roof heaped on top of us. With no small damage and risk of our lives we freed ourselves, and were dragged out covered with dust and dirt, scarred all over, a sorry sight! We were carried to our houses, one with an injured back, another with a broken leg: some had internal injuries, some were so terrified that they thought death imminent. The meeting was broken up, those present fled in alarm, and the people outside, hearing what had happened and the tumult within, believing it to have been a trap prepared beforehand to kill the bishops, rushed madly to the palace carrying bludgeons and arms. They found the doors shut, they set them on fire, the palace was wrapped in flame, and the mob pouring in slew the wretched Chil Osman, with eighteen of his followers. They sacked and robbed the palace of all they could find, whether it belonged to Government, to the murdered Governor or his train—a terrible tragedy.[1]

In 1821 a far more terrible tragedy was staged in Nicosia. The Governor, a certain Kuchuk Mehmed, heard of the successful Greek risings against the Moslems all over the Hellenic world. He therefore determined to forestall any such revolt in the island he ruled, not that there was danger of any such risings; the Governor's real reason was his

[1] *Excerpta Cypria*, p. 357.

desire to seize the lands and goods of the bishops and notables of the churches and monasteries. He was jealous, too, of the power the Orthodox Church had slowly been gaining during the past fifty years.

July 9th was the date chosen by Kuchuk Mehmed for his bloody *coup d'état*.

The officials brought out into the square in front of the Governor's palace the Archbishop Cyprianos and the three other bishops. The first they hanged on a tree opposite the gates of the palace, the others they beheaded. With them were beheaded some of the Christian notables, and the bodies of all were left lying on the ground for some days. During a space of thirty days after they ceased not to massacre, and often to hack off the limbs of living victims. Two hundred of the leading inhabitants of the towns and villages were sacrificed: those who fled were almost the only ones saved. The property of the slain and the fugitives alike was confiscated and sold.[1]

On July 1, 1878, Vice-Admiral Lord John Hay, commanding a British squadron then at Suda Bay in Crete, received a telegram from the Admiralty, commanding him to take over the island and raise the Union Jack in Nicosia. These instructions he duly carried out, driving in a waggonette from his landing-place at Larnaca, accompanied by two mules laden with sacks of new English sixpences with which to settle the arrears of pay of the Sultan's officials.

DESCRIPTION OF THE CITY[2]

The Paphos Gate [1] was known in the Middle Ages as the Porte Domenico, from the monastery and royal castle of St. Domenico which stood near by. This famous monastery was founded in 1226 by Alix. Countess d'Ibelin, while Nicosia was without walls and open. It was fortified by Peter II, and here he lived. The château was destroyed by the Mamluks in 1426, but the abbey escaped. The castle was repaired, and within its walls died King John and his Queen, Helena Paleologus, in 1458. Unhappily both the

[1] *Excerpta Cypria*, p. 466.
[2] The numbers in brackets refer to the plan of Nicosia.

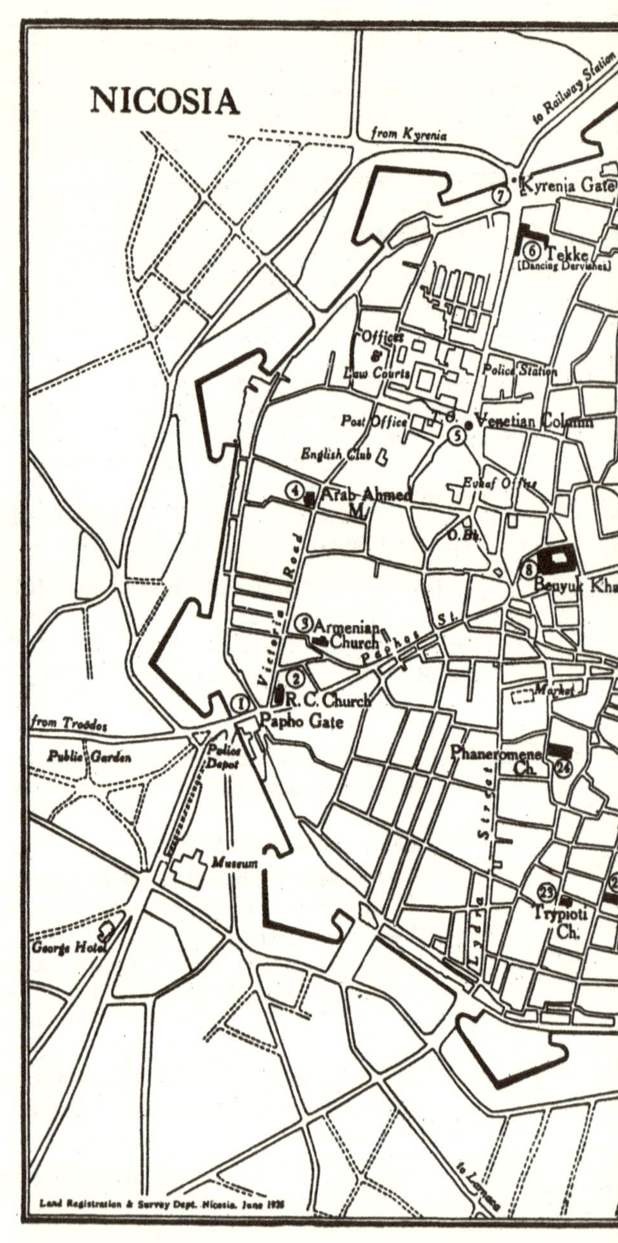
NICOSIA
from Kyrenia
to Railway Station
Kyrenia Gate
Tekke
[Dancing Dervishes]
Offices & Law Courts
Police Station
Post Office
Venetian Column
English Club
Evkaf Office
Arab Ahmed M.
O. Bk.
Beuyuk Kha
Victoria Road
Armenian Church
Paphos St.
R. C. Church
Papho Gate
Market
from Troödos
Public Garden
Police Depot
Phaneromene Ch.
Museum
Lydra Street
Trypioti Ch.
George Hotel
to Larnaca
Land Registration & Survey Dept. Nicosia. June 1935

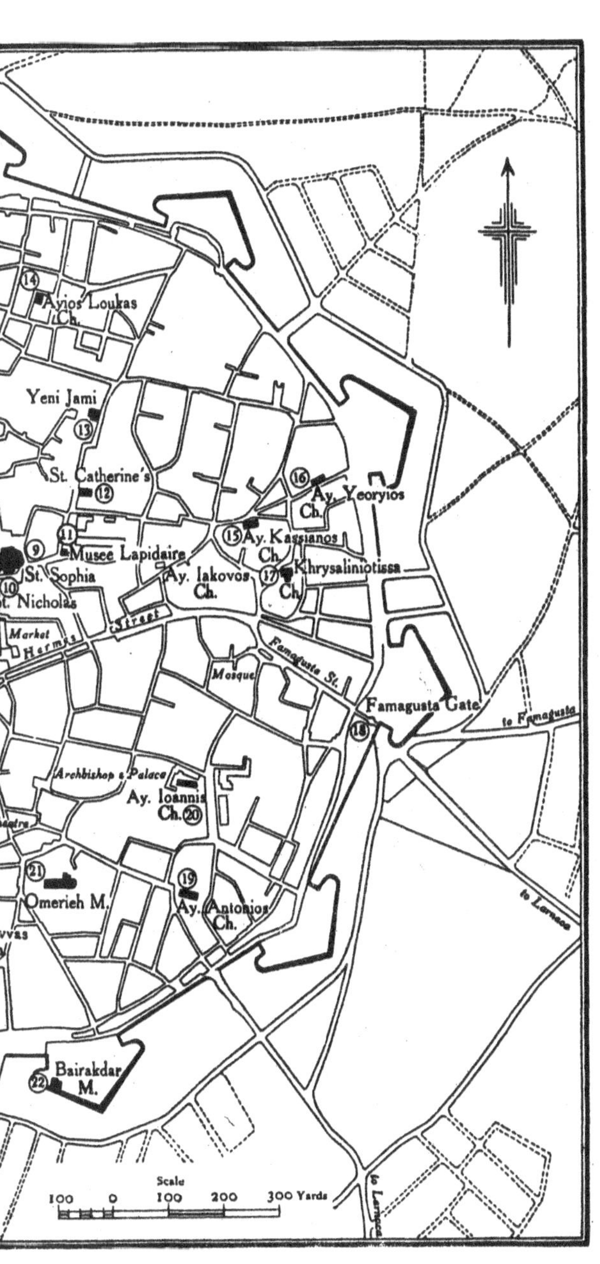
Ayios Loukas Ch.
14
Yeni Jami
13
St. Catherine's
12
16
Ay. Yeoryios Ch.
11
15
Ay. Kassianos Ch.
9
Musee Lapidaire
St. Sophia
Ay. Iakovos Ch.
17
Khrysaliniotissa Ch.
10
St. Nicholas
Market
Hermes Street
Famagusta St.
Mosque
Famagusta Gate
18
to Famagusta
Archbishop's Palace
Ay. Ioannis Ch.
20
21
Omerieh M.
19
Ay. Antonios Ch.
to Larnaca
22
Bairakdar M.
Scale
100 0 100 200 300 Yards
to Larnaca

abbey and the palace were destroyed by the Venetians when they remodelled the city walls in 1567.

The abbey must have been the finest building in Nicosia; it was the St. Denis of Cyprus, for within its walls were interred most of the kings and queens of Cyprus. Splendidly gilded and sumptuously adorned memorials of marble and alabaster recorded the names of Hugh II, Hugh IV, Peter I, Peter II, James I, Janus, and John I, with his two wives, Medea, daughter of the Marquis of Montferrat, and Helena Paleologus, daughter of the Despot of the Morea; here also was buried Louis, son of St. Louis of France, who died in the island during his father's first crusade.

Nor were the kings and their consorts alone in finding a last resting-place in the abbey. Here lay those who had held the most splendid titles of the kingdom, constables, marshals and turkopoliers, admirals, judges and seneschals, auditors and butlers of Cyprus. There could be seen memorials of those whose names were a roll-call of the chivalry of the Lusignan kingdom: nobles whose blazons and coats of arms were known far beyond the narrow confines of Cyprus—names famous on battlefields of Europe and the Holy Land, and whose territorial titles seem to bring back the days of Richard of England and St. Louis of France. The princes and seigniors of Beyrout, Edessa, Galilee, Antioch, Sidon, Jaffa, Caesarea, Tripoli, and Thoron. Here, too, beneath the great vaulted roof slept the sons of the proud families of Babin and Balion, della Baume and de Brie, Neviles and Nores, Montgesait and Milmar, Provosto and Poret, peers of the kingdom, Counts of Morfu, Viscounts of Nicosia, and Lords of Karpasia. Nor was this all the noble dust to fill the chancel and the nave; princes of the Church were laid side by side with princes of the blood. Sixteen patriarchs, archbishops, and bishops waited for the resurrection, their bodies slowly mouldering to decay. At Mass there mingled with the smoke from the high altar the dust of long-dead kings and queens and the proud nobility and clergy of their realm.

To-day not even the exact site of St. Domenico is known. All that remains are travellers' descriptions.

The conventual church is right royally adorned, and in it is the burial-place of the kings of Cyprus. It has two cloisters with marble pillars throughout their circuit, and all the offices of the monks are very good and convenient. Above are well-lighted dormitories, paved with marble.[1]

That royal monastery, to which were attached two cloisters full of oranges and paved with fine marbles, and the church adorned with the grand tombs of the Royal House, and other princes and lords, and on its walls and floor with many fine, broad and large marbles. . . . Then the dormitories, refectory, hospice, paved with marble: it had, too, the other offices to such a monastery, for in the time of the kings it held eighty monks. Then it had the chamber of the king on one side, and that of the queen on the other, which they visited often.[2]

The Paphos Gate was closed by the English in 1878, when they made a new cut through the walls. At the same time the gateway was blocked up and is now the resting-place of two red and gold fire-engines, manned by the police, whose barracks are above.

The Roman Catholic Church of St. Cross [2] is in the charge of the Franciscans. It is a large modern church of no interest. The barn-like interior is lavishly decorated with painted plaster and imitation marble. The church is under the protection of Spain, and the royal arms of Aragon and Castile are painted on the vaulted ceiling and embroidered on the cope of the Father President.

The ancient Franciscan church was destroyed in the great siege and the Order exiled, but in 1642 the Turks allowed them to return and they built a little church on this site.

In the cloister of the present building are a few memorials of the mediaeval church, which are built into the walls. The most interesting are two bas-reliefs: one is an Italian work dated 1555, and shows the Madonna and Child within a floriated arched niche, beneath is a coat of arms on a field croisy, a lion rampant crowned. The second relief is a work of great charm and beauty; it represents a land-

[1] Felix Faber, 1483, *Excerpta Cypria*, p. 44.
[2] Lusignan, Ibid., p. 120.

scape with palm-trees, in the centre is St. Mamas riding his lion, before him kneels a donor supported by an angel, at the bottom of the panel is the date March 15, 1524. The other fragments here include a shield with the royal Lusignan coat of arms.

The Armenian Church of the B.V.M. [3] was formerly the Benedictine Abbey of Our Lady of Tyre. During the siege of 1570 the Armenians, who hated the proud Latins, assisted the Turkish army, and on the fall of the city were handed this church as a reward.

The original church was probably founded in the thirteenth century, after the fall of Jerusalem and the expulsion of all religious Orders from that city. Soon after it had been first built it was destroyed by an earthquake, but was rebuilt by King Henry II (1285–1324). The revolt of the Prince of Tyre brought the work temporarily to a standstill. The Abbess was devoted to the cause of the King, and during his exile offered prayers for his return. This was reported to the usurper, with the additional malicious information that she had at the same time cursed him and his wife, the Princess of Tyre. In 1309 Sir Simon de Montolif assassinated the prince, and the enemies of the Abbess, always on the watch to do her some harm, reported that the murderer had taken refuge within the precincts of the church. At once a number of soldiers rushed into the building, ill-treating and insulting the Lady Abbess and her nuns. Not content with insults, the soldiers proceeded to burst open every door and cupboard, and carried off much valuable property. The Abbess, as soon as she could, went to the Legate and swore before God that neither she nor her nuns had any knowledge of the whereabouts of Montolif. The Legate persuaded the Abbess to return to her post, sending with her a body of his own men to safeguard her from further insult and the church from despoliation.

The present building was erected in the fourteenth century, and still retains a number of Gothic details, for it seems to have been but little damaged in the siege of 1570. A strange feature is a vaulted cloister on the north side, with a curious arrangement of outside arches, which support nothing; there seems no reason for this unless it was the beginning of some rebuilding which was never carried out. At the east end of this cloister are two most interesting funeral monuments, which at some period have been rearranged as an outside altar: the upper part consists of a heavily carved stone arch with moulding and leafage, while at the foot is a perfectly preserved tombstone of a Benedictine abbess. According to an inscription, it is the memorial of the most noble Eschive de Dampierre, Abbess of the Cross of Antioch and of Our Lady of Tyre, who died in 1340. The Abbess is shown giving a benediction with her right hand and holding a pastoral staff in her left; she wears a veil, over which is a round cap; at each end is the coat of arms of the Dampierre's—two fish adorsed.

The noble House of Dampierre was of great antiquity, and John de Dampierre was brother-in-law to King Hugh VI, for both had married daughters of the House of d'Ibelin.

The interior of the church has not been improved by covering up the tracery of the window with wooden sashes and coloured glass; indeed, it is only possible to study the tracery at all from the exterior. The remarkable collection of tombstones on the floor have probably never been removed from the position in which they were originally laid down. They are covered by a large carpet, which can easily be removed, and the best examples are by the semicircular step to the sanctuary. They include Mary de Bessan, who died in 1322; the costume is interesting, and the lady holds a book in her hand. The family of Bessan was one of the great princely crusading families, and took its title from the town of Bethsan in Palestine. To her right is the tomb of John Thenoure, 1362, who is represented in plate armour; on his shield he bears a coat of arms of four quarterings, one and four a fess, two and three a lion rampant. To the left of Mary de Bessan is John de Tabarie, 1402. The armour is unusual, and the tightly drawn in waist and the long pointed shoes should be noticed. In the inscription he is referred to as Marshal of Armenia. By the north door lies the tombstone of three ladies: Alice de Tabarie, 1357; Isabelle de Nevilles; and Mary de Milmars, 1393. All three ladies seem to have been buried in the same tomb, and are represented on the tombstone by a female figure in the costume of the period, with long hair falling over her shoulders. There are a number of other tombstones, more or less damaged, and a full account of them, with drawings, is given by T. J. Chamberlayne, *Lacrimae Nicossienses*, Paris, 1894.

Above the window in the south wall are the remains of a mediaeval fresco of the Virgin and Child. Inserted into the altar is a portion of the sarcophagus of the Mirabel family; this fragment is so completely embedded in the woodwork that only the front with shields within arched panels, with a coat of arms of the family, can be seen. The present holders of the church can give no reason why this fragment should be placed here. The altar platform is decorated with blue and white tiles, probably of the eighteenth century, exactly like those used in the Armenian church in Jerusalem.

The Arab Achmet Mosque [4] is built in the Byzantine style, and was erected in 1845. A mediaeval church must have once stood on this site, for a collection of gravestones, dating from the fourteenth century, is used as paving-stones for the floor. The best preserved is that of Louis de Nores (1369), who is represented in plate armour.

The family of de Nores was one of the best known of the crusading families established in the Near East, and it has been suggested that the English family of Norreys are of the same stock. The two last members of this family escaped from Nicosia after the siege of 1570 to the mountains, but it is unknown what their ultimate fate may have been.

There is also a tombstone of Francesco Cornaro, a member of that illustrious Venetian family which gave a queen to Cyprus.

In the graveyard lies buried Kiamil Pasha, born in 1833 at Pyroi, a village half-way between Nicosia and

Larnaca, where his father, Captain Salih Agha, was a police officer. Under the Turkish Government he was Commissioner of Larnaca, and later served in Constantinople, where four times he held the post of Grand Vizier, the most exalted rank in the Ottoman Empire and next to the Sultan himself. The monument to his memory above his grave was erected by Sir Ronald Storrs in 1927.

Close by lies buried a Turkish admiral, a certain Issak Pasha, who must have been exiled to Cyprus in the middle of the nineteenth century, for some fault, fancied or real, and died here.

Near the Law Courts and in the centre of the Konak Square is the Venetian column [5], the symbol of domination erected by the Republic in the various colonies which she held, and which was once crowned by the Lion of St. Mark. The column was taken down by the Turks and for many years stood in the courtyard of the Serai Mosque, but was re-erected in its present position in 1917. It is a single monolith of grey granite and doubtless once came from a temple at Salamis.

According to Jeffery[1] the coats of arms at the base are: (1) under the ducal cap, Donato or Dona Delle Rose. (2) Contarine. (3) Passaro. (4) Michiel. (5) Querine. Number six is missing. An inscription, a beautiful piece of Italian lettering, is cut on the upper step which supports the column and reads:

> FIDES INCORRUPTA NON PULCHRITUDO NON
> HUJUS UBERTAS SPECETUR INCOLAR.

Close by is the office of the Delegates of Evkaf—a large modern building. In the garden behind are the tombs of two of the Turkish generals who were killed in the street fighting which followed the fall of the city in 1570. They are plain whitewashed tombs lying side by side. Above them spread the branches of a large almond-tree, which is always the first to blossom in Nicosia, and which, while all the other trees in the city are in bud, has already shed its blanched petals so that they form a soft pall over the

[1] G. Jeffery, *Historic Monuments of Cyprus*, Nicosia, 1918, p. 50.

graves of the two warriors whose names and deeds have long passed away from the stories and legends of Cyprus. But these unknown dead are not forgotten; every night through winter or summer an old man comes and lights a flickering wick in a glass of oil, which burns till the next morning. Now one afternoon, a few years ago, Hassan, for such was the old man's name, had a marriage to attend, that of his daughter, and in the thrill and excitement he forgot to light the lamps. Tired out by his long day, he fell into a heavy slumber; suddenly he felt a hand roughly shake his shoulder. Stupid with sleep the old man opened his eyes and saw standing before him a tall man with a brown beard, wearing long flowing robes and girt with a scimitar; but what he chiefly noticed was the mingled look of anger and disappointment on the dark face. Still bewildered and dazed, Hassan heard the apparition say: "Why have you forgotten to light the lamps that burn over the tombs of my companion and myself, who died nearly four hundred years ago? Is a soldier's grave to be forgotten?" Hassan tried with trembling lips to reply, but before he could utter a word the vision vanished. Staying but to seize a box of matches, the old man, without thought of clothes, ran through the deserted and sleeping streets and with nervous hands lit the tiny wicks. Hassan has never forgotten, nor has the grim warrior risen from his grave again to remind the guardian of his duty.

The street opposite the front of the Evkaf leads to what is supposed to be the Church of St. George of the Latins, now used as a Turkish bath. Nothing remains save the elaborately carved door, richly ornamented with a motive of interlacing branches filled with birds. Owing to the decay of the neighbouring buildings, this door is sunk about six feet below the level of the street.

The Mevlevi Tekkye [6], or Mosque of the Dancing Dervishes, was built in the early seventeenth century, on land given by a certain Emine Sultan. The dancing-floor has been recently rebuilt. A long domed corridor leading from it contains the tombs of the fifteen sheikhs who have held that post in this mosque. Each tomb has at the end a painted plaster representation of the camel-hair hat with a green band at the base, which is still worn by the sheikhs.

The first tomb is that of Ahmed Pasha of the early seventeenth century, while the last holder of the dignity died in 1930. In the garden of the mosque is a white marble sarcophagus inscribed with the name of Augustino Canali, who, according to an inscription, was a member of the Supreme Council which governed the island under Venice, and who died in 1553.

Every six weeks or so a service is held in the mosque, and can be witnessed on application to the Director of Evkaf.

The Sheik sat on a carpet in the centre at the top of the oval, and the Dervishes on the floor, along the wall opposite us. With eyes shut and palms extended the Sheik murmured a long prayer, all the Dervishes bowing to the ground at the utterance of certain words in it unintelligible to us. After that an individual who, with a few musicians, occupied a square gallery at the end opposite to the Sheik, repeated or read a long tirade in a sort of nasal recitative, in that up and down quavering tremolo which the Turks affect, and which I have heard is intended to imitate the vibrations of an organ.

This exordium, which was rather trying both to the ear and to the patience, was followed by some feeble music on a limited range of notes, after which the Sheik slowly rose, bowed low to the carpet before he left it and bowed to it again when he reached the opposite end of the space. The Dervishes, following suit, all walked slowly round the space three times, and the Sheik regained his seat on the carpet; the time of the music changed, the Dervishes slipped off their cloaks, and each in turn approaching the Sheik bowed low and forthwith commenced whirling, at first with hands crossed, but soon with arms extended, to balance himself as he span smoothly and rapidly round, his long garment of spotless unbleached cotton standing out in a stiff circle, inflated by the rapid movement. The robe had a bodice of the same, confined by a coloured sash-belt. They wore open jackets and knee-breeches of the same cotton, with neat white stockings and black shoes, and their hats, as well as the Sheik's, which he never removes, are of brown felt, conical except at the apex. The costume was well made and most absolutely clean.

The Dervishes were for the most part young men, but there was one verging on age who had a worn and ghastly look as if hardly able to bear the strain. This went on for perhaps half an hour or more with only one pause, during which they prostrated themselves by the wall, and an attendant acolyte, in black, who could not see their faces but knew the coloured order of their cloaks, passing behind them, threw over each Dervish his own special cloak. Then the music stopped and they all passed slowly before the Sheik, kissing his robe as they passed, after which they met and bowed to each other in turn, kissing each other on either side of the breast in a very dexterous and curious manner, each with a simultaneous, double, sideways peck at the other.[1]

The Kyrenia Gate [7] was the third of the entrances into the city erected by the Venetians. Recently the gate has been isolated and two new entrances have been cut through the walls each side of it. The gate was originally known as Del Proveditore, after the Proveditore Francesco Barbaro. It was repaired by the Turks in 1821, when the square chamber above it was added. Over the arched doorway was a large panel with verses from the Koran cut on it. During the recent restoration this panel was taken out, and when it was turned round it was found that the reverse had on it an inscription recording the Venetian building of the walls and gate, and it is this side which once more is visible.

Close by is the Barbaro bastion, and on it are a number of English guns of the time of George III. Apparently they were brought out from England by Sir Sidney Smith, to defend Acre against Napoleon. They afterwards passed into the hands of the Turks who brought them to Cyprus, but did not trouble to remove them when they handed over the Island in 1878.

The Beuyuk Khan [8] was doubtless once a mediaeval building, but was rebuilt soon after the siege of 1570, and adapted as a khan. Mariti, who was in Nicosia in the middle of the eighteenth century, says:

[1] Mrs. Lewis, *A Lady's Impressions of Cyprus*, 1894, p. 198.

In the middle of it is a khan, or vast courtyard, round which are many rooms: the gate is of marble, built up of ancient remains. This khan was built for the benefit of foreigners generally by Muzaffer Pasha, who imposed to this end a tax of two paras (about two crazie) on every Cypriot. The impost was small indeed, but unjust, and, although he had the merit of having been with Mustafa Pasha at the taking of Nicosia, he was beheaded. He would not have been so punished in our days. The place is known as the khan of the Alajotes, because it is chiefly used by traders from Alaja in Caramania.[1]

From the original building remain the very interesting octagonal stone chimneys. These most unusual features in a mediaeval Cyprus building can be best observed from the garage behind the khan.

In the centre of this khan is a small domed mosque supported on marble pillars. By the steps which lead up to it is the empty and desecrated tomb of some unknown Turk, perhaps the builder.

At the end of the same street is a smaller khan, known by the delightful name of the Khan of the Itinerant Musicians. It is formed out of fragments from other buildings, though the main gate seems to be late sixteenth century.

St. Sofia [9], formerly the cathedral and now the principal mosque of Nicosia, is the most remarkable monument still existing in the capital. It stands in the centre of the city, and its twin minarets form a prominent landmark for many miles round. The cathedral, as we see it at present, was begun by Archbishop Eustorge de Montaigu (1217–1249), the fourth occupant of the See, but there was undoubtedly an earlier building on this site, and a few fragments of twelfth-century work can be found built into the present edifice. Work on the unfinished building was given a fresh impetus by the arrival in 1248 of St. Louis, the Crusader king of France, with numerous artists and architects in his train. It was followed, however, by a great setback caused by the death of Archbishop Eustorge in the camp of St. Louis in Egypt.

In 1319 the Archbishop Giovanni Del Conte completed

[1] Mariti, *Travels in Cyprus*, London, 1791, p.101.

a nave and built the magnificent narthex; and on November 5, 1326, the cathedral was solemnly consecrated. At that time St. Sofia must have presented a picture of the utmost splendour; descriptions still remain of the interior: the vault painted with golden stars on a blue background, the great high altar with its precious relics covered with gold and set with precious stones, its elaborate tombs and the silken tapestries hanging from its walls. Unhappily this glory was short-lived, for during the Genoese invasion of 1373 the cathedral was pillaged, and a similar misfortune occurred when the Mamluks won the Battle of Khirokitia in 1426. In spite of these events the cathedral towards the end of the fifteenth century still retained much of its magnificence.

Earthquakes caused much damage in 1491 and again in 1547, and it is recorded that after the latter so low had the Catholic Church in Cyprus sunk that it was with difficulty that the Lieutenant-Governor of Cyprus could find a chaplain to perform divine service within the cathedral walls. The last scene in the history of the building as Christian cathedral was enacted in 1570. The Turks were thundering at the gates of the city while the heroic Bishop of Paphos, Francesco Contarini, preached a sermon exhorting the people to resist to the last.

". . . every motive, both human and divine," he urged, "bids you display invincible valour, and that with a resolution the more bold and intrepid, inasmuch as you, freemen and the scions of a noble and illustrious race, are called upon to contend with slaves, an ignoble and unwarlike rabble, accustomed to achieve victory more by the number than by the valour of its soldiery; an advantage which they will not now enjoy, since this city is surrounded by very lofty walls and defended by an artillery so numerous that it alone will be able to repulse the enemy, who are of such a sort that, rest assured, if you only bear off their first attack, when they have screwed up their courage to deliver the assault, the victory will certainly be yours. For the succour cannot long delay its arrival, which you have heard is being prepared with a very powerful fleet by our republic, as she will never hesitate to send all her forces for the defence of this kingdom, which is regarded as the noblest portion of her dominions and is most dear to all. These human measures, though of themselves sufficient for your protection, your prayers, your faith, and your firm resolve to forsake your sins will render altogether invincible, while you, chastened more by fear than by actual punishment, will have time and cause to praise, honour and glorify the most High God, Who, with singular kindness showing you the appearance only of His anger through the rage of this Ottoman barbarian, has been pleased to provide for the safety of your souls and for the obtaining of the heavenly riches, and at the same time for the preservation of your lives, your native land and property, to the intent that you may henceforth devote all these things to the glory of Him who is your true and bountiful Lord and the giver of all good gifts."[1]

This was not only the last sermon to be preached in the cathedral, but the last Christian service to be held within its walls. On September 9th Nicosia fell and the brave Contarini was slain. The Turks lost no time in converting the cathedral into a mosque.

They began to clear out S. Sophia, the Latin cathedral, and arrange it after their own fashion, removing the choir, destroying the altars, and so forth. On the following Friday, September 15th, the day called Juma, which they keep as a Sunday, the Pasha went with his suite to worship God, as their wont is on that day, and to thank Him for so great a victory.[2]

St. Sofia is built after the plan of a French cathedral of the thirteenth century, and is carried out in the purest early French pointed style. The chief glory of the building is still the Galilee or parvis. Its three superbly decorated doorways are worthy to be compared with the cathedrals of Europe, and the central door, nearly twice as wide as those that flank it, consists of four orders of deeply carved moulding, an enrichment now unfortunately lost to some extent, having been partially filled with plaster by the Turks. In panels of the tympanum of white marble no traces of paintings have survived. At each side, however, still remain two charming reliefs of angels swinging censers, perhaps

[1] J. Hackett, *The Church of Cyprus*, London, 1901, p. 180.
[2] Calepio, 1573, *Excerpta Cypria*, p. 141.

the sole survivors of the statuary with which the cathedral must once have been so lavishly adorned. The door itself has panels on either side decorated at the top with a curious representation of a pair of hands holding a crown, doubtless the hands of God crowning a group of saints, or, as it has been suggested by Mr. Jeffery,[1] the figures may have been those of the twelve apostles.

The two doorways north and south of the central entrance have the same architectural conception, though the design in each is different. The north doorway is the most elaborate and had at one time a number of miniature statues under canopies in the moulding of the jambs. Here the carving of the arch is bolder and finer than the other doors in its floral design, an unusual effect being the use of the clematis as an architectural motif. The south doorway is interesting for the number of graffiti and coats of arms carved on the lower panels, the work perhaps of pages waiting for their lords during the long services of the church.

The interior at first sight seems bare and unrelieved, for all the sepulchres, altars, and screens of Latin workmanship were swept away by the Turks when they turned the structure into a mosque. At the same time the walls were pierced for a lower series of windows and various platforms were erected so that the church was orientated towards Mecca and not Jerusalem.

The interior plan consists of a nave and aisles of five bays, terminated by a semicircular apse encircling both the aisles and nave. The pillars in the nave are cylindrical, with capitals and bases, both painted green during a recent Turkish restoration. The vaulting of the ambulatory rests on four granite columns—probably taken from a temple at Salamis—with four florid marble capitals of the Byzantine period painted an unpleasant dark green. For some reason or other one of these granite columns was too short, and the deficiency was made up by the insertion of an inverted early Gothic capital which may very well have belonged to the first cathedral.

[1] *Monuments of Cyprus*, p. 69.

Originally the choir was divided from the rest of the cathedral by a marble screen standing, no doubt, in line with the fourth pair of pillars from the west end. The high altar stood in the apse, formed by the pillars of the ambulatory, with the choir stalls between it and the screen. The cathedral has five structural chapels attached to its sides. The south transept, where the Mihrab or Moslem altar now stands, was the Lady Chapel founded by King Hugh III in 1270. That on the north side may have been dedicated to St. Nicholas, and its altar was in a semicircular apse now occupied by a flight of stairs. This wooden stairway leads to the women's gallery from whence, in the Turkish period, the ladies of the Governor's household could watch, seeing but unseen, the great services of Bairam and the other Moslem festivals. Above, in the vaulting, is a great boss, the green paint formerly covering it having nearly all flaked off, so that its decoration the "Agnus Dei" can once more be seen. A passage cut in the wall leads to a tiny chapel of great charm and interest. This was the Treasury of the cathedral, and for this purpose were built the cupboards in the west wall. One of them, approached by a ladder, was doubtless intended as a strong-room. The two-light window on the south side, with window seats beneath it, was probably used by the cathedral sacristans to watch the high altar, and to see that the reliquaries and other objects exposed for the veneration of the faithful were untouched; it may also have served for exposing the relics of the church to the congregation.

The Chapel of St. Thomas Aquinas opens out of the church in the second bay from the west end on the south side. St. Thomas was a friend of King Hugh III of Cyprus, to whom he dedicated his book, *De Regimine Principum*, about the year 1275. Felix Faber, a Dominican monk, who visited his chapel 250 years after it had been built, gives the following description:

On the right of the church is a chapel dedicated to S. Thomas Aquinas, in which the legends of the holy doctor are exquisitely painted, while a gilt plaque on the altar sets forth his acts. In this chapel I saw a remarkable monument, which I will describe.

For at the side there stood, and still stands, a large and beautiful tomb, of great value, made of precious jasper. I measured it with my own hands, and found it twelve palms or spans in length, seven in depth, and five broad, and one in thickness, the whole of solid stone. It has a cover of the same dimensions, "à dos d'âne," in the usual form, of the same stone and price. The colour is generally green, but the stone which is polished is spotted with other colours, which add to the beauty of such marble. It is said to have as many virtues as it has spots, and these spots, which are innumerable, are red or rosy as though the stone had been sprinkled with blood. Those who carry it about chastely will find in it these virtues. It drives away phantoms, checks fevers, cures dropsy, helps women in childbed, preserves a man in danger, allays inward heat, stanches blood, represses passion and its consequences, cures inveterate ulcers, purges the eyes, and strengthens and comforts their use, is proof against witchery and spells, and more efficacious set in silver than in gold. It is found only in the mountains of Scythia, where it is of excellent quality, and whole cliffs and rocks of it exist. But lest so precious a treasure should remain unguarded, and its plenty render it valueless, God has set round those mountains very strong and fierce guardians, the gryphons, most savage beasts who resist the approach of strangers, running and flying upon them, and tearing them with their beaks and claws, so that no one can come near the stone until he has overcome the gryphons. Jason had to battle with them for the golden fleece, and Hercules for the golden apples of the garden of the Hesperides. These gryphons are most fierce creatures, with heads of eagles and the bodies of lions, they fly like the one and run like the other, and have such daring and strength that they attack an armed horseman, and carry off both man and beast whither they will; they are indeed huge and savage beasts. The head, beak and wings are fashioned as those of an eagle, their forefeet also, which have long claws; the hinder feet and the tail are those of a lion, but the legs are shorter, and the claws short and so large that drinking cups are made of them. It is said these beasts are never found except near mountains which teem with gold and precious stones; these they dig up, and take an extraordinary pleasure in gazing at and playing with them, defending them most savagely against others. In Asiatic Scythia, a rich but uninhabitable land, and accessible only to the Arimaspians, these savages, who have a single eye in their foreheads, arm themselves against the gryphons, and go and carry off the gems. Jerome, in his letter to the monk Rusticus, speaks of the way gold and gems are guarded by the gryphons. . . .[1]

Opening out of the third bay on the south side is a small square chapel, completely detached, its entrance being a wooden door. It is now used for the storage of lamps and various rubbish. On the south side is an arched tomb niche with a coat of arms, on a shield three pine cones. The same coat of arms is repeated on the exterior wall, and is probably the badge of the famous family of De Pins, which in the fourteenth century gave a Grand Master to the Order of St. John of Jerusalem.

There remains yet to be noticed the curious wall passage carried on the arches of the side aisles and below the windows. No very satisfactory explanation has been given for this. Standing at the east end and looking down the cathedral, the full glory of the west window can be appreciated, blocked though it is with gypsum brightened with fragments of Turkish glass inserted in the openings. In the south-west corner is a small door leading to a circular staircase which ascends to the roof. At the first opening it is possible to cross the west end of the cathedral by a narrow passage that runs beneath the great window. From this gallery a comprehensive view of the interior is obtained and the curious crookedness caused by the steps, platforms, and carpets being placed diagonally—i.e. Meccawards—across the floor becomes very noticeable.

Continuing the ascent, the north-west staircase leads into the gallery above the narthex, where it becomes obvious that the south tower has never been finished. This gallery was used for the exposition of relics or the pageantry pertaining to royal coronations. It is possible from here to ascend by the south minaret and so reach the roof of the south aisle, where the roof beneath the flying buttresses can be explored.

The east door was originally on the south side, having been removed to its present position in the last century.

[1] *Excerpta Cypria*, p. 42.

It is almost certain that the doorway dates from the cathedral of 1209. The tympanum of the arch is now filled with an inscription from the Koran and the seal of Abdul Aziz.

A number of mediaeval tombstones still remain on the floor, but as in the case of the Omerieh Mosque the majority of them are broken and a number are placed upside-down, and it is hoped shortly to rescue them from their present position and to place them in a more worthy site. For it must be remembered that none of these tombstones is *in situ*, for the Turks took up the whole floor and threw out the bones that lay beneath into the street, relaying the floor with the tombstones to save themselves the trouble of finding new stone.

The tombstones at present visible include that of Arnati Viconti (1347), which is far and away the best preserved example of the plate armour of the period. There is also the tombstone of Dame Marguerite Gapsel (1400). Her costume is interesting, with long sleeves and pointed shoes. The rest of the tombstones are broken and scattered all over the church, and it is hoped when the floor is taken up to be able to join a number of them together.

Dietrich von Schachten, who accompanied the Landgrave of Hesse on his visit to Nicosia in 1491, visited the cathedral just after the earthquake of April 21st. He gives the following account of the destruction caused to the cathedral, and of the finding of the king's tomb.

The earthquake did great damage everywhere, and especially in Nicosia, where it threw down a large part of St. Sophia, on which occasion a great miracle occurred as follows: when the earthquake came, it threw down the choir, immediately behind which was the tabernacle, in which was hanging a burning lamp: it broke the tabernacle and the Holy Sacrament remained entire, the lamp being found quite unbroken under the stones which had fallen from the choir—the which was a great miracle,

On the same occasion they found a king's grave (Hugh II, 1267) and documents in the grave, which was never yet known. This same king was quite fresh, as though buried six months before, in his golden coat with boots and spurs, with his gold inlaid sword, and his fine golden crown on his head: and in his right hand a golden apple with the cross, as a king should sit in his majesty: and in the document it was found that it was two hundred and some years since he died. And as soon as he came out of the grave he fell in pieces, as I, Dietrich von Schachten, have also seen. The Venetians took over the gold treasure, but for the use and honour of the church. At the same time many other churches and houses were overthrown, to an estimated number of four thousand in this town alone.[1]

It is interesting to observe that the imperial orb is termed by the writer the "apple", as it is also called in modern Greek to this day.

Opposite the east door of the cathedral is the Turkish library founded by Sultan Mahmoud in the early years of the last century. The interior consists of a single chamber; round the walls and above the bookcases runs an inscription from the Koran, in gilt letters on a blue background. The heavy top of the great bookcase is painted in the same colours, and the carved woodwork is in the style of the First Empire, as seen through Turkish eyes. Some of the books are of interest, and one or two are nearly seven hundred years old. Some have frontispieces and ends painted with flowers in the Persian manner.

At the south-east corner of the cathedral and near this library is a mediaeval building, once the chapter house of the cathedral. It has recently been rescued from becoming a garage, and the rich moulding of its windows has been repaired.

Opposite the north door of the cathedral is a fragment of the Latin archbishopric; little remains save a door and two small windows. On the façade are various coats of arms, including that of Donato, with a mitre above it.

The Bedestan [10] is merely a Turkish word meaning a market; the building was, before the conquest in 1570, the Orthodox metropolis of the Venetian period in Nicosia, and is separated from its Latin neighbour by the width of a street. There is no mention of it in existing records till the first years of the sixteenth century, when it was referred

[1] R. Rohricht and H. Meisner, *Deutsche Pilgerreisen nach dem Heiligen Lande*, Berlin, 1880.

to as the "Greek cathedral". The plan of the building consists of two churches built side by side, that on the south being much the earliest, and consisting of two aisles with two apses. The decorated capitals of the pillars which divide these two aisles have shields with a coat of arms of three bends. The west end has been destroyed at some period, and the building as we now see it is only half its original size. In 1906 a carved doorway from this west end was removed, when the squalid shops that had usurped its position were being rebuilt, and is now in the gardens of Government House. In the early sixteenth century was added the northern part of the building, which consists of two large aisles, the larger of which ends in a five-sided apse and is crowned with an octagonal cupola, the whole a curious mixture of Byzantine and mediaeval styles. The vaulting at the west end of this nave is faulty and of poor construction, and must have been added at a later date. The chief interest of the building lies in its northern façade, which faces the cathedral, and the eye is at once drawn to the great doorway which is a copy, on a smaller scale, of the marble archway of its Latin neighbour on the other side of the road; but on close examination it becomes only too apparent how Cypriote mason-craft had deteriorated during the two centuries that had passed since Archbishop Giovanni Del Conte had built the Galilee of St. Sofia.

The lintel of white marble is surmounted by a panel with the figure of a saint in the centre, with on either side a row of three coats of arms. Mr. Jeffery[1] has suggested that reading from left to right they represent the following families: (1) Da Ponte; (2) Da Ponte or Canali; (3) Basegio. (4) Pisani; (5) Verdizotti. Number six is defaced.

The second doorway on the north wall is also a copy of Gothic work, and is perhaps influenced by the neighbouring Church of St. Catherine. Between these two entrances stands what, at first sight, looks like a blocked doorway, but is almost certainly an external iconostasis or the stand on which the icon of the day would have been placed and thus be visible to the passer-by in the street.

[1] *Monuments of Cyprus*, p. 87.

In the centre of the marble lintel is a charming relief of the Dormition of the Virgin, which has managed to escape the mutilation which has overtaken so many of the sculptures and decorations of the churches in Cyprus. This fragment probably dates from the fifteenth century; it is possible that the whole of the stonework of this iconostasis may be formed from the doorway of some earlier building.

Quite close to the St. Sofia there is another beautiful building which was dedicated to St. Nicholas, bishop, as one sees from a figure of the said saint in bas-relief still remaining over the door. This church also had three aisles, and columns on which are painted various saints, much damaged. The place is now called Bezesten, a kind of market, where all kinds of goods are sold. It is the business resort of the chief merchants of Nicosia, Turks, Greeks, and Armenians.[1]

A misapprehension has grown up round this building, and still persists to the present day, that it is the Church of St. Nicholas belonging to the Order of St. Thomas the Martyr, founded in memory of the martyred Archbishop, Thomas a Becket. Its distinguishing badge was a mantle bearing a red and white cross. Originally established at Acre during the Third Crusade, it was transferred on the fall of that city in 1291 to Limassol. In Nicosia the Order had a church mentioned in documents of the period as the "Church of the Blessed Nicholas of the English", for St. Nicholas was the murdered Archbishop's patron saint; but there is no reason to identify the Bedestan with the Church of St. Nicholas, for the only connection with the English Order is the figure of the saint in the centre of the panel of the great north door, which may or may not be that of St. Nicholas. The Order of St. Thomas had left the island before the Venetian occupation, and it is almost certain that their church, if still standing, was one of the many destroyed when the Venetians reduced the circuit of the walls.

Here at present is kept a collection of mediaeval tombstones taken from the floor of the Omerieh Mosque,

[1] Mariti, *Travels Through Cyprus*.

formerly the Augustinian church. The majority of these tombstones were broken by the Turks when they turned the church into a mosque and relaid the floor, and unfortunately a great number of pieces are missing.

The Musée Lapidaire [11] is a charming fifteenth-century house, which has recently been repaired and put in order. The first storey is lighted with square windows, which have balconies supported on carved corbels, each decorated with a device, flowers, the head of an old woman, heraldic beasts, and with a delightful Dick Whittington-like figure of a youth, with his bundle on his stick over his shoulder, wearing a broad-brimmed hat, and apparently trudging forward to seek his fortune.

This house now contains mediaeval and Gothic fragments from the vanished palaces and churches of Nicosia; lintels with coats of arms from the houses of nobles and the sarcophagi of powerful families. The great window in the north wall is from the royal palace, pulled down at the beginning of this century. This arched window with its flowing tracery is all that remains of the royal residence.

> The house in which the King of Cyprus lives is fine; it has a courtyard as large as that of the new castle at Naples, and many fine apartments round it, among which is a large hall. At the end of that hall is a very beautiful throne with many fair columns and ornaments of various kinds. I fancy that few things or none will be found more beautiful than that throne. Around the hall runs a kind of arcade, beautifully adorned with columns. Such daring had I that I went right up to the entrance of the king's room, and had the door been open I was ready to enter and talk with him.[1]

A later traveller gives the description of the palace reminiscent of a picture by Panini:

> The Palace, formerly the residence of the Kings of Cyprus, is large and beautiful: above the entrance you see the arms of the house of Lusignan, crowned, and quartered with those of

---

[1] Martoni, 1394, *Excerpta Cypria*, p. 22.

Savoy. The Pasha or Viceroy lives there. In front is a spacious and fine square, in the midst of which is a pyramid or obelisk like those one sees at Rome. The Turks exercise their horses here every Friday.[1]

Here, too, is preserved the tomb of Adam of Antioch, Marshal of Cyprus, which was found when the Church of Paliouriotissa was being rebuilt; the coped lid is carved with a representation of a funeral pall. Opposite stands the fourteenth-century sarcophagus of the Dampierres; this work of art is well preserved, and is one of the most important mediaeval relics left to us. This bone chest must have once stood in a church, perhaps in the private chapel of the Dampierre family. The reason for these bone chests was that after a member of the family had been dead for about three years, his skull and bones were taken up, washed, and placed in them.

St. Catherine [12], now known as the Haidar Pasha, is, after the cathedral, the most important Gothic building remaining in Nicosia. It was erected towards the end of the fourteenth century in what is known as the flamboyant style. Except for the low windows pierced at floor-level in the walls and the minaret erected by the Turks, it is changed little from the day it was first built. There are two fine doorways: the west door has a marble lintel with a rose between two dragons repeated three times, and the central side pillars are also of marble. The south doorway is of heavier work, and seems to detract somewhat from the lightness and grace of the window above it. On the lintel are three defaced shields, in all probability the Royal Arms. In front of the door lies a gravestone, but passing feet have worn away the effigy and the inscription once incised on it.

The interior has recently been cleaned of the whitewash that covered its walls, and traces of painting can be seen on the wall shafts, while the piscina shows remains of the original colouring. The drain from the piscina runs through the walls, and the rinsings of the chalice were carried into a tiny chamber in the angle of the apse.

[1] Stochove, 1637, *Excerpta Cypria*, p. 215.

North of the apse is a sacristy; the lintel of its door has a defaced shield between two roses. The vaulting of the sacristy is supported on corbels with finely carved human heads which have remained unharmed during the transition of St. Catherine from a church into a mosque. Above this sacristy is a curious lofty chamber, once divided into two storeys by a floor. The lower of these has a window looking into the church, while the upper has windows in the external walls. The former was entered by a doorway from the roof of the Conventual building which once extended along the whole north side of the church. The latter has long since disappeared. It is hard to assign a reason for this chamber, but it may have been a treasury, and the window looking into the church may have been used for the exposition of the precious relics which belonged to the church.

The Yeni Jami, or New Mosque [13], was formerly a mediaeval church, but was turned with the cathedral and many others into a mosque in 1571. The original church was probably built in the fourteenth century, but in the eighteenth it was torn down by a rapacious Turkish official, who believed that there was treasure buried beneath its floor. The only part spared was the south-west corner, with its turret staircase, and the only reason this survived the general demolition was because it had the minaret erected on it.

For many years the marble lintel, with a decoration of dragons' heads and roses, lay on the ground, but this fragment has now been removed to the gardens of Government House. Near here are three Turkish tombs, which are small domed buildings beneath the vaults of which are florid marble sarcophagi, with long Arabic inscriptions at the head and foot. Two are resting-places of a father and son, Mentish Ismail Aga, and across the road his son Hassan. They died in 1734 and 1749 respectively. The father is said to have been a dishonest and knavish high official, and seems to have spent his time in oppressing the widows and robbing the fatherless; but at last he was found out and committed suicide rather than expiate his crimes on the gallows. The third tomb is of Hassan Hilmi, who was a poet and Grand Mufti of Cyprus, and died about 1800.

The Church of St. Luke [14] was built in the time of Archbishop Philotheos in 1758. The north and west doorways are in the mediaeval style, and doubtless come from some earlier building. The southern portion of the iconostasis is contemporary with the building, though it contains icons of an earlier date, the most interesting being an early sixteenth-century icon of the Annunciation in the Italian manner, with a donor, his wife and son, the latter wearing a black tunic and red hose, while round his waist is a belt with a short sword attached to it. On the north wall of the church hangs a large rood cross, dated 1692. In the gallery are a collection of icons which must all have come from a former church. Two of them are of great interest, and probably date from the fifteenth century. These icons are painted on both sides, and obviously were meant to be carried in processions, though the poles on which they were mounted have long since disappeared. Both show the same scenes, on one side the Crucifixion and on the reverse the Virgin. The larger of the icons is the better preserved, and the drawing of the figures grouped at the foot of the cross is by a skilled hand. In each case the semi-halo surrounding the Virgin's head is of gilded gesso.

Two other icons which lie here are of interest: a large panel of St. Barnabas with a donor priest who wears a cope with an elaborate "chequer-board" pattern and black skull-cap. This icon probably dates from the first half of the sixteenth century. The second is later, and shows the Virgin with upraised hands, and at the foot four donors, a man, his wife, and a son and daughter. The father wears a curious green head-dress reminiscent of a Turkish turban, while the ladies wear white hooded cloaks with green dresses underneath.

St. Kassianos [15] is a modern church, built perhaps on the site of a Latin church destroyed in 1570. Fragments from an earlier building have been re-used in its construction, of which the most interesting is in the narthex—a small bas-relief of the Virgin and Child under a canopy, probably dating from the fifteenth century. The great interest of this church lies in the collection of icons which it contains. On the west wall in glazed frames are three of the best: the one nearest the door is a superb example of post-Byzantine painting, and shows the Ascension of our Lord; the colours are still of great beauty, especially the blue and white robes of the angels behind the Madonna. This icon probably dates from *c.* 1456, and is one of the finest examples of icon painting that has come down to us.

The subject of the next icon is uncertain, but is almost certainly the "Doubting Thomas." There are two kneeling donors, a man and his wife. According to a much-damaged inscription, the man appears to have been a secretary of the Queen, and it is possible that the person here represented was the Greek secretary or translator to Queen Catherina Cornaro, or Queen Charlotte.

The third of these icons is unlike the two former, in that it is entirely in a Cypriote style, and shows the "Presentation of the Infant Christ in the Temple". The costumes of the donors are interesting. To the left are the father and his son; the latter wears a rich red dress, with a black cloak and scarlet hose. To the right kneel the wife and three youthful daughters; the mother in a black dress, with puffed sleeves, her neck covered with thin muslin, stiffened probably with whalebone. Her hair is confined by a net, attached to which is a veil, which falls behind her head to her feet. The daughters' dresses are of the same fashion, but richer and embroidered with gold. Two of them wear circular gold brooches in front of their head-dresses. From the style of the costumes this icon would appear to belong to the first quarter of the sixteenth century.

On the same wall, but unframed, is a large icon, *c.* 1520, of the Transfiguration, with a youthful female donor in a red dress with black sleeves; her bright yellow hair, covered by a thin veil, falls behind her.

In the centre of the church and in a glass case is not only the earliest but the most interesting icon in the building. Said traditionally to come from St. Sofia, it is of unusual size, and shows the Virgin and Child. At her feet are a group of supplicant priests in white robes, who may perhaps be Dominicans. At each side of the icon are a series of small pictures, eight each side, with Latin inscriptions underneath; most of these scenes are unfortunately much damaged, and it is difficult to state with certainty what they represent. The first scene shows a king on his throne with his Court in front of him, and subsequent pictures seem to depict the adventures of the king in search of some relic. A female saint appears to accompany the pilgrims and is present in most of the pictures. The second scene on the right is curiously like the Bayeux tapestry. It is extremely difficult to date this icon, but some of the costumes worn, especially those of the ladies of the Court in the first scene, are reminiscent of Europe in the first half of the fourteenth century.

The iconostasis is mostly of the eighteenth century, as indeed are the icons in it, and three only are of interest:

(1) St. Kassianos, covered with silver repoussé work and dated 1783. On the right-hand side is shown the helmet traditionally said to have been worn by St. Kassianos at the time of his martyrdom. The helmet itself, covered with silver, lies on the altar within the apse.

(2) A much repainted icon of Christ supported by the Virgin and St. John the Baptist, with a female donor in the right-hand corner.

(3) The Virgin and Child, also unhappily restored, but showing in Our Lady's face and the attitude of the Child the true Byzantine style.

In the women's gallery lie a few more early icons, the most interesting being an icon of the Virgin and Child, while in front is the model of a church with flamboyant Gothic windows and a tall campanile. To left and right of the church are two angels, while in front kneel the donors, a man and his wife. The icon is dated 1529, and the model of the church may represent the actual building for which this icon was intended. There is also an early sixteenth-century icon of St. Catherine, with two donors and a much damaged St. George dated 1599. At the end of the gallery also is kept one of those curious canvasses brought back by pilgrims to Palestine, and showing in a series of small pictures a most amazing number of facts connected with the Holy Land: the Creation and Deluge, the Life and Passion of Our Lord, and even the parable of the Lost Sheep. Nor are the sacred sites forgotten, for there are pictures of the Holy Sepulchre, Jaffa, and the Monastery of St. Catherine on Sinai; and as if this were not enough, room has been found for a most lurid "Day of Judgement" and the portrait of the Virgin painted by St. Luke. This pleasantly barbaric example of rustic art is dated 1811.

Till within the last few years an effigy of Judas was burnt in the churchyard on Good Friday.

In a street near the church lived Captain H. H. Kitchener, while he was in charge of the survey of the island. A tablet recording the fact that the future Field-Marshal lived here was placed on the house by Sir Ronald Storrs in 1927.

The small Church of St. George [16] is close to that of St. Kassianos. It is a simple barrel-vaulted building, and consists of a nave and north aisle, and probably dates from the seventeenth century, though fragments from an earlier building survive in its walls. Over the west door is a portion of the panelled front of a fifteenth-century sarcophagus, with three coats of arms on it, the centre belonging to the Syrian family of Gourri. On either side of this central coat of arms is a shield bearing three chevrons. The iconostasis was, according to an inscription on it, built in 1812, during the time of Archbishop Kyprianos. There are some large early seventeenth-century icons, which are kept in the north aisle. The icon of St. George and his martyrdom on the south wall was painted in 1719 but restored in 1851. In the iconostasis screen there is a noble icon of St. John the Baptist, dated 1700. The walls of the church were probably once painted, but all the paintings have been whitewashed over, and only a fragment can still be seen above the icon of St. George, already mentioned.

The Church of the Panayia Chrysaliniotissa [17] is

traditionally said to have been built in 1450 by Helena Palaeologus, daughter of the Despot of the Morea and wife of John II of Cyprus, whom she married in 1440. The present church is a building of different periods, and was once surrounded by a monastic enclosure, of which only a fragment now exists. An unhappy restoration a few years ago swept away a large portion of this enclosure, and at the same time the narthex was rebuilt. The church is of a curious plan, with a considerably elongated southern transept. The doorway into this transept and the exterior arcade are built of fifteenth-century materials, but the church must have been remodelled in the Venetian period, and the coat of arms on a white marble panel inserted on the northern wall may be that of the rebuilder. In the bema lie fragments of mediaeval tombstones, one showing a portion of the upper part of the figure of a knight in fourteenth-century costume, while others are in the Italian style of the fifteenth and sixteenth centuries, but too much defaced to allow of any description. The iconostasis is a patchwork of various periods and styles; the four lowest panels to the left and right of the holy doors in the central portion would seem to be of the early sixteenth century. Like those of St. Kassianos, the icons of the church are of considerable interest; the miraculous icon of the Virgin, said to have been found in the field of flax on this site, and which gave the church its name, has long since disappeared.

Starting from the north end of the iconostasis the most interesting are: (1) the Resurrection, with a portrait of the donor, Menicos Pelicanos, in Venetian costume and dated 1563. (2) St. Nicholas, represented in the Byzantine tradition, though the three donors wear Flemish costume of the early sixteenth century. (3) A long panel of St. Paraskeva with a youthful donor at the foot probably dating from the latter half of the fifteenth century. (4) The Virgin and Child, revarnished but otherwise in a good state of preservation and showing strong Italian feeling in the treatment of the Virgin's robes, *c.* 1520.

In a large chamber at the end of the elongated south transept is a collection of icons, which were found in one of the rooms of the fragment of the monastic building which still remains, and which were cleaned and placed here by Professor and Mrs. Talbot-Rice and the author in 1934. The gem of the collection is undoubtedly the long icon in the glass case. Painted in 1365, this is a fine example of the best late Byzantine workmanship. Above is seen Christ Pantocrator, the Creator of All. Below Him are two archangels. Below them are the donors of the icon, Manual the lay-preacher and his wife Eupheia. Last of all comes the Princess Maria; her face and blue eyes are painted almost in the style of a miniature; she wears a golden head-dress, long ear-rings, a necklace, and her fingers are covered with rings; her dress is of bright scarlet, elaborately decorated with golden fish *dos à dos*. Undoubtedly this is the actual portrait of some Byzantine princess, but whose daughter she was and where she came from is unknown. The other icons, though not unique, as that of the Princess Maria is, are still of great interest. They are (1) St. Elef-therios, a long panel of the same shape and period as that of St. Paraskeva in the iconostasis. (2) A large and crudely painted early sixteenth-century icon of St. Mamas, riding his lion, with a donor priest, his wife and child. The priest is tonsured and carries the Gospel in his hand. (3) The Virgin and Child, a large icon painted in a heavy wooden fashion. The costumes of the six kneeling donors, who appear to be a man, his wife and four children, are interesting. (4) The Liturgy, the giving of the Bread and Wine; an inscription on the bottom of the picture refers to the Orthodox See of Amathus. At the sides are heraldic shields bearing a coat of arms, a lion gules rampant. (5) Christ in Glory, with four donors who wear black dresses trimmed with fur, not unlike the pictures of wealthy European merchants of the early sixteenth century. (6) A beautiful panel in the Byzan-tine rather than a Cypriote style, at the top Christ seated with His foot on a red and gold cushion, blessing with the right hand and holding with the left an open book inscribed with a sentence from one of the Gospels; to left and right are the Virgin and St. John the Baptist. Below are St. Peter and St. Paul, and at the bottom four other saints and a small kneeling donor. The colours in this icon are still amazingly bright.

In the bema is also kept a large collection of icons, only a few of which are of interest. The two most important are in glazed cases: (1) An unusual panel, in the centre the Crucifixion, while to the left and right are the Annunciation and the Nativity. This icon shows foreign influence in the position of the mourning figures at the foot of the Cross and the kneeling angel in the Nativity. It is probably late fifteenth-century work. (2) A fragment like the Princess Maria already described, but here the Princess wears a much less elaborate robe and the painting is more damaged, though the figures of the donor priest and his wife are well preserved. (3) A large icon of the triumphal entry into Jerusalem with four donors painted in pure Cypriote style. There is an architectural background meant to represent Jerusalem, and consisting of a pleasant medley of architecture; amongst other buildings can be seen a domed church in the Byzantine style, an Italianate palace with columns, and a Gothic belfry.

The Famagusta Gate [18] was the chief gate of the city, and is the principal monument of the Venetian era in Nicosia. It was built by Giulio Savorgnano in 1567, who copied it from the Lazaretto Gate at Candia in Crete, designed by Michael Sammicheli. The gate was known as Porta Giuliana, after the builder. It has suffered from a Turkish restoration, but the modern aqueduct carried across it, which masked the façade, has recently been removed, and it is possible to see the six coats of arms mentioned by Mariti in 1791. The central dome, so strongly reminiscent of the Pantheon in Rome, is as perfect as on the day it was built.

It is uncertain whether the heavy wooden gates that guard the inner entrance are Venetian or date from the Turkish era, but in all probability they are contemporary with the building of the gate.

The Church of St. Antonios [19] is a building of but little architectural character, and was restored by Archbishop Philotheos in 1743. In the narthex is a tombstone of a woman in sixteenth-century costume, possibly brought from a Latin church on or near this site. The iconostasis is contemporary with the church, and a good example of the elaborate baroque carving of the period. In the bema is kept an unusual seventeenth-century icon of the Virgin seated on a carved and gilded throne, and with the Child in her arms. A curious grandfather clock with a ship on its pendulum is kept in the body of the church.

The Orthodox Archbishopric, or Church of St. John, [20] is almost certainly built on the same site as the Abbey of St. John the Evangelist of Bibi, where was preserved in its treasury a finger of St. John the Baptist. The abbey belonged to the Benedictine Order, but seems to have passed out of their hands during the period of the Latin supremacy and probably became Orthodox property when the Benedictines left the Island in 1426. It was repaired in 1655 by Archbishop Nikephoros, the same archbishop who, in the previous year, tried to persuade Duke Carlo Emmanuele II of Savoy to reconquer Cyprus from the Turks, urging that there were but 5,000 Turks in the whole island and that the 40,000 Greeks would rise as soon as the Duke's soldiers set foot on its soil. The Duke, however, was satisfied with the empty title of King of Cyprus and Jerusalem, and had no intention of acquiring by force a heritage left to his house by Queen Charlotte.

The church as we see it to-day owes much to Archbishop Silvestros, under whom it became the cathedral of the diocese and the archiepiscopal residence, but it was at an earlier period that the dedication of the church was changed from St. John the Baptist to St. John the Divine. At the west end is a spacious narthex, and above the west door are fragments from some older building which was almost certainly the original Church of St. John Bibi. Most interesting of these is a sculptured panel originally forming the front of a sarcophagus. This panel is divided into five arched compartments. In the centre is the Crucifixion with St. Mary and St. John on either side, while the two end panels are filled with the figures of a man and his wife kneeling in prayer. The former is represented in plate armour, with a sword at his side, and his wife is habited in a long veiled costume. In the spandrels of the arcade are four shields containing coats of arms.

It is difficult to date with any exactitude this curious specimen of Cypriote sculpture, but it probably belongs to the beginning of the fifteenth century. Immediately above the west door are three coats of arms. The Lusignan bearings (but with the crosses of Jerusalem in the first quarter defaced) are in the centre, and a lion rampant regardant appears on each of the two side shields. A later inscription on the slab recalls the rebuilding of the church from the foundations by Archbishop Nikephoros in 1665.

In the narthex lie fragments of a mediaeval gypsum tombstone. Above the south door is a block of marble in the centre of which is a shield, the coat of arms defaced, surrounded with a wreath of foliage in the Italian style of the late fifteenth century. The iconostasis is an example of the over-elaborate woodwork of the mid-eighteenth century.

The vault and walls of the church are entirely covered with paintings, the majority dating from 1730, but a number in the west end are considerably later. Above the south door is a spirited representation of the Day of Judgement, with the sins of man being weighed in a huge balance, and devils underneath trying to pull down the fatal scale. The condemned are escorted by demons to an enormous mouth breathing out a tongue of flame. In the hottest part of the flame and apparently being boiled in a cauldron with other famous sinners and heretics is a richly dressed figure of Salome, who from her features would seem to suffer no inconvenience from the temperature.

On the north side is a large picture of the Creation, with various birds, animals, and fishes, while opposite is a Tree of Jesse, also represented in the much earlier buildings of Antiphonitissa and Kalopanayiotes. The most interesting fresco is a composition of four scenes, to the right of the archiepiscopal throne, representing the legend of "The Invention of the Relics of St. Barnabas". In the middle of the four pictures is an inscription explaining their meaning. According to this "The Autonomous Church of Cyprus by the Apostolic tradition, and in accordance with the third Oecumenical Council, and after the discovery of the body of Barnabas and of his Gospel, was permitted by the Emperor Zeno to carry such marks of dignity as here are seen".

Constantine the Great, for convenience of administration, divided his empire into thirteen dioceses. The first of these, called the East, had its capital at Antioch, and was further subdivided into fifteen provinces, of which Cyprus was one. The Church at Antioch claimed that the Church of Cyprus came under its rule, and therefore was no longer independent. This contention was not, however, supported by the Council of Ephesus, whose decision was given in favour of Cyprus. The matter was not reopened till the reign of the Emperor Zeno (A.D. 474–491), when Peter the Fuller, who occupied the patriarchal throne, asserted that Cyprus, having originally received the faith from Antioch, should be subject to that See, which was an Apostolic foundation.

There is little doubt the attack against the liberties of the island Church would this time have succeeded, but for the opportune intervention of its patron saint. The Emperor favoured the cause of the heresiarch, whom he had restored to his diocese after being twice expelled during the reign of Leo. Though Anthemios, then in possession of the archiepiscopal see, resisted the pretension to the utmost of his power, he must eventually have succumbed to the powerful influences brought against him. Assistance came from a most strange and unexpected quarter. The Apostle Barnabas, suddenly appearing in a vision to the archbishop, urged him to lay his case in person before the Emperor at Constantinople, and at the same time revealed the place of his sepulchre. On the morrow, accompanied by his clergy and a great concourse of people, Anthemios went in procession to the place, which had been so miraculously indicated. After engaging in prayer they commenced to dig beneath a carob-tree, marking the supposed site of the burial. They soon came upon a cave, wherein they found a chest containing the remains of the saint, with a copy of St. Matthew's Gospel in Barnabas's own handwriting upon the breast, where it had been placed by Mark.

The most sceptical could no longer doubt that the Church of Cyprus was equally as apostolic as that of Antioch, and, therefore, of equal rank. Overjoyed at the discovery, Anthemios set off at once with the precious relics for Constantinople, where he reported the marvellous occurrence, and requested the Emperor's protection against the Patriarch's tyranny. Zeno, on hearing what had taken place, ordered Akakios, the Patriarch of Constantinople, to convene a meeting of his Synod to decide the matter in dispute.

The opponents of Cyprus began the discussion by claiming the pre-eminence for Antioch from its having been the first See of the Apostle Peter. Instructed by Barnabas, Anthemios retorted that his Church was equally as apostolic, as it also possessed an apostle for its founder. The Antiochenes, struck with the cogency of this reasoning and being unable to urge anything in reply, retired from the contest in confusion, leaving the archbishop master of the situation. Zeno, to mark his sense of the importance attaching to the discovery, conferred upon the Cypriote primates certain privileges, which they have most jealously guarded ever since. Among these favours they received the right of signing in red ink, a mark of distinction only otherwise enjoyed by the emperors, of wearing a purple cloak at the festivals of the Church, and of carrying an imperial sceptre in place of the ordinary pastoral staff. The copy of St. Matthew's Gospel, presented to the Emperor by Anthemios, was sumptuously adorned with precious stones and metals and conveyed to the Chapel of St. Stephen in the imperial palace, where it was read annually on Good Friday.[1]

On the staircase leading to the Archbishop's house is a white marble column, apparently a Jewish tombstone inscribed in Greek. This is the most curious and difficult to explain of all the many fragments from ancient sites which have been re-used in the erection of later buildings. On the top of the staircase is a charming early Byzantine carving on a marble panel of a palm-tree between two sheep.

The Synod Hall, a nineteenth-century structure, contains a chair said to have been used by Napoleon during his Egyptian campaign.

The Omerieh Mosque [21] was originally the Augus-

[1] Hackett, *Church of Cyprus*, p. 24.

tinian church and was turned into a mosque in 1571. According to a legend, the Prophet Omar once visited Nicosia and lodged in the porch of a church. Mustapha, the victorious Turkish general, for some reason best known to himself, identified the Augustine church as the resting-place of the prophet, and at once converted it into a mosque.

The church was damaged in the siege of 1570, and cannon-balls destroyed the vaulting of the roof so that it collapsed in ruins. The west door still survives more or less undamaged, and is a good example of Gothic work of the early fourteenth century.

Attached to the west side of the church is a chapel, now reserved for the Turkish women. It has been but little structurally altered, and the tracery of its rose window is unharmed. This was almost certainly the shrine of St. John de Montfort, one of the most famous of the Latin saints of Cyprus.

Sir John was of noble family, and was born in France; he accompanied St. Louis on his last fatal journey. Louis left France on his way to the Fourth Crusade, and reached Limassol on September 17, 1248, after a voyage of only twenty-three days, which must have been in those times almost a record. On the advice of his barons he decided to pass the winter in Cyprus and camped on the seashore, but his troops were decimated by fever and a vast number of his men died, besides more than 250 nobles and prelates. Amongst this company was John de Montfort, and on account of the great piety of his life his body was placed in a magnificent tomb, which befitted both his rank in this world and his position in the hierarchy of saints. So great was his reputation, and so numerous the miracles attributed to his power, that pilgrims came from all over Europe to pray at his tomb, where his body lay unchanged and uncorrupted by time. One such pilgrim was a noble German lady, whose ancestors had been of the same family as the saint. With a great retinue the lady arrived in Nicosia, and was taken to the tomb. The grating was removed and she knelt for a long time apparently in deep prayer. So fervent was her piety that she seemed to kiss the shoulder of the body, but in reality she bit out a piece of the arm of the corpse and hid it in her bosom. She at once returned to her ship, which lay at Larnaca, but although the sails of every other ship bellied out those of the German lady hung limp and slack at the yards. The sailors saw that this must be the anger of God, and began to search the cabins and baggage of all the passengers. They could find nothing, and at last determined to search the lady herself. They found the morsel wrapped in a little cloth, and she confessed the truth. When the king heard of this he forced the lady to return to Nicosia, and made her walk in penance clad in a shift and holding a lighted candle in her hand, back to the church. There with tears the lady contritely placed the fragment she had torn out with her teeth back on the body, and lo! it miraculously grew into the flesh again.

A large number of tombstones were removed from this mosque in 1935 by the writer. When the Turks took the church and converted it into a mosque, they tore up the floor, which was covered with incised tomb slabs, and threw away the bones of those who lay buried beneath. They then relaid the floor, after the manner of crazy paving, some stones downwards, some still the right way up, the head in the apse and the rest of the tombstone at the west door.

With the help and permission of the Honourable M. Munir Bey, Director of Evkaf, these most interesting memorials of the Lusignan nobility were rescued from further damage, and placed temporarily in the Bedestan, till such time as a Byzantine mediaeval museum is formed.

A number of these memorials have therefore remained face downwards since the sixteenth century, and now see the light of day after a lapse of more than 350 years. Among the slabs rescued was a complete and life-size one of Sir Hugh de Vis, in the interesting armour of the period. There were memorials, too, of Augustinian monks, which should settle once and for all the question as to which monastic Order held this church during the Middle Ages.

Here were also found tombstones of especial English interest, for buried here were members of the noble families of Neville and Daubigny. The former still flourishes in England, where the present head of the family is the Marquis of Abergavenny, while the latter has died out and is only represented by heiresses in the female line. It may at first sight seem curious to find members of English families at the Lusignan Court; for besides Neville and Daubigny, cadets of the Houses of Nores and Grey took service in the Kingdom of Cyprus. The reason is that there were but few openings for the younger sons of noble birth, trade was impossible, and there was not always fighting in England. The kings of Cyprus were always delighted to welcome men of coat armour at their Court, and not only received them well but granted them titles and land. The Cypriote branch of the family of Neville at one time held the Viscountcy of Nicosia, while Louis de Nores married Heloise of Brunswick, widow of James I.

Near the east end of the church is the remains of a two-storeyed building, almost certainly the monastery. It is an unusual mingling of Gothic and Venetian architecture, but the window-frames are pure Venetian and must from their style be late sixteenth-century work. This is, therefore, one of the last buildings of any consequence erected in Nicosia.

The Mosque of the Standard Bearer [22] is a picturesque building situated on the former Costanza bastion, and is where the first Turkish standard was planted in the siege of 1570. Hardly had the intrepid Turk placed his flag on the top of the bastion when he was struck down by a Venetian, but the city fell that same day and his body was found and a tomb was reverently built over it.

At some later period a mosque was built, of no architectural character. In a small chapel to the north sleeps the standard-bearer, under a heavy tomb. Here, too, is the standard he carried: the flag has long since mouldered to dust, but the brass top of the pole still remains.

Sozomeno, a Venetian Cypriote of noble family, served through the siege and was made prisoner. He was ransomed, and after his return to Italy wrote an account of the fall of Nicosia, which he dedicated to the Grand Duke of Tuscany. His account of the fatal September 9th is as follows:

> The last assault was made on the ninth of September, and began at dawn with tremendous vigour and men innumerable, so that the attacks never slackened for want of fresh troops, and all four bastions were assailed at once. At the Podecattero, Caraman Pasha [whose family name was Remoliti] led the Caramanian troops. At the Constanzo was Muzaffer Pasha and his men. At the Avila and Tripoli bastions were Mustafa and Ali Pasha, one of the commanders of eighty galleys of the fleet. All these led at the same time most furious charges. The defenders of the Constanzo, Avila and Tripoli bastions withstood the attacks, and repulsed the enemy without allowing them to get over the parapet. The slaughter was great on both sides, but much more on that of the Turks. In the Podecattero bastion, however, I know not from what lack of arrangement, neither the commanders nor the soldiers were of the temper needed for so great a task, so that without check from our men the Turks got in and made themselves masters of the platform and the reduit. The few Italians who were there present fought with spirit and were cut to pieces, as well as the nobles with them. But the country folk of the cernide, and those who were collected at the last moment in the city, behaved badly: some of them let themselves down through the embrasures and along the curtain and fled into the country.[1]

The Tripioti Church [23] is one of the principal Orthodox buildings of Nicosia, and is dedicated to the Archangel Michael. According to an inscription over the south door, the church was built by the Archbishop Germanos in 1690. The most curious feature of the church is the number of fragments from mediaeval buildings built into its walls and especially noticeable in the three doorways. Of these the southern is the most remarkable and is difficult to date. The panel forming the lintel has a low relief on it, representing a human being with its lower extremities turning into floriated scrolls, which it grasps in its hands; at each side are two lions. This panel gives an impression of great age, and is almost certainly in the style of building

[1] *Excerpta Cypria*, p. 84.

prevalent in Romanized Europe between the classical and Gothic periods. The frieze-like capitals supporting the lintel are of the same period and style.

The north door is covered by a marble lintel of Renaissance design, with a coat of arms in the centre. This coat of arms is also over the door of a house near the Archbishopric.

The third, or west, entrance has a lintel of yet another period, and is formed of a block of marble carved in the French style of the fourteenth century, with a series of eight trefoil arches, under crocketed gables and pinnacles. This curious fragment would seem to have come from an altar tomb destroyed or thrown out of some Christian church converted into a mosque by the Turks. Another mediaeval fragment is a coat of arms over the east gable, consisting of a shield with six fleurs-de-lis.

The interior is of little interest, though carefully built. The well-cut stone has assumed a rich brown colour, and there are fragmentary remains of wall painting in the apse. The iconostasis is a good example of mid-eighteenth-century work, and its gilding has been pleasantly mellowed by time. Only one icon is of interest—a large panel of the Archangel Michael, dated 1634. The altar is dated 1741, its lower panels are painted with figures of angels, and it has an elaborate domed baldachino with a picture of the Christ Pantokrator in the centre.

The Tripioti was built at a time when the Orthodox Church had recovered from the effects of the Turkish invasion, and shows that it was by now wealthy enough to raise buildings of importance and considerable size.

The Church of the Phaneromene [24] is a large modern building erected in 1872 with stones from the ruins of the Castle of Leondari Vouno, three miles distant from Nicosia. A few fragments from the former church have been used up in its construction, especially the curious gargoyles on the roof.

In the bema lie buried the bishops executed by the Turks in 1821, one of the blackest blots in the history of Moslem rule in the Island. In 1820 a certain Kuchuk

Mehmed, a man only too notorious for his cruelty, was appointed Governor of Cyprus. Although it was very unlikely that the insurrection started in Greece would have spread to Cyprus, an island surrounded by Mohammedan countries and garrisoned by Turkish troops, the Governor determined to take no risks, and at the same time saw an opportunity to enrich himself at the expense of the Orthodox Church and its more wealthy citizens. He therefore submitted to Constantinople a long list of names, comprising those of the archbishop, bishops, abbots, and leading citizens, accusing them of aiding and abetting the rebels, and received from Constantinople orders to put the accused to death, and seize the property of those whose names were on the list. On July 9th the gates of Nicosia were closed, and the bloody work began in the square in front of the Konak. Before killing the ecclesiastics, the executioners saddled them like horses, breaking their teeth by thrusting bits into their mouths, and goading them with spurs. The archbishop and his archdeacon were hung on trees, and the Metropolitans of Paphos, Kition, and Kyrenia were beheaded. On the next day their co-religionists were allowed to remove the bodies and bury them in the Phaneromene.

The church contains an extremely fine icon of the Virgin and Child which, though badly restored, is probably one of the earliest and most important icons in the Island, and dates from the thirteenth century.

In the treasury is kept a carved Byzantine wooden cross surrounded by gilt filigree work of a much later period, and dated 1779. In the centre of the cross is a tiny piece of wood said to be a fragment of the True Cross. In the offices of the church opposite the north door are kept the iconostasis and icons of the original building. The iconostasis and proskenetarion are fine examples of seventeenth-century wood-carving; some of the icons are earlier, and there is an interesting one of St. Paraskeva, with two donors, a certain Antonio Sakellari and his wife, *c.* 1480.

The word Phaneromene means "Revealed", and was used in connection with the building, by Marie d'Ibelin, of an Orthodox church between Nicosia and Ay. Dometios, which contained fragments of the True Cross.

The Church of St. Savvas [25] was, according to the inscription over the south door, built in the middle of the last century, and is of no architectural interest. The interior, however, contains icons and furniture from an earlier building. In the west end of the church is an eighteenth-century proskenetarion of wood decorated with tiny alternate squares of red tortoiseshell and mother of pearl. All the ancient icons were unfortunately repainted in the usual barbarous manner by a local artist in 1850. Two objects, however, escaped his unskilled hand. They are the large rood cross, painted by a priest named Paul, signed and dated 1659, and a curious gilded panel with a portrait of a man on it. This panel is unusual, for it is not a donor icon, as no figure of a saint can be seen. It is a portrait of a man dressed in a rich furred robe, and with a Persian head-dress. He is represented in a sitting attitude, while to the left is an inscription which refers to the benefactions to the church of this donor, a certain Demitrios, in the year 1514.

The church also contains a very fine silver-gilt chalice of 1501.

IV

FAMAGUSTA

> For Famagusta and the hidden sun
> That rings black Cyprus with a lake of fire.
> *The Old Ships*—FLECKER

THE Ammochostos of the Greeks (from the two Greek words *Ammos*—sand: *chono*—to hide) is one of the finest examples of mediaeval architecture still left and is worthy of comparison with Carcassonne or Ragusa. The early history of the town is obscure; it is said to have been founded by King Ptolemy Philadelphus of Egypt (285–247 B.C.) and was repeopled in A.D. 648 by Greek refugees from the neighbouring Salamis. At the time of the early Crusades it was but an inconsiderable village with a harbour and castle. Indeed, William de Oldenburg, who visited it in 1211, refers to it as being "slightly fortified".[1]

After the fall of Acre in 1291, King Henry II of Cyprus offered it as an asylum to the many Christian refugees from that city, and Famagusta rapidly became one of the richest and the most important cities in the Levant. Here were the business houses of the great trading organizations of Italy and France; here all the great religious Orders had their convents; the various religions of the Near East their churches—Nestorian, Greek, Jacobite, Jew, and many another. Famagusta was regarded as the principal mart of the Mediterranean and an ever-increasing stream of wealth flowed into the city. The nobility was the richest in the world, and regarded an income of 3,000 gulden with no more respect than a few shillings would be in other places. There was a Count of Jaffa who kept 500 hounds and a servant for every two dogs. Indeed many nobles did not have less than 200 servants as falconers and huntsmen.

[1] *Excerpta Cypria*, p. 13.

Concerning the city of Famagusta. The third city of Cyprus is called Famagusta, situate on the seashore: here are the harbours of all this sea and realm, and a concourse of merchants and pilgrims. It lies directly opposite to Armenia, Turkey, and Acon. It is the richest of all cities, and her citizens are the richest of men. A citizen once betrothed his daughter, and the jewels of her head-dress were valued by the French knights who came with us as more precious than all the ornaments of the Queen of France. A certain merchant of this city sold to the Sultan a royal orb of gold, and thereon four precious stones, a ruby, an emerald, a sapphire, and a pearl, for sixty thousand florins; and anon he sought to buy back that orb for a hundred thousand florins, but it was denied him. The Constable of Jerusalem had four pearls which his wife wore by way of a clasp, and, when and where he would, he could pledge it for three thousand florins. In this city in one shop is more aloe wood than five carts could carry away. I am silent touching drugs, for they are as common there as bread is here, and are sold as commonly. But I dare not speak of their precious stones and golden tissues and other riches, for it were a thing unheard of and incredible. In this city dwell very many wealthy courtesans, of whom some possess more than one hundred thousand florins. I dare not speak of their riches.[1]

Nor was it only the nobility who were wealthy: the merchants outvied them. Makhairas says of that great, slightly vulgar, and *nouveau riche* merchant prince, Sir Francis Lakhas, the Whittington of Cyprus:

I shall tell you something of the wealth which Sir Francis Lakhas had at Famagusta. He often invited King Peter to his house at Famagusta; and one invitation he made to him and to all the lords as well, and to the knights. It is true that all the Syrians in Famagusta were in the habit of doing this to the knights, but this Sir Francis especially, and very often to the King. Once he came to his house [in January], and Sir Francis of his pleasure and to show his wealth had instead of logs three or four loads of the wood of aloes, and so they cooked the food. And when the King with the barons and all the lords had finished supper, they sat on low seats and played dice. And he wanted to show them a portion of his wealth: and he ordered

[1] L. von Suchen, 1350, *Excerpta Cypria*, p. 19.

a great dish to be brought in, carried by four men; it was loaded with pearls in the rough, and stones beyond price, and full in the midst of it were four light-stones, that is, carbuncles: and in the corner of the hall he poured out treasure, pouring out ducats as if they had been corn; and in the other corners gros and seraphs. It was cold weather, and in the chimneys were logs of aloes wood and [he laid down] eighty silken carpets, and on some of these they were sitting. Now the ducats and the coins were covered up; then he gave orders, and they put out the torches and brought the tray right into the midst of them and uncovered it, and the light-stones were shining like burning coals. And he gave them refreshments, and instead of sweetmeats as presents he gave away the pearls. And he did not admit to the feast any men of no fortune, but only the King and his brothers and twelve knights. And many of the knights were greedy and poor, and reached out their hands, and every one snatched at what he pleased, and they took from him great store: and all that they took seemed to him as nothing. And this man according to his faith did much charity for the good of his soul, and also built the Nestorian Church from the foundations. And one day he did a great stroke of business, and sent the King a present of ten thousand ducats because King Peter had made a bond of brotherhood with him; and he sent him word: Yesterday I did a stroke of business and gained thirty thousand ducats, and these I am sending to your lordship, and I beg you take it not amiss.[1]

Such was the golden age of Famagusta. But in 1372 a calamity befell the city from which it never recovered. It was the custom that the Lusignan kings of Cyprus should receive the crown of Cyprus in the Cathedral of Nicosia, and that of Jerusalem (but an empty honour) in the Cathedral of St. Nicholas of Famagusta. Now there was an established tradition that the King should ride to the cathedral on a horse and that the horse should be led by the representatives of Venice and Genoa, the former holding the left-hand rein and the latter the right-hand. On the ill-starred occasion of the coronation of Peter II, hardly had the King appeared than the Venetian representative tried to seize the bridle on the right-hand. This was stoutly resisted by the Genoese,

[1] *Chronicle of Makhairas*, p. 83.

and in the arising confusion a riot arose in which many Genoese were massacred and their loggia sacked and pillaged. The proud Republic of Genoa could not stomach such an insult and sent a fleet under Admiral Fregoso to avenge their people. The Island was ravaged and Famagusta became to all intents and purposes an appendage of Genoa. Indeed they held it till driven out by King James II in 1464.

Martoni, who was in Cyprus in 1394, gives an account of Famagusta during the Genoese occupation:

On the 27th of November [1394] I landed at Famagusta. Famagusta belonged formerly to the King of Cyprus, and is situated in the kingdom of Cyprus. Cyprus is a good island, with a circuit of five hundred miles. But now the Genoese hold the said town. The city of Famagusta is large, as large I reckon as the city of Capua, but a great part, almost a third, is uninhabited, and the houses are destroyed, and this has been done since the date of the Genoese lordship. The said city has finer walls than I have seen in any town, high with broad alleys round them, and many and high towers all round. This city is jealously guarded day and night by the Genoese through fear of the King of Cyprus. There are seven hundred armed soldiers in the pay of the Genoese who guard that city with great punctuality.

The castle of the city is fine, and is nearly all in the sea, except perhaps a fourth part on the city side, and there are fine ditches there constructed on either side which are filled with the sea water, and remain always full of the said water, making the said castle impregnable.

The city of Famagosta has a pretty fine harbour, protected from every wind. And in this harbour in front of the city is a wooden jetty, a stone's throw in length, and vessels come up to this jetty, and therefrom merchandise is carried to the vessels.

In this city live a certain number of Genoese, and a large number of Greeks, because the whole island of Cyprus is peopled by Greeks; and there is made a great quantity of camlet. There is one custom in force in this city, and throughout the island, that no woman can go out of the city of Famagosta without the leave of the Commandant, and cannot escape giving bail in the Commandant's court for her return to the city: and this is rarely granted to any woman. The reason alleged is that men cannot live in that city, but for the women who spin and prepare wool for the camlet, for they have hardly any other means of living. There is another reason too for keeping up the men in the city, which for decency's sake I pass over in silence. But the air of the city is very bad; at all seasons of the year there is mortality, and men die in great numbers, of the Genoese far more than of the Greeks.[1]

During the Genoese occupation there is little known of Famagusta. Through the marriage of James II with Catherine Cornaro, daughter of a wealthy Venetian merchant and adopted daughter of the Seigniory of Venice, Cyprus became little more than a Colony of the "Mistress of the Adriatic".

James II and his tiny son died, not without suspicion of poison, and Catherine was allowed to hold the crown for a few more years. But it was an uneasy crown to wear. She was surrounded by conspirators who wished to see Charlotte regain the throne. One day armed men broke into the palace, and her physician, her uncle Andrea Cornaro and a cousin were murdered before her eyes. An expedition arrived from Venice and put down the revolt. The Seigniory determined to get complete control of the affairs of the Island and appointed two Councillors and a Civil Commissioner, nominally to help the queen but in reality to get a firm grasp of affairs in Cyprus.

As time passed on, they gradually assumed absolute power, and the position became intolerable for the unfortunate queen. She wrote lamentable letters to the Doge of Venice, complaining of the insulting conduct and actual persecution of these envoys, both to her father and herself. And others in authority took their cue from them, for even the Archbishop, "without respect or reverence, would enter her chamber when he would", and she was constantly molested by brawls in her own palace. Years passed in this way, for with the achievement of their purpose certain in the end, the Senators of the Republic could afford to wait. At length, when the time was ripe for action, they won over to their side her brother Giorgio Cornaro, and sent him to persuade Caterina to abdicate in their favour. With him they also despatched General Diedo, with instructions that, "by wise

---

[1] *Excerpta Cypria*, p. 22.

and circumspect, cautious and secure means, they should get the queen on board a galley and bring her here to us at Venice".

This elaborate diplomacy was successful, and the unhappy lady yielded at length to persuasion and threats. Her brother had arrived on his mission in October 1488, but it was not until February 26, 1489, that the banner of St. Mark's floated over the castles of Cyprus.

An ambassador was at once sent to the Sultan of Egypt to announce that the event had taken place "with the full and free determination of our most serene and beloved daughter Caterina Cornaro", and also to ask for his friendly alliance. There is an Italian proverb, "A nemico che fugge, ponte d'oro", and so it was in this case. Magnificent fêtes and ceremonies were arranged in honour of the fallen queen, in which as much as two thousand ducats were freely spent. All the population of Nicosia found their way down to the shore to witness the departure of Caterina, which was of the most triumphal description. The Doge had sent his own state *Bucentaur*, on which he was wont on Ascension Day to perform the solemn ceremony of wedding the sea. In this splendid wooden ship, with oars for many rowers, gorgeous with gilding and intaglio, and costly damask hangings, the poor deposed queen set forth on her homeward journey. With what other hopes had she passed that way more than sixteen years before, in her sumptuous youth and the gay prime of her beauty, now to return to the home of her childhood, widowed, and robbed of all save the glare of outward show; like the Dead Sea fruit, beautiful without, but dust and ashes within! The white moaning sea-birds which hovered around her in the salt sea breeze must have been more in sympathy with her mood than the festive music on board the splendid *Bucentaur*.[1]

The queen was given the domain of Asolo, and there for more than twenty years she held her mimic Court.

She became a munificent patroness of the arts, Titian and Bellini painted her portrait. Beatrice Duchess of Milan, Isabelle d'Este, and Theodore of Aragon were her guests. Cardinal Bembo wrote of the philosophy of love at her Court, and Lorenzo Lotto was commissioned to paint an altarpiece for the Church of Asolo.

On July 10, 1510, she died in the Cornaro Palace in Venice.

[1] Hare, *The Most Illustrious Ladies of the Italian Renaissance*, p. 195.

Caterina died in Venice on the 10th of July, 1510, fifty-six years old. On the 11th a bridge of boats was made across the Grand Canal from the Cornaro Palace to the other side. The dead queen was followed by the patriarch, the signory, the vice-doge, the Archbishop of Spalato, and an immense crowd of citizens with torches in their hands. There was something fitting in the manner of her burial, for the night was a stormy one, with heavy wind and rain. On her coffin lay the crown of Cyprus—outwardly, at least, Venice insisted that her daughter was a queen; but, inside, her body lay shrouded in the habit of S. Francis, with cord and cowl and coarse brown cloak. Caterina was carried to the Cornaro chapel, and next day the funeral service was performed. Over her grave Andrea Navagero, poet, scholar, and ambassador, made the oration that bade farewell to this unhappy queen, whose beauty, goodness, gentleness, and grace were unavailing to save her from the tyrannous cruelty of fate.[1]

Venice held Cyprus for eighty-two years, 1489–1571, and moved the capital from Nicosia to Famagusta, where the Island was administered by a "Captain of Cyprus".

The Venetian period was an unhappy time for the Island, for it was little more than a military occupation, and, as no measures for its proper maintenance were taken, the prosperity of the Island visibly declined throughout the whole period. Trade languished, manufactures almost ceased, landowners abandoned their property, schools closed, the population emigrated, cultivation was neglected, the streams were allowed to overflow and form infectious marshes, and the national wealth rapidly diminished.

The only lustre shed by this period is indirect, for in 1505 the Lieutenant-Governor was Cristoforo Moro, immortalized as the hero of Shakespeare's tragedy of *Othello*. But the final scene is drawing near. In 1570 the Sultan, Selim II—inflamed by the accounts of the excellence of the Cypriote wine—despatched a vast armada to conquer the Island. Nicosia was taken on September 9, but Famagusta did not fall till August 6, 1571.

The defence of Famagusta is one of the most glorious

[1] Horatio F. Brown, *History of Venice*, p. 91.

in history, worthy to be ranked with Londonderry and Verdun, and the name of its defender, Marc Antonio Bragadino, is inscribed in letters of gold on the Roll of Fame. There is not space here to go into the history of the siege—the attacks and counter-attacks, the bravery of the garrison, the slow starvation and the final surrender with flags still flying; the only provision left within the battered city being the hoards of rats which infested it. It is said that over 100,000 cannon-balls were fired into the city by the Turks, till hardly a building was left standing. The Turkish general, Mustafa, promised to allow the garrison to embark and sail for Crete with full honours of war, taking with them whatsoever they liked.

This was arranged and Mustafa entered the city, but when he saw how small and feeble was the company which had kept his army at bay, he was seized with a sudden fury and determined to destroy the remnants of a force which had defied him for so long and slain 50,000 of the flower of the Turkish army. He asked Bragadino and his captains to come over to the Turkish lines and discuss the terms of surrender.

Calepio, who was Superior of the Dominican Convent at Nicosia and captured by the Turks at the fall of that city, tells us:

> In the evening Signor Bragadino, accompanied by Signor Baglione, S. Alvise Martinengo, S. Gioan Antonio Querini, S. Andrea Bragadino, Cav. dell' Haste, Captain Carlo Ragonasco, Captain Hettor da Bressa, Captain Gierolamo di Sacile, and other gentlemen, with fifty soldiers, went out: the officers wore their swords, the soldiers had muskets. So they went to Mustafa's tent, who at first received them courteously and made them sit down. They passed from one subject to another, then a complaint arose that during the truce Signor Bragadino had caused certain slaves to be put to death. There was not a word of truth in it, but Mustafa, rising in anger, would scarcely listen to what his visitors said, and ordered them to be bound. They were defenceless, for they were compelled to lay aside their arms before entering the tent, and thus bound were led one by one into the open square before the tent, and cut to pieces in Mustafa's presence. Then twice and thrice he made Signor

Bragadino, who showed no sign of fear, stretch out his neck as though he would strike off his head, but spared his life, and cut off his ears and nose, and as he lay on the ground Mustafa reviled him, cursing our Lord and saying, "Where now is thy Christ that He doth not help thee?" The general made never an answer, but with lofty patience waited the end. Count Hercule Martinengo, one of the hostages, was also bound, but was hidden by one of Mustafa's eunuchs until his chief's fury was passed. He did not slay him, but doomed him, as long as his soul cleaved to his body, to continual death in life, making him his eunuch and slave, so that happy he had he died with the rest a martyr's death. There were three citizens in the tent, who were released, but the poor soldiers bound like so many lambs were hewn in pieces, with three hundred other Christians, who never dreamed of such gross perfidy, and impious savagery. The Christians who were already embarked were brutally robbed and thrown into chains.

The second day after the murders, August 7th, Mustafa first entered the city. He caused Signor Tiepolo, Captain of Baffo, who was left in Signor Bragadino's room, to be hanged by the neck, as well as the Commandant of the cavalry. On August 17th, a day of evil memory, being a Friday and their holiday, Signor Bragadino was led, full of wounds, which had received no care, into the presence of Mustafa, on the batteries built against the city, and for all his weakness, was made to carry one basket full of earth up, and another down, on each redoubt, and forced to kiss the ground when he passed before Mustafa. Then he was led to the shore, set in a slung seat, with a crown at his feet, and hoisted on the yard of the galley of the Captain of Rhodes, hung "like a stork" in view of all the slaves and Christian soldiers in the port. Then this noble gentleman was led to the square, the drums beat, the trumpets sounded, and before a great crowd they stripped him, and made him sit amid every insult on the grating of the pillory. Then they stretched him on the ground and brutally flayed him alive. His saintly soul bore all with great firmness, patience, and faith, never losing heart, but ever with the sternest constancy reproaching them for their broken faith: with never a sign of wavering he commended himself to his Saviour, and when their steel reached his navel he gave back to his Maker his truly happy and blessed spirit. His skin was taken and stuffed with straw, carried round the city, and then hung on the yard of a galliot was paraded along the coast of Syria with great rejoicings. The body was quartered, and a part set on each battery. The skin, after its parade, was placed in a box together with the head of the brave Captain Hestor Baglione, and those of S. Luigi Martinengo, G. A. Bragadino, and G. A. Querini, and all were carried to Constantinople and presented to the Gran Signor, who caused them to be put in his prison, and I was a captive chained in that prison as spy of the Pope, on my liberation tried to steal that skin, but could not.[1]

For some years the skin of Bragadino remained in Constantinople, but was bought at a great price by his brothers and sons, who reverently laid it in SS. Giovanni e Paolo, in Venice, where it rests till this day.

The Turks repaired the walls of Famagusta, but under them it became little better than a prison. There came to exile Grand Viziers who offended their Sultans, or Ambassadors who had misunderstood the orders of the Porte. One of the most romantic prisoners before the English occupation of 1878 was Kattirdji Yanni, the Robin Hood of the Levant. It is said of him that he never committed a murder, or permitted one to be perpetrated by his band. He and his band were in the habit of lying in wait for the parties who they knew were travelling with large sums of money and kindly relieving them of its charge. They also frequently captured persons of wealth and detained them until a ransom was paid. Kattirdji Yanni would often give this money in alms to the poor, and we are told he presented about one thousand young Greek girls with marriage portions.

When the British arrived in 1878 they found various State prisoners within the walls. The most distinguished of these was Subh-i-Ezel, successor of the murdered Mirza Ali Mohammed, who had founded the Babi sect. During his leadership there were dissensions and the Babis were divided, one-half following Subh-i-Ezel, the other his half-brother, Baha-u'llah. Both sections were deported from Turkey: the Baha-u'llah to Acre, the Ezelis to Famagusta. The former sect has grown and now numbers over two millions of adherents; on the other hand, the Ezelis have dwindled to a mere handful. When the British came,

[1] Calepio, *Excerpta Cypria*, p. 156.

Subh-i-Ezel was free to leave Cyprus, but he preferred to remain and lived till just before the war, when he died at the age of eighty-two. He had two wives, each of whom had a separate house, and every day, at four in the afternoon, the first wife took him to the door of the second wife's house and handed him over. After twenty-four hours had passed, and punctually at 4 p.m., the second wife took Subh-i-Ezel back and handed him over to the safe-keeping of the first wife.

But it was during the middle of the nineteenth century that the most damage was done to Famagusta. The builders of Port Said were in need of materials, and complete churches were torn down and their stones transferred to that city to build its quays and hotels.

DESCRIPTION OF THE CITY[1]

Famagusta is surrounded by walls of which many a stone is still perfect. On an average the walls are 50 feet in height and are in some places as much as 27 feet thick. It is more or less a square. One of the walls faces the sea and harbour; the other three overlook the plain. Round these landward walls runs a fosse. There were two main gates—the Sea Gate, opening on the harbour, and the Land Gate.

The Sea Gate, [1] or the Porta del Mare of the Venetians, is still in a very fine state of preservation and was built by one of the Venetian captains of Famagusta, Nicolo Prioli, in 1496; the wooden doors, covered with iron, date from the Turkish period, but the large iron portcullis, which could be raised and lowered by the chains, still visible, dates from the Venetian era. The lion of Venice and the name and date of the builder and his arms are still preserved on the façade, and the coloured marbles which form a background may come from the ruins of Salamis.

Close to the land entrance of the Porta del Mare are two large stone lions of uncertain period: the larger, which stands on a base of grey marble, being credited with miraculous powers by the superstitious inhabitants. It is said to have once stood on the quay.

[1] The figures in brackets refer to the numbers on the map.

Between the Sea Gate and the Citadel is a portion of the curtain wall which abuts on to the sea, unhappily pierced by needless entrances soon after the British leased the Island from Turkey in 1878. Indeed, it is said that Victorian vandals would have torn down the whole Sea Wall if they had been allowed.

The Citadel [2] was originally a building of the fourteenth century with four round towers at the corners and was once surrounded by a moat. On the first bastion is a large marble lion of St. Mark. The main entrance has over it the winged lion of the Republic and the name of the Venetian Captain—Nicolo Foscarini—who remodelled the citadel and removed the upper floor in 1492. This is the so-called "Othello Tower". Shakespeare only mentions "a seaport in Cyprus", but the citadel is always pointed out as the scene of the tragedy. Othello is supposed to have been a certain Christoforo Moro—Lieutenant-Governor of Cyprus from 1506–1508—whose name and canting coat of arms of three mulberries sable (*moro* means both mulberry-tree and Moor) gave rise to the story which changed him from a Venetian to a Moor.

The principal building remaining in the Citadel is the Great Hall [3] or refectory, which is 92 feet by 25 feet and dates from the fourteenth century. The arms of the Kingdom of Jerusalem are still visible on the keystones.

The Cathedral, [4] dedicated to St. Nicholas, is now used by the Turks as a mosque under the name of St. Sophia. It is a magnificent example of early fourteenth-century Gothic and resembles the cathedral at Rheims. Within its walls the Lusignan kings of Cyprus received the crown of Jerusalem—an empty honour; here lie buried the last two sovereigns of that house, James II and his infant son James III. There, too, Catherine Cornaro, widow of James II, renounced her royal rights and ceded the kingdom to Agostino Barberigo, Doge of Venice, in 1489, before she retired to Asolo. The extremely interesting coronation ceremony in Famagusta Cathedral has been preserved by Bouston.

Not only did the Church owe its inception to the royal initiative, but it also looked to the occupant of the throne for

1 Sea Gate
2 Citadel
3 Great Hall
4 Cathedral
5 Venetian Palace
6 Ruined Church of St. Francis
7 Museum
8 Church of St. Peter and St. Paul
9 Church of St. George of the Greeks
10 Ayia Zon i
11 Church of St. Nicholas
12 Church of the Stavros
13–14 Ruined Churches
15 Land Gate
16 Nestorian Church
17 Church of St. Anna
18 "Tanners" Mosque
19 Carmelite Church
20 Armenian Church
21 Martinengo Bastion
22 Churches of the Templars and Hospitallers
23 House in Italian Renaissance style
24 "Biddulph's Gate"
25 Church of St. George of the Latins
26 Djamboulat Bastion

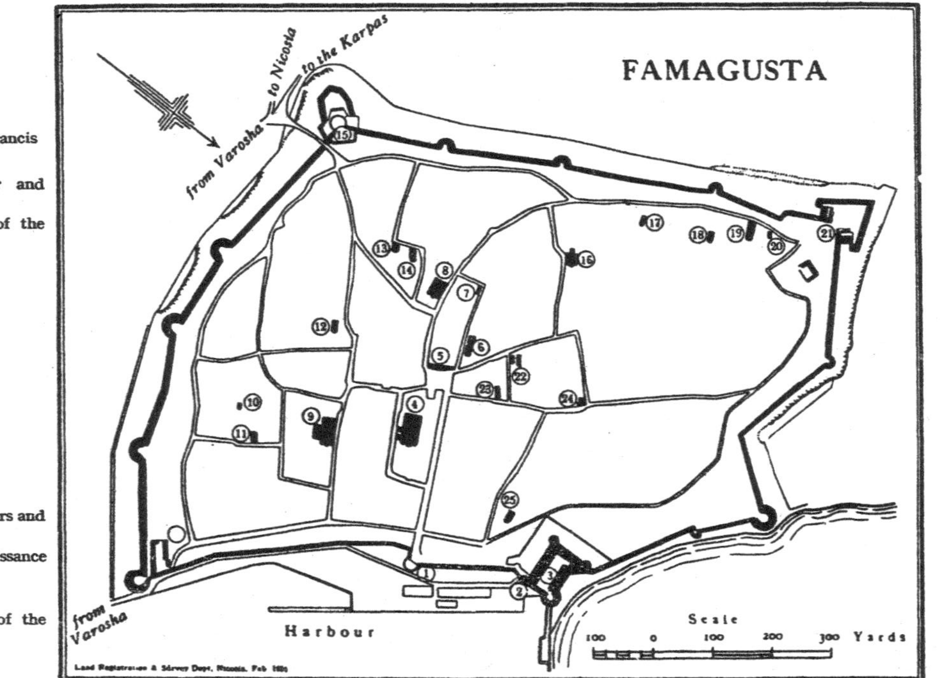

the time being to protect and maintain those rights and privileges which had been bestowed upon it. This was the first duty which the new sovereign at his accession was pledged to perform, as we learn from a description of the ceremonies observed upon such an occasion. On the day appointed for his coronation the candidate, vested in the surplice of a deacon, proceeded to the western entrance of the cathedral, where he knelt upon the threshold, surrounded by the great officers of state. There he was met by the Archbishop, or bishop, whose duty it was to perform the ceremony, attended by his clergy. After the officiating prelate had recited certain prayers over the head of the candidate, the latter stood up and, with his hands upon the Gospel, made oath as follows: "I . . . who by Divine providence am about to be crowned King of Cyprus, promise you, my lord . . . Archbishop of Cyprus and your successors, in the presence of Almighty God and of all the clergy, prelates and barons, who are here assembled, that from this time forward I will be your faithful protector and the defender of your person against all comers in the realm of Cyprus. The possessions and privileges of our holy Church and of all the Churches appertaining to it, the possessions and privileges, I mean, of which they were in the enjoyment in the time of the kings of blessed memory, my predecessors, and those which they may hereafter lawfully acquire in my time, I will maintain and defend. The canons and ancient privileges and the divine laws, with their decrees, and the ancient customs of the franchises I will observe, and I will maintain the persons of ecclesiastics in their exemptions. To widows and orphans I will render justice. The privileges granted by the royal benefactors, my predecessors, and the assizes and customs of the realm I will observe and protect. I will uphold the Christian population of the realm in their rights and justice, as a Christian king should do in his realm. And all the aforesaid things I will faithfully observe, so help me God and His Holy Gospels."[1]

The exterior of the Cathedral has three large doorways at the great west front, with straight-sided gabled canopies overhead. Over the centre of those is a superb window of six lights, with a wheel in the tracery; above the side doors are long double-light windows. To the left of the parvis, or square, in front of the Cathedral lies a small Turkish grave-

[1] J. Hackett, *A History of the Orthodox Church of Cyprus*, p. 471.

yard and a small domed building erected out of ancient fragments and formerly used as a Moslem school. There, too, are the two Venetian columns, once crowned with the badges of the Republic. They are monoliths of grey granite and doubtless came from a public building at Salamis. It was between these columns that the heroic Bragadino was flayed alive by the inhuman Mustafa after the fall of the city in 1571. Opposite the north wall of the Cathedral are the remains of the Archbishop's palace. The little building, which projects from the north wall of the Cathedral, is later than the rest of the building and may have been used as a sacristy.

Though much damaged by the bombardment of 1571, the Gothic detail on the apse will give some idea of the vast amount of carved stone work with which the Cathedral was once decorated. East of this apse lies a small ruined building which may have served as the private chapel of the archbishops. The ground outside the apse was cleared in 1928 and a large number of human bones were found; it is said that there was an early Turkish cemetery here and the bones were afterwards removed to a Moslem graveyard outside the walls.

On the south of the Cathedral wall lie two small chapels, and near them the south door which was blocked up by the Turks. On a buttress to the left is a surprisingly well-preserved inscription recording the partial construction of the Cathedral by Bishop Bauduin in 1311.

Guy d'Ibelin, who was Bishop of Famagusta from 1298–1308, had collected 70,000 bezants towards the building of the Cathedral, but his successor in the see, Antonio Saurano, was one of the most arrant knaves who ever disgraced a bishop's throne. As soon as he was enthroned he took 20,000 of the bezants so carefully collected by the late bishop and spent them on his own private pleasure. He also despoiled the Cathedral of its property, and sold the church plate: indeed, the see would have been bankrupt if death had not put an end to his evil life after he had held it for a year.

To the right of the façade is an arched door and vaulted

hall, which now contains a fountain for Moslem ablutions. The former use of this building is uncertain; it was once of two storeys, of which only the lower now remains. It has been suggested that it might have been an open-air grammar school supported by the Bishop. There is a highly decorated doorway on the north side and two circular windows with Venetian coat of arms on shields of white marble above—a chevron between three roses—probably those of the builder.

Beneath the circular window nearest the Cathedral lies a remarkable fragment of a classical frieze representing various animals chasing each other. Near by is a slab—once the tombstone of some Frank—on which the bodies of dead Turks are laid out.

The interior still retains a certain dignity, though its frescoes and paintings are hidden beneath the all-prevailing whitewash; its altars and tombs have been swept away, the stained glass has gone from its windows, and the hangings from its walls, but it must be remembered that even if this building has passed out of Christian hands and is now a shrine of Islam, it has been spared the baroque additions and nineteenth-century "restorations" which have ruined so many European cathedrals, and it is possible to see the original design reduced to its bare and unrelieved architectural outlines.

A few mediaeval tombstones lie in the north aisle, but in 1571 the Turks tore up most of the tombstones and cast the remains beneath them into the sea. Perhaps one slab is still *in situ*, and that is the one commemorating Bishop Itier de Nabinaux, which lies in the apse of the north aisle. It is said this prelate died through a chill caught while bathing in the sea in 1365.

In the south aisle a door leads into a small side-chapel which may have been a funeral chapel and is separated from the main building by a wall of Turkish construction. It contains a tomb niche over which rises an arch of heavily carved design with a shield with a coat of arms in the centre.

The modern glass in the great west window is an unhappy and ill-advised restoration of about thirty years ago. The remaining windows are filled with tracery of plaster of paris, and are recent Turkish work.

Opposite the Cathedral and across the square is the façade of the Venetian Palace or Palazzo del Proveditore. [5] Nothing now remains of the Royal Palace of the Lusignans, in which the kings of Cyprus, till the reign of Peter II in 1369, lodged. This Venetian façade is a magnificent piece of architecture and consists of three arches supported by four grand columns (from Salamis). Over the central arch are the arms of Giovanni Renier, Captain of Cyprus in 1552.

The courtyard of the Palace is now used by the police, and in it are piles of cannon-balls from the siege. At the base of the flight of stairs and over the entrance to the police stables is a large lintel of marble with three coats of arms. In the room above this was imprisoned, in the middle of the last century, Kemal Bey, the most famous and best known of all the Ottoman poets—still called the "Shakespeare of Turkey".

The Turks destroyed the Palace, and all that now remains is the shell of its western portion—a large L-shaped building of the early sixteenth century. The bronze cannon in front of this wing was found by sponge fishers in Famagusta Bay in 1900, and has the arms of the Emperor Charles V and the date 1534.

To the right of the Palace lies the ruined Church of St. Francis. [6] The Franciscans first appeared in the Island about A.D. 1226, and at one time seem to have held considerable property. The most interesting part of this church is the south chapel, which contains its altar and a collection of mediaeval tombstones, some of which may still be *in situ* and date from 1314 to 1474. One or two have the effigy of the deceased carved in relief on them, but are of poor and clumsy execution. A disused Turkish bath lies round the apse.

The Museum [7] is a small unidentified chapel of the fifteenth century and houses various antiquities and architectural fragments found in the city. To the left of the door is a well-preserved Venetian lion of the late fifteenth century, while to the right lies a door lintel with the arms of the

Kingdom of Cyprus. Opposite is a large hooped proto-cannon mounted on wheels and some small mortars, all early fifteenth century. On the south wall is a collection of armour said to have been found in the moat and mostly of the sixteenth century. Below lie Gothic finials, etc., from the Cathedral.

Room No. 2 contains a collection of coats of arms, tomb-stones, etc., of the thirteenth to sixteenth centuries. In the middle is the life-size figure of a cleric found outside the Cathedral in 1930, and which may be of the fourteenth century. On the south wall hangs the chain used for closing the mouth of the harbour, and below is a stone carving of a fifteenth-century tilting helm. In the courtyard lie various larger and less interesting antiquities, including a large marble lion now in fragments.

The Church of St. Peter and St. Paul [8] is said to have been built out of the proceeds of a single trading venture by a merchant of the town during the reign of Peter I (1358–1369). It is a well-preserved though heavy building, and the flying buttresses which support the vaulting of the nave are ugly and clumsy. The church was used as a mosque at one time and owes its preservation to this fact. The great north doorway is a good example of European Gothic and was once decorated with coats of arms, which have been erased.

The interior contains little of interest and is now used as a store. A few fragments of tombstones lie on the floor and a wooden gallery stretches across the west end and connects the roof aisles.

The Church of St. George of the Greeks [9] has recently been restored, and is a large and handsome building. It was once the Orthodox Cathedral of Famagusta. On the south side lie the remains of the original Byzantine cathedral, a small building of two apses with fragments of painting. There, it is said, was once buried St. Epiphanios (A.D. 310–406), the celebrated Archbishop of Salamis (or Constantia) and rightly regarded as one of the brightest ornaments of the Cypriote Church. His body was taken by the Emperor Leo, about the year 900, to Constantinople.

The mediaeval Orthodox cathedral received the full brunt of the Turkish bombardment, and its dome, north wall, and columns of the nave have long since disappeared.

Founders' tombs remain on the side walls with fragments of painting in the arches. There are also considerable remains of paintings of the fifteenth century in the three eastern apses. They are much faded, but the subjects are quite distinguishable. In the upper rows are scenes from the Passion and other New Testament subjects, while below are a series of saints and fathers of the Orthodox Church. M. Enlart carried out some excavations here and found a large quantity of coloured glass roundels, set in plaster of paris, white, blue, green, and purple in colour. This method is more or less the same as that used by the Turks to the present day, as can be seen in the neighbouring Latin Cathedral of St. Nicholas.

Two other small churches are situated in what was the Orthodox quarter of the city. Ayia Zoni [10] is a small fourteenth- or fifteenth-century building in the Byzantine style and is dedicated to the "Holy Girdle", or Zone of the Blessed Virgin Mary. It was covered with painting and traces of a huge Archangel Michael still remain on the wall. Close by is another church of the same period and style—St. Nicholas, [11] a small double-aisled church. It is ruined, and all that remains is the east end, with two semi-circular apses and the greater part of the south nave, originally covered by two small domes. It was once completely covered with mural painting, but now only a few fragments survive.

The Church of the Stavros, [12] or Holy Cross, is used by the Turks under the name of the Mustafa Pasha Mosque. It is a well-built church of the sixteenth century and has a barrel-vault and a well-carved west doorway; the coat of arms on the marble lintel has been erased. The interior contains nothing of interest and is now used as a store. Near the Land Gate are two ruined churches [13] and [14]. They are both in the last stage of decay and no records remain of their dedication, or even to what Christian faith or religious order they belonged. They would seem to date from the fifteenth century and, ruined though they are, are lucky to have escaped the contractors and house-breakers who tore down and sold so many churches and buildings, wholesale, in the second half of the last century to build the quays and hotels of Port Said.

The Land Gate [15] is perhaps the oldest part of the city after the citadel. The present bridge and entrance is modern and passes through a gun chamber which once flanked the ravelin. During the siege the hottest fighting was here and both the bastion and the ravelin were much damaged by Turkish guns and mortars. The original gateway can still be seen, an arch 30 feet in height. On either side within the archway are coats of arms painted on plaster; they are now much decayed and damaged, but according to a local tradition are known as the Genoese Badges.

Passing through this archway it is possible to appreciate the size and design of this immense ravelin. On one of the near walls is a marble slab with the four quarterings of the royal coat of arms; two angels support a crown above it, while below are two swords, the badge of the Order of the Sword, one of the oldest orders of chivalry in the world and founded by Guy de Lusignan in 1194. The original foundation decreed that a naked sword must be worn round the neck as long as the Holy Land remained in the hands of infidels, but this seems to have given place to a smaller badge. Count Capodilista visited Cyprus in 1458, and he and his friends while in the Island were taken to see the King. "He was in a convent of monks, and received them with gracious kindness, and gave to the honourable Miser Gabriele his Order, fastening it on his breast with his own hand. It is a sword encircled by the legend, 'Pour Liute Mantener'."[1] Felix Faber, who was in the Island a few years later, refers to the order as follows:

> It is an ancient custom that the knights of the Holy Sepulchre present themselves to the king of Cyprus and make with him a kind of pact. He calls them his companions, and enters their names in a book, and gives them a silver dagger in a sheath with

---

[1] Capodilista, *Excerpta Cypria*, p. 36.

a belt for it, and at the end of the dagger hangs a silver flowret like a violet, in token of the alliance between them. For this reason my lord Georius de Lapide, whom I never left, with other nobles entered Nichosia and stayed there three days. But because the kingdom of Cyprus has now no king, the nobles begged of the Queen to be received into the companionship of the kings of Cyprus. She summoned them to a large banqueting hall, and when they were set before her proposed to them through an interpreter the statutes of that companionship, which are: that they should strive to help the kingdom of Cyprus in its need, since it lies midway between Saracens, Turks, and Tartars. They pledged their faith to the Queen with their hands, and she delivered to them the daggers, and allowed them to depart.[1]

The bastion itself is dated 1544 and is planned with an immense ravelin to protect what was the main entrance to the city.

The ruins which lie between the great archway and the modern entrance are those of an unimportant Turkish mosque. Along the land wall is a series of churches more or less undamaged. The first is the Nestorian Church, [16] which has lately been handed over to the Orthodox community. This is the church referred to by Makhairas,[2] who says of Sir Francis Lakhas, the great Nestorian merchant prince: "and this man according to his faith did much charity for the good of his soul and built the Nestorian Church from the foundations". This was in 1359. The Nestorians or, as they called themselves, Chaldeans came from Syria. They used the Chaldean language in their liturgy and admitted the dual nature of Christ. They are now represented by the Assyrians in Iraq.

Outside the western door lie several marble bases of statues of the Roman period, which doubtless originally came from Salamis.

The interior is now but of little interest. The magnificent paintings which once adorned the walls have been destroyed; many of them, alas, since 1899, when M. Enlart visited the church. The iconostasis is quite modern. In a glass case on the south wall hangs an icon of the Transfiguration dated

[1] Felix Faber, *Excerpta Cypria*, p. 36.
[2] *The Chronicle of Makhairas*, p. 83.

1725. According to Hackett,[1] the Chaldeans in Cyprus, under the leadership of Timothy, Archbishop of Tarsus, acknowledged the supremacy of the Holy See in 1445, but the understanding lasted for only five years.

The Greek community now call this church "Ayios Georghios Xorinos" or "St. George the Exiler". The legend is that anyone who would get rid of an enemy collects some dust from the floor of this church and leaves it in the enemy's house, who within a year will either die or leave the Island.

The next church is St. Anna, [17] a well-preserved building with an unusual and heavy belfry. The interior contains considerable remains of mural paintings with Latin inscriptions underneath. Near by is the "Tanners" Mosque [18]. Nothing is known of this church, which would seem to have been built in the sixteenth century. Acoustic vases are built into the vaulting and traces of painting may be observed on the walls.

Next is the Carmelite Church, [19] dedicated to St. Mary of Carmel. Martoni, who visited it in 1394, gives the following account. "In the same city is a monastery of S. Maria de Cammino. The church is very fair and dignified, vaulted with chapels round, with very beautiful scenes and pictures, and a right fair cloister with oranges and other fruits. There is also a dormitory, and many other rooms for the use of the monks. In this church I saw the undermentioned holy relics, to wit:

The head of the blessed Ursuline, very beautifully shrined in silver.
A bone of the shin of S. Leo, Pope.
The head of S. Cufinus.
The head of S. Sosius.
And a piece of the wood of the holy cross of our Lord."[2]

The body of the Blessed Peter de Thomas, Latin Patriarch of Constantinople, is said to have rested here. He came to Cyprus in 1359 as Papal Legate and in the same year crowned

[1] *A History of the Orthodox Church of Cyprus*, p. 533.
[2] Martoni, *Excerpta Cypria*, p. 23.

Peter I as King of Jerusalem in Famagusta. A wholehearted and sincere bigot, he tried to convert by force the Orthodox clergy in Cyprus, and serious riots resulted in which he nearly lost his life. In 1361 a serious plague raged at Famagusta and the Legate, convinced it was a punishment from God for the sins of the city, organized a solemn procession in which not only all the Christian sects but Turks, Saracens, and Jews walked barefooted beseeching the mercy of Heaven.

This "Favourite of Heaven" died from a wound received at the siege of Alexandria in 1366 and was buried in this church, his last request being that "his body might be laid at the entrance to the choir, so that all, even goats and dogs, might walk over it".

The interior contains some most interesting paintings on the north wall, a series of patriarchs and bishops; while below are the coats of arms of various countries—England, France, etc.; and in the nave are figures of various female saints. It would seem as if Carmelite churches regularly had coats of arms painted on their walls, as N. le Huen, who visited the church of the Order in Nicosia, says: "Our Carmelite house is near the king's Palace and was founded by the lords of France, for you can see a proof in the church, by the arms of the King of Jerusalem, of the King of France, of the Duke of Normandy."[1]

The Armenian Church [20] dates from the middle of the fourteenth century. The Armenians were settled in Cyprus before the arrival of the Lusignans. Their bishop resided at Nicosia, and at one time there was a second prelate at Famagusta.

On the death in Paris of Leo VI (de Lusignan) without male heirs, in 1393, the title of King of Armenia was assumed by James I of Cyprus and was retained by the sovereigns of Cyprus till the Venetian occupation.

The interior has the earthenware jars which were built into the ceiling, and were supposed to prevent the acoustic defects of vaulted buildings. The walls still have fragments of mural paintings of rows of apostles and saints within

[1] N. le Huen, 1487, *Excerpta Cypria*, p. 51.

niches, while on the north wall are scenes from the Passion; the inscriptions are in Armenian.

The Martinengo Bastion [21] is one of the best examples of military architecture. Its walls are 13 to 20 feet thick. In its vaulted casements are still visible the holes for the escape of the powder smoke. The builder is said to be Giovanni Girolamo Sammicheli, nephew of the celebrated Veronese architect, Michele Sammicheli. He was sent to Famagusta about 1550 by the Republic of Venice to design the new fortifications, died here in 1559 at the age of forty-five, and was buried in the Cathedral.

The bastion doubtless received its name from Signor Hieronimo Martinengo, who was chosen by the Seigniory to command the troops in Cyprus on the outbreak of the war with Turkey in 1570; but on his way he fell ill and died in Corfu.

It is a superb monument of military art, and commanded an area over a mile square and was almost impregnable. The Turks in 1570 seem to have made no attempt to assault it. The ventilation shafts for the escape of the gunpowder smoke of the cannons still remain, as do the small recesses in the walls of the gun chambers for the kegs of powder and shot.

It is dominated by the so-called "Cavalier", on the east, which has a large platform for guns. A magnificent view can be obtained from the top, and the whitewashed domes of the Church of St. Barnabas, the burial-place of the Apostle, are a conspicuous landmark on the horizon.

Across the town are the twin churches of the Templars and Hospitallers. [22] These two little fourteenth-century churches have recently been carefully restored, when the marble lintel with the arms of the Hospital was replaced over the west doorway. The sockets for flagstaffs can be observed on the gables of the chapel. The interiors have little of interest; traces of paintings can still be observed in the Hospitallers' Church.

Besides the Palace, little remains of domestic architecture except a house, [23] a well-preserved example in the style of the Italian Renaissance. Nothing is known of its history. Further along the same street is a doorway [24] known as "Biddulph's Gate", after Sir Robert Biddulph, High Commissioner of Cyprus in 1879, who saved it from being pulled down. It has an elaborate cornice and columns on either side.

St. George of the Latins [25] is the most picturesque of the Famagusta churches and is built in the best French style of the late thirteenth century. It has been a fortified church, which would seem to indicate that it was built before the city was walled round. Little remains save the north wall, and the sacristy, which still retains its vaulting. Mr. Jeffery considers that remains from some classical temple have been used in the building of this church, and adds: "The most curious detail of construction is the way in which the circular drums of the Classic columns have been adopted as the stones on which to cut the slender shafts of the Gothic style."[1]

A pleasant conceit is shown in the capital of one of the wall shafts on the north side, which is in the form of a cluster of bats.

The Arsenal or Djamboulat Bastion. [26] It was here that there took place some of the fiercest fighting in the siege, and the Turks very nearly succeeded in capturing this corner of the city; indeed, Djamboulat Bey, one of their bravest generals, was able to place a Moslem standard on the bastion. The story goes that the Venetians had here a machine formed of a wheel covered with knives that cut to pieces any Turk who tried to force his way through the narrow entrance. Djamboulat Bey, seeing how many of his men had been killed by this machine and how despondent they were becoming, decided to destroy it, even at the cost of his own life. Mounting his white horse, he rode forward, urging his steed straight at the machine. He and his mount were killed at once, his head being cut off and the horse torn to fragments; but he had accomplished his desire, for the Venetian machine was put out of action. Nor was this the only thing which emboldened the Turks to press forward the conduct of the siege. Wherever the fighting was hottest, or the

[1] *Historic Monuments of Cyprus*, p. 128.

Venetians appeared to be gaining, there was the ghost of Djamboulat, plain for all the army to see, one hand waving a sword, the other holding his head tucked under his arm. When the city at last fell, Djamboulat was buried by the bastion, for which he had given his life, and there his tomb can still be seen.

Nor is this the end of this miraculous soldier, for a fig-tree grew from his grave and to this day childless couples go and eat of its fruit so that their dearest wish may be satisfied: indeed, many of the population of Famagusta owe their being to Djamboulat and his fig-tree.

V

LARNACA

THERE is no doubt that Larnaca is one of the most ancient cities in the Island, and was founded originally by the Phoenicians. According to an ancient legend it was founded by Kittim, the great grandson of Noah, who colonized Cyprus after the deluge. Larnaca is the Chittim of the Bible: from Chittim, Balaam prophesied that ships would come to afflict Assyria.[1] Isaiah said that the ships of Tyre would come to it,[2] while Daniel foretold that the ships of Chittim would advance against the kings of the north.[3]

The principal claim to fame that Larnaca has is the fact that Zeno, founder of the Stoic school of philosophy, was born there about 336 B.C. His father is said to have been a merchant in the town, and while engaged on a trading voyage in the Levant, Zeno happened on some of the writings of Socrates, which fired his enthusiasm for philosophy. He went to Athens, where he studied and later founded the Stoic school named after the Stoa, a colonnade of the Athenian Agora, where he lectured. He was held in great respect by the Athenians, but died by his own hand in 264 B.C. It was here, too, in 450 B.C. that the famous Athenian general, Cimon, died while besieging the town.

The town is hardly mentioned during the Roman occupation of Cyprus, and indeed it was also of but little account during the Middle Ages. It probably first gained its importance after the Genoese captured Famagusta, when it was used as the principal port for Nicosia. It was then known as Salines, from the neighbouring salt lake, and was used as a landing-place by various pilgrims, who stayed at Cyprus on their way to and from the Holy Land.

Nicholas de Hune, when he visited Cyprus in 1487, says: "August 29th we landed at Salines. There is a church founded

[1] 1 Numbers xxiv. 24. [2] Isaiah xxiii. 1. [3] Daniel xi. 30.

by St. Lazarus, the seat of a bishop. There are no other dwellings than a house for a tavern. There we found bread and wine, grapes and pomegranates. We slept inside the church like good sheep."[1] The Turks landed here in 1570 and marched to Nicosia, and after the Turkish conquest Larnaca came into prominence as the residence of all the foreign consuls. But even as late as 1599 the Dutch traveller Jean van Kootwyck found the town ruinous and destroyed.

From the church of Lazarus to Arnica we saw nothing but ruins, wide plains full of the caper plant, and fields generally deserted. That Arnica or Arnicum was once a remarkable and very populous city is sufficiently attested by the remains of public buildings, and ruined houses. Now there is nothing to see but some small buildings, few and poor, of one storey only. There is still a Governor's palace, large and stately, of rustic work in squared and smoothed stone, constructed, I should say, by the Venetians, but now ruinous and almost destroyed, for the four walls only are standing. Opposite this is a fine building, once a Christian Church, dedicated to S. Roch, now profaned and turned into a grain store. Standing close to it is a high square tower, and a porch adorned with marble columns. Between the church and the porch lies a wide court, in the middle of which stands a marble column which was formerly crowned by the marble figure of a winged lion, the badge of Venice.[2]

DESCRIPTION OF THE TOWN[3]

Of the ancient Larnaca little can be seen to-day, except the remains of walls. During the middle of the last century the foreign consuls seemed to have amused themselves—for time must have hung heavy on their hands—by digging for ancient remains, and their reports are full of the tombs and treasures which they found. But they were not the first persons to dig, the Venetians of the fifteenth century being the earliest excavators. Indeed, it is said that the name of the town has changed from Salines to Larnaca on account of the number of sarcophagi found, for Larnax is a Greek

[1] *Excerpta Cypria*, p. 52. [2] Ibid., p. 190.
[3] The figures in brackets refer to numbers on the plan.

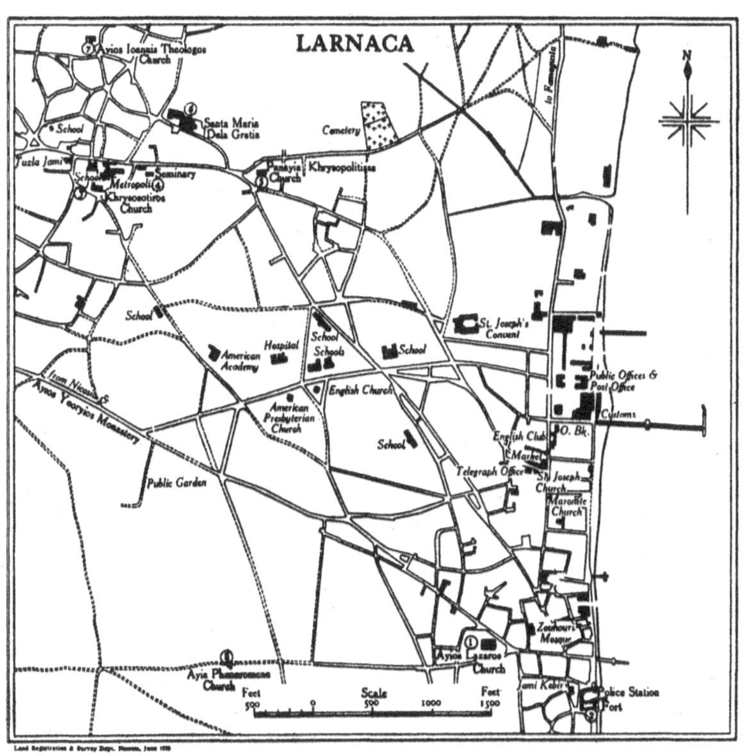

Land Registration & Survey Dept., Nicosia, June

word meaning a coffin. It is interesting to note in this connection that the famous banking-house of Fugger kept a representative in Cyprus, who collected antiquities for his master, and some of his acquisitions, including a beautiful classical sarcophagus, can still be seen in the Vienna museum.

A few tombs of the classical period still survive scattered over modern Larnaca. Pococke, who stayed some time in Cyprus in 1738, says:

> They have discovered a great number of antient sepulchres in and about the city of Larnaca; I saw some built of hewn stone; in one of them I observed the stones were laid along at top like large beams, and others laid over them like a floor; there is another which ends at an angle, and both are of excellent workmanship, and finished in a most perfect manner.[1]

The first of these tombs referred to is probably that now known as Cobham's tomb and scheduled as an ancient monument. Of the Phoenician remains nothing is left save a site known as Banbula, which lies close to St. Joseph's convent. This is the site of a temple, and was excavated by the Swedish Expedition in 1930, who found a number of archaic statues of Hercules. It would seem to have been an important open-air temple, such as was usually built by the Phoenicians at each of their trading stations.

The principal monument of Larnaca is the Church of St. Lazarus. [1] According to a legend, Lazarus was, after his resurrection at Bethany, expelled by the Jews, and was placed with his two sisters in a frail barque and committed to the mercy of the sea. His tiny boat came ashore at Kition, and he was consecrated first bishop of that see by the Apostles, who then chanced to be in the Island. There he remained for more than thirty years, and there he was buried. In A.D. 890 his tomb was miraculously discovered, and his remains were, by the orders of the Emperor Leo VI, transferred to Constantinople. They were subsequently stolen from there by the French and carried to Marseilles, where they rest to this day. The present church is said to have been built by the Emperor Leo VI. At the time of the

[1] *Description of the East*, London, 1745, p. 213.

Turkish invasion it was taken by the Turks, but was repurchased in 1589 for three hundred aspers, and was used in common by both the Latin and the Orthodox. This arrangement seems to have lasted for some years, and even as late as the eighteenth century it seems to have still continued.

The church originally belonged to the Latin clergy. It was taken from them under an order of the Grand Signor, but they always preserve a right to the side chapel on the left, and twice a year in token of their right the Fathers of Terra Santa go to celebrate the Holy Mysteries there.[1]

The church was restored in the seventeenth century, but the plan of construction is probably very much the same as that of the original building. A number of Corinthian capitals are reused in the construction of the walls and piers, and the church has a bold and graceful campanile, one of the few permitted by the Turks in the Island. Belfrys were not generally allowed in the Turkish Empire till 1857, as the ringing of the bells was regarded by the subject races under the Ottoman Empire as a tocsin and signal for a rising against their masters; and to prevent any likelihood of this the Turks, except on rare occasions, had forbidden any Christian church to be graced with a campanile.

Pietro della Valle, a Roman nobleman, who visited the Island in 1625, gives a good description of the church, which is probably very much then as it is now, though his references to the Armenians are obscure.

I returned early to our vessel, and stopped on the way to see a Greek church in the Marina, called S. Lazarus. It belonged originally to the Armenians, and in a buttress of its outer walls all the stones are inscribed with Armenian letters. Why it is held now by the Greeks is possibly because there are no Armenians here, as there must have been formerly. It is very ancient, entirely of stone, its arrangement fantastic though common among the Greeks, for there are three aisles with a roof supported on four piers only, and three domes in a row over the middle aisle, and three apses without. Within, the space between the

[1] Mariti, *Travels in Cyprus*, London, 1791.

piers is used by men, the aisles on either side by women only. Behind the altar they show underground a tomb like a small grotto, which can be entered through a square opening like the mouth of a vault. This, they say, is the grave of Lazarus who was restored to life by Christ: adding that he built the church, of which he was bishop; that he died here, and that his body was carried later to Constantinople and thence to Marseilles, the truth of this being proved by the miracles which are daily worked at the tomb, the sick are healed, and the like.[1]

The tomb of St. Lazarus can still be seen, and consists of a marble sarcophagus placed behind the iconostasis beneath the floor of the bema or sanctuary; a short flight of steps leads down to it.

Jacques le Saige, a draper of Douai, visited Larnaca in 1518. He states in his Journal that he saw the Church of St. Lazarus and then witnessed a most curious ceremony.

Wednesday, September 14th, we went to hear mass in a chapel where they sing in Greek. Then we came to dinner, and after dinner heard a crying and singing. They were carrying a young woman to her grave. There were four or five women crying so that it was piteous to see them. They had put a mask on the corpse, painted like the face of a beautiful dead woman. They had clothed her, too, in a fine black robe; she even had a fine scarf of black silk round her, and they told us that when a poor person dies they borrow for her beautiful clothes which she wears up to the mouth of the grave. We did not go to see her buried, because there had been deaths from the plague pretty close to the place.[2]

The iconostasis itself is a good example of baroque wood-carving of the end of the eighteenth century; the majority of the icons were painted in Crete in the first few years of the nineteenth century. At the end of the iconostasis on the south wall is a pleasant icon of the Raising of Lazarus; it is curious to note how the workman who removes the lid of the coffin holds his nose, recalling the words "Lord, by this time he stinketh, for he hath been dead four days."[3]

[1] *Travels*, London, 1665, p. 291.

[2] *Excerpta Cypria*, p. 60.

[3] John xi. 39.

At the north end of the iconostasis is an icon of St. George and His Martyrdom, painted in 1717. In the body of the church, in an elaborately carved woodwork setting, is a Russian icon of the B.V.M. covered with silver gilt and set with semi-precious stones. In the west end of the church are preserved a few icons: St. George, dated 1694; St. Onoufrios, dated 1696; and a quaint late seventeenth-century icon of the Raising of Lazarus, the drawing pleasantly out of all proportion, and with vast scarlet tulips growing on the hill in the background.

In a room opposite the west door of the church is a small museum, containing old and damaged icons; they are mostly decayed work of the seventeenth century. There is little else that calls for notice, save a pair of royal doors dated 1659, and a large rood cross of about the same date.

Behind the church is the English cemetery. The graves are those of members of the Turkey or Levant Company, and of British consuls and their families. The Levant Company was incorporated by charter by Queen Elizabeth in 1581, and preceded by twenty years the foundation of the East India Company, and is therefore the parent of those undertakings which have done so much for the development of the British Colonial Empire. The tombs of the English merchants include Ion and William Ken, who died in 1693 and 1707 respectively, before they had reached the age of thirty. They were nephews of the famous Bishop of Bath and Wells. The consuls include George Barton, who died in 1730, Michael de Vezin, who was consul from 1785 to 1792, and Dr. James Lilburn, who was consul from 1840 to 1843. Here, too, are buried Captain Peter Dare, commander of the ship *Scipio*, who died in 1685, and the Reverend Lorenzo Warriner Pease, an American missionary, who died in 1839.

The tiny English colony at Larnaca is mentioned by nearly all the eighteenth-century travellers. Its members seem to have lived a pleasant and easy life, and with little if any work, though they were touchy about the order of precedence and kept up an almost fantastic state. There is no space here to quote even a part of the references to this

English colony; but one or two of them give some idea of the life of the period. Captain Light, who came to Cyprus in 1814, says:

> I was often amused by the assumed dignity of the different representatives of European nations at Larnica, where the Austrian, Neapolitan, French, and Spanish consuls had their residence, and where etiquette of precedency was pushed to a degree not known in our own country; all except the French consul were engaged in trade; and of course their own interest prevailed over that of the country they represented. The only English merchant on the island resided at La Scala: he had to contend with the united phalanx of Levantines, who had no inclination to admit a competitor in trade.[1]

In 1815 William Turner, who was attached to the staff of Sir Robert Liston, the English ambassador at Constantinople, touched at Larnaca while voyaging in the Levant. He was entertained by Mr. Vondiziano, and stayed at the English consulate, which had two janizaries.

> The cheapness of living in Cyprus is extraordinary, considering the declining state of the island. Mr. Vondiziano, with all the expenses of the consulate, a wife and five children, a large house, six servants, two janizaries, a carriage, horse and mule, spends only 5,000 piastres a year. Servants' wages (men-servants the dearest) a few years ago were only from fifty to sixty piastres a year; but now they are generally ten, and sometimes even twenty, piastres a month.
>
> In the morning I went with Signor Vondiziano (who put himself in grand state, with a large cocked hat which he always wears, even in the house, a gold-headed cane, and preceded by a janizary) to visit the Austrian consul, who lived in a good house near us. He has lately married a young lady of the country, who was tolerably pretty. He was now much frightened by a report brought two or three days ago by a ship from Constantinople, that Austria, in conjunction with Russia, had declared war against the Porte; from which fear I delivered him.[2]

Even as late as 1827 Captain Colville Frankland found that the British representative kept up an outward show of state.

[1] *Travels*, London, 1818. [2] *Journal*, London, 1820, vol. ii, p. 40.

After dinner we all went to call upon the Mutesellim in the house of the Khoja-bashi. Our procession from the Consular residence to the Khoja-bashi's house was rather ludicrous, but appeared to produce a very grand effect upon the minds of the good inhabitants of Larneca, who all came out of doors, to stare at us. I could hardly retain my gravity on witnessing the awkward attempts made by an old Turk of the Consulate, in his long scarlet robes and grey beard, to stand up behind the rickety carriage of the Consul (*à la chasseur*) with a large truncheon in his hand, as an emblem of his office and dignity.[1]

The fort, [2] now used as a police barracks and prison, was erected by the Turks in 1625. It is of but little interest, and Mariti, who lived here in the middle of the eighteenth century, says:

On the shore is a town called also town of the Salines, whose length is greater than its breadth. It contains a fort built by the Turks in 1625, armed with several good pieces of artillery, which bear the arms of the republic of Venice. It is a wretched building, and almost in ruins on the sea side; it has, however, a guard of Janissaries, and its Disdar or Commandant. It is square without any bastion. Now its principal use seems to be to fire salutes to the war vessels of the Christian Powers, and to return those of the Grand Signor's.[2]

Close to the fort is the mosque which was once a Latin church dedicated to the Holy Cross. A number of columns and Gothic details from this building can still be observed.

The Khrysosotiros Church, [3] and the Monastery and Church of the Saviour, is the residence of the Orthodox Bishop of Kitium. The church was largely rebuilt in the nineteenth century. To left and right of the north door two marble tomb slabs have been let into the exterior wall: that to the left is dated 1779, while the one on the right is in memory of a Greek girl who died in 1831. This monument is an elegant, almost European, piece of work, with a large vase surmounted by a bird sculptured in relief, in black and white marble. The church contains a large number of icons, mostly eighteenth century, but none of out-

[1] *Travels*, London, 1831, vol. i, p. 321.
[2] Mariti, *Travels in Cyprus*, London, 1791.

standing interest save a large icon of the B.V.M., in the Italian style of the seventeenth century. The most interesting piece of church furniture is the pros-kenetarion, or icon stand, which, according to an inscription, was the gift of an inhabitant of Larnaca in 1730. It is not unlike Coptic work in style, and is formed from wood inlaid with small diamond-shaped pieces of mother-of-pearl and red tortoiseshell. The throne of the bishop, supported by two fierce and snarling lions, was erected in 1779.

In the monastic buildings several marble columns and capitals support the balcony and the roof.

Close by is the tiny Chapel of St. George. The buildings which surround it are used as a school, the first floor of which is supported by three delightful arches resting on stumpy black marble columns from some ancient site.

A few yards from the Metropolis, and nearly opposite a small police station, is a seminary, [4] formerly the British Consulate. Unfortunately it is now in a poor state of repair. It was built before 1720, and the Dutchman Heyman, who visited the Island in that year, says: "The English consul's house is the best on the whole island. It has also the largest hall I saw in any part of the Levant." Heyman, however, was shocked by the behaviour of the English consul: "I once saw the English consul very readily offer his hand to the wife of the first dragoman of the French consul and led her upstairs; a civility to which a Smyrna consul would by no means have condescended."[1]

This consulate is again referred to by Hassilquist, the Swedish naturalist, who came to Cyprus in 1749. "Mr. Treadway, an English merchant, had built at Larnaca the finest house in the island of Cyprus, in which was one of the most spacious saloons that I had seen."[2]

This room still survives and contains a fireplace executed after the Italian manner in stucco, with an overmantel decorated with large putti, intended to contain a portrait. Above is the coat of arms of some British consul, an eagle displayed on a chief of three escallops. A pleasant story still exists of Mr. Treadway. He was greatly in debt and

[1] *Excerpta Cypria*, p. 250.

[2] Ibid., p. 307.

owed money to all the principal inhabitants of Larnaca. One day he invited all his creditors to a grand banquet in the great saloon. All accepted, looking forward not only to an excellent dinner but hoping that the consul would at last settle up the debts he owed them. Hardly had they sat down when the consul begged them to excuse him for a moment. Leaving the house, he rushed down to the shore and went on board a ship, the captain of which was a friend, and where he had the previous night, under cover of darkness, bestowed all the most valuable of his possessions. As soon as he was on board, the sails were hoisted and the ship sailed away from Larnaca. Meanwhile the guests waited impatiently at the table, and to add insult to injury, not only was the consul never seen again, but the dinner never appeared, and such goods and furniture as were left behind when sold paid but one or two of the creditors.

The Church of the B.V.M. Khrysopolitissa [5] was erected in 1815. It is a building of two aisles, the roof supported by a row of high columns in the centre. The interior of the church has recently been repainted in so painful a manner that on entering one is irresistibly reminded of the reception-room of some cheap German hotel. Against one of the pillars hangs a charming seventeenth-century icon of the B.V.M. and Child; a text on it is inscribed to the Madonna, and runs: "Rejoice, for you hold him, who holdeth everything." The church font is formed from a section of a white marble column, and is mounted on four wheels so that it may be easily moved about the church. The arcading of the south cloister is supported by marble pillars from some former church.

The Latin Church of the Franciscans, Santa Maria della Gratia, [6] was built in 1843, and replaced a church built by the Latins in 1702, the foundation-stone of which lies in the narthex, with an inscription stating that this stone was laid by the French consul and consecrated by the Superior of the monastery, Marco Biturico, on June 21st. The organ in the present church is said to have been presented by the Emperor Leopold to the former building.

In the west end of the church are a few tombstones of the eighteenth century, including one of a consul of Ragusa to the Kingdom of Cyprus in 1759. Michael de Vezin, British consul from 1788 to 1792, in his report says:

> The republic of Ragusa has also a consul who is in business. He has no salary, but takes 2 per cent like his Venetian colleague. In accordance with an agreement with the Porte, Ragusans pay only this 2 per cent as duty: but then they are tributaries of the Porte. All Christian vessels, except those of Ragusa, pay half-yearly fifteen piastres anchor money, which is divided between the officials of the Custom House and the fort and the consul.[1]

It is interesting to observe how the title of the Kingdom of Cyprus remains, though it had ceased to be that for more than 200 years.

The Latin convent seems to have been re-established soon after the Turkish conquest of the Island. Jan van Kootwyck, in 1598, refers to the Latin convent of Larnaca.

> For they have no goods or lands to provide for their food and the necessary expenses of the convent, and are thus compelled to live on the alms of the merchants living at Arnica, the bounty of seamen who put in at the neighbouring port, and the munificence of travellers. Hence the custom has grown up among the Venetians that every one of their vessels which calls here pays a Venetian ducat, or gold sequin, to the aid and support of the convent. They are also at liberty to board the ships in harbour to collect an alms from the sailors and passengers, who are liberal and even munificent to them; and rightly so, for it is very meet that they who sow spiritual things should reap carnal things.[2]

The Roman Catholic cemetery is close to the Monastery of St. George on the road to Nicosia. Here are said, on very good authority, to be buried two persons connected with a crime that, in the last century, deeply moved the world.

In 1882 Lord Frederick Cavendish and his secretary Mr. Burke were assassinated while walking across Phoenix Park in Dublin. The British Government were determined to punish the perpetrators of this revolting crime, and offered

[1] *Excerpta Cypria*, p. 379.

[2] Ibid., p. 191.

a reward and immunity to anyone who would turn Queen's evidence. At last three members of the gang came to the police and offered to give the necessary evidence which would convict the rest of the murderers.

After the trial it was easy enough for the British Government to carry out the first half of their promise, but immunity was a different matter. For a time the men were kept in prison for their own safety. At last one was sent to South Africa under an assumed name; hardly had he set foot on the docks in Cape Town when he was shot dead by another Irishman, as a traitor.

The British Government then came to the conclusion that the only part of the world where there were no Irish, and over which they had jurisdiction, was Cyprus. So they at once sent the two informers there, under assumed names, giving them small posts in the Public Works Department. But in six months both men were dead, of remorse and drink it was said, and they were buried in the Roman Catholic cemetery at Larnaca.

The Church of St. John the Divine [7] dates from the seventeenth century, though it was much repaired about 1850. The iconostasis is *c.* 1700, but the contemporary icons have unhappily been repainted. A certain number are stored beneath the altar, of which the best is a seventeenth-century Madonna with a carefully painted embroidered dress. The women's gallery, which dates from the mid-nineteenth-century restoration, has charmingly painted panels decorated with flowers. A beautiful pair of Italian bronze floor candlesticks of the sixteenth century stand in front of the iconostasis; they are decorated with putti, etc., and doubtless come from some Latin church, but have unhappily recently been covered over with cheap gold paint. The proskenetarion is of the same Coptic work as that in the Church of the Saviour, and is dated 1737. The original Venetian black and white marble door has been removed and built into a room by the narthex; it is decorated with fine dog-tooth moulding. Opposite the west door is an open-air pulpit erected in 1849, in which the Gospel is read at Easter in various languages.

Not far away is the modern chapel of St. Luke, which must replace a mediaeval building, as gypsum coffins of that period are frequently found in the near neighbourhood.

The Phaneromene Church, [8] a structure of colossal stones, was originally a very early tomb. The huge stone which forms the roof of the inner chamber is slightly squared and hollowed out inside. The tomb has not been improved by being turned into a church, and the original dromos and entrance chamber have disappeared. The place is credited with various magical properties: thus those who suffer from headaches or malaria walk three times round it and leave a fragment of clothing or a piece of their hair on the grill in front of the south window. It is also much frequented by girls whose lovers are overseas, who come here to pray for their safety.

Two monasteries lie near Larnaca, St. George the Near and St. George the Distant. The latter, which is close to the aqueduct built by Bekir Pasha in 1747 to bring water to Larnaca, is a small domed church supposed to have been built in the twelfth century. The Monastery of St. George the Near was rebuilt by Bishop Leontios in 1833. The iconostasis is a patchwork of two periods, the lower portion being probably early eighteenth-century work. The icon of St. George, covered with silver gilt, was given by a certain Michael in 1818, when Meletios was Bishop of Kitium. Outside the south door lies the marble base of a Roman statue. Any child who is late in learning how to walk is brought here by his mother and taken three times round the church and his shoes left behind on or under this base. It is hard to explain how or why this belief started, the only possible suggestion being that on the base is the matrix of the feet of the statue which once stood on it, and it is possible that these outlined feet may have suggested the idea to the simple mind of the local peasantry; whatever may be the reason, the fact remains that this custom is still frequently practised as is witnessed by the large number of children's shoes which can be seen.

About three miles from Larnaca is the salt lake and Tekke of Umm Haram. This salt lake was at one time a source of great revenue to the Island—indeed, it was said to be worth £10,000 a year—but now the salt is only used for local consumption. The salt is collected in huge heaps from the compact coat of salt which forms to the thickness of about eight inches on the bottom of the lake. Zuellart, a late sixteenth-century traveller, gives the following account of the salt lake:

There is a lake of about nine miles circuit, in which are springs of salt water, which, with waters from the winter rains, and kept enclosed during summer, by the heat and ardour of the sun, they harden and congeal into a very beautiful salt, white like snow, without it being necessary to refine it. In certain points it is more than 1 foot thick, and seems, when you see it, like ice, which is so white that it dazzles the eyes of the passers-by, and of those who gaze at it. This salt is broken and collected with iron implements during the moon of the month of August, then it is heaped on the banks of the said lake, resembling to small mountains of snow. This salt is the principal treasure, from which is derived the greatest revenue of the island, as every year a great quantity of vessels are loaded with it, and it is carried to several places, and even as far as Venice.[1]

The origin of the salt lake, according to the villagers, is that St. Lazarus, when he was once walking in the vicinity of Larnaca, met a woman and asked her for some of the grapes which she was carrying. She answered him mockingly, saying: "that more salt than wine was likely to be got from the soil". To which the saint replied: "Then let it be so; from henceforth the soil shall produce salt, not the juice of the grape."

The Tekke Umm Haram stands at the far side of the lake surrounded by palm-trees, and its domes and minarets stand shadowed in the calm waters. The Lady Umm Haram was the daughter of Milhan, the contemporary and relation of the Prophet Mohammed. She was twice married; her first husband was killed in battle, and her second, named Umbada or the Pot Bellied, was Cadi of Palestine and died at Jerusalem about 655. With her husband she visited Cyprus in

[1] Zuellart, *Voyages*, 1598.

A.D. 694, and died by a fall from her mule, or, according to the chronicle, "falling from her beast she broke her pellucid neck and yielded up her victorious soul, and in that fragrant spot was at once buried".[1] The actual tomb is at the far end of the mosque, and must be entered through it. The tomb itself, as far as can be ascertained, is a trilithon consisting of two uprights more than fifteen feet in height, and a third stone of great size resting on them, after the manner of Stonehenge. It is almost certain that this was an ancient cromlech, and may date from the early period of Cypriote history. The actual dolmen is now roofed over. The entrance doorway, with its dog-tooth moulding, must come from a mediaeval building. The doorstep is formed of a fragment of a classical marble frieze, and the door handles are of solid silver. The trilithon is now so covered with curtains and trappings that it is impossible to see anything of the stones themselves, but in the time of van Bruyn in 1674, it was possible to see it uncovered.

> Near the Salines is a mosque which the Turks state to be the grave of Mina, mother of their prophet Mahomet. The sepulchre is enclosed by three huge stones, two of them upright, and the third resting on them above. The first two are thirteen palms broad, and at least as high again. But the stone is covered with lime, and can no longer be seen.[2]

According to a Moslem legend, the three stones were brought from Palestine by the hands of angels, like the Holy House of Loretto.

In the cloister outside is the tomb of the second and Turkish wife of King Hussein of the Hedjaz, who died in Cyprus in 1930. Outside the main entrance gate of the Tekke lies a white marble slab, with a beautifully cut inscription referring to Baldassare Trivizani, who was the Venetian Lieutenant-Governor of Cyprus from 1489 to 1491. The Tekke is clearly visible from the sea, and all Turkish vessels as they pass dip their flags in homage to one of the most holy places in the Mohammedan world.

[1] *Journal of the Royal Asiatic Society*, January 1897.
[2] *Voyage to the Levant*, London, 1702, p. 272.

VI

KYRENIA

THE Castle of Kyrenia is one of the most ancient buildings in Cyprus, and played a large part in the history of the mediaeval kingdom. It was never taken by Turkish assault, though besieged many times, but only surrendered through starvation or change of policy. It was built about the beginning of the Latin occupation, between 1192 and 1211, when it is noted by Wilbrand von Oldenburg. "We first touched at Kyrenia, a small town but fortified, which has a castle with walls and towers. Its chief boast is its good harbour."[1]

The first siege of the castle was in 1220, when the supporters of Frederick II surrendered it to the Lord of Beirut, but in 1232 it was again garrisoned by the imperial troops, who took as hostages a number of ladies of noble birth, including Queen Alix de Montferrat, wife of King Henry I, who had just attained his majority. The Queen died here, and during her funeral in St. Sofia, Nicosia, a truce was arranged between the two armies. The captain who defended the fortress on this occasion was Philip Chinard, whose family came from Champagne in France; but he was forced to surrender to the King, and the garrison, reduced by famine, was allowed to sail to Palestine and join the other Lombards there. Thus ended the imperial pretensions to be overlords of Cyprus. In 1349 King Hugh IV imprisoned his two sons, Peter and John, here. They were young boys, and seized with a desire to see the world ran away from their father's Court, accompanied by their tutor, Sir John Lombard. They were, however, captured, and Sir John, by orders of the King, had his hand and foot cut off before being hung on the gallows. The sons were only imprisoned for three days, as the

[1] *Excerpta Cypria*, p. 13.

King suddenly died and was succeeded by his eldest son, Peter I. Not unnaturally, perhaps, the new king wished others to sample the dungeons with which his father had given him an acquaintance, so in 1368, yielding to his natural vivacity, he lodged the ambassadors of the Sultan of Cairo as guests in the castle.

In 1374 the Genoese force, sent by that republic to avenge their merchants massacred at the coronation of Peter II, laid siege to the Castle of Kyrenia, which was held by the Constable of Cyprus, afterwards King James I, on behalf of the royal family. The young king Peter II, and his mother, Eleanor of Aragon, widow of Peter I, had been captured by the Genoese at Famagusta. Queen Eleanor had at first intrigued with the Republic, regarding them as a means of avenging herself on the murderers of her husband, but when she discovered that they intended to dispossess her son of his kingdom she quickly changed her plans. She offered to lead the Genoese soldiers to an attack on the Castle of Kyrenia, and set out from Nicosia at their head, having previously provided herself with her late husband's mule, the strongest and swiftest in Cyprus, which she rode astride, her spurs concealed by her flowing robes.

And the queen mounted on the wonderful mule called Margarita, which had belonged to her husband King Peter, and she sat upon the wonderful mule as women do; and she ordered her squire who was called Putsurello to bring her spurs with him. And she said to him: "When I make a sign to you, turn my foot over so that I sit like a man, and put on my spurs." And she was happy to think that the armies were waiting for her. And when she came near to Anykhia, the Genoese were keeping in step close by her side, and were thinking how they would guard the castle when they took it, and who they would put to guard it. And when the queen came to the hill, she made the sign to Putsurello, and he turned her foot and put on her spurs, and she pressed her mule and was off. Then they shouted: "Let him come with us who will, and who will not, let him go hang." And immediately the queen fell in with the [Constable's] army, and they received her with great honour.[1]

[1] *Chronicle of Makhairas*, p. 460.

The Genoese when they reached the castle found to their astonishment the queen inside the fortress, and defying them from the wall. The Genoese invested the castle closely, even attacking it from the seaward side with floating batteries, but the defenders were as determined as the attackers, and repelled every attack.

And conspicuous above all the others was a youth who was skilled with the crossbow, and he could string the bow well, and he used to string the bow for the constable: and he was a very good shot and never wasted a bolt. And on that day they killed four hundred of the Genoese. And the man who strung the bow so stoutly was Nicholas Makhairas: and he said to his companion: "Shoot at that Genoese and hit him in the head." And the man stood ready, and shot and hit the Genoese. The Genoese felt the pain, and knowing that it had pierced him, put his hand up to feel his basinet: and Nicholas immediately let fly with his crossbow and pierced the palm of his hand, and the bolt went through the basinet, and he died.[1]

Worn out by their efforts, the Genoese decided to raise the siege and arranged a truce, by the terms of which the Constable James was permitted to go to Europe. But the Republic broke their oath and captured him while on his voyage, at Rhodes, and took him prisoner to Genoa, where his enemies avenged themselves for his gallant resistance by torturing him.

In 1426 the Mamluks having won the Battle of Khirokitia and taken the King prisoner, advanced to Nicosia. The Cardinal, Hugh de Lusignan, took refuge in the Castle of Kyrenia with the sister and children of the King, bringing with him the Crown jewels and as much of the royal treasure as he could collect. The Mamluks followed him, but decided that the castle was too strong to attack.

In 1460 the usurper James II besieged in the castle his half-sister Charlotte, the last Queen of Cyprus, and wife of Louis of Savoy. Queen Charlotte Lusignan is one of the most tragic figures in history. She was the only legitimate child of King John II and Helena Palaeologus; she married first John, Prince of Portugal, who shortly

[1] *Chronicle of Makhairas*, p. 459.

after his arrival in Cyprus was poisoned by his mother-in-law. To avenge her husband the princess hired a couple of Sicilian bandits to assassinate the Chamberlain of Cyprus, who was the confidant of the Queen and had been privy to the murder, because the Prince of Portugal had restored the power of the Latin clergy over the Orthodox, of which Church the Queen was a member. On the death of her father in July 1548, Charlotte was crowned Queen of Cyprus, Jerusalem, and Armenia in Nicosia, but during her return to the palace the superstitious remarked that the Queen's horses stumbled and fell, causing the crown to fall from her head. Shortly afterwards Count Louis of Savoy, to whom she had been betrothed before her father's death, arrived in Cyprus, and they were married. Louis was a poor, miserable creature, and the majority of the Island had no wish to be ruled by Charlotte and her mean-spirited husband. The other claimant to the throne was James, illegitimate son of the late King by a Greek lady, Mary of Patras. This lady had had an unfortunate meeting with Queen Helena, who in a sudden moment of temper had bitten off her rival's nose. This bastard James was from his earliest youth a boy of high abilities, but of ungovernable temper. Queen Helena seems to have realized this while James was but a boy, and saw that one day he might prove a rival to her child Charlotte; she therefore persuaded her husband to appoint him, at the early age of sixteen, to the Archbishopric of Nicosia, and trusted that by devoting him to the Church she would keep him from mischief, but her precautions were in vain. James had at first supported Charlotte, and had assisted her in the assassination of the Chamberlain, whom she believed responsible for the death of her Portuguese husband. But this crime had filled even the Cypriots with horror, and the Archbishop was forced to fly to Rhodes. He soon found his exile irksome, and suddenly returning to Nicosia in 1547 scaled the walls and at once proceeded to the house of Jacques de Gourri, Viscount of Nicosia, who as a creature of the Queen was one of his bitterest enemies. Bursting open the door, he rushed into the room where the unfortunate man was sleeping, and stood by while his confederates dispatched the Viscount with repeated dagger thrusts. James then retired to the Archbishopric, which he held with a body of armed men. Unhappily the King, his father, was weak, and though at first he made a show of bringing his son to judgement for this second crime, he actually forgave him. Charlotte, however, forbade the Archbishop to officiate at her coronation service. This affront was more than James could stomach. He rode to Larnaca and took ship to Egypt, and on his arrival at Cairo he persuaded the Sultan to proclaim him King of Cyprus, and to assist him to regain his inheritance. On September 18, 1460, escorted by the Egyptian fleet of eighty ships, he landed once more in Cyprus. Everywhere he was welcomed with open arms, for the Cypriots were disgusted with the overbearing conduct of Louis and the train of Savoyards he had brought with him. On the news of his approach Charlotte and her husband abandoned the capital and took refuge in Kyrenia. The castle was well furnished with victuals, engines of war and munitions, and it was not till the garrison was half starved that the captain, a certain Sicilian called des Nares, surrendered it. Charlotte was not in the castle, having left for Italy, where she attempted to persuade Pope Pius II to influence the other European princes on her behalf.[1] Boustron, however, says that the price of des Nares' perfidy was the hand of a natural daughter of James, called Charlotte. It is true that des Nares was afterwards appointed Prince of Antioch and Constable of Cyprus.

The Queen retired to Rome, where she eventually died in 1487, having bequeathed her claims to the House of Savoy. Her renunciation was made in the Sistine Chapel in the presence of the Pope and Cardinals, and it was read at the coronation of Charles V. She was buried at St. Peter's between the Chapel of St. Thomas and Our Lady.

Venice reconstructed the castle in 1554, but when the Turks arrived in Cyprus in 1570 she apparently made little, if any, attempt to defend it.

[1] George Boustron, *History of Cyprus*, Venice, 1560, p. 469.

The present entrance of the castle is across a modern bridge, which replaces the drawbridge that originally stood there. An inclined path leads up a covered way to the main barbican; just before the top a doorway on the left leads down a dark passage to the tiny Chapel of St. George, built in the thickness of the wall. This is a square vaulted building, the dome of which has recently been replaced. The dome is supported on arches, carried by three marble columns with Corinthian capitals. The extremely interesting early windows and a north door have been recently rediscovered by Mr. Caroe. Fragments of the marble geometric floor still remain. A small door in the west end leads down into the interior of the great round tower of the Venetian rebuilding, which is now used as a store by the Public Works Department. The only reference to this chapel is in the will of a certain Lady Piemadabena of Ferrara, widow of Antonia di Bergamo, who left five bezants in her will, that masses should be said for her soul here.[1]

Returning to the main guard, above which are two shields with the royal Lusignan coat of arms, the great court of the castle is entered through a modern iron gate, near which is a Turkish tomb, said to have been that of the Turkish admiral to whom the castle was surrendered by the Venetians. During the Turkish period this court was used as a prison, and this has considerably damaged its character. The west side, with its vaulted apartments, still remains, above which were the royal rooms occupied by Queen Charlotte when she was besieged here. The north or sea wall remains intact with arrow slits in the lower stages; though the buildings along this side are later and largely date from the conversion of the castle into a convict prison. The doorway and windows at the north-west end are Venetian work of the sixteenth century. At the north-east corner is a square tower, dating from the thirteenth century, and containing two halls, one above the other. The rooms are lighted by long, deeply splayed arrow slits, and the original crenellation still exists on the roof.

[1] Enlart, *L'art Gothique en Chypre*, Paris, 1899, p. 574.

Passages in the south-west corner lead down to gun chambers and dungeons, mostly blocked up when the castle was converted from a fortress into a prison. In one of the last stages is a well, which must have supplied the garrison with water during the numerous sieges of the castle. The upper storey, above the barbican, was occupied by a chapel, of which the plan is easily traced, and the vestry on the north side is in an excellent state of preservation. To the right was once a large room. The stone-carved supports which can still be seen jutting out into the main courtyard probably supported a gallery or covered walk.

DESCRIPTION OF THE TOWN

The town of Kyrenia must also have been fortified, but only two mediaeval towers still remain. The larger formed the south-west corner of the town wall, while the smaller may possibly have defended the main gateway of the town. The little harbour of Kyrenia has, since the British occupation, been furnished with a quay and a sea wall. In the centre are the ruins of an ancient lighthouse, the path to it from the shore being formed of circular inscribed Roman cippi.

The churches of Kyrenia are without interest, except that of Chrysopolitissa, a small building in the centre of the town. On the north side is a doorway, now blocked up, which originally belonged to a Gothic building. The iconostasis is probably seventeenth century, but the icons are without interest.

Kyrenia existed long before the Latin occupation, and was once a capital of the nine kingdoms into which the Island was divided in ancient times. It is said that it was originally founded by Cyrus, King of Persia, when he captured the Island. Simon, who carried Our Lord's Cross to Calvary, is supposed to have been born at Kyrenia. From these ancient times date the quarries which lie east of Kyrenia, and contain relics of both pagan and Christian times. Here are found tombs of the classical period and chapels of Byzantine and mediaeval date, but nearly all the former were destroyed when stone was quarried to build the castle. There survive, however, the remains of a chapel dedicated to St. Mavra, which was formerly a Roman tomb. Traces of paintings still remain in the apse, cut in the solid rock. Near the sea is the tiny mediaeval chapel of Chrysocava. There are no architectural features by which to date it, but it was probably built during the fifteenth century. A curious founder's tomb projects from the exterior south wall, and there is a crucifix carved above the lintel of the door on the same side. The local inhabitants repair to this chapel to pray for their loved ones who travel by sea, and commend to the Madonna not only those who go in local sailing ships to trade in Asia Minor but also those more venturesome sons or fathers who emigrate to America or England. Close by are the remains of a classical tomb, with heavy moulding cut in the rock over the arch, and a tiny niche above, where it is said that the mysterious Queen of Chrysocava sits, and the women of Kyrenia, both Greek and Turk, keep a lamp perpetually burning to propitiate one who has such power over the sea. A little farther south is a holy well attached to the church, with a huge fig-tree growing from it. The water is much esteemed for its powers, and those who suffer from headaches come and collect some of it in a vessel and then pour it over their heads and cut off a piece of hair, which they tie to the branches of the fig-tree.

There is a small English cemetery belonging to the War Office at Kyrenia. It contains a most curious tomb, a Byzantine sarcophagus with crosses on its side; on its coped top is the following inscription:

> No. 141. Sergeant Samuel McGaw V.C., 42nd Royal Highlanders (Black Watch), died on the line of march to Camp Chiftlik Pasha of heat apoplexy, 22nd July, 1878. Aged 40 years.

Beneath is a carving in relief of the Victoria Cross.

About a mile west of Kyrenia is the Church of the B.V.M. Glykyotissa. It is a plain building without any character, with a cloister on the north-west side. Here is kept a large obliterated tombstone, which is supposed to represent the engineer who completed the fortifications of the castle, a certain Caesar Kariotis, who died in 1546. The effigy on this sepulchral stone shows the dead man in European costume, and on either side is his coat of arms, three serpents surmounted by a cross.

VII

LIMASSOL

ALTHOUGH this is the second largest town in Cyprus, it contains little of archaeological interest. It was probably first built soon after the arrival of the Latins in Cyprus, but it was at old Limassol, the present Amathus, that Richard Cœur de Lion landed. Richard was on his way to the Crusades, and in another ship accompanying his fleet was his intended bride, Berengaria of Navarre, and his sister Joanna, Queen Dowager of Sicily. The whole fleet put in at Crete and thence attempted to cross to Rhodes, but a storm arose and the fleet was scattered, and the ship containing the two queens was driven with several others to take refuge in the harbour of Limassol. Cyprus was then ruled by a certain Isaac Comnenus, a man of evil life, who oppressed the people and was cordially hated by all who came into contact with him. This tyrant, on hearing of the distinguished persons who had been driven into his harbour, tried to get the two queens into his power, but they, mistrusting the sincerity of his friendly overtures, refused to land at his invitation. Isaac, therefore, sent four armed galleys to attempt by force what he could not effect by strategy. At this critical moment the ships of Richard appeared over the horizon. The King of England was furious at the insults offered to his bride and sister, and at once demanded satisfaction and the release of those Englishmen who had been captured when one of the smaller ships had been wrecked. To these requests the Emperor sent insulting messages and refused to surrender the captives. Benedict of Peterborough, the contemporary historian of Richard I, has left the following account of the battle which ensued:

Meanwhile the Emperor had occupied the shore in every direction with his men. Many of them were armed, but still more had no arms at all. But the King of England and his men, as soon as they had armed themselves, disembarked from their large ships into their boats and galleys, and came to land with a rush. The king, accompanied by his bowmen, was first to land, the rest followed, and as soon as they reached the shore one and all flung themselves upon the Emperor and his Griffons. The arrows fell like rain upon the grass. After a prolonged conflict the Emperor, having lost a multitude of his men, fled, and all his host with him. The King of England, exulting in his great victory, pursued, and made a very great slaughter of all who resisted, and, had not night fallen soon, he would have taken the Emperor himself that day, either alive or dead. The king and his men, however, knew not the roads and mountain paths by which the Emperor and his followers made their escape, and would not pursue them further, but returned with a great prey both of men and animals to the town of Limezun, whence the Griffons and Herminians [Greeks and Armenians] had fled, leaving it empty.

On the same day [May 6th] the King of Navarre's daughter and the Queen of Sicily, who was sister to the King of England, entered the port of Limezun, attended by the king's fleet. The Emperor, having rallied round him his men, who were scattered amid the thickets in the mountain valleys, pitched his camp the same night on the banks of a river about five miles distant from the town of Limezun, declaring with an oath that he would fight the King of England on the morrow. The report whereof was brought by scouts to the king, who long before daylight armed himself and his men for battle, and advancing silently came upon the Emperor's men, whom he found asleep. Then, with a loud and terrifying shout, he charged into their tents, and they, suddenly awakened from sleep, were as dead men, knowing not what to do, nor whither to fly. The Emperor himself escaped with a few men, naked, and leaving behind him his treasure, his horses, his armour, his magnificent tents, and his imperial standard wrought all over with gold, which the King of England at once dedicated to the blessed Edmund, King and Martyr of glorious memory.[1]

After the defeat of Isaac, King Richard on May 12th, the feast of SS. Nereus Achilles and Pancras, married Berengaria, and later in the day caused her to be crowned Queen of England by John, Bishop of Evreux, in the

[1] *Excerpta Cypria*, p. 13.

presence of the Archbishops of Apanea and Auch, the Bishop of Bayonne, Guy de Lusignan, afterwards Lord of Cyprus, Bohemund III, Prince of Antioch, Raymond III, Count of Tripoli, and many others.

It is interesting, having seen the account of the historian, Benedict of Peterborough, to read the account given by a local historian, St. Neophytos, who was also alive at this period:

England is a country beyond Roumania on the north, out of which a cloud of Anglish with their sovereign, embarking together on large vessels called smacks, sailed towards Jerusalem. For at that time the monarch of the Germans, it is said with 900,000 soldiers, was making his way to Jerusalem; and passing by the land of Iconium, and coming through the eastern counties, his troops perished from the length of the journey, and from hunger and thirst. And their sovereign, as he was riding, was drowned in some river. But the English king, the wretch, landed in Cyprus, and found it a nursing mother: had it not been so he, too, perchance would have suffered the fate of the German. But how Cyprus was taken, this too I will briefly relate.

When it became necessary that the most pious sovereign Manuel Comnenus, of happy memory, should send a garrison to the royal strongholds in Armenia, he sent one of his kin, quite a youth, Isaac by name, who, after guarding the fortresses for some years, engaged in war with the Armenians. He was taken captive by them and sold to the Latins. They held him for many years bound with chains, for his uncle, the Emperor Manuel, was dead, leaving his realm to his son, Alexius, also a child. Whereupon his uncle Andronicus, who reigned with him, killed the boy and seized the kingdom. But at the entreaty of the assembly he sent a very large ransom, and bought the said Isaac out of the hands of the Latins. Isaac came to Cyprus, took it, and was proclaimed king. He ruled over it for seven years, and not only utterly despoiled the land and perpetually harassed the lives of its rich men, but by every way he hounded and oppressed its nobles, so that all lived in distress, and sought how by any means they might protect themselves against him.

While things were so, lo, the Englishman lands in Cyprus, and forthwith all ran unto him! Then the king, abandoned by his people, give himself also unto the hands of the English.

Him the English king bound in irons, and having seized his vast treasures, and grievously wasted the land, sailed away to Jerusalem, leaving behind him ships to strip the country and to follow him. But King Isaac of Cyprus he shut up in chains in a castle called Marcappus. The wicked wretch achieved naught against his fellow wretch Saladin, but achieved this only that he sold our country to the Latins for two hundred thousand pounds of gold. Whereupon great was the wailing, and unbearable the smoke, as was said before, which came from the north.[1]

One of the lesser-known incidents of this campaign is the story of the daughter of Isaac. After his defeat he was imprisoned and bound with silver chains in the castle of Margat, in Lyna, which belonged to the Hospitallers. His daughter became lady-in-waiting to Queen Berengaria, and accompanied her to Acre. One of the conditions exacted by Henry VI, the German Emperor, for the release of Richard was that she should regain her liberty. The grounds upon which Henry VI claimed the liberation of Isaac's daughter were those of relationship, for Isaac had married a sister of William II of Sicily, and was therefore uncle by marriage to Constantia of Sicily, Henry's wife. This daughter of Isaac became the wife of Raymond VI, Count of Toulouse, who later divorced her. In 1202 she was living in Marseilles, and met and married there a French knight, a relative of Baldwin, Count of Flanders. This new husband appears to have had ambitious designs, and with his bride went to Cyprus, where he demanded the restitution of the crown of Cyprus in the right of his wife. Amaury, the Lusignan King of Cyprus, at first treated the matter as a jest, but later informed the claimants that unless they left the Island at once he would have them executed.

Limassol, after the fall of Acre in 1291, passed into the joint guardianship of the Hospitallers and the Templars, but with the departure of the Orders seems to have fallen on evil times. It was destroyed by the Genoese in 1373, and again by the Saracens in 1426. Earthquakes, too, seem

[1] *Excerpta Cypria*, p. 11.

to have damaged the town, and travellers in the sixteenth century have left depressing descriptions of it.

The master took us to Limisso, a village in a beautiful plain and close to the sea. The houses are built chiefly of earth covered with rushes and fascines, of a single storey, and so low that one must stoop to mount two or three steps. They make their doors thus low so that Turks on horseback or an angry crowd may not enter. We landed and found on the beach a number of Turks who had come to see us. They all had in their turbans roses, violets, and other flowers. After having a good look at us they left on horseback with their Cadi, all carrying a scimitar at their side, and a long dart or javelin in their hands: some had a bow and quiver, with an iron mace hung at their saddlebow, and in this array they paraded all the afternoon, managing their horses, as is their wont, with graceful dexterity. Then we walked about the village. There was nothing worthy of mark. About five years since an earthquake threw down all the houses, which have been rebuilt by the Turks after the fashion of pigsties. The poor Christians are no better lodged than the Turks, or even worse. They have indeed built a little church fifteen feet high, where they say the mass of the Greek rite. You may see, too, the baths where the Turks bathe every day, and the sepulchres in which they are laid after they have descended to the Paradise prepared for them by their false prophet Mahomet. The sun was low in the west, and reminded us to return to supper and sleep on our vessel.[1]

Another traveller writes towards the close of the sixteenth century:

Limassol is situated upon a sinuosity of the sea, that produces a beach instead of a port. It was formerly adorned by many beautiful buildings, churches, and monasteries, Latin as well as Greek, being once one of the four episcopal towns of the island. One of its bishops was the good Father Leontide, who wrote the life of St. John the Almoner. But all those churches and monasteries, as well as the Fortress, are now into ruins. The spot and site of the sea was very convenient to navigators, going or willing to succour the Holy Land, as there are but

---

[1] Villamont, *Excerpta Cypria*, p. 171.

150 miles till Jaffa or Joppe. Even now, most of the vessels going towards the East, use on their passage to anchor there. The air is good, and there is a beautiful plain with sweet water in abundance; but the town is without walls, but only ruins are to be seen, and some houses rebuilt with one storey only, by fear of earthquakes. There also still remain some vestiges of a fortress, which was pulled down by order of the Senate of Venice in 1539. It is therefore now nothing else but a town, or big borough, still bearing traces of fire. The entrances of modern houses, especially of the richest, are for the greatest part with degrees or steps, and have a stone in front of the doors, as in those quarters is practised before the entrances of the cemeteries of the churches; and the object of this is to prevent Cavalry, or Turkish or Arab soldiery, to enter there at will.

There reside the Agents of Venetian and French merchants, and some Christians, remnants of the ancient Cypriots, and even Turks and Moors, who mix themselves in the traffics, act as interpreters, and spies to the Turks, to let them know which Christians, of the various nations, are arriving. The resident Christians have recently built a vaulted church. The Turks, too, have one mosque and baths.[1]

DESCRIPTION OF THE TOWN

It is not surprising, therefore, that the modern Limassol has little of interest to show. The chief monument is a fortress now used as a prison, the oldest portion of which is a great square hall in the centre, probably dating from the early fourteenth century; it was remodelled at some period, when the central pillar which supported the vaulting was removed. The rest of this building and its wall, in some places three feet thick, dates from the Venetian era. It was partially demolished by Francesco Bragadino, the Venetian Governor of Cyprus, in 1525, owing to the fact that it had been seized by Turkish pirates. An absurd and totally untrue legend has grown up, that the great hall of the castle was the scene of the marriage of Richard and Berengaria.

The Orthodox churches are also without interest. The

[1] Zuallart, *Voyages*, 1586, p. 33.

principal one is dedicated to the Holy Handkerchief of St. Veronica, and is an enormous modern building in the Byzantine style completed in 1903. It replaced a small rustic church built in 1738, the walls of which were completely covered with mural paintings. The interior of the present church with its crude painting and gilded marble is garish in the extreme. A number of icons survive from the former building, and are kept in the apse; they are mostly eighteenth century, and only one is dated, that of Christ in Glory, painted in 1740 by the priest Joannikou.

A tombstone in the graveyard commemorates Esther, infant child of the Rev. Joseph and Lady Georgiana Wolff, who died in 1828, aged nine months.

Dr. Wolff was one of the grand eccentrics of the early nineteenth century. He was the son of a rabbi, and was born in Germany, but while a student at Weimar he changed his religion and became a Roman Catholic, entering a monastery in Switzerland. Full of his new-found zeal, he determined to submit to all the rules of the Order; these included flagellation. This penance was carried out in the dark, and Wolff gave himself the first lash, but not liking it turned round to see how the other monks were faring, and to his amazement observed they were merely beating the walls. This was more than Wolff could stand, and he at once applied his whip to the shoulders of the monk nearest him.

Next day the Superior turned Wolff out of the monastery, and shortly afterwards he became a Protestant missionary, and during his work in the Near East came to Cyprus.

Later he journeyed to Bokhara in the days when travelling was most difficult, and the country wild and the people fanatical. He was regarded by the inhabitants as mad, and was treated with the respect which Moslems show to those who are thus afflicted.

That the people of Bokhara had some reason for imagining him insane must be admitted, for he entered their city in a surplice and mortar-board, reading the Church of England service.

Dr. Wolff married Lady Georgiana Walpole, daughter

of Lord Orford. One of their sons was Sir Henry Drummond-Wolff, the politician and ambassador.[1]

There is also a small church dedicated to St. Antony, and built in 1870. In the gallery are kept some icons from a former church, of which the best is an emaciated St. John the Baptist, in the style of El Greco, painted by the priest Thomas in 1693, and presented to the church by a certain Styli. The holy doors were painted by the same priest in 1694. The original iconostasis of the same date has recently been removed to the neighbouring Chapel of St. Mamas; it is an extremely good example of the gilded and carved woodwork of the period, and has never been repaired or touched in any way; indeed, it is probably one of the best late seventeenth-century iconostases still surviving in the Island.

[1] The above facts about Dr. Wolff's life are taken from *Under Five Reigns*, by Lady Dorothy Nevill, niece of Lady Georgiana.

VIII

PAPHOS

THE modern town is known as Ktima, while the ruins of the Roman and mediaeval city near the sea are known as Nea Paphos. The latter is supposed to have been founded by Agapenor, who was wrecked here in 1184 B.C. when returning from the Trojan wars. During the Roman era the city was decorated and adorned with magnificent temples and public buildings, and it is here that the first person of any distinction to become a Christian was converted. Hitherto those won to the new religion had been simple folk, but Paul, by the startling conversion of the Roman Governor, captured the attention of the ruling classes.

And when they had gone through the isle unto Paphos, they found a certain sorcerer, a false prophet, a Jew, whose name was Bar-jesus:

Which was with the deputy of the country, Sergius Paulus, a prudent man; who called for Barnabas and Saul, and desired to hear the word of God.

But Elymas the sorcerer (for so is his name by interpretation) withstood them, seeking to turn away the deputy from the faith.

Then Saul (who also is called Paul) filled with the Holy Ghost, set his eyes on him.

And said, O full of all subtilty and all mischief, thou child of the devil, thou enemy of all righteousness, wilt thou not cease to pervert the right ways of the Lord?

And now, behold, the hand of the Lord is upon thee, and thou shalt be blind, not seeing the sun for a season. And immediately there fell on him a mist and a darkness; and he went about seeking some to lead him by the hand.

Then the deputy, when he saw what was done, believed, being astonished at the doctrine of the Lord.[1]

Paphos was the port for Kouklia and the Shrine of Venus, and it was here that countless pilgrims landed to

[1] Acts xiii. 6–12.

visit and worship at the great shame and glory of Cyprus: glory for its buildings and treasure; shame from the unrestrained licenses of the priestesses, who wantonly flaunted their prostitution.

Nea Paphos was destroyed by an earthquake in the time of the Emperor Augustus and remained in ruins till the Latin era. During the First Crusades pilgrims landed here and rested before proceeding to the Holy Land, and some even died and were buried here. In this town, so far distant from their homes and so strange, for ever rest Guelph, the fourth Duke of Bavaria, Eric I, King of Denmark, and Amadeus, Count of Savoy. The Bavarian Duke died in 1101, Eric four years later, and the Count of Savoy in 1148.

According to *Saxo Grammaticus*,[1] it was impossible to bury bodies in Cyprus, as a demon dug them up at night and brought them back to their houses; but that with the burial of Eric the Good this unpleasant trouble ceased.

Before the end of the Lusignan kingdom, Nea Paphos seems to have been so damaged by earthquakes that it was almost deserted. A Dominican monk, who visited it in 1480, says:

> How vast this city was, and how stately the churches which stood there, the extent of the ruins and the noble columns of marble which lie prostrate prove. It is now desolate, no longer a city, but a miserable village built over the ruins; on this account the harbour too is abandoned, and ships only enter it when forced to do so, as was our fate. As the city was laid low by an earthquake so it lies still, and no king nor bishop gives a hand to raise it up again.[2]

It was also supposed to be unhealthy, so the town was moved inland on to the bluff above the harbour, the modern Ktima.

The first mention of the new town is made by the Spanish noble, Pero Tafur, who rested here in 1436. He stayed at "the house of Diego Thenorio, an esquire of Castile, and had much pleasure with him", but adds, "the Port of

[1] Bk. 12, Ed. Holder, pp. 408–9.

[2] *Excerpta Cypria*, p. 45.

Papphos, where I had embarked, is a very unhealthy place: the very day I arrived the bishop, Angelo de Narmi, and two of his esquires had died".[1]

After the Turkish conquest Nea Paphos was almost completely abandoned, save for a few families who lived in the ruins, and Ktima became the capital and chief town of the district.

DESCRIPTION OF THE TOWN[2]

The ancient walls of Nea Paphos can still be followed on the west and north sides, and there are traces of gateways with rock-hewn steps. Near the great quarries is the Church of St. Agapetikos, [1] a tiny chapel cut from the soft sandstone, and perhaps in its curious dedication still recalling Venus, for St. Agapitikos is the saint of love. Of the church only the apse remains. According to a local legend, the Queen of Paphos loved a certain strong man called Dhiyeni, and promised to marry him on the condition that he brought fresh water to the city. This he accomplished, but the Queen changed her mind and refused to carry out her promise. In anger he retired to Ktima and threw at her a great rock, which is to this day called Petra tou Dhiyeni, or the Rock of Dhiyeni.[2] The Queen, not to be outdone, threw her spindle, and a great granite column is still pointed out as the spindle of the Queen. After this example of masterful wooing the Queen consented to marry, and the couple lived in the cave which later became the church. To this day lovers go secretly at night and light here a candle or lamp in the belief that they will thus win the love of those they desire to marry.

Close by is another chapel dedicated to St. Misitikos, or the saint of Hatred. In reality the names of these two saints are a corruption of two local holy hermits, St. Agapetos and St. Themistos, who lived here at an early period.

The Church of St. Marina [3] is a ruined building of the fifteenth century. In the interior lies a white marble column

[1] *Excerpta Cypria*, p. 33.
[2] The figures in brackets refer to numbers on plan.

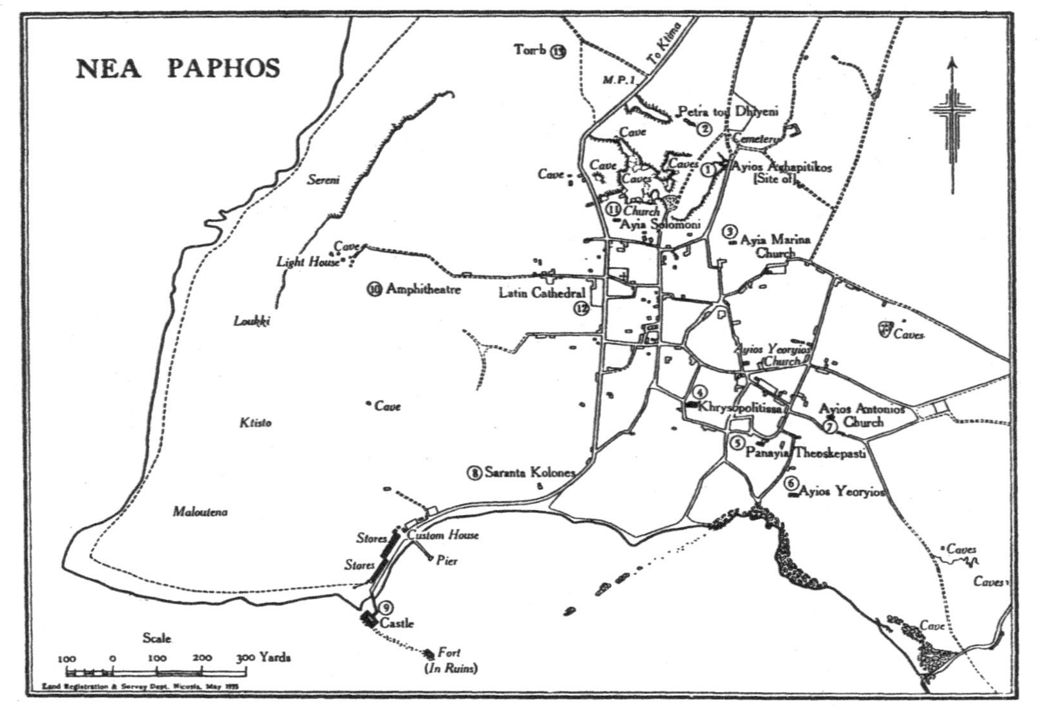

NEA PAPHOS
Torb 13
To Ktima
M.P.1
Petra tou Dhiyeni
2
Cemetery
Cave
Caves
1 Ayios Aghapitikos [Site of]
Cave
Caves
11 Church
Ayia Solomoni
3 Ayia Marina Church
Sereni
Light House
10 Amphitheatre
Latin Cathedral 12
Caves
Loukki
Ayios Yeoryios Church
4 Khrysopolitissa
Cave
Ayios Antonios 7 Church
Ktisto
5 Panayia Theoskepasti
8 Saranta Kolones
6 Ayios Yeoryios
Maloutena
Stores
Custom House
Stores
Pier
Caves
Caves
9 Castle
Cave
Scale
100 0 100 200 300 Yards
Fort (In Ruins)
Land Registration & Survey Dept. Nicosia, May 1935

with a Greek inscription, recording the gift of a certain Deacon Isidoros.

The Church of Chrysopolitissa [4] was originally erected in the eleventh or twelfth centuries, but has been remodelled and rebuilt. The foundations of a larger and older apse can still be seen encircling the present bema. The iconostasis is modern, and the only object of interest which the church contains is a fragment above the screen in the right aisle; it is now painted over, but carved on it is a shield with a coat of arms, a phoenix displayed. There are also two seventeenth-century processional icons of St. George and Christ. A most important Roman temple must have stood here to judge from the large number of granite columns which lie scattered around or stand upright. It is uncertain whether the upright columns are actually *in situ* or not. Near the west end of the church is a stump of a pillar surrounded with an iron railing. Here, according to a late and untrustworthy legend, St. Paul was bound and beaten before the conversion of the Roman Governor.

The Church of the B.V.M. Theoskepasti, or the Madonna Covered by God, [5] takes its name from a legend that when the Arabs attacked the town under Abu-Alur in the seventh century A.D., they advanced to sack and desecrate the church, but the Virgin shrouded the building in a thick mist so that the raiders were unable to see it, and retired leaving it unharmed. Unhappily the original church has been destroyed and the new one erected in the usual mean, vulgar form. In the interior is an icon almost completely covered with metal repoussé and said to have been one of the seventy painted by St. Luke.

The Church of St. George [6] is now completely ruined and little remains save fragments of the ribs of the vaulting lying amongst the débris. Here, too, can be seen two mediaeval tombstones, one of which is a memorial of a certain Harior Beduin and his father. The family of Beduin was one of the earliest Latin families to settle in Cyprus, and a certain Thomas Beduin is mentioned as having a position at Court in the year 1223.

The Church of St. Antony [7] was originally a double-aisled building built in the Byzantine manner. At some period the south aisle has been destroyed and a common narthex added. In the interior stands a fine fluted white marble pedestal of the Roman period. Of the Roman remains the most impressive left is the Saranta Kolones or Field of the Forty Columns.[8] This is supposed to be the site of the principal temple dedicated to Aphrodite.

Tradition points at this day to a mound close to the north-west side of the harbour as the site of such a temple; at a rough estimate its summit measures 200 ft. from north to south by 250 ft. east to west: fragments of about twenty monolithic columns of grey granite, 22 in. in diameter, lie on the surface, protrude from the sides, or are built into fences hard by, and from these native exaggeration has given to the mound the name Forty Columns. No other remains lie above the surface, but three holes have been sunk into the mound whereby massive foundations and substructures have been exposed; that on the south reveals a vaulted chamber 12 ft. high, the southern wall of which has fallen away; to the east of this a narrow stairway runs down from the surface of the mound to a doorway choked with earth; a massive wall can be traced for some feet further, the returning wall being also visible on the east of the mound. In the centre of the summit a shaft has been sunk into similar substructures of a very massive order, and there is evidently a labyrinth of staircases, vaults, and passages underlying the whole mound and awaiting a persevering explorer. As to the date of some portions at any rate of the Temple of which they formed the basement, indications are afforded by the Roman granite columns, already mentioned, and coarse plaster which may be picked up in quantities; but the existence of blocks with a raised panel in the centre and chisel-draft round the edges, similar to those in the lower courses of the Parthenon basement and in pre-Roman work of the second period at Old Paphos, suggests an earlier date for the original building erected on this mound.[1]

These underground passages mentioned by Hogarth have still never been explored, though at the beginning of the last century they would seem to have been much more accessible than they are now. William Turner, in his *Journal*, tells the following story.

[1] Hogarth, *Devia Cypria*, p. 5.

Signor A. told me that twenty years ago a Turk who had murdered another, and was hotly pursued, took refuge in these subterraneous chambers, to which despair made him find the passage, not then entirely choked up; after wandering three days underground in utter darkness he came out at Afrikee, about a quarter of a mile distant from the hill of the temple; his report was that he had passed through chambers full of stones, with some skulls and other bones.[1]

The castle [9] or fort was completely rebuilt by the Turks in 1589. It is a small unimportant building and till lately was used as a store for salt. The sea wall is much ruined, but probably dates from the thirteenth century. Apparently the mediaeval castle stood close by, as van Bruyn, who was here in 1683, says: "On the shore is a fort under which vessels moor, to get the protection of its guns. The old castle is on a hill close by, a mere ruin."[2] North of the fort lie the ruins of the Roman town, but little remains except piles of stones, marking where buildings stood and here and there fragments of mosaic floor. Nothing can be identified for certainty, but a place close to the lighthouse is pointed out as the amphitheatre.[10] The arena is not more than 250 feet in circumference and no trace of its stone seating is visible.

The Church of St. Solomoni [11] is one of the most curious monuments of Paphos; formerly a Roman tomb, it was at some early period converted into a church. Traces of painting still remain in the apse cut from the solid rock, and fragments remain of the stone iconostasis. Attached to this chapel is a holy well, which is frequented by those who suffer from ophthalmia: having washed, they then tear off fragments of their clothing and tie them to the large tree at the head of the flight of steps which leads down to the church. This may possibly have been the Chapel of the Seven Sleepers or the Seven Maccabees.

Nearly every mediaeval traveller to Cyprus seems to have visited that monument, but their descriptions are not clear enough to decide with any certainty where the tomb was.

[1] *Journal of a Tour in the Levant*, London, 1820, p. 562.
[2] *Voyage to Levant*, p. 276.

Even the legend has become involved. According to some it was the scene of the martyrdom of a mother and her seven sons, called by the name of the Heroic Maccabees; this legend is evidently derived from 2 Maccabees vii, where a mother and her seven sons were tortured and slain for refusing to eat swine's flesh at the order of Antiochos Epiphanes. Other writers hold that this was the resting-place of the Seven Sleepers. The Byzantine Church commemorates the Seven Sleepers on August 4th under the title of the "Seven Holy Children of Ephesus". They are said to have lived in A.D. 252 in the reign of the Emperor Decius, who, when he arrived at Ephesus, tried to force them to forswear their Christianity and to offer sacrifices to idols. Rather than yield to his wishes they hid in a cave, which was walled up at the Emperor's commands. There their bodies remained undisturbed till A.D. 446, when the owner of the field in which the cave was situated wished to build a sheepfold; while collecting stones for this, he pulled down the entrance to the cavern, and at once the Seven were miraculously restored to life, having undergone no change either in their persons or their raiment during 194 years. When they did eventually die their bodies were taken to Marseilles, and a large stone sarcophagus in the Church of St. Victor is pointed out as containing their remains. André Thevet, who visited Paphos in 1590, saw the tomb

> in a very deep grotto in the chapel called by the vulgar the Seven Sleepers. Of these seven sleepers the simple folk tell a thousand stories; among others, they are so deluded that they believe that these seven sleepers are still alive, their priests having always kept them in this error. This chapel is between the town of Paphos, now mostly ruined, and the tower near the sea, on the top of which can still be seen the arms of Savoy carved in white marble.[1]

Of the Latin cathedral [12] nothing remains except the south angle of the west end. It was probably built in the fourteenth century and was restored by Francesco Contarini, last Latin bishop of Paphos, who was murdered by the

[1] *Excerpta Cypria*, p. 180.

Turks on the fall of Nicosia. The most famous occupant of the Latin See of Paphos was Jacopo Pesaro, who held it from 1496 to 1502, when he became Admiral of the Papal fleet under Alexander VI against the Turks. He died in Venice in 1547 and is buried in the Church of the Frari in that town. Close to his tomb is the famous altar-piece by Titian, known as La Pala dei Pesari. The bishop ordered the picture in 1519 and the artist received ninety-six ducats for his work, the most magnificent ex-voto picture in the world.

The great necropolis of the Greco-Roman period extended from the north wall of the city along the seashore for about two miles. All the tombs have been robbed, but near the police rifle-range is a tomb [13] which has recently been discovered and is in a good state of preservation. The key of the iron gateway which protects the entrance is kept at the police station. The largest tombs of all are at a site known as Paleo Castro, about a mile due north of the tomb mentioned above. They are all of Roman date, and one or two of them still retain their colonnaded entrances decorated with plain architectural details. There are more than a hundred of them, and the description given by William Turner in 1815 holds good to this day.

These ruins are called by the general name of Palaio Castro, and their appearance is most extraordinary. They occupy a spot of ground, about a quarter of a mile long, and very nearly as much broad, which is covered, except in a few spots where the communication is broken, by a mass of solid rock, more or less high, but seldom more than 40 feet, and hewn into numerous caves, which appear to have been catacombs, but are now so choked up that it is impossible to see whether they all communicate with each other.

These caves are more or less large, and within them are others cut of a shape evidently meant for tombs, about ten feet long, three broad, and four high. We entered most of these caves, and found them of various sizes, some about 20 ft. square, but in general they were smaller, i.e. those above ground, for there are some subterraneous ones which Signor Andrea, who probably was a better fisherman than antiquary, did not advise us of.

Sometimes the rock was so low, and the ceiling consequently so thin, that the excavated part, to prevent its falling in, was supported by Dorick fluted columns, 10 feet high, hewn out of the rock, which the Turks have broken off and carried away to adorn their mosques, leaving however frequently enough of the capital and shaft to see what was there. There are many small excavations, one or two feet deep, and three or four feet square, like the ground of a basso-relievo, which were probably devoted to the reception of images: over the entrance to many of the caves are carved architraves, slightly adorned in various ways.

Many stairs are cut on and towards the top of the rocks. The rock is of a very soft grey sandstone, and the ruinous state in which it now is must have been produced by some earthquake or tremendous convulsion of nature, as immense masses of it are severed, and lying at some distance from the main body. On the top of the rock nothing is visible. The excavated caves are on every side of it. There are above fifty of the larger ones, and above one hundred of them in all. As their floor is generally of earth, much I have no doubt might be discovered by exploring and digging them, but the watchful jealousy of the Turks being carried in Paphos to a most rigid excess their passages are blocked up by dirt and dust, and they serve as stables to the donkeys of the neighbourhood; we dislodged at least a hundred of these animals, nor did we observe any other cattle among the ruins.[1]

The modern town of Ktima contains little of interest. The churches are modern, though the Mosque of St. Sofia was in all probability originally a Latin church. In the court-yard of the police station are a number of relics and fragments from the ancient city, which include a large white marble Hellenistic sarcophagus and two mediaeval tomb-stones.

About two hundred yards south of the police station is a large rock-cut tomb of the Hellenistic period consisting of several chambers, on the walls of which can still be seen fragments of the original painted plaster. Outside the tomb lies a large mutilated stone lion, which was discovered inside.

[1] *Tour in the Levant*, vol. ii, p. 557.

IX

THE VILLAGES, CASTLES, AND MONASTERIES

AGRIDHAKI (xi)[1]

THE church is dedicated to St. Haralambos, and is a modern building completed in 1920. It contains nothing of interest save an icon of Christ, dated 1804. The ruins of its predecessor lie near by, but would appear not to be earlier than the late eighteenth century.

A local superstition records that oil from the lamp which burns in front of St. Haralambos will cure the diseases of cattle and other animals.

AGRIDHIA (xxxvii)

The church is dedicated to the Prophet Elijah, and is a large double-aisled structure almost entirely reconstructed in 1811. The vault is decorated with late eighteenth-century porcelain plates. Unhappily the usual fatal restoration has robbed the church of much of its interest, and the finely carved early seventeenth-century iconostasis has been vilely repainted in every known colour and hue.

The long panel above the holy doors has a most unusual motif carved on it of birds and mice nibbling at bunches of grapes. In a large wooden frame, carved after the Gothic manner with crockets and finials, is kept a fine eighteenth-century icon of the Prophet Elijah. The remainder of the icons in this church are without interest, except a seventeenth-century processional one of St. Paraskeva.

AGROKIPIA (xxix)

The church is dedicated to the B.V.M. Chrysopantanissa. It is an ancient building which has been much repaired, and the apse is modern. The west door and

[1] The Roman numbers in brackets refer to the map of Cyprus at the end of the book.

a blocked-up window on the south side survive from the original building.

About two miles from the village lies the large eighteenth-century monastery dedicated to St. Panteleemon. The church has the unusual feature of a gabled roof covered with small brown tiles. The contemporary iconostasis is an extremely good example of gilding and wood-carving, and is as brilliant as in the year it was first painted, namely, 1774. The icons mostly date from the eighteenth century, while the icon of St. Panteleemon himself is covered with silver gilt repoussé, and is dated 1792.

AGROLADHOU (xxviii)

A small Turkish hamlet, now in the last stages of decay. Two small Christian chapels still remain in the vicinity, but a modern restoration has not improved them. One is dedicated to St. Barbara, and is a small early seventeenth-century building containing an unusually well-painted seventeenth-century icon of Christ. It is treated symbolically, the body being shown after the Deposition—an unusual subject in Byzantine iconography.

AGROS (xxxviii)

In recent years a vast new building, in the Byzantine style and dedicated to the Virgin, has taken the place of the original village church. Luckily, the original iconostasis and icons are preserved, and are a delightful example of eighteenth-century work.

At the far side of the village is a building dedicated to St. John the Baptist (*c.* 1760), which is of unusual proportions, being 114 feet in length and 21 feet in width. It contains little except a well-painted eighteenth-century icon of the Transfiguration in an elaborately carved frame.

AKAKI (xxix)

The principal village church, dedicated to the Virgin, was almostly completely restored in 1858. Of the original building little now remains except the flying buttresses on the north and south walls, and the arches and two founders' tombs on the south side.

The iconostasis is a peculiarly revolting example of varnished woodwork, but contains an icon of St. John the Divine painted on the back of a seventeenth century one of the same subject.

The village also contains a tiny chapel dedicated to the Archangel Michael, built on the site of an earlier church, of which only a fragment of the apse now survives. This earlier church must have had a frescoed interior, for fragments of painted plaster can still be seen on the stones used in the rebuilding.

AKANTHOU (vi)

The Church of Our Saviour is a vast new building, but it is in better taste than most modern churches in Cyprus. Its predecessor, built in 1862, still stands by its side, but is shortly doomed to destruction.

About two miles north, and by the seashore, lie the ruins of the ancient city of Aphrodisium. Little now remains, as the site had been plundered since the memory of man for building material. Half a mile west along the coast is to be found a large deposit of the fossilized bones of the pygmy hippopotamus.

About three miles from Akanthou are the remains of an ancient village. Of the village itself nothing remains save piles of stones, but the church, dedicated to the Madonna of Pergamon, is in an excellent state of repair. It is in the mediaeval style with a central dome, and was once completely frescoed with mural paintings of a good style; but these are now much decayed and damaged. Near the church is a tiny chapel cut in a rock, measuring 16 feet by 13 feet. In it is an iconostasis. In the centre is a doorway, and on either side a window, and then a door. There are no architectural features, and it is impossible to give any date to this unusual little building. On a neighbouring hillock are the remains of the acropolis of the ancient settlement, and half of the marble lid of a sarcophagus with a crudely cut face in relief, imitated from an Egyptian mummy case and dating from about 400 B.C.

In a thicket close by lie the ruins of an ancient and small village, squared blocks, smooth pillars of sandstone, and many stones from a vault. On a low rocky rise a hundred paces to the north are more old foundations, and bigger heaps of squared stones, broken sarcophagi, and fragments of tiles lying about the fields.[1]

AKAPNOU (xlviii)

The principal church of the village is dedicated to St. George and was built in 1857. It is of little interest. Outside the village, however, lies the small and ancient Church of the Virgin of Kambou. It was probably abandoned at some period, as a passing visitor has cut his name and the date, 1777, on one of the wall paintings, of which a considerable number still remain.

In the interior two beams run the length of the church on the north and south walls, which support the roof. On each of the beams are painted eighteen roundels of various saints, which are possibly late sixteenth-century work.

The iconostasis is much repaired, and contains a processional icon of the B.V.M., of the late sixteenth century, and three long panels, seventeenth century, of St. John the Baptist, St. John the Divine, and St. Peter, well painted.

The mysterious Queen of Cyprus known to folk-lore is connected with this village. Here her army fought with a rival force composed entirely of black troops, while in the neighbouring village of Vikla is a pile of stones which the Dhiyeni, or twin brothers, are supposed to have thrown at the queen and so caused her death.

AKHELIA (li)

During the Middle Ages this was a village of considerable importance, and the centre of the sugar industry of the Commandery of the Knights of Rhodes. The name Akhelia is a corruption of the mediaeval French name of L'Eschelle,

[1] Ross, *Reisen Nach der Insel Cypern*, Halle, 1846.

which is the equivalent of La Scala or the Port. To-day it has sunk to a small hamlet of half a dozen houses, but two important mediaeval churches still remain. Near the road is an early sixteenth-century building dedicated to St. George, which was restored in 1743, when the narthex was destroyed.

The icons include an early sixteenth-century Virgin and Child in almost pastel shades, untouched by restoration. There are also a St. Mamas and a St. George, both of the early seventeenth century. Of the magnificent woodwork which once decorated the church, and of which an account is given by Hogarth,[1] nothing now remains save the lower pillars which once supported the Baldachino, for about forty years ago the iconostasis, pulpit, and all the carved and painted woodwork of the church were carried off and sold in a London auction room for a small sum.

The other church, still remaining, is dedicated to St. Theodosios, and is a very early cruciform building with a number of frescoes still on its walls. In the south transept the altar is formed from a marble fragment of a Roman temple with egg and dart moulding. On the floor lie the fragments of a mediaeval tombstone with a coat of arms—a lion passant—on a shield. The church has recently been restored in a barbarous manner.

There is also close to the sea a small chapel dedicated to St. Leontios, but now deserted and containing nothing save an altar formed from a Corinthian capital. A number of marble pillars and capitals lie scattered round the church, and it is probable that this is the site of some small Roman town.

AKHYRITOU (xxxiii)

Called by the Turks Kuverjinlik, or The Place of Pigeons. This is one of the numerous instances of a place-name in Cyprus referring to the bird of Aphrodite.

The village church is dedicated to the Saviour, and is quite modern, but contains a number of icons of earlier date from other churches in the vicinity. The most interesting of these are a seventeenth-century Madonna from the

[1] D. G. Hogarth, *Devia Cypria*, London, 1889, p. 45.

ruined village of Trapeza, a St. George of 1759, and twelve icons of the Apostles dated 1709 from the Chapel of St. George. There is also a noble and unusual icon of Agios Georghios Tou Sporou (St. George the Farmer), dating from the early seventeenth century. His anniversary is November 3rd, and a festival is still held in his honour before the sowing of the harvest takes place.

Close to the Church of the Saviour lies a small chapel dedicated to St. Marina, built in 1758. According to an inscription on the iconostasis this chapel was built by a certain Andronicos Karides, of Larnaca, who owned a *chiflik* (small farm) here. Finding that the mediaeval church was being used by the Turks as a stable he sought and at last obtained permission from the Pasha to build this chapel, on the condition that it was smaller than its predecessor. The consecration of the building was carried out by Archbishop Philotheos (1734–1759), whose dedicatory cross still remains painted on the south wall. Mariti, who wrote of Cyprus in 1760, notes:

> Turning south you reach on something of a hill Acerito, a village thickly inhabited and well cultivated. It is the property of Signor Andronico Caridis, (by Berat) honorary dragoman to H.I.M. the Apostolic Queen of Hungary. Near his residence is a little chapel dedicated to St. Marina, of rough Greek construction, but embellished with fine old pictures of saints bought by him from houses in Famagusta at the price of the panels on which they are painted.[1]

Kept in the church is a fragment of a very early icon of St. Nicholas, with scenes from the Saint's life round the border. Only two of these little scenes still remain, but in each the attendant priests and acolytes are shown with a tonsure and what appear to be Latin vestments. It is difficult to date this fragment, but it may belong to the early years of the fifteenth century.

A number of chapels surround the village, and the most interesting of these is a tiny Byzantine Church of St. George, probably dating from the thirteenth century. At some period

[1] *Travels in Cyprus*, London, 1791.

the narthex and south aisle have been destroyed, but the interior still shows sign of the original painting.

About three miles from the village, and close to the main road, lies the little Monastery of St. Kendeas, one of the fourth-century saints of Cyprus. The simple church probably dates from the sixteenth century, and is without interest save for the early seventeenth-century holy doors. Near by, and surrounded by giant olive-trees, is the Ayasma, or holy well of the monastery—a long tunnel in the side of the hill filled with water, the mouth protected by a small square chamber with a door, which is used as a tiny chapel. The water in the tunnel is regarded by the surrounding villages as a sovereign cure for all manner of diseases.

About twenty-five years since a woman in a distant village had an only child afflicted with a terrible skin disease. Doctors were of no avail, and she prayed to St. Kendeas, who appeared to her in a dream and described his monastery and its well. He told her that if she brought her child and washed it in holy water it would be cured at once. Next day the poor woman told the village priest, who was amazed that she was able to describe so accurately and with such a wealth of detail a place that she had never seen in her life. So impressed was the worthy father that he accompanied the woman and her child to the monastery, where the child was immediately cured.

About two miles north of Akhyritou lie the ruins of the mediaeval town of Trapeza, which was ravaged and destroyed by the Mamluks in 1426. Nothing now remains except the ruins of two important churches, one of which is fairly well preserved. This church, dedicated to the Virgin, is designed on a plan of three aisles with an east end composed of a central apse, and a square-sided chapel on either hand. The roof is constructed of barrel-vaulting, with two domes. The building is a curious mixture of the Byzantine and Gothic styles, the only date shown being 1563, which must refer to a half-hearted attempt by the Venetians to restore it. The other church is completely ruined.

The only local tradition still surviving of what must have been a town of considerable importance is that Trapeza once boasted seventy-two taverns. Near this village extensive irrigation works were carried out in 1899, and in the course of these remains of a Venetian dam were discovered. It appears that the Venetians had tried to deal with the problem of irrigation in Cyprus on quite an extensive scale.

AKOURDHALIA, PANO AND KATO (xxxv)

The principal church is dedicated to the B.V.M. Chryseleoussa, and is a small sixteenth-century building with a vaulted narthex. The interior was once completely painted, but has recently been whitewashed. The lower village was, until a few years ago, Turkish, but contains a ruined chapel dedicated to the Panagia. It is also known as the Church of the Hill Covered with Shrubs.

A curious legend lingers in the village of a wealthy and eccentric Englishman who lived here in the early years of the nineteenth century, and his house is still pointed out by the villagers.

AKROTIRI (lviii)

The village Church of the Holy Cross is a large, ugly, modern building, but contains a few icons from its predecessor. The finest of these is a large early seventeenth-century one of a pair of youthful saints with robes of red, gold, blue, and gold Brusa embroidery. A large painted wooden cross of the same period hangs on the north wall.

The village is situated above the salt lake, which is the haunt of innumerable wild-fowl, while the ornithologist can watch, in the early summer, a variety of birds from flamingos and ibis to the Kentish plover and dunlin.

A mile west, over the flat salt marshes, lies the fifteenth-century Church of St. George, a simple monotholos with semicircular apse and three narrow lancet windows. The interior contains remains of painting. Over the south door are SS. Cosmas and Damian, while to their right is St. Mercurios and the remains of a long inscription.

The story of St. Mercurius is perhaps the most dramatic of all the Greek legends. Julian the apostate had sold his soul to the devil, and became not only a cruel heathen but a wizard and a necromancer. One of his evil actions was to slay his faithful officer, Mercurius, for his adherence to the Christian faith.

The legend then relates that when Julian led his army against the Persians, on the eve of battle St. Basil the Great was granted a vision.

He saw the Virgin seated on a throne surrounded by a myriad angels; and she commanded one saying: "Go forth and awaken Mercurius who sleeps in his tomb that he may slay Julian, that stiff-necked and proud blasphemer of me and my Son."

In the morning St. Basil went to the sepulchre where Mercurius had been laid with his armour and weapons, and lo! the tomb was empty.

Early next day he returned and there lay the body of Mercurius, but the lance was stained with fresh blood. For on the day of the battle, as Julian led his army, suddenly an unknown warrior appeared, of a pale and ghastly countenance, mounted on a white horse. Spurring his charger through the soldiers he reached Julian and, raising his lance, pierced the Emperor through the body and then vanished as suddenly as he had appeared, before the terror-stricken royal guard could prevent him.

Julian was carried to his tent and, in his dying agony, took a handful of blood which flowed from the gaping wound, and threw it in the air so that it bespattered those who crowded round the death-bed and, raising himself, cried with his last breath: "Thou hast conquered, Galilean! Thou hast conquered!"

Then the demons received his spirit, but Mercurius lies secure in his tomb.

An inscription on one of the lower panels of the iconostasis refers to a restoration in 1793.

Two miles east of the village lies what was one of the most interesting monasteries in Cyprus—the monastery of St. Nicholas of the Cats, probably dating from the early years of the fifteenth century. It is referred to by nearly every mediaeval traveller. The monastic buildings are now but heaps of stone. The only architectural features remaining in the church are the doorways of the west, north, and south sides, which show moulding and carving in the mediaeval style, or of genuine mediaeval workmanship. The doorway on the north side has a most remarkable lintel supporting the tympanum of the arch. This lintel is carved with a cross in the centre, and with two shields with coats of arms on either side. According to Jeffery they are, from left to right:[1]

1. On a shield a pigeon cote, or perhaps a ciborium.
2. On a shield the lion rampant of the usual Lusignan variety.
3. On a shield a cross Potencee.
4. On a shield a cross, on the four angles of which are four keys erect, the wards outwards.

Mr. Jeffery suggests that the coats of arms Nos. 1 and 4 are doubtless personal ones, while the other two shields probably represent the free rendering of the Lusignan royal badge, which not uncommonly occurs on the Orthodox buildings of the Middle Ages.

The interior of the church is a mournful sight—the floor dug by treasure-seekers, the iconostasis destroyed, and all the icons mouldering to dust. Indeed, only one icon can still be identified. This is a large seventeenth century one of St. John the Divine.

Monsieur Enlart has some interesting suggestions to make on the subject of the Cats.[2] He suggests that they may be a special breed like the sacred cats of Egypt. There is a famous temple of Pasht near Zagazig, in Egypt, where the cat-headed goddess, prototype of the classical Diana, was worshipped 1,000 years before Christ, and it is possible that a shrine of the cat-headed goddess may once have stood on the Peninsula of Akrotiri. So many travellers refer to the monastery and the cats that it is only possible to give extracts from a few of the more interesting mediaeval writings:

[1] *Monuments of Cyprus*, Nicosia, 1918, p. 371.
[2] *L'art Gothique en Chypre*, Paris, 1899, p. 460.

And so conversing together we arrived at the abbey of S. Nicolas. It is close to the sea, and remains almost whole, having received no injury from the Turks when they took Cyprus from the Venetians in 1570. But they slew or drove away the monks of S. Basil who occupied it, nor have they from that time forth allowed anyone to dwell there, so bitterly do they hate the Christian faith. My companion told me that the said monks kept a number of cats on purpose to catch the snakes, which are found all about the plain in greater numbers than in any other part of the island.

These snakes are black and white, at least 7 feet long, and thick as a man's leg, so that I could scarcely believe that a cat could overcome so big a beast, or that they would have the patience to go to hunt them, and not to return until the bell rang for mid-day, and as soon as they had dined to resume their chase until evening, if it were not that the monk swore that he had seen it. His story was confirmed later by other persons of honour who had seen the same. The abbey is left deserted, and the cats are dead for want of food, but their memory lives in the name Gape delle Gatte, the Cape of Cats.[1]

Above Nimona is a certain wooded spot so full of serpents and noxious animals that no one can live there. Nevertheless in the middle of the wood some ancient fathers built a monastery, so that, being surrounded with serpents, they might be less exposed to the visits of worldlings, which are known to disturb devout monks. But lest the serpents should molest the inmates of the convent they maintain a number of cats, who naturally make a prey of snakes, mice, dormice, and rats, and do not allow such to approach the walls: and daily war is waged between the cats and the snakes to drive the latter from the walls. At night they remain within, and roam about the offices lest any reptile be hidden there, but during the day they hunt in the wood, and when their dinner-hour comes the monk on duty rings a bell, at the sound of which they all run to the place where they are fed. For the mouse catcher has good hearing and better smell, but best of all is his sight, which can pierce the shades of night, hence he is called cat: for *cattus* means cunning, and the ancients thought that cats were akin to the *Genii* or *Lares*, saying that *Genii*, though unseen by men, could not remain invisible to cats.[2]

---

[1] Villamont, 1589, *Excerpta Cypria*, p. 171.
[2] Felix Faber, 1483, *Excerpta Cypria*, p. 36.

I heard a marvellous thing. From the said city of Lymisso up to this cape the soil produces so many snakes that men cannot till it, or walk without hurt thereon. And were it not for the remedy which God has set there, in a short time these would multiply so fast that the island would be depopulated. At this place there is a Greek monastery which rears an infinite number of cats, which wage unceasing war with these snakes. It is wonderful to see them, for nearly all are maimed by the snakes: one has lost a nose, another an ear; the skin of one is torn, another is lame; one is blind of one eye, another of both. And it is a strange thing that at the hour for their food at the sound of a bell all those that are scattered in the fields collect in the said monastery. And when they have eaten enough, at the sound of the bell they all leave together and go to fight the snakes.[1]

ALAMBRA (xxxix)

The village church was erected in 1837 and was dedicated to St. Marina. The north and west doorways are in the Gothic manner, and serve as admirable illustrations of the length of time the mediaeval tradition has lingered on amongst the stonemasons of the Island.

Close to the village lies a Bronze Age necropolis, excavated by Cesnola.

Twenty minutes' ride west of Dali lies the small village of Alambra, situated on the rocky slope of a hill which commands a beautiful view of the plain below. In former rambles I had remarked a curiously shaped mound facing the village, and separated from it only by a craggy ravine worn by a winter torrent. Making enquiries of the peasantry concerning this mound, I learned that some twenty years ago a tomb cut deeply into the rock had accidentally been opened there; of course, the usual fable was appended of the finding of much gold therein. I hired some labourers, and started to explore the place. It proved to be a mass of rotten limestone, the portion most exposed to the heat of the sun being cracked and crumbling into dust. I soon ascertained that its slopes contained a number of tombs, similar in size and form to those of Dali, except that they were cut in the rock.[2]

[1] Suriano, 1484, *Excerpta Cypria*, p. 48.
[2] *Cyprus: Its Cities, Tombs and Temples*, London, 1877.

ALAMINOS (l)

The Church of St. Mamas is an ancient building with a modern narthex. The interior was once completely painted, but the majority of the frescoes have been whitewashed. The dome, however, still contains a noble bust of Christ Pantokrator, while beneath is a frieze of angels. On the south wall is a fragment of a colossal fresco of St. Mamas himself, but only the head now remains.

In the Turkish quarter of the village stands a well-preserved mediaeval tower. According to Enlart:

> Alaminno was a casal belonging to Philip D'Ibelin, seneschal of Cyprus. In 1307 the Prince of Tyre, usurping the kingdom of his brother, Henry II, confined the seneschal, and remained faithful to the king in this place, afterwards exiling him to Armenia. In 1464 James II gave the Lordship of Alaminno to Giovanni Loredano.[1]

The tower is similar to the one at Pyla; it is built of rough stonework, and the entrance door is on the first floor. The most curious thing about it is the long narrow recess in the west face, which extends from the door-sill to the top of the tower and into which the drawbridge—it must have been of exceptional length—fitted. The tower probably dates from the fifteenth century.

ALEKHTORA (lii)

This is now a Turkish village, but there must have been a Christian settlement of some importance here in mediaeval times, to judge by the ruins of several churches which lie in the vicinity. The best preserved is one dedicated to St. Kassianos, an early mediaeval building, though now much ruined. The interior shows traces of wall paintings. St. Kassianos, who was one of the German saints who came to Cyprus in the fourth century, is said to be buried here. A church dedicated to him in Nicosia contains the helmet in which he is supposed to have suffered martyrdom. Makhairas says: "By Alekhtori, at a place called Glyphia, is the grave of St. Kassianos, and they keep his feast on

[1] *Art Gothique*, p. 669.

September 16th."[1] Near by is a church of the same period dedicated to St. Constantinos.

Three miles from the village is a *chiflik* called the Well of the Franks, which now belongs to a farmer from Pissouri, who has built himself a house after the manner of a Scotch shooting lodge. Near this lies a small early sixteenth-century church dedicated to St. George, a simple barrel-vaulted building with a semicircular apse. Within are the remains of a painting of St. George under an arched stone canopy.

From the name of this locality it is possible that this was originally a Latin chapel. The well, commemorated in the name, has a certain air of antiquity about it, but no inscription or fragment of sculpture remains.

A few miles from Lakkos tou Frankou is the Randidi site, explored in 1910 by Doctor Zahn, of Berlin, who found a number of stones with a syllabic inscription on them. They are as yet undeciphered, but can be examined in the Nicosia Museum.

Between this village and Pissouri lies the mediaeval church of St. George, a large building without any architectural details save a cross cut on a key-stone above the west door. It is thus not easy to assign the church to any definite date. It appears to have been a building of some importance, for it is much larger than the usual rustic chapel. The interior was once painted, but all is now blackened and destroyed through shepherds lighting fires in the interior during the winter.

AMARKETI (xlvi)

Near this village in 1887 Mr. Hogarth excavated a small temple of the classical period dedicated to Apollo. Like the majority of shrines of that period the Temple of Amarketi consisted of an enclosure built of mud brick, without architectural detail. The finds were numerous, principally statuettes and figures of soft stone and terra-cotta, but nearly all of the crudest description. They were of all sizes and might belong to any age.

From the inscriptions found Mr. Hogarth conjectured

[1] *Chronicle of Makhairas*, p. 32

that the shrine was dedicated to Apollo Melanthius, or Apollo who Healed the Sick with the use of drugs extracted from the Melanthium, a species of poppy known to botanists as *Nigella sativa*.

The virtues of the Melanthium and of its oil are set forth by Dioscorides; it appears to have been accounted potent against an amazing variety of disorders, such as headaches, toothache, the itch, eye complaints, tumours, worms, bites of spiders, difficulty of breathing, and affections of the urinary organs.[1]

The village church is dedicated to the B.V.M., and was built in 1882. It contains a few eighteenth-century icons, including one of Christ dated 1773. There are also some pleasant though modern gargoyles on the north and south walls.

AMBELIKOU (xxviii)

Or the Place of Vineyards, is a small and uninteresting village situated above the ruins of Soli. Both the Church of St. George and the mosque are modern. Near the coffee-shop lies a fine Corinthian marble capital from Soli, and various other stone fragments from the same site lie scattered round. A large number of Roman tombs surround the village.

ANALIONDA (xxxix)

There must have been a considerable Roman settlement here, as numberless tombs of that period are to be found in the vicinity, and a great many inscribed cippi are built into the walls of the village houses.

The church is dedicated to St. Marina, and probably dates from the late eighteenth century. It has an attractively carved west door. The interior is bare save for a few paintings on its walls. In the iconostasis is a seventeenth-century icon of the three Patriarchs, while in the women's gallery lies a collection of damaged and decayed icons. The most interesting of these is one of Christ robed in elaborately decorated vestments.

[1] *Devia Cypria*, p. 25.

About a mile west of the village, and on a small hill, lies the monastery of the Archangel Michael built by Chrysanthos (Archbishop of Cyprus, 1767–1810) in 1769. The interior contains a number of wall paintings. One on the south wall shows the Archbishop himself presenting a model of the church to God. The Archbishop, who is attended by a deacon, wears a brown robe trimmed with fur and carries an ivory-headed stick in his hand. There is a very large icon of the Archangel Michael in an elaborately carved frame, and this, according to an inscription, was painted by a certain deacon called Lavrendi, and was the gift of the Archbishop himself to the monastery.

The contemporary iconostasis contains three well-painted icons which would appear to be earlier than the foundation of the building. These are of the Baptist, Christ, and the B.V.M. The church also contains a delightfully painted grandfather clock case, though the clock itself has long since disappeared. The bronze chandelier hanging from the roof is almost certainly contemporary with the building of the church. The monastic buildings surround the church on all four sides, and must at one time have sheltered a large community of monks.

The church and monastery are now rapidly falling to decay, and stand deserted, the last priest having died about ten years since. The monastic property still belongs to the Archbishopric, and consists of about a thousand acres and more than a thousand olive-trees.

ANAPHOTIA (l)

The village church is dedicated to St. Photeine. The iconostasis has the date 1743 on one of the lower panels, which is probably also the date of the erection of the building. A vast new church, dedicated to St. Dimitrianos, is in process of being built, but it is so badly constructed that it may well fall down long before its central dome is finished.

The Franciscan nunnery at Nicosia was also called St. Claire, or St. Photeine, and was connected with one of the more disreputable incidents in the history of Cyprus. It was here that Queen Eleanor of Aragon, during the absence of her husband, King Peter I, in Europe, forced the King's mistress, Jeanne l'Aliman, widow of the Seigneur of Choulou, to take the veil. The King on his return, finding his partner in guilt within the convent walls, made her renounce her vows and resume her position at Court.

ANARITA (li)

The village Church of St. Marina is now in process of reconstruction. Not far from the village lies the completely ruined Byzantine Monastery of St. Nisiforos. According to tradition St. Nisiforos was born in Constantinople, and became in the course of time an admiral in the service of the Byzantine Empire. Towards the end of his life, however, he wearied of fighting and, giving up all position and power, came to Cyprus as a humble hermit; he lived at Anarita, where he later died and was buried.

ANAVARGOS (xlv)

The Church of St. George is quite modern, and is without interest. About a mile below the village lies a large Roman tomb, excavated from a level rock. It has a square courtyard, sunk to a depth of about eight feet and open to the sky. On the south and east sides are covered colonnades, each supported by eight square pillars. From these two sides are various chambers cut from a rock, which contained the bodies. The entrance to the central chamber on the south side has a doorway with carefully carved decoration. Traces of painting and crosses show that this tomb was in later times used by the Christians as a chapel. According to the villagers a certain King Anav was buried in this tomb.

ANAYIA (xxx)

The Church of SS. Vichinos and Nomon was built in 1866, and the ruins of its mediaeval predecessor lie to the north. From a former church comes an early eighteenth-century rood cross, and above the west door a sixteenth-century marble shield with a coat of arms of four quarterings. St. Vichinos is a saint of complete obscurity. It is possible that a Latin chapel, dedicated to St. Vincent, stood here, and on the expulsion of the Latins in 1570 passed into the hands of the Orthodox, who adopted St. Vincent with the Orthodox name of Vichinos. Whatever the truth may be, these saints have a great local reputation as infallible curers of coughs, colds, and croup.

St. Nomon was a hermit who lived in the Troodos hills till he died of extreme old age, and was buried at Tamassos.

ANDROLIKOU (xxxv)

The mosque of this Turkish village is built on the site of the Church of St. Andronicos, of which a few fragments can still be seen built into the walls. In the side of an oven in a village house is a portion of a mediaeval tomb slab of the early fifteenth century. This portrays a woman in an attitude of prayer, and has an inscription of three lines, but now so much decayed that it is illegible.

ANGASTINA (xxii)

The church is dedicated to St. Therapon, and is a building which has been much restored. The date 1796 above the south door may be either the date of the original building or of a restoration. The iconostasis, which is of the usual type, is dated 1814. A pleasant silver repoussé icon of St. Therapon bears the date 1804.

St. Therapon (May 14th) was the son of a noble German family who renounced all the advantages of rank and wealth and spent his time in the diligent study of Holy Scripture, and in a frequent attendance at church. So exemplary was his life that at an early age he was chosen to fill the see rendered vacant by the death of his bishop. After he had presided over his diocese for several years his flock was divided by the action of the iconoclasts. Therapon took a firm stand against these enemies of the faith, but was defeated, tortured, and exiled by them.

He visited Jerusalem and then came to Cyprus, where his holy life and the miracles he performed so impressed the Archbishop that he appointed the Saint Bishop of Constantia. In 632 the Island was invaded by the Arabs, and the bishop was butchered in the church while celebrating the Eucharist. In 690 his remains were translated to Constantinople.

ANGOLEMI (xxviii)

A miserable Turkish hamlet of no interest except for its curious name. It is highly probable that a knight from Angoulême settled here during the Middle Ages, but though the place still retains its ancient name no sign of any castle or church remains.

ANOYARA (lii)

The village contains several churches:

1. That of the Archangel Michael, a building of 1794. The iconostasis, icons, and the well-preserved women's gallery are all contemporary with the building. An unusual feature is a sundial with an inscription round it on the exterior south wall, which must come from some earlier building. The west door is a good copy of Gothic work. The church contains a plate of the early sixteenth century, which has on it an angel holding two shields in high relief.

2. St. Barbara.—The extremely interesting Byzantine church has recently been pulled down, and a miserable modern shed, without architectural detail or charm, has taken its place. It contains, however, a few early eighteenth-century icons from the former building.

3. The Holy Cross.—A large Byzantine mediaeval monastery, now deserted. The church itself would seem to have been much larger, but part of it was at some period reconstructed as a series of monastic cells. Fragments of painting cover the walls of the building. There are also founders' tombs, two in the north and two in the south walls of the narthex, and two north and south of the altar. Above the tomb in the north wall of the narthex are the remains of portraits of two female donors. The paintings above the south door show marked Italian influence.

Opposite this church there are the foundations of a small Roman temple, and the remains of a mosaic pavement. A large fragment of a stone cornice lies near by, and a Doric capital.

APESIA (liii)

A considerable number of Roman tombs lie in and around the village, all open and robbed long since by generations of treasure-seekers. All that survive are the inscribed cippi which they once contained. Nearly every yard and house has one, the best preserved lying round the church and the schoolyard, the latter containing an unusually large one with an inscription of four lines.

The early nineteenth-century Church of St. George is without any interest.

APHENDRIKA (i)

About six miles from Rizo-Carpas lie the ruins of Aphendrika. Nothing now remains save three churches. The largest of them is the B.V.M. Chrysiotissa, and is an example of the Romanesque style of the twelfth century. It must have been of considerable size, for it measures 75 feet long by 45 feet wide, and the central apse is 24 feet across. This church must have been destroyed at an early date—perhaps by pirates—for in the fourteenth century a smaller edifice was built in its ruins, filling up the three western bays of the central nave.

This second church is in an excellent state of repair. It contains nothing of interest save a few architectural fragments from the earlier building, which lie on the floor. The most interesting of these is a square plaque with a figure of a woman with upraised hands sculptured on it.

To the south lie the ruins of another Romanesque church of the same period, dedicated to the B.V.M. Asomatos. Of this only a portion of the principal nave and south aisle remains. A curious feature in the construction are two small arched passages, just big enough for a man to pass through, connecting the central apse with those on each side.

Close by are the ruins of an unnamed domed church in the Byzantine style, the west end of which has completely disappeared. About a mile north lies the harbour of the ancient city, now silted up with sand. To the west is the necropolis, most of the tombs cut in the rock and some of considerable size. Still farther west was a temple, if one may judge by a huge headless statue half buried in the ground, and various architectural fragments which lie about. But of the pre-Christian city the most interesting remains are those of the citadel which is situated to the east of the churches already described.

The summit of this rock bears the ancient remains, as interesting and perhaps as primitive as anything in Cyprus. The entire ground-plan of the building, whether palace or fortress, which once crowned it, has been preserved by the fact that the lower portions of all its chambers were excavated in living rock to a depth of from two to four feet. The walls are, therefore, so far intact as to determine the position of the doorways and the character of the approaches; the outer walls are generally 2 to 2½ feet thick, and the party walls vary from 1 to 1½ feet thick, but no trace is left of the masonry which must have been superimposed. The building is approached from the south-east by a gate and wide passage, on the left of which are two chambers; a flight of four steps and another gate with sockets remaining led into an inner chamber, which again opens into a third, the largest of all. On the east a considerable margin of uncut rock has been left, and a smaller one on the right, but on the north, overlooking the city, the precipice falls away sheer from the outer wall of the chamber.[1]

APOSTOLOS ANDREAS (ii)

The monastic buildings and the church are modern. Indeed, the whole cult of St. Andrew is of recent origin in Cyprus. By the sea cliff remains the original Gothic fifteenth-century chapel, which is nearly square with a central round pillar with no capital, from which spring the square ribs of the vault. It is possible that this may have been the crypt of the original church.

The large modern church contains nothing of interest, but is visited by thousands of pilgrims annually. The wonder-working icon of St. Andrew is covered with silver-gilt, and on the curtain which covers it are hung a vast number of offerings in silver, representing hands, legs, fingers, eyes, or whatsoever portion of the body

[1] Hogarth, *Devia Cypria*, p. 85.

the afflicted person desires to be cured. In a glass case near by is a most curious collection of objects left behind by pilgrims—watches, necklaces, earrings, spoons, coins, medals, tresses of hair, and hanks of silk. Every two years or so this collection is sold, and last time it realized as much as £1,500.

At the west end of the church are a number of wax effigies, some life-size, all sent or brought by those who wished to be cured, and in some cases intended to be actual portraits of the sick person. In their wooden, coffin-like cases, and with their staring glass eyes, they have a most eerie appearance. Here, too, are hung models of ships, for St. Andrew not only cures the sick but guards those who travel by sea. St. Andrew is prayed to by both Christian and Moslem alike, and endless stories are told in the villages of well-authenticated cases of the cures he has worked. Indeed, the writer himself knows of a case of a child who had always been completely blind, and whose sight was restored as soon as he had crossed the threshold of the church. But St. Andrew is a jealous saint. Once a Turk was bringing his blind child, and had promised a great present to St. Andrew if he would but cure his son. As soon as the child came within sight of the church he was able to see. The Turk at once turned back, but hardly had they passed the monastic boundary when the child was blind, and no amount of prayers or gifts could make St. Andrew relent.

Numerous other stories are told of the saint and his miraculous powers. Not so long ago thieves from a neighbouring village broke into the church and opened the safe. As soon as they took the money out, the doors of the church disappeared, and they were hemmed in by blank walls. Trembling, they returned the money, and at once the doors appeared and the thieves fled, never to rob or steal again.

At the monastery are always a certain number of people who give their work free as the result of being either cured or helped by the saint. When the writer was there in 1935 there was a boy who was going to work for two years without fee or remuneration of any sort at all. He had been motoring, and while overtaking another car on a narrow road with a steep cliff below had gone too near the edge, and had felt the car turning over. In the actual moment of danger he prayed to the saint, and though the car overturned and fell to the bottom of the cliff the boy was unhurt.

Another story records how a mother came all the way to pray to the icon of the saint that her son should not become a sailor, as it was such a dangerous life, but should stay and help his brother, who was a chauffeur. The saint granted the mother's wish and the boy stayed at home, but a week later was killed in a motor-car accident.

The principal historical interest of the monastery is due to the fact that it was here that Isaac Comnenus surrendered himself to Richard Cœur de Lion in 1191.

Four miles distant from the monastery is Cape Dinaretum, the farthest extremity of the Island, where rises the mass called Castros. Here are the remains of the Temple of Aphrodite Acraea.

> Married women were excluded from its rites, while maidens there underwent the initiation which Herodotus records at Babylon. We are never likely to learn more of it. There is no scope for excavations, the site having been too thoroughly plundered to build the monastery, or, like Famagusta, to make the quays and hotels at Port Said.[1]

APSIOU (xlviii)

The principal church is dedicated to the B.V.M., and was built in 1740. Both the iconostasis and icons are contemporary. There is a fine early seventeenth-century icon of the Madonna, but unfortunately partially painted.

About three miles from the village lies the monastery of the B.V.M. Amyrou. The story goes that a certain rich man who lived abroad found that his sight was fast failing, so he prayed to the Virgin to help him. She appeared to him in a dream and bade him take ship and sail to

[1] *Devia Cypria*, p. 83.

Amathus in Cyprus, and as soon as he landed he would see a little light on the hills beyond the town. So he sailed from his country, and it all fell out as the Madonna had foretold. Guided by the villagers—his sight was now dim—he proceeded towards the light on the hills. When he reached the place he found that the light came from a lamp hung in a tree. Taking oil from the lamp, he rubbed it on his eyes, and his sight was at once restored. In gratitude, Amaril, for such was his name, built the monastery which is called after him.

In the sixteenth-century church there is no architectural feature at all save the west door, which is Venetian in style. The chief interest lies in the icons. The iconostasis itself is partly sixteenth and partly seventeenth century, and the holy doors are dated 1647. Inscriptions on two panels in a lower portion of the iconostasis refer to a restoration in 1698 and 1706.

Of the icons there is a two-sided processional one of the B.V.M., but only a fragment of painting, though of good quality, remains on the reverse. This icon would appear to be contemporary with the foundation of the monastery, and has inset a small icon of the Madonna, said to have been given by Amaril himself. The frame of the icon is studded with gilt rosettes after the Italian manner. Underneath this icon is an inscription stating that in 1776, the time of Makarios, Bishop of Kition, and by the desire of his archimandrite, Jacovos, the church was restored by the abbot, and that "the monks' rooms were embellished", and adds, "Accept, Holy Mary, his prayer, and render him worthy of the Kingdom of Heaven, and to see the God-like face of your Son."

The other icons in the screen, reading from the left, are St. John the Divine, 1679; the B.V.M. and Christ, the former repainted, but both *c.* 1680; and an icon of the Baptist, dated 1567, with a kneeling donor, much destroyed, in the left-hand corner. The donor is said to be Amaril himself, who is shown as a youth dressed in black with a stiff white lace ruff.

The Baldachino above the altar is eighteenth century,

though the ceiling, with its painting of the Virgin and the four emblems of the Evangelists at the corner, is much earlier. The rood cross dates from 1659.

The inscription on the Baldachino would appear to read, "Remember your servant Yerasimos, monk and abbot of this holy monastery."

The only relic the church contains is an ancient bronze lamp with four nozzles, said to have been the actual one whose oil cured the founder.

Most of the monastic buildings have long since vanished, and the whole foundation is now deserted and disused save for some passing shepherd who drinks from the fountain, whose waters still run as they did when it was built by one of the abbots in 1713.

ARADHIOU (xxix)

The ancient village church is dedicated to the B.V.M., and is built on a small hillock the other side of the river. It probably dates from the late fifteenth century.

There are founders' tombs in the north and south walls, and fragments of a painting on the north wall of St. George with remains of kneeling donors. The iconostasis is dated 1695, and contains a fine icon of St. Nicholas, *c.* 1520, and an icon of Christ dated 1643.

In the village is a modern church dedicated to St. George, containing little save an icon of that saint with a donor priest dated 1831. It is interesting to note how long the custom of depicting the donors on icons lasted. Both of these churches contain sixteenth-century plates, that of the Virgin having the Annunciation in relief on it.

All the fields round the village are covered with fossil sea shells, and it is not uncommon to pick up sharks' teeth and fragments of the bones of whales.

ARADHIPPOU (xl)

The principal church of the village is dedicated to St. Luke, and was built in the middle of the nineteenth century. It contains a silver gilt repoussé icon of that saint dated 1817. Above the icon hangs a mirror, and those who are paralysed are brought here every day for forty days to gaze into the mirror and repeat at the same time a prayer to St. Luke.

About a mile and a half from the village is the tiny modern Chapel of St. George, built on an ancient site. It contains a fine triptych of the Madonna and Child (perhaps originally a Latin altar-piece), with St. Athanasius to the right and St. Cyril to the left. The figures stand in frames of carved wood, and there has been at some time a top rising to three points, which has now disappeared. Beneath the main figures are portraits in arcades of the Twelve Apostles. This unusual work of art probably dates from the late fifteenth or early sixteenth century.

Not far from St. George is the Chapel of the Madonna of the Vineyards, again a modern rebuilding, though the apse of the former church is still visible. A number of ruins and a large cistern lie near by, and may possibly be the ruins of the royal villa called La Cour de la Despotissa, which existed here in the fourteenth century and belonged to the Lady Margaret de Lusignan, grand-daughter of Amaury, Prince of Tyre, and sister to Leon VI, King of Armenia. She was the wife of Manuel, the despot of the Morea, son of the Emperor John Katakauzinos. We know from Makhairas[1] that she visited Cyprus in 1372 for the coronation of her cousin, King Peter II. In 1425 the villa was destroyed by the invading Mamluks.

ARAKAPAS (xlviii)

The village contains the remains of what was apparently an important Latin church. The original building appears to have been a three-aisled church, but at some period it became disused and fell into ruins. In 1717 it was repaired by placing a large shed roof over the whole, rebuilding the apse, the north and south walls, and west end, so that now all that remains of the original church is the arch at the west end and the pillars and arches dividing the main aisle from the two side ones. Even these few fragments, however, show how magnificent the original building must

[1] *Chronicle of Makhairas*, p. 63.

have been. The side arches bear paintings of saints and angels, and architectural motifs, also floral designs, of which the chief is one of wreaths of laurel bound with red ribbons. These arches are carried on pillars, also painted, and with curious capitals, Ionic in feeling. All the paintings are far above the average, and show marked Italian influence. The spandrels of the arches contain figures of evangelists, etc. The west and south doors probably come from the original building. In the church itself lies the root of a vast tree, which is said to have provided the timber for the rebuilding of 1717.

There are two curious side chambers to the north and south of the apse, the habitation of numberless bats. In the southern chamber was found a most peculiar icon, now preserved in the neighbouring modern church—also dedicated to the Virgin. The icon is unique in that it is not painted on wood or canvas, but is made of leather. A painted figure of the Virgin and Child of the same material stands out in relief against an elaborate background of stamped leather painted with a floral design in red, gold, and silver. The whole is strangely reminscent of a Spanish screen of the sixteenth century, which indeed must be the date of this curious relic.

ARGAKI (xx)

The ancient Church of the Baptist was rebuilt in the late nineteenth century. The west door is from the original building. The church contains a good early eighteenth-century baroque iconostasis, and some quite pleasant icons of eighteenth century or earlier date, all of which have, unhappily, undergone a disastrous and fatal restoration. A wooden rood cross which once crowned the iconostasis now hangs in the apse, and is dated 1650.

ARKHIMANDRITA, PANO (lii)

The village church is dedicated to St. Theodosios, and is a small building of uncertain date. A number of drums of columns lie scattered about, with an average circumference of seven feet, which would seem to argue that the building which once stood here must have been one of considerable importance, but it is difficult to judge to what period they may have belonged.

The church contains nothing of interest save an icon of Christ, slightly repainted and dated 1568. Close by lies perhaps one of the strangest monuments in Cyprus, a large Roman tomb, converted into a chapel. All the walls were once painted with pictures of saints, but only the figure of St. Onouphrios is now recognizable. In a large niche in the north wall lie hundreds of skulls and bones, said to be the remains of 318 saints driven by persecution from across the sea. Some of the skulls and bones have taken on a rich brown polish from the frequent osculations of the faithful. This little chapel is dedicated to the Holy Fathers, but who these 318 saintly men were and whence they came no one knows. The village tradition is that they were holy men who came across in a boat from Syria and landed at Pissouri at night (whence its name, for Pissouri means dark or black). At dawn they reached Alekhtora, when the cocks were crowing (Alekhtora—meaning cock), and led by an archimandrite came to this village, where they were massacred by the heathen. A site near the village is shown with the footprints of these holy men and their horses; also a spot where the only woman who accompanied them was found to be suffering from leprosy and at once slain in case she should infect the others—though this would hardly seem to be the action of Christian men.

ARMENOKHORI (liv)

A small Turkish village with magnificent views of Limassol, the salt lake, and the sea. An eighteenth-century church of the Archangel Michael is here, and about two miles distant a chapel of the same period dedicated to St. Marina. This was at one time one of the many Armenian villages in Cyprus, which contributed the "Herminii" to the army of Isaac Comnenus, referred to in the chronicles of Richard Cœur de Lion's landing at Limassol and his conquest of the Island.

ARMINOU (xlvi)

Outside the village lies the Church of the Holy Cross, built in the middle of the eighteenth century and now deserted. Its chief treasure, a cross, has been taken to the modern Church of St. Marina. This relic is a large wooden cross covered with silver gilt. In the centre is a repoussé plaque of Christ crucified, which is of an earlier date. It is said that the cross was kept at Souskiou, and came to Arminou of its own volition many years ago. Not unnaturally, perhaps, the people of Souskiou came at once to demand back their precious relic, and there was nearly bloodshed between the two villages. The people of Arminou, however, had a small Chapel of St. Marina, and this they gave in exchange for the cross to the people of Souskiou, who own it to this day.

ARMOU (xlv)

The Church of St. Barbara is a large modern building from which a superb view of the Plain of Paphos and the sea can be obtained. Two large Corinthian capitals lie outside the church, which contains nothing except an icon of St. Barbara dated 1797. A large marble bowl, said to be from an ancient church, lies near by beneath an oil-press.

It was near this village that Hogarth found a remarkable Roman trough, shaped at one end into the semblance of a dolphin's head. It is said that in the stream that runs by the ruined Chapel of St. Mavra small particles of gold are found. This is one of the few places in Cyprus where even minute portions of this metal appear, though nearly all the ancient writers refer to gold being discovered in considerable quantities in the Island.

ARNADHI (xxiv)

The Church of St. Andronicos is a small eighteenth-century building with an illegible inscription over the west door. In the women's gallery lie fragments of beautifully carved woodwork from some former iconostasis, and two seventeenth-century icons of Christ and the Virgin. The well-painted robe of the latter is of Brusa embroidery.

The chief treasure of the church is a carved wooden cross set in a silver, gilt, and enamel covering of 1717. The cross itself is much older, and probably dates from the sixteenth century. All the semi-precious stones on the covering, save a single torquoise, have long since been removed and replaced by glass.

ARODHES (xxxv)

A double village, the upper part being Christian, the lower Moslem. The mediaeval name of the village was Rhodes, from the fact that it was the property of the Knights of St. John of Jerusalem, whose headquarters were until 1522 in the island of Rhodes.

The Christian village contains an eighteenth-century Church of St. Kelandion, an early bishop of Paphos. To the north side of the church lies the large stone sarcophagus of St. Agapiticos, while the companion one of St. Misiticos is to the south. The village legend is that those who wish to win the love of a person, be it girl or boy, come secretly at night and chip off a fragment of the sarcophagus of St. Agapiticos. This is powdered and introduced into the loved one's drink, who will immediately reciprocate the donor's passion. Conversely, should a person desire to quarrel with another, he merely carries out the same procedure with powdered stone from the sarcophagus of St. Misiticos. It is interesting to note that the latter is far more worn away than that of St. Agapiticos, but this is explained by the fact that its powers are much in request by young men and women who wish to change their lovers.

ARSOS (xxxi)

A large temple site was excavated here in 1917, and the finds, including a superb cornelian and gold necklace, can be seen in the Cyprus Museum. Many of the large statues were either too damaged or too big to be moved, and two, of the Roman period, lie outside the village coffee-shop, while numberless fragments and torsos of various periods are built into the wall on the left of the road to Troulli.

Both the church, dedicated to the Virgin, and the mosque are modern. A small mediaeval chapel is dedicated to St. Phimianos, and shows traces of wall paintings.

ARSOS LIMASSOL (xlvi)

The village is situated in the centre of the wine industry. Cyprus has always been famous for its wine. It is said that the champagne grape originally came from this island, and we know that

> Simon the Cellarer kept a good store
> Of Malmsey and Malvoisie,
> And Cyprus, and who can say how many more.

Nearly all the early travellers in Cyprus refer to its wine:

> The wines of Cyprus are naturally red, and after a year they grow white, and the older they are the whiter they grow; they smell well, are wholesome and very strong, and unless largely mixed with water are hardly fit to drink.[1]
>
> Also in that island and province of Cyprus there is a native wine called Marea. If it were drunk neat the heat of the wine would burn up a man's entrails. It does not appear so strong to the taste, anyone who would drink it must put one glass of wine to four of water, and even so it is strong enough.[2]
>
> From this isle of Rhodes men go to Cyprus, where be many vines, that first be red, and after one year they become white: and those wines that be most white be most clear and best of smell. . . .[3]
>
> The island is rich indeed in all the fruits of the earth, and its more useful products. Its wines are very luscious and wholesome; as they grow old they turn from black to white, they are fragrant and of pleasant taste. One finds wine of eighty years and more, and a vintage that had graced a grandee's table gets fresh honour as a medicine, for its health-giving and preservative virtues, which are those of a balsam. One needed to drink but

---

1 W. von Boldensele, 1333, *Excerpta Cypria*, p. 15.
2 J. de Verona, 1335, Ibid., p. 16.
3 J. Maundeville, 1356, Ibid., p. 18.

a tiny measure in a large quantity of water. I do not mean that this wine only is rich and good, but all the wines of Cyprus may vie with those of any country, and they are appreciated accordingly in Venice and Rome, wherever indeed they reach.[1]

The principal church of the village is dedicated to St. Philip, and is a vast modern building on an ancient site. It contains a large seventeenth-century icon of that saint and his martyrdom. The icon has been ruined by the figure being clumsily repainted, but is still resorted to by all the neighbouring villagers, as the oil from a lamp which burns in front of it is said to be an infallible cure for earache.

Outside the village lies an ancient church, recently rebuilt and dedicated to the B.V.M. It contains two well-preserved icons of the early seventeenth century of the Madonna and Christ; also a seventeenth-century icon of St. John the Baptist with two lines of inscription.

ASHA (xxii)

During the Middle Ages this village belonged to the family of De Nores. It was here that the Genoese rested after they had pillaged Nicosia of its treasures. It was here, too, that the councillors of the Venetian Government met in 1570 to decide what action and plan of campaign should be taken against the Turkish invaders who had already landed and were advancing on the ill-fated city of Nicosia.

The village contains two churches, of St. John the Baptist, and St. George, both built in 1861 and of no particular interest.

About half a mile from the village lies a church dedicated to the B.V.M., which may be fifteenth century or even earlier. The remains of paintings on the arch above the apse are of good quality, and show signs of foreign influence. There is also a fine late seventeenth-century rood cross. The font is formed from a portion of a fluted marble column, and stands on a Corinthian capital. The coat of arms and tomb slab mentioned by Jeffery have now disappeared.

[1] T. Porcacchi, 1576, *Excerpta Cypria*, p. 162.

ASINOU[1] (xxviii)

The Church of the Virgin is the most interesting Byzantine memorial still existing in Cyprus. It stands about three miles from Nikitari, in an isolated position on a tiny shoulder overlooking the valley of the Asinou river. No human habitations are near, and it must be many years since a service was celebrated within its walls.

The original church was erected in 1105, and a domed narthex was added about 1200. In 1300 the vault of the naos was rebuilt, and the central bay strengthened with internal buttresses.

The chief glory of the church is its frescoes, amazingly preserved; they seem almost as brilliant as the day they were first painted.

The probable chronology of the church and its painting may tentatively be summarized thus:

1105. Erection and frescoing of the naos and bema. Of the original frescoes nineteen survive; most of those in the central bay of the naos were repainted about 1350.
c. 1200. Erection and frescoing of the narthex.
c. 1225–50. The conch of the bema was restored and painted. The south door of the narthex was walled up, and the frescoes of St. George, etc., were painted.
c. 1300. The central vault of the naos was rebuilt.
1332. Painting of the dome and most of the frescoes in the narthex.
c. 1350. Most of the frescoes in the central bay of the naos and in the narthex were painted with silvery haloes in relief.
c. 1620. On the north buttress of the east apse the fresco of Christ in a chalice was painted.

The principal entrance to the church is the west door, which leads into the narthex. A most important painting is in the half arch above the entrance into the nave, the Virgin portrayed with the palms of both hands uplifted, in the medallion between her arms is the head of the Infant Christ with a cruciform nimbus; to the left is the Servant

[1] I am much indebted to Mr. W. H. Buckler for his account of the church published in vol. lxxxiii of *Archaeologia.*

of God, Barnabas, vested in an alb, a dark stole, chasuble, and dark cuffs; to the right a white and a black hound, from the ring of the collar of each runs a leash, which is tied to a spear or stick set upright behind them; in the background are seen mountains and two moufflons. An inscription gives the date of this painting as 1332.

Above the west door is a Throne of Judgement, to the left Adam and Eve kneeling, on the right an angel swooping down towards a group of the Unjust.

Turning to the south side of the narthex we have one of the finest frescoes in the whole building, a fresco in the full flower of the Byzantine style: St. George mounted with lance poised; above the horse's hindquarters is the following inscription:

> A tamer of horses, Nicephorus the pious, moved by warm heartfelt devotion, with like feeling painted the effigy of George, very greatest of all martyrs; and reverently he did it in this monastery of the Phorbia, longing to find as helpers at the judgement that most brilliant victor-crowned martyr and the supplications of those dwelling here. Prayer of Nicephorus, son of (?) Kallias.

We now enter the naos of the church. On the north wall is a large painting of the Forty Martyrs of Sebaste, with the following inscription:

> It is flesh that here bears the winter's cold: thou shalt hear the martyrs' sobs and groaning. They are steadfast as they suffer under the sharpness of the frost; at the clouds they look, and not upon their pangs.

The rest of the wall is covered with the paintings of various saints, and scenes from the life of Our Lord. On the south wall, above the blocked doorway, is a most interesting painting of Nicephorus, founder of the church, and his wife. The inscription runs as follows:

> Having been blessed in life with many good things of which thou, Virgin, wast seen to be the provider, I, Nicephorus magistros, a wretched suppliant, with devotion erected this church in return for which I pray that I may find thee my champion in the terrible day of judgement.

To the right are St. Constantine and St. Helena, and below an inscription, partially built over, which reads:

This sacred church was built by the contribution and the great devotion of Nicephorus magistros the Strong when Alexius Comnenus was emperor in the year 6614, indiction 14 (December 15, 1099).

The west wall of the naos shows the Dormition of the Virgin, while in the apse is the Virgin in Glory, supported by the archangels Michael and Gabriel.

It is possible that the Nicephorus mentioned in the inscription was the son-in-law of the Emperor Alexius I.

The rank of Magistros was fourth in the list of honours known to the Byzantines.

ASKAS (xxxviii)

The principal village church is dedicated to St. John the Baptist, and was restored in 1763. A considerable number of wall paintings remain in the interior, which consists of a central nave and side aisles divided by arches carried on small columns with decorated capitals. The wall paintings would appear to be of two periods. Those in the apse, such as the Virgin in Glory, supported by archangels, and the fathers of the church, would appear to date from about 1510, while the paintings in the body of the church probably date from the end of the same century. One of the most delightful of these is of Dives and Lazarus, complete with the dog licking the sores of the poor man.

The iconostasis is modern, but contains two interesting late sixteenth-century icons of Christ and the B.V.M. Hodegetria. In the apse is kept a beautifully carved early sixteenth-century lectern with what appears to be a coat of arms on three of its sides.

The village also contains the Church of the Holy Cross. The interior is on the same plan as that of the Baptist, although in this case the capitals are of wood and more elaborate than the stone ones in St. John.

The iconostasis is ugly and modern, but contains a large silver gilt cross of early eighteenth-century work, while another wooden one, with a cavity for a relic in the centre, lies in the apse. On the south wall is a late painting of St. George and his martyrdom, the donors being dressed in Turkish costume. The gilt cover of the Gospel, representing the Crucifixion, may be mediaeval, but it is difficult to tell as the ancient designs were so frequently copied later. The soldiers at the foot of the cross wear armour, half chain mail and half plate armour, and from European standards one would be inclined to date it as an example of the late fifteenth century.

About two miles from the village lies the little Chapel of St. Pareskeva. An inscription over the small window in the south wall records its building by a certain Constantine Mardakes and Mandelon his wife, in honour of St. Christina, in 1411.

On the north wall is a large painting of St. Christina, with these two pious donors kneeling at her feet. The whole church was once completely decorated with paintings, but time and damp have much injured them. Of those which remain, the Virgin in Glory is the best.

ASOMATOS (lviii)

A mile from the village lies the Church of the B.V.M. Galoussa, repaired in 1780, but probably originally a Latin chapel. The Proskenetarion is supported by a marble pillar and Corinthian capital. There is a semi-hexagonal Piscina in the bema. The icons are of little interest, but the painting on the holy doors is of a finer quality than usual and dates from late seventeenth century.

ASPROYIA (xxxvi)

The Church of St. Epiphanios is a charming building with a steep-pitched roof, which is weathered dark grey, and with the tiles covered with patches of dark green moss. An inscription in the interior records that the church "was rebuilt from the foundations in 1723".

There is a noble icon of Christ Pantokrator, given by a certain Karia and his family in 1523; and of the same date is an icon of the Madonna and Child with their gilt haloes in relief. In the apse lies an early red and blue "Rhodian" tile. It is curious that it should have found its way to this obscure little village.

ASTROMERITIS (xx)

The Church of St. Auxibios was built in 1876. The iconostasis and icons of the former church lie in the gallery. The present iconostasis is a good example of modern wood carving, and has not as yet been painted that ugly shiny dark brown which is so admired by the Cyprians.

Jeffery suggests that the name of this village is supposed to refer "to a deep well, at the bottom of which the stars can be seen at midday", but this is unlikely.

St. Auxibios was born in Rome of wealthy heathen parents, and against their wishes he became a Christian. Leaving his family he embarked on a ship bound for the east, and landed at Limne, near Soli. Here he met St. Mark, who was hiding from the Jews, after the martyrdom of St. Barnabas. Mark was so impressed and pleased with the youth that he immediately consecrated him Bishop of Soli. He was later appointed Archbishop of Cyprus, a post he held for nearly half a century.

ATHIENOU (xxxi)

This village was for centuries the home of the Muleteers, who carried on the transport of the island, and was until the advent of the English and the new road which they built the half-way house between the capital and the sea. Near here General Cesnola, in 1860, discovered a vast temple site, and an immense number of statues, some of heroic proportions, which are now one of the principal glories of the Metropolitan Museum in New York.[1] A large number of fragments from these excavations still lie scattered about the village.

The principal church is dedicated to the B.V.M., and was built in 1711. It contains a good baroque iconostasis of the same period. Against the south wall is a curious painted fragment 7½ feet long, representing Christ with

[1] See *Cat. of Cesnola Coll.*, edited by J. M. Myres, New York, 1914.

eight saints. The stone above the small east window of the apse is a door lintel laid the wrong way up with three mediaeval coats of arms on it. The other churches in the village are without interest. The Chapel of St. Photios, mentioned by Makhairas, has now disappeared.

All the inhabitants of this village of 150 houses ply the trade of muleteers, in Turkish, Kiraji—the Turks call the place Kiraji-Keuy. According to an unauthenticated tradition these Kirajis are of distinguished ancestry, for they say that at the capture of Famagusta, after all the principal Venetians had been executed by the Turks, there were still a number of poorer nobles, to whom the victors, tired of bloodshed, granted their lives. Helpless and poor, without the means to return to Venice, to which their families were now for several generations strangers, these patricians turned to the calling of guides and muleteers.[1]

ATHRAKOS (xlviii)

The church, built in 1858, is dedicated to St. George. Like many churches in this part of the Island, the weathered tiles give a completely false air of antiquity to a building frequently less than a hundred years old. From the name of the village it is probable that there was a watch tower here at some period.

ATHNA (xxxii)

Near here in 1882 six sanctuaries were explored, which yielded over 1,000 stone and terra-cotta figures. Many of these are now in the British Museum.[2] The figures were chiefly female, and ranged in size from nine feet down to tiny statuettes. The majority of them probably dated from before the third century B.C. Many of the terra-cotta and even stone figures were fully coloured. From these excavations come two large headless statues of the Roman period, which now lie outside the police station.

The village itself is not on an ancient site, for the mediaeval village lies about a mile to the south. The principal church, the B.V.M. Trasha, is a sixteenth-century

[1] Ross, 1846, *Reisen nach der Insel Cypern*, p. 23.
[2] Myres, *Catalogue of Cyprus Museum*, Oxford, 1899.

building with a founder's tomb in the north wall, and in quite a good state of repair. The remains of a belfry can still be traced on the roof.

Close by are the ruins of a small nameless church of the same period. The modern village contains the Church of St. Marina, a large building of 1885. Here is kept a much damaged icon of the Virgin, *c.* 1550, which originally came from the B.V.M. Trasha. In times of drought this icon is taken back to its former church, where a service is held and prayers for rain offered. After the service the icon is returned to St. Marina. The last time this ceremony was carried out was in 1932, and the next day rain came.

In the boundaries of the village is a small Chapel of St. George of the Threshing-floor, whose icon is much resorted to by those who lose anything from a thimble to a calf, for the saint has a wonderful power of restoring things that are lost in the house or animals that have strayed. Nor is this the only miracle that this icon works. A few years since a woman from Prastio was stricken with blindness, and prayed to the Virgin to help her. That night the Virgin appeared to her in a dream and told her that if she took her necklace of gold coins which she always wore and hung it over the icon she would be cured. Fully believing, the woman went next day and was cured, and her necklace can still be seen hanging over the icon as a proof to those who scoff at the powers of the Virgin of Trasha.

AVGOROU (xxxii)

The principal church is dedicated to St. Peter and St. Paul, and is a vast and pretentious modern building without style or charm. It contains, however, two double-sided icons—St. John the Divine, on the reverse St. George, seventeenth century, and St. John the Baptist, on the reverse the same, dated 1679. There is also an icon of Christ dated 1629.

There is also an ancient Chapel of St. George, which has a later raised narthex with steps down to the body of the church. On the south side is an arched cloister, on one of the pillars of which is a small roundel of St. George and the Dragon. Built into the south wall is a Byzantine marble plaque with two crosses in relief on it, and another lies in the churchyard.

About a mile from the village lies the Church of St. George Terrachotis, or St. George of the Caroub-trees, its dome a conspicuous object in the flat landscape. It is a fine mediaeval building, though the narthex and north and south cloisters have disappeared. Over the west and south doors are coats of arms, perhaps those of the family of d'Ibelin. The interior has recently been restored in the usual fatal way. Only a fragment of the original frescoes survives on the north wall; the remainder has been repainted in the most distressing manner. The story goes that many years ago a holy man was walking near St. George reading his breviary While thus engaged the devil appeared to him and began to plague him, twitching his cloak away and snatching his book from his hand. The holy man was unable to rid himself of this unwelcome acquaintance, and at last taunted him, saying that if he was really a great devil he could do something more spectacular than to annoy a poor harmless old man, and suggested that he should uproot the many caroub trees which grew in the vicinity. While the devil was thus occupied the monk escaped, later returning to build the church as we see it to-day, in memory of his strange adventure.

AVLONA (XX)

The village Church of St. Marina is of the eighteenth century, and has remains of frescoes on the ribs of the vault. The iconostasis is seventeenth century, but nearly all the icons have been repainted. There remains, however, a delightful naive icon of St. Symeon Stylites, who is shown sitting on the top of his column with his feet dangling over the edge, for all the world like a small boy in a tree. The icon is dated 1730, and in the right corner is the donor, Germanos, who is dressed in a green cloak with a yellow girdle and red shoes. In a corner of the church is a large carved wooden candlestick of the sixteenth century.

Just outside the village lies the ruined Church of St. George, once completely painted. It was restored in 1535, when the late fourteenth-century frescoes were completely painted over. Of the original series of paintings little remains save one on the south door with a figure of a donor, dimly discernible, in a long dress ornamented with black and red checks. Of the paintings remaining from 1535, the best preserved is the Raising of Lazarus, on the south wall, and the Virgin in Glory, with attendant angels, in the semi-vault of the apse.

AYIA ANNA (xl)

The Church of St. Anna is quite modern, but probably replaces the church mentioned by the traveller, Felix Faber, who visited this village on his descent from Stavrovouni in 1485.

> We could not leave the place at once, for it had grown very hot and the sun burned like fire. So we went over to a Greek church hard by, to pray and to rest a little in the shade. While we were sitting there a certain clerk came, who said to us in Latin, "What are you doing in a Greek church? close at hand is a Latin church in which you should pray and rest". We rose and went with him to the Latin church. He produced from the treasure of the church the arm of S. Ann, mother of the Blessed Virgin Mary, decently set in silver. He brought out also a nail likewise sheathed in silver, which he said was one of the nails with which Christ was nailed on the cross. We kissed these relics, and pressed our rosaries against them, as I said before.[1]

AYIA IRINI (xxxvii)

The Church of the Holy Cross is a small building with considerable remains of wall paintings. The actual frescoes are in a very good state, but unhappily the plaster is falling from the walls. On the south wall is the Nativity and the Archangels Michael and Gabriel. In the apse are three series or rows of paintings. In the semi-vault is Christ in Glory, supported by the Virgin and St. John the Baptist. Below are the Fathers of the Church, while the lowest row of all

[1] *Excerpta Cypria*, p. 38.

is of the Twelve Disciples Receiving the Bread and Wine. Above the semi-vault is the Crucifixion It is most difficult to date the paintings, which in the case of those in the apse are above the average, but they are probably work of the last years of the fifteenth century.

Below the church itself lie a large number of rich Byzantine tombs.

AYIA IRINI (x)

In 1930 a Swedish archaeological expedition excavated a most interesting temple site here, which yielded an amazing number of terra-cotta figures, nearly all male, and of all sizes, dating from 600 B.C. The majority of these statues, together with the scarabs and minor objects, are preserved in the Nicosia Museum.

The Church of St. Irini was built in 1832, and is without interest. In the churchyard lies an elaborately carved Roman cippus with four lines of inscription. In the rocky walls above a small ravine close to the village are numberless fossilized bones of the pygmy hippopotamus.

AYIA MARINA (xx)

The church is an unimportant modern building, but one and a half miles from the present village lies the remains of the Byzantine town of Floudi. It is said that there were once seven churches here, and it is true that the remains of three can still be traced.

The Church of St. John Kokinochromos has recently been rebuilt. It receives its curious name from the rose-pink cliff which overshadows it. Here during the rebuilding were found large marble slabs with incised crosses on them, Byzantine work of the twelfth century, and remains of a geometrical marble pavement of the same period.

AYIA NAPA (xlii)

The monastery was probably one of the last buildings erected by the Venetians before their expulsion from the island in 1570. Above the entrance to the monastery are shields with coats of arms, but too worn to be legible, while to left and right and above are standard sockets. In the centre of the monastic enclosure is a superb octagonal marble fountain covered by a large dome carried on four open arches. Between the arches are raised stone seats. The marble basin itself is decorated with heavy floral swags carved in high relief. Above each swag are various decorations—bulls' heads, a lion facing a stag, a crowned head, etc., and at alternate corners are either putti or florid Italian shields bearing coats of arms. All these are defaced save one which bears three pales, a coat that was borne by both the families of de Bries and de Veit in Cyprus. The water is conveyed to the monastery by an ancient aqueduct, which was probably of Roman construction, although it has undergone many repairs. It ends in a marble boar's mask, the water gushing from the open mouth. This piece of sculpture is probably of the Roman period.

The church itself is partially excavated from the living rock. The main entrance is by the south door, above which is a coat of arms. This entrance leads into a long passage with stone seats against the walls.

To the east of this lies a small Latin chapel referred to by Pietro de la Valle in 1625.

This, like all which I have seen in Cyprus, was almost destroyed, partly by the usual tyranny of the Turks, partly through the great pestilence which had wasted the island a few years before, killing most of its inhabitants. The church itself, built, perhaps, out of respect to the pirates, somewhat like a square castle, is still standing. There is a large quadrangle with rooms round it, the church being on the left as you enter, reached by many steps, as well as the underground chapel which is formed out of the very grotto in which the sacred image was found. A Papas or Greek priest takes care of the church, and officiates in it, and there are certain Calogrie or nuns, who have abandoned the world and devoted themselves to the service of God: they are decently clad in black, but are not cloistered. In the middle of the courtyard is a fountain of spring-water, built up as we might build one, and not badly, of marble. Over this, at no great height, they have placed a dome on four pillars, with raised seats or platforms of Eastern fashion right round it, a cool and shady resting place. . . . Next morning, Mass after the

Greek rite was sung in church, at which I assisted as far as the end of the Gospel. Within the church, in a corner apart, is an altar where our Latin priests, if any should come here, say Mass. The church is just a small grotto, the image ancient, the altar adorned after the Greek rite in the usual way.[1]

This Latin chapel is again mentioned by Mr. Consul Drummond in 1745:[2]

Sancta Nappa is much admired by the people of the country, though for what I do not know: the convent is rendered agreeable within by a fountain of water, round which the people can sit and solace themselves under a large cupola; but there is nothing beautiful in or about the place. Here I found a Latin inscription on a marble stone: by which it plainly appears to have been a Roman convent: and I found a place called the Latin chapel, under the same roof with the Greek church, part of which is dug out of a rock.

At the west entrance of the monastery is a very fine specimen of the *Ficus sycomorus*, the sycamore of the Bible.

This convent is called Sta. Napa, and gives its name to the village. It belonged to the Latin Church before the conquest of the island by Selim II, and was given to the Greeks by Mustafa Pasha, but is now in a dilapidated condition. Its architecture proves that it was built under the Lusignan dynasty. The Royal Crusaders must have richly endowed it, as it still owns thousands of acres of fertile land, much of which lies untilled for the want of manual labour. Its possessions extend as far as the village of Ormidia. In the gardens of the convent are two large stone reservoirs, fed, chiefly during the winter months, by the water of a spring, the source of which is some four miles north-east. The water is conveyed by an ancient aqueduct somewhat similar to those at Amathus, Curium, Citium, and one or two places on the north side of the island. The aqueduct of Sta. Napa, like that of Citium, has undergone many repairs, and the greater part of the construction, as it now appears, is according to the Roman system; but while following its course I found several air-shafts, showing that the water had been originally conveyed to Throni in a more direct way, and by the ancient Greek system

[1] *Travels*, London, 1665, p. 289.
[2] *Travels through several parts of Asia*, London, 1754.

of tunnelling. I explored some of these shafts, which were pointed out to me as ancient tombs which had been opened before, and found that the rock beneath had been excavated some 16 inches square for the passage of the water.[1]

AYIA VARVARA (xxxix)

The Church of St. Barbara is a nineteenth-century building, and contains nothing of interest save two icons which, as village tradition has it, were rescued from a Turkish village where they had been taken in 1570. One icon is of St. George, and the buckles, gems, etc., on his dress are represented by pieces of coloured glass. The second icon is a sixteenth-century one of the B.V.M., and is in a good state of preservation.

AYII OMOLOYITADHES (xxi)

The Church of the Holy Cross was built in 1674, but was much repaired and altered in 1894, when the narthex was destroyed. On the north wall is a marble plaque with a florid Venetian coat of arms, and above the window in the apse is a large slab of marble decorated in the Byzantine manner of the twelfth century.

The iconostasis is contemporary with the building. The icons include the Holy Confessors, 1663; St. Nicholas, 1763; St. John the Baptist, 1761; Christ, 1770, etc. Beneath the church is a shrine cut from a rock and formerly a Roman tomb. It is excavated to a considerable depth below the west end of the church, and is entered by a steep narrow staircase through a trap-door in the floor. This shrine consists of a central chamber with four recesses in the form of a cross, each recess being about six feet square and about the same height. The middle of the central chamber is a shallow well of water.

Immediately south-west of the village are the extensive grounds of Government House. Here is kept an extremely interesting relic which was discovered by a sponge-fisher in Famagusta harbour in 1907. It is one of the nineteen cannons presented by King Henry VIII of England to

[1] L. P. D. Cesnola, *Cyprus, Its Cities, Tombs and Temples.*

de l'Isle Adam, Grand Master, 1521–1534, of the Order of St. John of Jerusalem.

It bears on it the badge of the House of Tudor as well as the coat of arms of the Grand Master.

AYII TRIMITHIAS (xxix)

The church is dedicated to SS. Cosmas and Damian, and was rebuilt about forty years ago. Little remains from the original building except a fine west doorway, and the fragment of another doorway is built into the north wall. The church contains an icon of St. John the Baptist dated 1780, and a small late seventeenth-century icon of the Virgin.

SS. Cosmas and Damian were brothers who were born in Arabia but lived in Cilicia. By profession they were physicians, and were famed far and wide for their charity and kindness to the poor and sick. They were martyred during the persecutions of the Emperor Diocletian.

These saints are known in Greek as Agii Anargyri, or the saints without fees, for during their lifetime they are said never to have accepted payments for their work among the sick.

A church was built to their memory by Pope Felix IV in 526 in Rome, and the saints are depicted in the mosaics in the apse being presented by SS. Peter and Paul to Christ.

SS. Cosmas and Damian were the patron saints of the Medici family, and Cosmo de Medici commissioned Fra Angelico to paint a picture, still at San Marco in Florence, of the legendary history of the saints.

One of the most delightful legends about them is that they once had to amputate a leg of a man, but after the operation the poor fellow was unhappy with only one leg and begged the holy brothers to see what they could do. Now as it happened a negro had just died, so they cut off one of his legs and grafted it on to their patient, where it fitted perfectly; but the saints had overlooked the fact that it was a negro they had taken the leg from, so that their patient for the rest of his life had one black and one white leg.

AYII VAVATSINIAS (xlviii)

The church is a large building of the middle of the nineteenth century, and is dedicated to SS. Cosmas and Damian. There is an icon of these saints dated 1765, while in the apse is kept a curious relic in the form of a sixteenth-century Italian chair, one of the few pieces of domestic furniture of that period still remaining in the Island. This is one of the prettiest villages in Cyprus, with its superb views. It is inhabited principally by charcoal burners. The name of this village means the "Place of the Mulberry-trees".

AYIOS AMVROSIOS (xiii)

The principal church of the village is dedicated to St. Ambrose, and is a vast new building with pepper-pot domes, strangely reminiscent of those on the wings of the National Gallery. The village must be built on an ancient site, as in several cases white stone tesserae floors of the Byzantine period can still be seen.

Three monasteries lie near the village, of which Antiphonitis is one of the most delightful monuments in the whole island. Deserted and unvisited, it has a charm of its own which is denied to many more famous buildings. It stands in a narrow, secluded valley, the steep sides of which are covered with trees, while far away below is the sea, and in the distance the mountains of Anatolia. During the early sixteenth century the Casale of Antifonti belonged to the Lusignan family. It is at present the property of the Monastery of Kykko. The monastery is dedicated to the B.V.M., and consists of a church of the Byzantine plan, covered by a large dome supported by eight columns. Four of these are detached, while the other four are attached to the side walls. At the end of the fifteenth century a narthex and loggia on the south side were added. This loggia is a delightful example of the architecture of that period. It consists of an arcade of pointed arches supported by octagonal columns with moulded capitals and bases.

The interior of the church was completely painted in the

fourteenth or fifteenth century, but the frescoes are much damaged by damp and obscured by dirt. The two most remarkable are the vast bust of Christ Pantokrator in the dome, and on the south wall a Tree of Jesse painted on a dark blue ground.

The iconostasis is a superb example of the carved woodwork, painted blue and gold, of the seventeenth century. The holy doors are dated 1650, which may possibly be the date of the whole screen. The majority of icons are seventeenth century, though only one, that of the Archangel Michael, 1659, is dated.

The Monastery of Apati lies about a mile distant from Antiphonitis. The monastic buildings have long since been pulled down, and nothing remains save the entrance doorway near the east end of the church. The church, dating from the early years of the sixteenth century, has recently been repaired and whitewashed, and the iconostasis is of a common type. A charming wrought iron candlestick is the only piece of church furniture with any pretence to antiquity.

The third of the monasteries is Melandryna, situated close to the sea-shore. The original Church of the Virgin was built in the fifteenth century, but it was repaired in 1731, when large flying buttresses were added externally. The holy doors are dated 1651. Part of the blue and gold iconostasis is earlier, and dates from the closing years of the sixteenth century. The church is supposed to have been built on the site of a heathen temple.

AYIOS ANDRONIKOS (iii)

The principal church of the village is dedicated to St. Photini, and is a large late eighteenth-century building of no special interest. About a mile from the village lies a tiny mediaeval chapel, dedicated to the Madonna, which possibly was once the Latin chapel of some casale and which has since disappeared. The interior still shows fragments of wall paintings, the Crucifixion at the west end and a colossal Archangel on the north wall, the former painting being of careful workmanship.

An unusual fragment of Italian woodwork lies in the

church, and consists of a long panel with a lion's mask at the top, while below are fishes, crabs, and other sea animals carved in high relief. The whole was once gilded. It is difficult to suggest how this fragment found its way here, and of what it originally formed a part.

AYIOS ATHANASIOS (liv)

The huge modern church, dedicated to St. Athanasios, is built in the worst possible style, with a hideous iconostasis and modern icons to match. Close by lies the original eighteenth-century village church, dedicated to St. Menas. The vault is decorated with porcelain plates, and on the south wall is an heroic full-length painting of the Archangel, which is not older than the middle of the eighteenth century. Such ancient icons as this church once possessed were recently removed by the bishop of the diocese.

Into a house in the village is built a small Roman altar and inscribed cippus, both found in a field in the vicinity of the village.

About three miles distant from the village is the monastery of the B.V.M. Sphalangiotissa, so named from a wonder-working icon able to cure the bites of the "sphalangi" or anthrax fly, but this and such other icons as this uninteresting monastery contained have also been removed to the metropolis of Limassol.

AYIA DHIMITRIANOS (xxxv)

The apse of the original church lies to the south of the present building, which was first erected in 1794 but has since undergone an almost complete restoration. Close to the church lie a number of important Roman tombs.

On a hill above the village a site is pointed out by the villagers as the palace of the mysterious Queen. Nothing can be seen save a few stone columns and débris of the Roman period, and it may be possible that this was the site of a heathen temple.

Between the two small villages of Aghios Dimitri and Fasuli I found the ruins of an elliptical structure measuring twenty-seven feet by sixteen. Its area was strewn with pieces of broken statues, upon two of which an eagle was carved. I discovered also on the bases of two life-size statues to which the feet still adhered, Greek characters roughly but deeply cut in the calcareous stone. I should have liked to explore this spot thoroughly, as these ruins are not improbably those of a temple dedicated to Jupiter.[1]

AYIOS DHIMITRIOS (xxxvii)

A very pretty village surrounded by fruit trees. The Church of St. Dhimitrios probably dates from the early eighteenth century. The iconostasis is modern save for the holy doors, which are dated 1715. The church contains a very interesting small early sixteenth-century icon of the Transfiguration, with two kneeling donors.

AYIOS DHOMETIOS (xxi)

The principal church of the village is dedicated to St. George, and is a huge and ambitious building in the usual tasteless modern style. In the apse, however, are a few old icons from some former church, including an interesting one of the B.V.M. with three donors at the foot (*circa* 1520).

Outside the village lies the Church of St. Dhometios, a single-aisled building of the seventeenth century, standing on a small hillock. There are the remains of painting on the north wall behind the icon of the saint. In the iconostasis is an icon of the Archangel Michael, dated 1733, and one of Christ, 1772. The latter has been painted on the back of the front panel of a dower chest. In the gallery lies a much damaged icon of the Virgin, dated 1545, and showing marked Italian influence. St. Dhometios is supposed to have been an early archbishop of Cyprus, but his name does not figure in any known list.

About a mile distant from the village is the small well-built Chapel of St. Paul, which has been damaged by fire at some period. The floor of the apse has curious Italian tiles with a coloured design carried out in green, yellow, and purple.

[1] Cesnola, *Cyprus: Its Cities, Tombs and Temples.*

About two miles west is the small Monastery of Makedhonitissa, with its spring of perennial water. It was founded in 1798 by the Archbishop Chrysanthos, and a painting of him survives in the tympanum of the south doorway. The picture represents the Madonna and Child on a throne with a blue background covered with red cherubim. Below is the figure of the archbishop holding a scroll, on which is written a record of the foundation of the monastery. At the base is a conventional representation of the church and monastic buildings, but the church is depicted with a dome and is completely unlike the existing building.

AYIOS EPIKTITOS (xii)

The Church of St. Epiktitos is a building of 1856 on an earlier site, and contains nothing except an early icon of that saint, who would seem to have been of German origin, a soldier and a companion of St. Auxentios, and to have lived the life of a hermit in a cave beneath the church. This cave can still be visited by an entrance in the south interior wall which leads down a tiny circular staircase to the supposed burial-place of the saint. It contains a ruined tomb and a channel for water.

By the sea-shore is the Tekke of Hazaret Omer, the reputed burial-place of seven Moslem saints, whose tombs are still shown, but no tradition lingers of who they were or from whence they came. This shrine is sacred to Turk and Greek alike, though the latter call it Ayii Phanontes.

Several tiny ruined chapels surround the village—St. Stephen, St. Nicholas, and the Prophet Elijah. At the last named the figure of the saint himself has frequently been observed by the villagers, and in broad daylight. He is seen dressed in a red robe and riding on a white ass.

AYIOS EPIPHANIOS (xxxviii)

The Church of St. Epiphanios is the usual hill-village type of eighteenth-century church, with a steeply pitched roof. The interior is a lamentable example of the craze for restoration. The delightful original iconostasis has been replaced by a crude screen painted a hideous dark brown, and with shiny photographic icons. The original icons of the church were given to the neighbouring village of Pharmakas, but in the gallery lie the holy doors and rood in a perfect state of preservation, so that even the excuse of dry rot cannot be advanced by the villagers as a reason for casting them out. These holy doors are well painted in a careful manner, and are far above the usual level of village art. They are difficult to date, but probably belong to the early years of the eighteenth century.

The church contains an unusual relic in the shape of a large bronze cross with repousse figures of the Madonna surrounded by the four Evangelists.

AYIOS JOANNIS (xxix)

An early nineteenth-century building, dedicated to St. John the Baptist, is the principal village church. A very fine fourteenth-century gargoyle in the form of a lion's mask, and a head of St. Mark from some vanished statue of the same period, are built into the wall of the churchyard, and come from a ruined chapel at Akhera.

The church itself contains little of importance save an interesting icon of Christ dated 1540, with five donors, all in an attitude of prayer, the parents on the left and the three daughters to the right. The man is dressed in burgess's robes, his wife in a puce-coloured costume with sleeves puffed out at the shoulders. The two elder daughters are in pale-green dresses with square Elizabethan stomachers, pearl necklaces and other jewellery, and their hair is confined by thin golden nets. The youngest daughter is similarly dressed, except that her robe is black.

An early Hellenistic necropolis was discovered here and ransacked by peasants in 1883. Later Richter excavated three more tombs for the Cyprus Museum, which contained Graeco-Phoenician pottery with concentric circles, and much jewellery, especially gold frontlets and animal-headed earrings.[1]

[1] *Catalogue of Cyprus Museum*, p. 6.

AYIOS JOANNIS AGROS (xlviii)

The vast new church, at present unfinished, is a conspicuous object. The original village Church of the Archangel was built in 1725 and is now deserted in favour of its newer rival. The iconostasis is dated 1757 and is well preserved, but a certain amount of its woodwork is earlier.

AYIOS JAKOVOS (xiv)

Now a completely Moslem village. To the north lie the remains of its mediaeval predecessor, which would appear to have had a circular wall round it. In 1928 the Swedish expedition excavated two sanctuaries here. The first, north of the village, dated from the Bronze Age (*c.* 1400 B.C.) and was once divided into two parts. The main entrance was from the north-west, and in the exterior court was a large terra-cotta basin. In and around this basin was found an accumulation of offerings consisting of gold rings earrings, and a magnificent gold necklace composed of seven hollow beads in the shape of pomegranates, and six large and two small hollow beads shaped like dates. In the centre was a Babylonian cylinder of solid gold mounting. The second, or Iron Age, sanctuary contained little beyond pottery and small terra-cotta figurines.

AYIOS NEOPHYTOS (xlv)

The monastery was founded towards the end of the twelfth century. The present building is situated on one side of a narrow gorge, the slopes of which are covered with groves of olives, cypresses, and other trees.

The church of the monastery is a large and well-built mediaeval edifice of three aisles. The barrel-vaulted roof is supported by columns, three on each side of the nave, crowned by capitals carved with curious thin acanthus leaves. The interior shows considerable remains of mural painting of two periods: those in the apse date from the sixteenth century, while those on the vaulting of the north aisle are earlier. A portion of the iconostasis is seventeenth century, and contains a repainted icon of the Virgin of *c.*1620, with a kneeling donor priest, a certain Joachim.

In a glazed cupboard in the north wall are kept some old icons, the finest being two angels in carved frames after the Italian manner. These are probably the icons referred to by Hogarth:

> On the seat was standing, when we visited the place, a small icon of an angel, painted on wood, certainly not in the usual Greek style, but strongly suggestive of Italian sixteenth century art; but whence it had come no monk could tell us.[1]

Near by is a large late seventeenth-century icon of the Dormition of the Virgin. In a wooden sarcophagus are kept the saint's bones, his skull is in a silver reliquary.

Above the west door of the church was an inscription giving the date and history of the church, but it was removed by the Abbot in 1878, who feared that the English were going to take over the building and use it for Protestant services.

Hard by the church are the three caves which formed the original dwelling-place of the saint, and are said to have been hewn by Neophytos himself from the living rock. The first cave consists of a chapel, the rough-hewn walls covered with paintings of various periods. Some of these, notably the angels (on the roof), St. Constantine, and St. Helena, the Passion and Resurrection of Our Lord, may be early thirteenth century, re-touched at a later date. The remaining fragments are dated 1503. The painting in the bema of St. Neophytos supported by angels is in the true Byzantine style. In the iconostasis screen are two late sixteenth-century processional icons.

The next cave was the dwelling-place of the saint. In this tiny room eleven feet by eight, is his empty tomb cut in the recess of the rock. Into this still climb the sick, who turn round three times, in the hope of being cured. Here can be seen his rock-cut table, and his seat, above which is a modern cupboard containing the skulls and bones of his earliest followers. On the wall above is a painting of Neophytos kneeling at the foot of Christ, who is supported by the Madonna and St. John the Baptist.

[1] *Devia Cypria*, p. 21.

The third of the caves is now disused, and its painted interior blackened and destroyed by fire. On the outside are the remains of a fourteenth-century doorway with a chevron ornamentation.

St. Neophytos was born at Lefkara, near Amathus. At an early age he decided to become a monk, but his parents had other plans for their son, and chose a bride for him. Rather than marry Neophytos ran away to the monastery of St. Chrysostomos, where he hid for three months till he was discovered and forced to return home. After much entreaty and argument he at last persuaded his parents to grant his dearest wish and to allow him to "embrace a monastic life rather than a bride". He journeyed to Paphos and near there at last chanced on a likely place of retreat:

The loneliness of the locality induced him, by its prospect of complete freedom from intrusion, to settle there for a while. It was on St. John Baptist's Day (24th June), 1159, when twenty-five years of age, that he first took up his abode in the cave, and by the following September he had decided to remain. Immediately on coming to this determination he commenced to enlarge his strange habitation, a work which he finished on 14th September of the following year. On its completion he dedicated the cave to the Holy Cross, and erected an altar within, as well as constructed a tomb for himself in its innermost recesses. There he continued to live in the strictest seclusion until the accession of Basil Kinnamos in 1166 to the See of Paphos. This prelate, who proved a warm friend and patron, after much entreaty persuaded him very reluctantly to enter the priesthood and to share his solitude with a companion. From that time the place, which had hitherto remained tenantless, save for the dweller in the cave, began to be occupied by human habitations, until in 1183 all the buildings necessary to the reception of the new community were completed. As time went on the fame of the recluse near Paphos so extended that pilgrims flocked in crowds to the spot. Annoyed by the ever-increasing numbers of his admirers, whose attentions he found it difficult to escape, he determined to leave the cell, which he had occupied for forty years, and with his own hands to construct higher up the cliff another retreat more inaccessible to the multitude. Though now well advanced in years, he laboured at the work with the same enthusiasm as he had shown when a young man.

His life was in constant danger from falling rocks, which became detached during the course of the excavations, yet in spite of the entreaties of the brethren he refused to desist. At length his efforts were crowned with success, and the new habitation, commenced on 24 June, 1199, was dedicated to St. John the Forerunner. His only means of communication now with the outer world was by a ladder, which was drawn up when not required. Here in this new retreat he continued to practise the most rigid austerities, only descending on Sundays for the instruction and exhortation of the disciples.[1]

AYIOS NIKOLAOS (xlvi)

The village is now inhabited entirely by Moslems, but contains an extremely interesting church dedicated to the Archangel Michael. It was until a few years ago a curious example of one of those double churches which were shared between the Orthodox and the Latin. The Latin half with a cross carved on the dividing wall has recently been pulled down. In the Orthodox part there remains a vast sixteenth-century painting of the Archangel on the north wall, and some interesting icons, St. John the Divine, 1562, with donors, and two late sixteenth-century icons of the B.V.M. and the Archangel Michael. A large decorated slab of marble lies in the apse, Byzantine work of the thirteenth century, and also a marble font. A portion of the much repainted iconostasis is of the sixteenth century.

AYIOS PHOTIOS (xlvi)

The church is a small and ancient building repaired in 1835. A bronze cross, apparently mediaeval and with a crucifixion in high relief on it, is inset into a triangular stone above the west doorway.

AYIOS SERGIOS (xxiv)

The Byzantine mediaeval Church of St. Sergios has numerous marble fragments from Salamis built into its walls and lying about in the churchyard. The icons include two excellent examples of mid-eighteenth-century work, a large one of SS. Sergios and Bacchus on horses, and the other

[1] J. Hackett, *History of Church of Cyprus*, London, 1901, p. 348.

of the Madonna and Child. The dated ones include the Nativity, 1680, and Christ, 1745. Built into the west narthex is a capital of the fifth century B.C.

St. Sergios was Bishop of Constantia in the middle of the seventh century, and was a vigorous opponent of the Monothelite heresy.

The village also contains a sixteenth-century church of St. Paraskeva. A fragment of a classical frieze forms the doorstep into the south narthex.

There was a tower here during the Middle Ages, and it is supposed to have stood at a locality known as Partzili.

The Genoese at the beginning of their invasion only held Famagusta, and a certain knight, Sir Peter de Cassi, raised on his own account a body of troops, and with these men watched the gates of Famagusta so that no provisions should pass into the city.

But after a time both Sir Peter and his troops got tired of guarding the roads to the city, and retired to the tower at St. Sergios.

Now many of Sir Peter's troops came from the neighbouring villages and used to return there every night, for it was thought impossible that the Genoese would sally forth from Famagusta.

But a certain peasant knew this, and came and asked the Genoese what they would pay to capture Sir Peter. At first the Genoese refused to listen to the man, thinking it was a trap; but at last he persuaded them, and the Genoese said they would give a great price. Then the peasant told them how at nights Sir Peter had but few troops with him.

That very evening the Genoese set out from Famagusta with many soldiers and, having come to St. Sergios, surrounded the town and captured Sir Peter and the small guard which was with him.

AYIOS SOZOMENOS (xxxi)

The village church is a plain rustic shed dedicated to the B.V.M., with fragments of painting on the exterior north wall. The interior contains a seventeenth-century fresco of the Madonna and two icons of the same period.

Close by lies the ruin of the early sixteenth-century Church of St. Mamas. In the side wall of the north aisle are two fine Renaissance founders' tombs. There is a well-carved west doorway with a cross above it. This church must have been in its original state a building of importance and of some architectural pretensions.

Close to the village is a cave cut in the face of the rock and the reputed tomb of St. Sozomenos. A considerable number of wall paintings remain in the bema and above the empty tomb.

AYIOS SYMEON (iii)

A small Turkish hamlet, near which lies one of the most curious sights in Cyprus, a great cave tomb of uncertain date. The entrance is difficult of access and it is advisable to take a guide and a rope.

It is while passing under one such hill, after abruptly descending from the central ridge and within sight of Elisis, that the traveller suddenly perceives high up in the cliff upon his right a dark patch, which a moment's scrutiny convinces him must be the mouth of an artificial cave. If he turns off his path, as we did on that blazing midday in July, and, tethering his horse at the foot of the hill, bursts his way for five hundred feet of ascent through matted thorns and over rocks so hot as to blister the bare hand, until he reaches the foot of the scarp which forms the crest of the hill, he will have had no bad foretaste of purgatory. And still the door of the cave—now evidently artificial—is fully twenty feet above his head. The rock is sheer, and even slightly overhanging, and for a few minutes he will see no way up its smooth face; but a long ledge in the cliff face, running obliquely across it and passing under the cave-door, ends in a turn of the cliff about fifteen feet above the ground, and careful search will reveal the possibility of reaching it by means of knobs and cracks on the face of the precipice; and, once therein, it is fairly easy, though most unpleasant, to wriggle the body along the ledge, which is not more than a foot wide, until immediately under the opening, and get into the latter with a sigh of relief, tempered by the consciousness of having to descend that sloping ledge again sooner or later. But, standing upright in the doorway, the climber will not regret his labour, for the largest of ancient Cyprian sepulchres lies before him.

It will be seen that this tomb is cut for 87 feet straight into the precipice. 12 feet is taken up by the passage which runs down to the door, and then the great hall opens out divided into a central nave, supported on four arches, and flanked on each side by aisles, from the farther sides of which run out the sepulchral chambers, four on the left and two more shallow on the right, the tomb never having been completely finished on the first plan. The whole is rather flatly vaulted, and not more than seven feet high: the floor is perfectly even, and covered with a couple of inches of coarse dust, the detritus of the roof; the cutting is in all parts regular and careful. On either hand of the entrance runs a narrow passage, opening out into a little chamber, which is lighted by a slit in the face of the cliff: these may be relics of a time when the cave was used as a refuge or stronghold, and seem to be of a later period than the rest. The peasants of Elisis have a tradition that robbers once used it, and the roof is in places blackened by smoke, while cinders and dung are to be seen on the floor. The beds in the sepulchral niches lie across the inner end, in shallow recesses. At the far end of the Tomb is a square arched recess containing what is apparently a well, cut perhaps in later times, and a stone which I threw down seemed to bound and rebound from its sides to infinity; but I had neither the means nor the will to descend the shaft, more especially as persuasion and threats had alike failed to induce my servant to follow me up the cliff. In no part of the tomb—and I looked most diligently—was there any sort of inscription, excepting only two or three names of modern Greeks who had climbed up in past years, and had carved the sides of the entrance after their manner. The whole cave is absolutely empty.[1]

AYIOS THEODHOROS (xlix)

The Church of St. Theodore was built in 1847 and contains little save a late eighteenth-century Venetian chandelier and a well-painted icon of Christ.

Four miles south, at Pendaskinos, is the ruined Church of St. Anthony, a large double-aisled building. Beneath the floor of the church lie two well-built tomb chambers, once painted and roofed with large gypsum slabs. They measure 10 feet by 4 feet, and to the side are arched niches where

[1] *Devia Cypria*, p. 72.

the bodies were laid. In the ruins lies a large cippus with an inscription of four lines, which probably supported the altar stone.

Between Ayios Theodhoros and Kophinou lies the Church of the B.V.M., the interior once completely painted but now much damaged and blackened from shepherds lighting fires inside. The paintings would appear to have been the work of the early sixteenth century.

AYIOS THEODHOROS (KARPASIAS) (XV)

The village Church of St. Theodore is an ancient but much restored building. There is said to be a mysterious underground passage beneath the church, but it has long since been blocked up.

About five miles from the village and close to the sea lie the ruins of Cnidus, the birthplace of the historian Ctesias. Nothing now remains except

> a wilderness of formless heaps extending round a small bay about half a mile and inland for some 400 yards. Large "oil stones" are seen here, and there are many traces of houses and a city wall, but no temple or very large building. But the most interesting feature lies about 150 yards to the east, and a like distance from the sea—a stone enclosure rectangular and oblong with the long sides lying nearly true east and west. . . .
>
> The north-west angle is composed of a great upright block, obviously a menhir, or emblem of fertility. Its full height from the ground is 6 ft. 9 in., and its width and thickness each 2 ft. 10 in. . . . That this is a Phoenician relic there can be little question. Stone enclosures with upright menhirs are frequent on the opposite coast, where the usual form is circular.[1]

AYIOS THEODHOROS (AGROS) (xlviii)

The village once possessed seven churches, but only two now remain. The only one that is of any interest is that of the B.V.M., an ancient building which has been restored and added to. It contains a magnificent iconostasis in a perfect state of preservation and dated 1667. There is a late seventeenth-century icon of the Prophet Elijah with a

[1] *Devia Cypria*, p. 66.

donor priest in the corner, and also a sixteenth-century one of the B.V.M. Khiotissa, which is one of the famous rain-compelling icons.

In the church is kept a Gospel of 1550. On a half-page is written a short contemporary account of the Turkish conquest of the Island by a certain priest called Simeon. In this Gospel are preserved three leaves from a fifteenth-century MS.

AYIOS THYRSOS (iv)

Half-way between Yialousa and Rizokarpaso is a tiny chapel close to the sea-shore. A local superstition is that anyone suffering from a skin disease should first wash in the holy well of the church and then again in the sea.

About two miles distant is the Church of Ayios Photios Tis Selinias. The usual fatal restoration has recently taken place, the south nave of the church has been wantonly torn down and all the interesting paintings in the interior have been whitewashed, so that now nothing remains save a portion of a vast painting of the Archangel Michael on the north wall.

About a mile from Ayios Thyrsos is a curious relic of a past age. Amongst rocks and juniper bushes in an uncultivated tract of land lie two colossal limestone female statues, one about 13 feet high and the other life-size. They apparently date from the late Roman period. There are no signs of a temple here, and one can only imagine that they were commissioned and hewn out of the rock for some neighbouring shrine, but either owing to their size or the introduction of Christianity into the Island the work was never finished, so that they lie just as the sculptor left them 1,600 years ago.

Near this site are the ruined lower stages of a mediaeval watch tower.

AYIOS TYKHONAS (liv)

The village is largely built from the ruins of Amathus, which lies a mile or so distant. The village church is dedicated to St. Tykhonas, second bishop of the See of Amathus. He was ordained deacon by the first bishop, whose name was Mmemonios, on whose death he was consecrated to the see by St. Epiphanios, and his memory is observed on June 16th.

The original Church of St. Tykhonas was at Amathus, but was pulled down by the last bishop of that see, who sold the stones to the Franks, who took them away by sea to Larnaca to build a church. The bones and relics of St. Tykhonas and the other bishops were thrown by impious hands into the sea, but retribution overtook this callous and wicked prelate, and within a year he died raving mad.

Cesnola has another version of the story, which a peasant told him.

> The church was dedicated (the peasant continued) to Aghios Tychona, who had been killed here, and to this shrine was attributed the miraculous power of curing epileptics. Many years ago there existed one of our bishops—a bad man, God forgive him!—who ordered the church (in danger of falling, I suppose) to be pulled down and a new one to be built with the same stones at a little distance, but the Saint would not permit such a desecration, and appeared in a dream to all the villagers of the neighbourhood in the same night, and told them to oppose so sacrilegious a demolition by force, which I assure you they would have done if the bishop had not desisted. As a punishment the bishop was afflicted with epilepsy, became crazy, and in a fit destroyed himself.[1]

The ruins of Amathus, perhaps the most ancient city in Cyprus and capital of one of the former nine kingdoms, are to-day but heaps of stone. It continued to be a flourishing town until the close of the Byzantine supremacy, when it was captured and destroyed by Richard Cœur de Lion, King of England. Its origin has been ascribed to Phoenician colonists, from whom it is said to have derived its name—from Amathus, the son of Hercules, or from Amathusa, the mother of Kinyras. In ancient times it was one of the centres of the copper mining industry, as well as being celebrated for the two famous temples, that of the Tyrian

[1] *Cyprus: Its Cities, Tombs and Temples.*

Heracles, who was worshipped under the name of Melkarth, and that of Aphrodite.

Amathus has been ransacked by treasure-seekers from an early period. One of the principal treasures of the Louvre is a huge stone vase with bull-headed handles from this site, which was carried off by the French in 1866, and a fragment of a second vase can still be seen on the top of the Acropolis. Cesnola excavated many tombs here, and found some interesting sarcophagi with sculptured panels in relief, which are now in the Metropolitan Museum in New York.

The Orthodox See of Amathus lingered for a long time after the destruction of the city. One of the last bishops mentioned is Esaias, who signed a letter with the other prelates in 1608 to the Duke of Savoy asking him to rescue the Island from the Turks.

But the town's chief claim to fame is that it was the birthplace, at the end of the fifth century, of the famous patriarch of Alexandria, John the Almoner, the original patron of the Order of St. John of Jerusalem. John was the son of Epiphanios, Governor of Cyprus, and was born in A.D. 609. His curious title of "The Almoner" was given him by reason of his great charity to the poor, 7,500 of whom he is said to have maintained at his own expense. At the taking of Alexandria by the Persians, John, instead of remaining to share the dangers of his flock, resolved to seek safety in his native Cyprus, justifying his desertion of it by the words of Christ, "When they persecute you in this city flee you into another...." Coming to his native city of Amathus, he immediately called for writing materials and bade his attendants draw out his Will, on the completion of which he died.

It is not to be expected that the death of one so highly favoured by heaven would take place without some strange portents occurring. It is gravely asserted that at the funeral of the saint in the church of St. Tychon, a former occupant of the see of Amathus, as the body was being lowered into the grave the corpses of two holy bishops already interred there side by side rolled apart and left a space between them for the newcomer.[1]

[1] Hackett, p. 394.

AYIOS VASILIOS (xx)

The Church of St. Basil is modern, but a portion of the iconostasis is of the late seventeenth century and comes from a ruined church at Kato Kopia. There are several large mid-eighteenth-century icons from the same source. In the apse is a sixteenth-century icon of the Madonna, which is supposed to have come from the deserted village of Palourakambos.

AYIOS YEORYIOS (LEFKA) (xxviii)

The church was until quite recently one of the most charming little mediaeval domed churches in the Island, but it has been completely ruined by a restoration which added on a west end and knocked in large windows on every side. Nor were the local vandals content with destroying the exterior, for the ancient iconostasis and icons have been swept away and the floor relaid with disgusting encaustic tiles.

AYIOS YEORYIOS (FAMAGUSTA) (xv)

The Church of St. George is a large early nineteenth-century building. The top of the altar is formed out of a portion of a sixteenth-century tomb slab, and consists of the head and part of the arm and dress of a woman. This curious fragment possibly came from one of the destroyed churches in Famagusta. There is an elaborate west doorway with a long inscription above it, but so worn as to be now completely illegible.

AYIOS YEORYIOS (KYRENIA) (xii)

Near the sea is the tiny rock-cut Chapel of St. Phanourios. Beneath this chapel the rocks are full of fossil bones, called by the villagers the bones of St. Phanourios, but in reality they are the remains of the pygmy hippopotamus.

St. Phanourios was a youth who lived in Asia Minor and heard the call of Christ, and came across from there to Cyprus. He sailed across in a small open boat with only his faithful horse as his companion, and, landing, tried to ride up the steep cliff, but his horse slipped and fell and he and his steed were killed, in token of which the horse's footprints are shown to this day.

The chapel is much resorted to by villagers, who dig out from the rock the fossil bones and, powdering them, mix them with a drink of water. This draught is said to be a sovereign cure for nearly every known disease.

BELLA PAISE (xii)

This Premonstratensian Abbey is the most remarkable Gothic monument still remaining in Cyprus. It has been known under various names, such as the Abbey de la Pais, or the Abbey of Peace, which became corrupted in the Venetian times into Bella Paise, the Abbée Blanche or the White Abbey, from the colour of the habit worn by the members of the Order. The Premonstratensian Order—also called the Norbertine—was an Order of Augustinian canons founded in 1120 by St. Norbert, Archbishop of Magdeburg, and its first monastery was in a deserted place called Prémontre, near Laon. The rules of the monastery were of great strictness, and the monks followed a life of deep austerity. At one time they held a certain amount of property in England, including Bayham Abbey in Kent. The strength of the Premonstratensians at present lies in Belgium, where the great Abbey of Tongerloo is still in the hands of the Order. Though the Abbey of Bella Paise had considerable privileges, its origin is obscure. Originally there were canons of St. Augustine here, but Archbishop Thierry (1205–1213) allowed them to become members of the Premonstratensian Order. In 1246 a very precious relic consisting of a fragment of the True Cross and a sum of 600 besants was bequeathed to the Abbey by Sir Roger the Norman, on condition that the monks should ever say masses for the soul of the testator and his wife Alix. But the principal benefactor of the Abbey was Hugh III (1267–1284), who was probably responsible for the building as we see it to-day. It was this king who granted to the head of the community the privilege of being a Mitred Abbot, and of carrying a gilded sword and wearing golden spurs.

Hugh died at Tyre, and his body was brought over to Cyprus and buried within the church. Towards the end of the Venetian era the monastery had sadly declined, and the Lieutenant-Governor was scandalized to find that the monks had taken wives—indeed some did not even restrict themselves to one—and that the only novitiates they would receive were their own children. In 1570 the Turks, when they captured the island, sacked and despoiled the monastery.

The monastery was defended by a fortified gateway, the present entrance, which still retains its machicoulis, though the drawbridge has long since disappeared and the belfry is modern. The church is without doubt the most ancient part of the building, and is in a superb state of preservation. It consists of a central nave and two side aisles. The style of erection seems to be early thirteenth century and the earliest part of the church is the choir and the windows of the nave. In the middle of the thirteenth century the pillars, vaults of the nave, and porch were added. No monuments remain, though many famous persons, including King Hugh III, were buried in the church. The body of the interior has been marred by a common type of iconostasis, recently erected by the villagers, for with the advent of the Turks the building passed from Latin into Orthodox hands. The only relic of the Latin period remaining is a bronze plate now preserved in the apse; in the centre is a running stag, surrounded with a circle of small bosses. The plate was probably made in Flanders or North Italy in the fifteenth century.

The apse and the porch of the church were originally enriched with frescoes, of which a few traces remain. On the south wall of the apse is a fragment of a medallion which once was painted with the busts of the Apostles. The frescoes in the porch are fragmentary, and are probably fifteenth-century Italian work. The large painting above the great west door is modern. The cloisters were built in the late fourteenth century: stone-robbers have, alas, wrenched out nearly all the tracery from the eighteen arches, but enough remains of the fragments to allow of a reconstruction of the design. Within one of the arches of the cloisters, and opposite the refectory doors, stands the lavabo, consisting of two Roman sarcophagi of marble placed one above the other, so as to allow the water from the upper one to run into the lower through six small holes carefully pierced, and once possibly fitted with metal taps. The upper sarcophagus is decorated with bulls' heads at the corner, while on the panels is a child supporting a heavy floral swag with lion masks above.

The crowning glory of the monastery is the refectory. It is entered by a door built in the style of the late thirteenth century; on the marble lintel are three shields bearing the royal Lusignan coat of arms. The refectory, as we see it to-day, was almost certainly built by King Hugh IV (1324–1329). It measures 90 feet by 32 feet; the arched vault is supported by fourteen pillars, seven on each side. In the north wall are six deep windows, which give superb views of the sea, and the distant hills of Anatolia beyond. The pulpit for reading during meals by one of the monks still remains unharmed; it is lit by a small window and is reached by a staircase built in the thickness of the wall. The pitting of the stonework of the east wall is said to be due to the fact that the refectory was used as a miniature rifle range during the early years of the British occupation. Against two sides of the refectory are the remains of a wall seat, which rises to a higher level at the east end; this suggests the presence of a dais for the high table. Under each of the windows on the north sides is a drain hole for the water used for washing the floor after meals. Outside the west end a worn staircase leads to the undercroft, which consists of two vaulted compartments. The rib vaulting is supported by octagonal columns with moulded capitals. Part of this was probably used as a cellar by the monks.

East of the cloisters lie the ruins of the common room and chapter house, with the monks' dormitory above. In every bay of the dormitory is a small window and a wall cupboard, so that each monk had thus, at the head of his bed, a place to keep his belongings, and a window through which to gaze over the green and smiling countryside. The chapter-house is a small square room with a central marble pillar and capital which supported the vaulting; this pillar was probably brought from the ruins of Lamboussa. The stone seats of the monks survive, and the carved corbels of the vaulting ribs show a certain ingenuity in their design. They include: a man carrying on his shoulder a double ladder; Ulysses between two syrens; a woman reading; a youth fighting two beasts; a girl holding a rosary; a monkey and a cat in a pear-tree, with a man holding a shield, the bearings of which are now much defaced; and finally a monk dressed in a cloak.

A staircase in the south cloister leads to the flat roof, where the small treasury is built against the south-west corner of the church. The little rectangular cupboards still remain, but their doors have long since disappeared.

CHAKISTRA (xxvii)

The village church is dedicated to St. Nicholas. A curious feature of the building is that the church boasts two north doors and no west door. In the apse are a number of wall paintings, the Virgin in Glory, etc., probably late sixteenth-century work.

The iconostasis and icons are a terrible example of the craze for restoration. All has been repainted in the crudest manner. Some of the icons have been brought here from ruined chapels in the vicinity, St. Mamas, St. Anastasia, etc.

CHATOS (xiii)

The mosque is modern, though built on the site of a mediaeval church, fragments of which can be seen built into its walls, including part of a fine doorway with dog-tooth moulding.

DALI (xxxi)

A large village built on the banks of the Yalias River. The large principal church, dedicated to St. Andronicos, was built in 1841, and is without interest. But even this will not serve the villagers, and an enormous temple with a conspicuous dome has been erected within the past few years in the centre of the village. It is a mixture of every style and period, and illustrates only too well the "incoherency" of architecture.

Close to the village lies the perfect small-domed Byzantine Church of St. Dimitrianos, still containing considerable remains of paintings. Above the west door is a picture of the donor, Michael Castouroubes (= Chateau Roux?) and his wife presenting a model of the church to Christ in 1316. On the north wall are the remains of a vast painting of St. George, with graffiti in Gothic script scratched on it.

The Church of St. George, which also lies close to Dali, is of the same period and style as St. Dimitrianos, but the interior paintings are not so well preserved. A number of fragments from the ancient Idalion are built up into its walls.

The Church of St. Mamas is probably a Latin church of the sixteenth century. It is now used as the Orthodox cemetery chapel. The doors, with their richly moulded pointed arches, are in the true Gothic style. The wall shafts which carry the vaulting are formed from marble columns, which may once have constituted part of one of the temples of the ancient city. The interior is whitewashed and without interest, and the only piece worthy of note remaining is the wooden door-handle of the south door, carved in the likeness of an owl and belonging to the Latin church.

The ancient town of Idalion is mentioned by most of the classical writers. The acropolis and sanctuary of Aphrodite is on a conspicuous limestone peak to the east of the village. Nothing now remains save traces of the city wall. During the eighteenth century the whole site was ransacked by various treasure-seekers, Cesnola himself tells us he opened more than ten thousand tombs here, and it was on the sharply pointed hill to the west, known as Ambelliri, that the Duc de Luynes found the bronze inscribed tablet, now one of the treasures of the Louvre.

About half a mile south of Dali village the path to the Paradisi valley passes between conspicuous limestone hills, between and on the north slopes of which lay IDALION. That on the east is crowned by the principal sanctuary of Aphrodite:

the city wall can be traced up the spur nearest to the path: the sanctuary of Apollo, excavated by Mr. Lang, is close to the path in the valley between the two acropoleis. The sharply pointed hill on the west, called Ambelliri, was within the city wall, which appears again north-west of it, and has a sanctuary of Athene and other signs of occupation: here were found the silver paterae now in the Louvre, and the inscribed bronze tablet of the Duc de Luynes. Further west, outside the town, on the north slope of the same high ground, is a sanctuary of Aphrodite Kourotrophos, found ransacked in 1883, with many stone statuettes on the surface; nursing-mothers, temple-boys, flower-holders, etc.[1]

Adonis is connected with stories of Idalion, and it was here that he was killed by the wild boar. Venus was so affected by the death of the beloved youth that she ordered the inhabitants of the city to keep the anniversary of his death as a day of mourning. To this day in the spring the fields are covered with the flowers which bear his name.

DELIKIPO (xxxix)

The tiny little church is dedicated to the Transfiguration. According to an inscription in the interior the foundations were laid in January 1723 and the building was finished in March of the same year, during the time of Archbishop Silvestros (1718–1731). Fragments from an older building were used in its construction, including portions of a mediaeval doorway. There is an icon of St. Dimitrianos, painted by the priest John in 1728, a Transfiguration of 1726, and St. John the Baptist, 1764.

The church contains a fine sixteenth-century alms plate with an Agnus Dei embossed in the centre.

DHEFTERA (xxx)

The churches of the twin villages of Pano and Kato Dheftera are without interest, but about a mile from Kato Dheftera and the other side of the Pediaes River is one of the most curious monuments in Cyprus—the Chapel of the Chrysospileotissa. Advantage has been taken of a natural

[1] Myres, *Catalogue of Cyprus Museum*.

cave in the face of the cliff, and it has been enlarged to form a church measuring about 30 feet by 24 feet. The interior was at one time completely painted, but little now remains owing to damp and the plaster falling away from the surface of the rock. The church must have been abandoned at some period, as is shown by the number of names and dates of the seventeenth and eighteenth centuries cut on the frescoes in the apse. The church wall, and the door which now encloses this church cave, is of recent date.

The church is approached by a pathway cut in the face of the cliff, and there must have been a drawbridge at some period so that in time of trouble the church could become a place of refuge and defence. The neighbouring villagers flock here in great numbers in times of drought to pray for rain, and in 1933 so successfully did the Virgin answer their prayers that the grateful farmers purchased an iron girder to take the place of the original drawbridge and make the shrine more accessible.

The church is always kept locked and the key must be obtained from the village.

DHERINIA (xxxiii)

A number of churches lie in and near the village. They are:

1. St. George.—A small mediaeval church with a dome. The interior walls were once completely painted, but are now much damaged. The best preserved fresco is of the saint and his martyrdom on the north wall.

2. The Blessed Virgin Mary.—An ancient building with a south aisle and narthex added during the nineteenth century. The paintings in the original church have been whitewashed, but two seventeenth-century icons, Christ and the Virgin, and a well-preserved carved wooden cross of the sixteenth century, seem to have escaped the hand of the restorer. A number of marble Corinthian capitals lie in the churchyard. The original Venetian blue and gold iconostasis has recently been torn from the church and lies in fragments in a shed near the school.

3. St. Constantinos.—A late eighteenth-century chapel of

the usual type. Outside the west door is a stone slab to support the icon of the saint, which is placed here on feast days and is much venerated by the villagers.

One and a half miles from the village lies the charmingly situated and wonderfully preserved fifteenth-century chapel of St. Marina, which is a perfect example of the village church of the period, the only restoration being to the south wall. The holy well lies beneath the church and is much frequented by persons suffering from skin diseases, who bathe therein and leave a portion of their clothing on a tree which grows near by.

Three miles from the village, near the main road, lies the little chapel of St. Nicholas of the sixteenth century. At some period the south aisle was destroyed and a narthex added. The building still retains traces of paintings and a founder's tomb.

DHIERONA (xlviii)

A picturesque village built on the side of a steep hill, so that the houses seem from a distance to look like tiers of birds' nests in a Chinese cavern.

The village church contains a few painted icons from the church of the Archangel Gabriel which lies outside the village. This large building is now deserted and dismantled. It is hard to assign any certain date to it, but it is still in a good state of preservation, the only reason for its desertion being its distance from the village.

DHIORIOS (xi)

The Church of St. Marina was built in the early years of the nineteenth century on an ancient site. Remains of the foundations of the previous church are still visible at the west end. It contains a well-preserved icon of St. Marina with a donor priest, probably *c.* 1670.

DHORA (lii)

The name of this village probably comes from the ancient Greek word for a skin. It has been suggested that in former times all the country here round the village was thickly wooded, and the deer which inhabited it were killed for the value of their skins.

The Church of St. Marina is carefully built of well-cut stone. On the south side is an arcade with five arches carried on square pillars. The south door has an inscription recording the building of the church in 1598. Above this is a tympanum with zigzag moulding. The interior is without interest save for an early sixteenth-century icon of Christ supported by St. John the Baptist and St. John the Divine.

Above the village is a large church dedicated to the Virgin. According to a local legend an ancient church stood here, but was destroyed some years ago. It contained a famous icon of the Madonna, still preserved in the present building. The icon is kept covered, as no one is supposed ever to see the face of the Virgin. It is apparently of the early seventeenth century, and according to an inscription at the foot was given by a certain Vroni Simvias and her children. It is one of the rain-compelling icons of the Island, and the church is supposed to stand in a direct line with Kykko. When the old church was pulled down the villagers wished to rebuild it in their village, so as to be spared the long walk to the top of the hill. But this the Virgin would not allow, and destroyed by night whatsoever building had been done during the day, so that in the end the villagers were forced to rebuild their church on the ancient site and the Virgin was contented.

DHRINIA (XXXV)

The Church of St. George was built in 1755 and repaired in 1842. Over the west door are a large marble lintel and two marble brackets, which are said to have come from a ruined church, and which certainly appear to be mediaeval work.

One of the lower panels of the iconostasis is formed from an icon of the Madonna (*c.* 1700). Near the church lies a large marble basin, which was probably once used as a font.

DHROMOLAXIA (l)

One of the villages destroyed by the Saracens in 1425. The Church of St. John the Baptist dates from the late eighteenth century. A number of marble Corinthian capitals lie about the churchyard, and the marble font is supported by another.

In the women's gallery is kept a large icon of the Baptist, damaged by fire at some period. At the bottom are donors and the date 1794.

DHROUSHA (xxxv)

The Church of St. Ephiphanios was built in 1754 and almost completely rebuilt in 1856. The north door alone survives from the original building. The interior is devoid of interest, save for a large Venetian chandelier of the late eighteenth century, which hangs from the roof.

About two miles from the village is the monastery of St. George, which was destroyed by fire in 1923 and has since been rebuilt.

On the sixteenth-century maps of the island is shown a place called Guardia Diurna, which probably is the high isolated hill near the village, and may have been the site of a mediaeval watch-tower, for from here signals could be seen either at Paphos or Akamas.

DHYMES (xxxvii)

The Church of St. John the Baptist was built in 1861 and contains a singularly hideous iconostasis varnished a sticky dark brown, and with garish icons painted by the monks of Stavrovouni. In the bema stands a seventeenth-century processional icon said to have come from a ruined chapel in the vicinity.

ELEA (KYRENIA) (xii)

The Church of St. Nicholas has been recently rebuilt. Placed against one of the buttresses of the north wall is a gypsum tomb slab with the life-size figure of a man in armour, with a coat of arms on his shield. From the style of the armour this probably dates from the end of the fifteenth century. The Greek inscription which runs round the edge is much destroyed and the only words still legible are "died February 23rd".

Another curious mediaeval relic is placed on the roof of the apse, a headless figure holding two shields with coats of arms. The armorial bearings are much destroyed but appear to be lions rampant

About a mile from the village is a small mediaeval ruined church dedicated to the Archangel Michael, with fragments of fresco still adhering to the walls. It is possible that a mediaeval château once stood here, for marble and granite columns lie scattered about the village, and on the ancient aqueduct is inscribed "F. Bale", with a space below for a coat of arms.

ELEA (LEFKA) (xxviii)

The mediaeval Church of St. George has been rebuilt and repaired. A fragment of a sixteenth-century tombstone lies outside the north door. The interior was once painted, but little now remains save a fine Dormition of the Virgin over the north door, and fragments of other scenes in the apse.

Part of the iconostasis is late sixteenth-century work, and contains an icon of St. George, dated 1650.

The village is completely Turkish, and the church is now deserted. Close by is a fine fountain built like a small monotholos church, with a marble lintel and two stone rain spouts on its façade. There is an eighteenth-century Turkish inscription, but this refers to a restoration, and the original fountain was in all probability Venetian.

ELIOPHOTES (xxix)

A small Turkish hamlet containing a rebuilt church dedicated to the five saints known as the Eliophotes. The plain modern iconostasis is patched with fragments of early seventeenth-century woodwork, and contains also two pieces of a large icon of the same date. Against the north wall hangs an unusual icon dedicated to the "Madonna of the Rose which never fades", below is part of an inscription, but unfortunately the date and the name of the painter, except for one or two letters, are destroyed. The icon probably dates from the last years of the seventeenth century.

In the west end of the church, and cut from the living rock, is a tomb of these completely obscure saints, empty save for a few bones. A large and much damaged early icon of the chief of these, St. Eliophotos, hangs above his grave. The oil from a lamp which hangs in front of this icon is credited with the power of curing rheumatism. St. Eliophotos, with four companions, came from Germany to Cyprus in the seventh century and died and was buried here.

EMBA (xlv)

The Church of the B.V.M. is a large Byzantine building and consists of three aisles crowned with two domes, the westernmost of which, with the narthex, was added in 1744. At the top of each dome is a small marble pillar apparently of the Roman period. An unusual feature is the external staircase which leads from the north of the narthex to the roof. The interior of the church was once completely frescoed, but in 1886 the paintings were nearly all redone in the vilest and crudest manner by some local artist without a shred of taste. Only the painting of Christ Pantokrator in the dome is original.

The seventeenth-century iconostasis contains several icons dated 1736, and also an earlier one of St. Simeon Stylites. The finest icon, on two panels, now hangs in a glass case on the south wall. It shows the twelve apostles, six on each panel. Below are Venetian coats of arms. It is extremely well painted, and shows first-class work; it probably dates from the early years of the sixteenth century.

In the aisles are preserved a collection of decayed and early icons, one or two of which may possibly be as early as the fifteenth century. In a chest in the bema is kept a Gospel printed in Venice in 1539, the leather binding of which has in the centre an embossed medallion of Christ.

On the north wall hangs a small sixteenth-century icon of Christ, with two kneeling donors.

About a mile south of the village lies the barrel-vaulted

Church of St. George. The interior shows two layers of frescoes, of which the latest appears to be sixteenth century. An unusual feature is a square apse with founders' tombs on the north, south, and east sides. In the spring the rocks near the church are a mass of cyclamen: indeed, the village of Emba is famous for its wild flowers, and in April the fields which surround it are scarlet with anemones and purple with Venus's looking-glass.

ENGOMI (xxiv)

All round the village are numberless tombs, for here was the necropolis of Salamis. The most important archaeologically are those of the Mycenaean period which lie about a mile west of the village. Here the Swedish Expedition dug in 1932 and found some superb gold ornaments—rings, necklaces, bracelets, etc. It was in the same field that the carved ivory box was found, now one of the treasures of the British Museum.

The village Church of the B.V.M. was rebuilt in 1736. The iconostasis dates from 1790 and contains an icon of the B.V.M. of 1703. Outside the church are two stone lions, perhaps the guardians of some ancient tomb. Close to the village lies a large artificial mound, not unlike a Scandanavian barrow, and it may be that one of these lions guarded the entrance to the tomb-chambers of this monument. This barrow was excavated during the last century, but nothing was found save a spade and lamp left behind by some previous tomb robber.

About a mile from the village lies the monastery of St. Barnabas. The ecclesiastical legend of the finding of the body of St. Barnabas by the Archbishop Anthemios has already been given in a description of the Archbishopric at Nicosia. As soon as he returned from Constantinople the Archbishop Anthemios founded a magnificent and sumptuously adorned edifice. Part of the ground plan of the west end of this church has recently been found outside the apse of the present building, no walls remain, but the beautiful marble geometric pavement is in a good state of preservation. The present church probably dates from the fifteenth century and is a large building with two conspicuous domes, which are a prominent feature in the landscape. A number of marble Corinthian capitals are re-used in the piers which support the domes, but with little or no effect. The south apse of the present church may once have been used as a Latin chapel. Into its south wall is built a spirally fluted column of green marble, which may come from the original fourth-century church The walls of the chapel have recently been covered with a series of crude life-size frescoes depicting the finding of the body of the saint and the bestowal of the privileges of the autocephalous Church of Cyprus by the Emperor Zeno. The iconostasis and icons are without interest save for a long panel of the late seventeenth century with portraits of various saints upon it; this icon is kept on a ledge in the north apse. Close to the church is the tomb cave of St. Barnabas, where the body of the apostle is said to have been found. The tomb, which is cut from the rock, was probably one of the many Hellenic sepulchres which surround Salamis. St. Barnabas is the most famous of all the saints connected with the Island, the patron and pride of the Church of Cyprus. He is mentioned in the Acts of the Apostles, where we hear of him selling all he had and bringing the proceeds to the Apostles.

> And Joses, who by the apostle was surnamed Barnabas, (which is, being interpreted, The son of consolation,) a Levite, and of the country of Cyprus, having land, sold it and brought the money, and laid it at the apostles' feet.[1]

Of the events which occurred during his visit to Cyprus accompanied by Paul and Mark, the few notices recorded in the Acts are all we possess; little is known of his subsequent career. According to a mediaeval legend, he is supposed, after becoming Bishop of Salamis, to have been sent by St. Peter to Italy, where he converted St. Clement, at Rome, and later became Bishop of Milan. He afterwards returned to Salamis, where he met with a martyr's death.

Between the monastery and Salamis lies "the tomb of St. Katherine". It was originally a Roman tomb and consists

[1] Acts iv. 36.

of a large hall covered with a dome-shaped roof composed of five stones, the middle one of which runs the entire length of the building; on the west side there is a small chamber roofed with a vast flat stone. St. Katherine of Alexandria is mentioned by many mediaeval writers; Lusignano gives the following account of the legend:

About A.D. 290 a certain King Costa lived in Salamis, in whose honour the city was called Constantia. In those days the Emperor Diocletian reigned, and a certain Achilles, ruling in Egypt, rebelled against the Roman Empire. So Diocletian proceeded to Egypt, where he killed Achilles, and calling Costa from Cyprus he gave him the government of the Kingdom of Egypt. King Costa, leaving his brother in charge of Cyprus, obeyed the summons of the Emperor, but being in Alexandria he fell ill and died, leaving an only daughter named Katherine, who, although young, was quite learned in the liberal arts. Katherine, on the death of her father, returned to her uncle in Cyprus, who, discovering she was a Christian and fearing Maxentius and Diocletian, thought it well to put her in prison (in the tomb in question at Salamis), and afterwards sent her to Maxentius in Alexandria, where in due course she was martyred.[1]

Close to this tomb is a grove of *Zizyphus spina christi*, which is supposed to be haunted, and through which no villager will pass at night.

EPHTAGONIA (xlviii)

The principal church of the village, dedicated to St. Marina, was built in 1914 and is of no interest. Close by is the poorly repaired Chapel of St. Photios, in which is preserved a superb iconostasis of the late sixteenth century in an excellent state of repair. In it are several interesting icons. That of the Virgin and Child has a coat of arms on it with the original tinctures. Unfortunately, it is impossible to identify the family who bore it. There are also icons of Christ, 1643 (repainted), and one of the Archangel Michael painted in 1693 and, according to the inscription, restored in 1713.

[1] *Chorograffia di Cipro*, p. 39.

On the altar is kept a small silver box containing relics of the SS. Photios and Anikitos, who are said to have been buried there. These relics are supposed to cure insanity; the last recorded case was in 1931, when a boy of fifteen was cured.

EPHTAKOMI (vii)

The Church of St. Luke is a small eighteenth-century building with an arcade on the south side. The iconostasis and some of the icons are dated 1770, which may well be the date of the erection of the church itself.

In a safe is kept a fourteenth-century manuscript Greek Gospel, written on vellum, and containing an illuminated picture of St. Luke.

EPISKOPI (lviii)

During the Middle Ages this village was known as "La Piscopie". In the thirteenth century it belonged to Jean d'Ibelin, Count of Jaffa, in the fourteenth and fifteenth centuries it formed part of the domains of the Cornara family, and from its owners acquired the name of "La Piscopie de Cornier". It must have been a village of considerable wealth and importance, as the ruins of the churches and chapels that still surround it testify.

The principal church of St. Paraskevi has recently been rebuilt. In the interior is a large mediaeval marble lion, unearthed when the foundations of the school were being dug. There is also a fine seventeenth-century icon of St. Paraskevi.

In the village is the small early chapel dedicated to the Virgin, now used as a store. Fragments of painting still remain on the north wall, and pieces of the late sixteenth-century iconostasis lie scattered over the floor. A stone slab with a Byzantine cross cut in relief is built in the south wall.

Close by are the ruins of a tiny chapel dedicated to St. Anthony, but nothing now remains save the apse with a charming double lancet window.

The mosque was formerly a Church of St. George. The Moslems have removed the apse, but the original paintings are still said to lie beneath the layers of whitewash which cover the walls. In the Moslem graveyard, close by, lies a large marble Hellenistic sarcophagus.

Outside the village are the ruins of a large and important mediaeval church dedicated to the B.V.M. Chrysanayiotissa, nothing of which now remains except the west end.

About one mile west of the village and near the cliffs of Curium is the small and ancient Chapel of St. Hermogenes. Inside the church is the tomb of the saint with a cippus at the head and foot, while another supports the altar. The present icon of the saint is modern, but on its predecessor was written a history of the saint who is supposed to have walked across the sea from Samos:

> The support of the Samians, keeper and guard of the people of Cyprus, Hermogenes our father, who crossed the sea as if on foot, mastering its waves and putting a bridle in its mouth as if it were a horse, Hermogenes, you who support Larnaca and Episkopi, glory to those who glorify you, glory to those who crown you, glory to those whom you cure.

St. Hermogenes is held in great repute at Episkopi and Lefkara and is said to cure fever and colds; his feast day is October 5th.

A vast Roman necropolis surrounds this curious tomb chapel, but the majority of the graves have been plundered.

Of domestic buildings little remains save a fine doorway close to the police-station, with a decoration of vine leaves in relief on it.

Close to Episkopi lie the ruins of the royal and ancient City of Curium, the earliest reference to which is made by the geographer Strabo in the last century B.C.:

> Curion then is the starting-point of the western course aiming at Rhodes; very near it is a promontory from which they hurl those who have touched the altar of Apollo: then Treta and Boosoura and Palaipaphos, built as much as ten stadia from the sea: it has a roadstead and an ancient fane of the Paphian Aphrodite.[1]

One of the earliest traditions connected with Curium is that it was founded by Greeks from Argos in the Pelo-

[1] *Excerpta Cypria*, p. 5.

ponnese: the founder himself is supposed to have been Koureus, the son of Kinyras, who settled his colony here in 1595 B.C.:

Travelling due west from the ruins of Amathus or Palaeo-Limassol, after a ride of five hours, mostly through a fertile and well irrigated plain, shaded by caroub and olive trees, in which are situated the large town of Limassol and the small picturesque villages of Kolossi and Episcopi, we reach the western shores of Cyprus, where once existed the royal city of Curium.

Built like an eagle's nest, on the summit of a rocky elevation, 300 feet above sea-level, and almost inaccessible on three sides, the city must have defied in former days all foes, and her inhabitants must have enjoyed from that eminence, with the fine bay stretching away from the foot of the mountain, the lovely scenery which still presents itself on every side.

At a short distance one would take this rock for the walls of a huge mediaeval castle in ruins, but if the traveller coming from Episcopi approach it nearer, he will be surprised at the patience, labour, and ingenuity of the people, who, having selected that excellent spot for their habitation, forced the gigantic rock to take the shape they wished, and that, too, with the poor tools at their command of which traces are still visible. The rock is of common calcareous sandstone, and has been cut on the east and south sides into a quite perpendicular face.

The city of Curium had three entrances, one on the south, one on the west, and a third on the north, near the present road to Paphos; the first and second are still visible. The southern flight of steps led up to the gate, bridge, or whatever else closed the entrance, which is still marked by the fragment of a column standing on its original base. Entering the city from this southern gateway, and walking a few minutes in a north-easterly direction, one meets with the ruins of a semi-circular structure, 720 feet in circumference, probably those of a theatre.[1]

It was close to this theatre that Cesnola declared that he found his treasure, now one of the glories of the Metropolitan Museum, New York. An endless controversy has raged as to whether General Cesnola did or did not find here his superb collection of gold and silver objects, or

[1] Cesnola, *Cyprus: its Cities, Tombs and Temples.*

whether they were but the proceeds of ransacking thousands of tombs all over the Island. Much has been written on both sides, and later excavators have often taken the trouble to dig again in the ruins to prove that the famous treasure chambers beneath the mosaic pavement never existed. Dr. Drummler, indeed, states that he examined the supposed site before numerous witnesses and found undisturbed earth at a shallow depth. The acropolis consists now of nothing but piles of tumbled ruins, marking where palaces and temples once stood. The Roman town was undoubtedly destroyed by an earthquake, but it was rebuilt and flourished till the fifth century A.D., as is proved by some magnificent mosaic pavements recently uncovered by the Pennsylvania Museum expedition.

To the right of the main road, at the top of the hill above the acropolis, are the remains of two important buildings, the Stadium, and an unknown temple. The former measures 1,300 feet by 84 feet, but nothing can now be seen save the ruins of the outside wall. The temple is about 300 yards from the road and is marked by a whitewashed forest beacon: to judge by the number of black and white marble columns which lie scattered about, it must have been a building of considerable size.

The principal temple of the city was that of Apollo, which lies in the midst of scrub about one and a half miles from Curium. It is best approached by following the track which leads from some ruined houses that lie to the right of the main road close to the sixty-fourth mile post. Little more than a few columns survive, for the site has been robbed for generations by the villagers of Episkopi. The original cave over which the temple was built can, however, still be seen; it faces south-east, and was connected with the temple itself by a passage running east and west, perhaps a natural vault in the rock. The original Curium may have been here, but in the sixth century B.C. it was transferred to the site now known as the acropolis. From the description given by Dr. Ross about ninety years ago, there must have been much more of the temple than we see to-day:

I found here plain drums of pillars, 50–70 cm. in diameter, and Doric capitals with two very broad and flat bands, and a little higher the remains of a large building, with inscriptions on bases of the Ptolemaic Era. The great ruins of the temple proper lie somewhat more to the west. On its southern side is a large cistern underground. On the same side one can trace for some distance the foundation of the walls of the temple court. These foundations are preserved on the north side also: the whole peribolos seems to have included four or five other smaller buildings. I came upon several fragments of round and square bases, but no more inscriptions, nor was a single bit of scuplture to be found.[1]

This Temple of Apollo was copied from the original one of Hylae in Greece, of which Pausanias gives a description:

There is a place called Hylae, and in it is a cavern sacred to Apollo, which from its magnitude does not demand much admiration; but the statue within the cavern is very ancient, and imparts strength in every undertaking. Hence men that are sacred to Apollo leap from precipices and lofty rocks without sustaining any injury, and having torn up trees of a prodigious altitude by the roots, carry them with ease through the narrowest roads.[2]

The story that those who profanely touched the altar of Apollo were killed by being thrown over the cliffs of Curium has a curious Christian parallel in the story of Philoneides, an early bishop of Curium:

Hearing that the heathen had received orders to debauch the Christians, Philoneides, wishing to escape such a fate, threw himself over one of the cliffs near Kurion and so ended his life. Shortly after his suicide the saint appeared to two men as they were walking at some distance from the city, running naked before them with a crown upon his head, his body anointed with sweet-smelling myrrh, and bearing a palm branch in his hand. On the spectators drawing near to Kurion the apparition vanished, when they found the spot where the body was lying. The heathen Greeks are said to have placed the remains in a sack and dropped them into the sea, which threw them on shore again, when they were discovered and buried by the Christians.[3]

---

[1] *Cyprus*, p. 84
[2] Jeffery, *Historic Monuments*, p. 382.
[3] Hackett, *Church of Cyprus*, p. 431.

One further curious feature of the ancient Curium deserves notice. About three miles from the acropolis, and at the far end of the Bay of Tripoli, high up in the cliff and almost inaccessible, is part of a passage cut through the living rock. Earthquakes and land-slides have destroyed both the entrance and exit, but a large amount still remains of this inexplicable monument. The passage is 160 feet long, 10 feet broad, and about 8 feet high, and shows traces of most careful cutting. No descriptions remain save traces of dim and fragmentary Byzantine inscriptions in red paint, which probably date from the time when it was inhabited by one of those early Christian hermits, whose only idea in life would seem to have been to make themselves as uncomfortable as possible after the manner of St. Simeon Stylites. It would seem, therefore, that the period and the reason for which it was built must for ever remain a complete mystery. The only inscription still remaining in the whole area of Curium is on the table-land opposite the acropolis on the far side, and to the right of the main road where, just above a small sheepfold, an inscription of three lines in the Cypriote syllabary is cut in the rock.

EPISKOPIO (xxx)

The Church of St. Mamas, on the site of an older building, contains nothing of interest save an eighteenth-century rood cross above the iconostasis.

The Chapel of St. George was rebuilt in 1841, but fragments of the original building survive in the apse. Mural paintings decorate the wall, but they cannot be much more than a hundred years old.

Groves of ancient olive-trees surround the village, whose rental contributes to the upkeep of the great mosque of Nicosia, a curious survival, as in the Middle Ages the same fields belonged to the Cathedral Chapter.

ERIMI (liii)

A large neolithic site was excavated here in 1933, the finds from which are preserved in the Nicosia Museum.

It consisted of a large settlement site; the stratification

extended to nine layers, showing the circular stone foundations of huts. The finds included pottery, stone, and flint implements, steatite idols, and a pick fashioned from a stag's horn.

A contracted burial was found outside a hut in the fifth layer.

The principal church of the village, dedicated to St. John the Baptist, is modern; but in the vicinity are two mediaeval churches, that of the B.V.M. Khrysopolitissa and that of St. George. The former is a well-preserved example of a mediaeval church of the fifteenth century. The interior was once completely covered with mural paintings, but little remains now; the best is the Dormition of the Virgin, over the south door. St. George's is a large sixteenth-century church now in ruins, save for the west end, in which the ribs of the vaulting are carried on pillars with plain capitals.

EVDHIMOU (lii)

The village is now completely Turkish, but during the Middle Ages it was the centre of a barony of the same name. A mediaeval writer informs us that it was founded by Ptolemy Philadelphus in honour of his sister Arsinoe, but this is unlikely. It is true, however, that it was the fief of Jean d'Ibelin, Count of Jaffa, and it was on the shore near the village that the Mamluks with 150 ships and more than 3,000 troops landed in 1426.

The principal mosque is erected on the site of the ancient church, a number of stones from which are built into its walls. Nothing remains of the mediaeval village, which lies half a mile south, save the gaunt walls of a large church dedicated to the B.V.M., and a curious stone corbel with two human faces carved on it, which had for many years lain in the ruins of the church, but which is now preserved in the police station.

EVRYKHOU (xxviii)

A large and picturesque village of some antiquity, though both the village churches of St. George and St.

Marina date from the last century. The former contains an icon of its patron saint dated 1743.

About half a mile north of the village is a most interesting fifteenth-century church dedicated to St. Kyriakos, which is an untouched example of the mediaeval tomb church for a local saint. On the north side is a small chapel which contains the altar tomb of St. Kyriakos. The archway above the entrance of this chapel has been painted with a geometric design of small shields, which probably bore coats of arms. A number of paintings are still visible through the whitewash, including two saints, with nimbi. The iconostasis is a good example of sixteenth-century work, and is surmounted by a large dark-green bronze rood cross, an unusual feature. There is a processional icon of Christ of the seventeenth century, and in the apse is preserved a fine but damaged sixteenth-century icon of the B.V.M.

EYLENJA (xxi)

The original mediaeval church was partially excavated in the face of the sandstone cliff which overshadows the village, but all that now survives is the south wall, with remains of paintings of two periods, of which a St. George of the second period is the best preserved. The building which has taken the place of the mediaeval church is a poor modern shed, and contains an icon of the B.V.M. dated 1609, in a very fair state of preservation. There is also a much damaged icon of St. John the Baptist of the same period.

The other church in the village is dedicated to St. George, and was built in 1866. It contains a large icon of its patron saint dated 1792, and a charming baroque proskenetarion.[1] This village was the headquarters of the Turkish army at the siege of Nicosia in 1570.

About one mile from the village is the Government farm Athalassa, and attached to this *chiflic*, or farm, is a Church of St. George, built in 1793. It contains a contemporary icon of that saint, which is much revered by the local inhabitants, who when they suffer from fever dip a piece of

[1] Stand like a lectern on which the icon of the day is placed.

cotton in the oil of the lamp which always burns in front of the icon, and take it away to wear next the skin till they are cured. Close to Athalassa is the curious-looking, flat-topped hill of Leondari Vouno, a conspicuous sight in the flat plain which surrounds Nicosia. The history of Leondari Vouno goes back to about 3000 B.C. In 1888 Mr. M. R. James excavated a number of Bronze Age tombs at the south end of the plateau. During the Middle Ages the hill was fortified and a castle was built by James I of Lusignan in 1385; little now remains save a portion of a great tower. Up till 1870 a considerable amount of the castle was still standing, including the vaulted hall, the curtain wall, and two towers, but in that year the majority of it was pulled down to build the Church of Phaneromeni in Nicosia. The castle was known as La Cava from a large cistern cut in the rock, measuring twelve feet by fourteen. Mr. James dug to a depth of forty-nine feet without reaching the bottom of this cutting.

GALATA (xxxvii)

This village is famous throughout the Solea valley for its churches. The principal church of the village, dedicated to St. Sozomenos, was built in 1513. It is completely painted inside, while a number of most interesting paintings still survive on the exterior north wall. These include the Tree of Jesse, to the left of the north door; to the right are paintings of the Early Councils of the Church, while in the foreground are the crouching figures of the various heretics who were expelled by them. According to an inscription over the door the painting was done at the cost of several contributors, thirteen in all, by the hand of Simeon, son of Auxentis, who was also the painter of the neighbouring Church of the B.V.M. Podithou.

A number of chapels surround the village. St. Paraskevi was built in 1511; the paintings in the bema include one of the B.V.M. in Glory. The sixteenth-century chapels of St. George and St. Nicholas were also once painted, and still retain their carved pew ends.

About one mile below the village lies the Monastery of

Podithou. The monastic buildings are fast falling into decay, but the two churches are in a perfect state of preservation; both of them owe their erection to the munificence of the Venetian family of Zacharia. The largest, dedicated to St. Paraskevi, is a shed-like building with a covered veranda on three sides. On the exterior wall above the west door is a fine painting of the Madonna in Glory with donors, a man, his wife, and daughter, presenting to the Virgin a model of the church; in the far right-hand corner are two other donors kneeling, and a coat of arms, three stars on an azure field. Below the centre picture of the Virgin is a fresco of Christ healing the sick, while on each side of the door are life-size figures of St. Paraskevi and Christ. The interior contains two magnificent mural paintings. The Crucifixion, above the west door, and the Virgin in Glory, in the semi-dome of the apse. The latter is a magnificent piece of work, and in a perfect state of preservation; the blue background is of extreme beauty, and seen through the iconostasis has the colour of a summer sky at dawn. The iconostasis, partially restored in 1783, is a good example of sixteenth-century wood carving; in the centre and just below the rood is the Venetian Lion of St. Mark. The upper series of icons of large size are almost certainly early sixteenth century, but they are placed so high that it is difficult to distinguish them. The church also contains the following icons: St. Nicholas with a donor in the right-hand corner, *c.* 1600 in the screen itself, and a Christ painted on the back of an elaborate carved panel in front of a late sixteenth-century dower chest placed on a ledge against the north wall. The church contains a candlestick 4½ feet high, carved in the Italian manner with swags of foliage and bunches of grapes.

The other church is dedicated to the B.V.M. Theotokos; it is a small building of rough, unhewn stone and sun-dried brick, roofed with tiles.

The entire surface of the walls is decorated, the names of donor and painter being recorded in the fresco over the north door. This shows Christ enthroned, with an open book on the left knee and blessing with the right hand, between the Virgin and the Baptist, both standing. Below kneel the grey-bearded donor, his wife, infant son and three daughters; he holds a model of the church (incorrectly drawn as having a door in the south wall), and from his right middle finger hangs the key; the wife holds a rosary, the eldest daughter an open book. In front of the donor is a shield, apparently with his arms impaling those of his wife; the blazon seems to be as follows: dexter, gules, a palm-tree (?) argent; sinister, bendy of seven argent and azure, a lion rampant gules: and between this and Christ's footstool the following inscription is painted, with many ligatures and abbreviations, in black on a white ground:

"There was erected the sacred church of the most holy God-bearing and ever-virgin Mary by contribution and at cost of Messer Stefano Zacharia and of his wife Luisa, and pray ye for their happiness, amen; and it was painted at cost of Messer Polo Zacharia and of his wife Maddelena and of their children, bless ye them by the Lord.

"Their portrait was completed on the 17th December, indiction 15, 1511 of Christ."

"Hand of Symeon son of Axentes (-Auxentios)."

Since children are mentioned in the case of Paul Zacharia and not in that of Stephen, the family here depicted must be Paul's. On completing the interior of the church built by Stephen —who may have been his father or brother—Paul evidently had himself painted as donor of the finished building. The dating and signing of this dedication-scene presumably apply to it only; this panel is by the master Symeon, whereas the other scenes were probably in part executed by his pupils or assistants.[1]

The iconostasis is probably contemporary with the building. On each side of the holy doors is the same coat of arms, three stars, as in the Church of St. Paraskevi. One or two of the icons are probably sixteenth-century work, but are much decayed.

GALATARIA (xlvi)

The Church of the B.V.M. Galatoussa is a delightful stone building of 1768, with a sundial on the north wall. In the bema is kept a very fine untouched icon of the B.V.M. Chrysogalactotrephoussa, with a kneeling male donor in

[1] Buckler, *Journal Hellenic Studies*, Vol. LIII, p. 107.

a black dress and a cape of about 1520. There are also two damaged icons, one of the B.V.M. Galatoussa of the sixteenth century, with scenes from the Madonna's life round the edge of the raised frame; the other also of the B.V.M. The former icon is much resorted to by owners of animals, both Greek and Turk, when the milk of their beasts fails; the other, painted in pure Byzantine style, may possibly be fifteenth century.

About two miles outside the village and near the river is a small chapel dedicated to St. Nicholas, built on the side of a vast mass of rock, which is a prominent feature in the landscape. According to inscriptions in the bema, it was built in 1550, and still retains its mural paintings, but these are much blackened by the smoke from the fires which the shepherds will build in it during the winter months. The handles of the south door are covered with hair from the tails of animals, for all the Turks and Greeks of the district firmly believe that if their beasts are ill they must cut off a few hairs from their tails and tie them to the handle of the church door, and then take oil from the lamp which burns in the church and anoint the animal with it. In order to make the cure even more efficacious, the beast, if possible, should be led three times round the church.

GALINI (xviii)

The small shed-like building of St. John the Baptist contains nothing save a large and fine icon of Christ of the late seventeenth century. Built into the exterior north wall of the apse is a fine marble statue of a woman, about half life-size, the head and shoulders missing, and of the second century B.C. This must undoubtedly have come from ruins of the temple of Isis at Soli.

GALINOPORNI (iv)

The village is inhabited by Moslems. About a mile outside and close to the ruined Church of St. Anna is a remarkable tomb not unlike that of Ayios Simeon, but far more easy of access. It has for long been used as a stable for goats and sheep, which accounts for the fact that it is filled with dust and dirt to a depth of 2 feet. It is 69 feet long, but, unlike the other great tomb at Ayios Simeon, it has no aisles, only side chambers which run from a central nave at right angles, each about 20 feet long by 10 across. It is about 9 feet high, and the cutting, which has been carried out with a small adze-like tool with blade about an inch broad, is hardly so careful.

At Galinoporni a hundred other rock-cut graves honeycomb the eastern slope on which the village is built: the houses are often built on to them, and they are used as inner rooms, as storechambers, as stables—indeed the natives are half troglodyte. Many of these tombs are square pits sunk into a flat plateau of rock, and would therefore have been open to the sky had they not been covered with a lid of some kind; the ledges on which this lid rested are seen an inch or two below the top of the tomb walls.[1]

GASTRIA (xv)

Little now remains of the Castle of Gastria save a few foundations of rock-cut cisterns about a mile from the village, situated on a promontory overlooking the sea. It was built by the Templars in 1191, and destroyed by King Henry II at the beginning of the fourteenth century. Amadi says that King Hugh III destroyed the castle in 1278, but it is still spoken of in 1310, and it was from a little port beneath the castle that Henry II was forced to embark for Armenia by the usurper Amaury, Prince of Tyre.

The principal church of the village is modern. The former Church of St. George is now used as a school but still contains a few early damaged icons. By the sea-shore is the ruined Chapel of St. John. Glass mosaic cubes can be picked up here in large numbers, and it is possible that a Byzantine church of some importance stood on the site.

GOURRI (xxxviii)

The Church of St. George was built in 1775, and the iconostasis is contemporary. It contains very little of interest save a large and fine rood cross of 1692.

[1] *Devia Cypria*, p. 76.

Some of the houses in this village would seem to be of the eighteenth century, and the doors, window frames, etc., are of well-carved woodwork.

The name of the village is interesting as identifying it with the great mediaeval family of Gourri. Their coat of arms, a sun displayed, is found in several places in the Island, Famagusta, Kellia, etc. One of the members of the family was Jacques du Gourri, Visconte of Nicosia, who was a great supporter of Queen Charlotte. He was assassinated in 1457 by the Queen's half-brother, James II, the last King of Cyprus.

GYPSOS (xiv)

The Church of St. John the Baptist was built in the late eighteenth century, and contains an icon of St. Peter dated 1719. Outside the south door lies a well-preserved late Corinthian marble capital.

In the centre of the village stands the sixteenth-century Church of St. George, a double-aisled building, perhaps originally a single-aisled church with a second aisle added at a later date, for the exterior of one of the apses is hexagonal, while the other is rounded. The altar is formed from a magnificent fragment of a Byzantine marble plaque carved with a geometric pattern, possibly dating from the twelfth century. The early eighteenth-century proskenetarion has an unusual feature, in that the lower panels are painted with portraits of the four evangelists. Outside lies a vast circular stone font, which according to village tradition was used for the baptism of those of riper years. The church is much frequented by those whose animals stray, for a candle lit to St. George will ensure that the wandering beast will return to its owner. The icon of St. George is also accredited with curing epilepsy.

INIA (xxxv)

The Church of the Archangel Michael in the centre of the village is ruined, but a fine boss with a cross in relief lies amid the tumbled stonework. Outside the village stands the Church of St. James, a small mediaeval building with fragments of frescoes on its walls. A most unusual feature is that a small Chapel of St. Agapios is joined to the main Church of St. James, the apse forming its west end; the only entrance is on the south side. It is impossible to explain this except by the supposition that the second church formed the tomb chamber of some saint.

KAIMAKLI (xxi)

The Church of St. Barbara is a huge building in the usual depraved early twentieth-century style. In the Women's Gallery is kept an early eighteenth-century iconostasis and icons from a previous building. Of these probably the most interesting are those of St. John the Baptist, late seventeenth century, the B.V.M. dated 1763, and a pair of well-painted eighteenth-century icons of SS. Theodore and Dimitrianos.

About a mile from the village is situated a small church dedicated to the Archangel Michael and dating from the eighteenth century. The vault is decorated with porcelain plates of the same period. In front of the iconostasis is a mediaeval tombstone bearing the effigy of a man and a coat of arms of three crosses, but it has been almost complately obliterated by the feet of the villagers.

In the apse is a fragment of another tombstone of the same period.

The village takes its name from the farm which was here and which supplied Nicosia with *kiamak*, or clotted cream, a favourite Turkish dish.

KAKOPETRIA (xxxvii)

One of the most picturesque villages in Cyprus, with its houses wandering up the valley in a long straggling cobbled street, which follows the course of a mountain torrent rushing through a narrow gorge. The woodwork of the houses is stained dark by the sun, and the roof tiles have weathered a deep brown. Like the neighbouring village of Galata, Kakopetria is famous for its churches and chapels. The principal church of the village is dedicated to the Transfiguration, and was built in the late eighteenth century, but a restoration has robbed it of most of its interest.

The Church of St. Nicholas lies about two miles from the village up the valley. The domed church probably dates from the fourteenth century; it has been covered with a shed roof at some later period. The interior is completely painted, the frescoes of various periods. Those in the narthex are probably to be assigned to about 1430, to judge by the costumes of the donors. In the north-east bay of the narthex lies one of the most interesting icons in the island. It is the same size and date as the icon of the Virgin in St. Kassianos, Nicosia, already described, and may well have been painted by the same hand. In the centre is St. Nicholas, while on either side are scenes from the life of the saint; in the left-hand bottom corner is shown the donor, a knight in full armour mounted on a horse, whose trappings bear his master's coat of arms, an eagle displayed gules. This icon is perhaps unique in that it is painted on vellum. A finely carved pair of doors leads from the narthex into the body of the church, also completely painted. The earliest frescoes, perhaps *c.* 1320, are in the south aisle; the majority of the remaining paintings are either 1623 or 1735. The donor of the former is depicted on a north-east pier supporting the dome, below a fresco of St. Peter. The other icons are of no special interest. At the west end is preserved a fine marble font.

The Chapel of the B.V.M. Theotokou has remains of mural paintings on the exterior north wall, and the fine frescoes in the interior date from 1511; the best is a painting on the north wall, the Dormition of the Virgin: she lies on her bed with head raised, with mourners to right and left; in the foreground the Archangel cuts off the hand of the Jew who impiously tried to touch the bier; behind stands Christ carrying in His arms the Virgin's soul, represented as a swaddled babe. Above the north door is a portrait of the donor and a dedicatory inscription. The paintings in the apse are in an excellent state of preservation, including the Virgin in Glory, in the semi-apse, and on the south wall Abraham entertaining the angels. The iconostasis appears to have been an open rood screen, like that of Pedoulas. A curious fragment is placed above the holy doors in the centre of the iconostasis, and is a portion of a panel decorated with conventional flowers, etc.; it shows a kneeling female donor being crowned by Christ, and also a portion of an inscription. This fragment probably depicts the wife of the original builder. In the iconostasis is an icon of St. John the Evangelist dated 1638.

North of the village lies a small early sixteenth-century Chapel of St. George, but a rebuilding of the roof has damaged the painted interior. Over the window in the south wall is a painting of a skeleton, perhaps a *memento mori*. In the iconostasis is a sixteenth-century icon of the B.V.M. with kneeling donors. A portion of the original floor remains, consisting of terra-cotta slabs stamped with a crude figure of some female saint with a halo. Work of this type is at present unknown elsewhere outside Cyprus.

KALIANA (xxxvii)

The Church of SS. Joachim and Anna was originally built in the sixteenth century, but has since been restored, and additions have been made to the west end. There are considerable remains of paintings on the north wall, of which the best preserved is a large fresco of the forty martyrs. On the central roof beam are seventeen squares, which have at some time contained painted coats of arms. As far as one can judge from those surviving there are only two coats, which are in alternate squares, viz. a lion rampant regardant, and a palm-tree. They have been repainted so that the tinctures are different in nearly every case. These arms are not unlike those borne by the family of Zacharia, which are depicted in fresco in the Church of the B.V.M. Theotokos, at Galata. Fragments of the iconostasis are of the seventeenth century, and there are two very well preserved icons of the B.V.M. dating from the late sixteenth or early seventeenth century.

KALLEPIA (xlv)

The ancient Church of St. George is now disused. It is a building of unusual shape, being as much as ninety feet long, but very narrow, and the walls are of great thickness. On the apse has been erected a headless female stone statue, probably from some Roman temple in the neighbourhood. All the icons and furnishings have been removed from the church and placed in a modern building, also dedicated to St. George. The only dated icon is one of the B.V.M. of 1740, but there are two fine seventeenth-century wooden candlesticks about three feet high.

On a hill above the village stands the ruined church of Monasterni, with traces of frescoes on its walls.

KALOKHORIO (DAGH) (xxxviii)

The Church of St. George was originally built in 1633, and was repaired 200 years later. The north door belongs to the original building, and on the south wall is a painting of St. George and his Martyrdom, dated 1655. The iconostasis is of several periods, the holy doors having been painted by the priest Paul in 1639. A few early dedicated icons are to be found in the Women's Gallery, the best of these is one of St. George, who wears a red and gold cloak.

Close to the village are a number of Roman mine workings, and at Zigonas are the remains of a temple site.

KALOKHORIO (LARNACA) (xl)

The Church of St. Basil was built in 1732, and the narthex has been added recently. The iconostasis dates from 1852, and contains an icon of St. John the Baptist, of superior workmanship, painted in 1714.

KALOKHORIO (KAPOUTI) (xx)

The original church of the sixteenth century, dedicated to St. George, was during the nineteenth century incorporated into a larger building of which it now forms the south aisle. A number of wall paintings still remain, of which the best is the Resurrection, which appears to be above the usual average of Cypriote mural decoration. The church contains a few eighteenth-century icons, notably a Transfiguration, dated 1783, and a Baptism dated 1793.

KALOKHORIO (LIMASSOL) (xlviii)

The Church of St. George was built in 1768. On the north wall is a fresco of the patron saint of the church, while at the bottom corner is shown a donor priest presenting a model of the church to the saint.

The brass chandelier, which seems to be contemporary with the building, is of fine quality, as are two icons, the B.V.M. supported by St. John the Evangelist, and Christ with St. John the Baptist.

KALOPANAYIOTIS (xxxvii)

The village contains a large number of churches and chapels, far and away the most important being the ancient Monastery of St. John Lampadistes. This church is one of the most interesting in Cyprus, in that it is not only untouched, but shows the curious custom of apportioning a church between the Latin and the Orthodox rites. In this case the Latin chapel is on the north and the Orthodox church on the south, both under the same roof, and with no division between them. The church is entered by the small south-west door which leads into the narthex, the east wall of which is completely covered with paintings. At the corner, by this door, four donors are shown, in front two priests in white albs, with black and white cassocks beneath, and behind them a civilian and his wife, dressed in black robes. The rest of the paintings on this wall consist of scenes from the Life of Our Lord, the Day of Judgement, etc. The whole of the paintings in the narthex probably date from the early fifteenth century. The church itself is also completely painted, but those in the north or Latin chapel are infinitely superior to those in the Orthodox portion, for they all show a hand skilled in the art of the Italian Cinquecento. They are perhaps true frescoes; in the Orthodox churches the actual technique of fresco, i.e. painting on the damp plaster, was practically never employed. The whole of the west wall is occupied by a painting of the Tree of Jesse, while the east wall has above the semi-apse a large painting of the Old Testament Trinity, i.e. Abraham entertaining the angels. The vaulted ceiling, with its painted ribs and bosses, has busts of the twelve Apostles against a blue background. The two small doors in this chapel are superb examples of contemporary wood-carving. The paintings in the Orthodox church are much rougher, and differ but little from the usual mural paintings of late fifteenth-century churches. The colours are harsh and crude and the drawings ill-balanced, but yet have a strength and power from their very crudeness and brightness of colour. The most interesting thing in this portion of the church is the iconostasis, which is almost certainly the original Latin rood screen. In the centre of the "ceiling" is the Royal Lusignan coat of arms, while to left and right are the blazons of the noble families of Cyprus, d'Ibelin, Damperre, Giblet, etc.; the whole of the background of the screen and the lower panels are powdered with badges and arms of various families, all in the original tinctures. This screen, hitherto unnoticed, deserves the closest study. The icons, too, are of considerable interest, the most important being (1) B.V.M., Hodegetria or Conductress, given by the priest Joannikou in 1562; (2) St. John the Baptist, given on January 4, 1542, by the priest Meletios; (3) St. Philip, 1658, with two kneeling donors, a priest and his wife; (4) the B.V.M. Eleoussa, *c.* 1500; (5) The Archangel Michael, late fifteenth century, the frame decorated with figures of angels; (6) St. Heraclidios, with a portrait of the donor priest, who with his wife and family gave the icon to the church on November 21, 1543; (7) St. John the Baptist, late sixteenth century; (8) St. Marina, late sixteenth century; (9) St. John Lampadistes, the earliest icon in the church and probably *c.* 1400; scenes from the life of the saint decorate the frame. A number of early but much damaged icons lie in the bema, and here, too, is kept the base of a large florid baroque candlestick painted red and gold, Italian work of the sixteenth century. The tomb of the saint lies between the two chapels, his skull, enclosed in an early eighteenth-century gilt casket, is kept in a small niche, which is covered with the names of believers from outside the Island, who came to be cured of epilepsy during the eighteenth century, for St. John Lampadistes had a reputation which far transcended the boundaries of Cyprus.

St. John was born in the village of Lampas near Galata; he renounced matrimony for monasticism at an early age, and suffered the loss of his sight owing to the enchantments of the parents of the girl he had slighted. He died at the age of twenty-two, and was buried in the monastery which he had founded. Florio Boustron suggests that the saint derived his cognomen from Lambadisto, one of the ancient names of Troodos, which it received from the glittering snow by which it is covered during the winter months.

The churches and chapels which lie in or around the village are nearly all of interest. They are: (1) St. Kyriakos, now deserted, built in 1722, and still containing remains of the original wall painting. (2) St. Andronicos, a small early sixteenth-century chapel. Most of the original mural paintings still remain. The best is a Crucifixion; and on the west wall there is a fine early seventeenth-century icon of SS. Nicholas and Athanasia, and a much-damaged processional icon of Christ, *c.* 1650. In the iconostasis is a curious long panel painted with scenes from the Passion. (3) St. Marina, a large building of the nineteenth century. In the iconostasis are icons of Christ, 1765, and the B.V.M., 1768. In the gallery is kept a damaged icon of the early seventeenth century, painted on both sides; on one side is the B.V.M., and on the other the Presentation in the Temple. Here, too, is kept an icon of Christ of the same period, and a large St. Stephen of 1641. (4) B.V.M.: the church is modern, but the majority of the iconostasis is of the seventeenth century, as is a much over-painted icon of the Madonna and Child, which is so holy that it is always kept covered. (5) St. George: this tiny chapel contains a superb icon, Christ Pantokrator, *c.* 1500, with a tonsured priest kneeling in the corner. There is also an icon of the B.V.M., 1671. On the altar is kept a Gospel, printed in Venice in 1550, with a contemporary red leather binding, in the centre of which, in high relief, is a bronze repoussé plaque of the Archangel Michael. This is probably earlier than the Gospel itself, and may even date from the fifteenth century. (6) A small chapel on the hill above the village, dedicated to the Archangel Michael. It contains an icon of St. Michael of 1509.

About three miles from the village are the ruins of the B.V.M. Moliboskepasti, or "covered with lead", which seems to have been originally a Latin church. The story goes that when the Turks came to the valley in 1570 the Latin women and children were placed in this church for safety, while their menfolk went out to fight the invaders. The engagement took place on the other side of the valley, at a field now called Magolio, or the place of the slaughter, for the invading Moslems were victorious, and slew all; and to this day the fig-trees that grow in the valley have fruit red from the spilled blood which watered their roots.

KALOPSIDHA (xxxii)

During the Middle Ages the village was a fief of the Counts of Jaffa. The principal church, dedicated to the B.V.M., is probably mediaeval. A hexagonal marble column with a Byzantine capital lies outside the west door. The church contains a well-painted icon of the Dormition of the Virgin, of the late sixteenth century, which has unfortunately at some period been damaged by fire.

There is also a Chapel of St. John the Baptist, a double-aisled building of the seventeenth century, and an important Bronze Age cemetery was discovered here in 1894, the contents of which are now in the Ashmolean Museum, Oxford.

The village was destroyed by the Saracens in 1426.

Porcacchi in 1576 tells us: "In the village Calopsida grows the herb from which they make soap, and that with which they bleach camlet, for this and other cloths are made in great quantity. Cotton, however, is the real staple of the island."[1]

In 1894 excavations were carried out here of a Bronze Age settlement:

[1] Ref., *Excerpta Cypria*, p. 166.

The high road after leaving Kuklia village, runs nearly eastwards to Kalopsida, skirting the limestone plateau, which is here invaded by a southward bay of the marshes of the Pidiàs river. About a mile from Kuklia it passes a deserted farm (Daud Chiflik) on a low ridge between two small streams. The necropolis begins on the moor west of the first of these streams. The next ridge east of the chiflik is considerably higher, and is cut through by the road to a depth of 10–12 ft. In this cutting masses of broken pottery had been exposed; all hand-made, of a red or brown colour, like that from the tombs, but it lay in a compact mass among loose earth and stones, some of which seem to retain a wall-like arrangement. What made it clear that a settlement was in question, was a well-defined layer of cockle shells, often broken, about 18 inches from the surface, and two or three inches thick: this layer could be traced for some yards, and on both sides of the cutting. A little trenching on the north of the road, and close to the west brow of the ridge, revealed a fragment of wall built of unwrought stones of the size of a man's head and under, bound together by a mud cement which was clearly recognizable, and itself full of scraps of pottery.[1]

KAMBI PHARMAKAS (xxxviii)

The Church of St. George was built in 1800; the delightfully carved and painted women's gallery is contemporary. The iconostasis comes from a former building, and contains an icon of the B.V.M. dated 1709.

About a mile and a half from the village lies a ruined Chapel of St. George: close by is a holy well, near which is a stone with an illegible inscription and cross cut on it.

KAMBIA (xxxix)

The village is slowly moving with a landslide which will, in the course of time, completely destroy it, and the inhabitants are rebuilding their houses on a flat plateau close to the high-road.

The Church of St. George is an ancient rustic structure, which has undergone a disastrous restoration, during which the north and south aisles were destroyed. A few paintings remain on the walls, but they are probably not

[1] Myres, *Catalogue of Cyprus Museum*, p. 7.

earlier than the late seventeenth century. The iconostasis is dated 1770, and bears an inscription telling how two of the icons in it, those of St. John the Baptist and St. George, were both painted by a certain priest, Leontiou, who placed them there. The holy doors are dated 1731.

KAMBOS (xxvii)

The Church of St. Kyriakos, a large building with a steep pent roof, was restored in 1881. A perfectly hideous belfry of white stone has been added recently. The interior consists of a central nave, and two side aisles. In the iconostasis are icons collected from the various ruined chapels in the vicinity, mostly of the seventeenth and eighteenth centuries: the best preserved are of St. Nicholas and St. John the Baptist, and a long, narrow panel of the B.V.M. is not without merit.

Near the village is a locality known as Androuklos, which probably derives its name from the *Arbutus andrachna*. This shrub is mentioned by a Russian pilgrim, Zosinios, who visited the Island in 1421.

KAMBYLI (xi)

The village contains a domed mediaeval church dedicated to the B.V.M.; it would seem to have had at some earlier period a south aisle which has since disappeared. It is a good example of a village church of the fifteenth century, except for the restored west end.

Though now a Turkish village, Kambyli was until quite recently inhabited by Maronites, and it is mentioned as a Maronite village by Dandini, who was sent to Cyprus about 1650 by Pope Clement VIII on an apostolic mission to that sect.[1]

KAMINARIA (xxxvi)

The Church of St. George stands in the centre of the village, and is a large building of the early nineteenth century. It contains a fine icon painted in 1712 of the Day of Judgement.

[1] *Voyage to Mount Libanus*, London, 1675.

A number of interesting chapels surround the village. They are: (1) the B.V.M., a tiny building of the early sixteenth century perched high above the village. It must have fallen into disrepair at some period, but was reroofed and the west door blocked during the early nineteenth century. A considerable number of mural paintings still remain, of which the most interesting is a fragment of four donors, a woman and three men, the latter wearing flat hats exactly like a Holbein portrait. (2) St. Hermolaos dates from the eighteenth century, and contains an icon of SS. Cosmos and Damian dated 1740. St. Hermolaos was Bishop of Carpasia at the time of the Council of Chalcedon in A.D. 451. (3) About a mile from the village is the deserted Chapel of St. Basil, built at the beginning of the sixteenth century; it is now fast falling into ruin. A number of frescoes can still be seen, including portraits of donors on the north wall. The contemporary icons still stand in the broken screen; though badly blackened by smoke from the oil lamps which burn in front of them, they appear to be good examples of early sixteenth-century work.

KANDOU (liii)

This is now a completely Moslem village, but three mediaeval chapels remain in the neighbourhood. Two of them are of the fifteenth century, namely the B.V.M. Khrysopolitissa and St. Marina. Little remains of the former, but the latter was once completely painted; St. George and his Martyrdom, on the north wall, is still in a good state of preservation. The third chapel, dedicated to Ayia Napa, the Holy Handkerchief of St. Veronica, lies about two miles from the village in the valley of the Kouris river. Save that the doors have long since disappeared, it remains a perfect example of a sixteenth-century chapel. The interior was completely painted, but time and damp have destroyed the majority of the frescoes, though it is still possible to discern dimly the Dormition of the Virgin, St. George, St. Paraskevi, etc., and on the north wall are the remains of an unidentifiable scene with what appear to be kneeling donors in the corner; one of them wears a curious green helmet with a white plume. This church, so isolated, so obscure, set in a poor cornfield covered with stones, which once doubtless formed the houses of the hamlet that it served, seems to have a claim and charm denied to others of the same period and style. There is something strangely moving in the gradual decay of this tiny building. Nothing now remains of its decoration save a few paintings rapidly flaking to decay and the cippus from some Roman tomb, which once supported the altar in its narrow apse, a curious example of the mingling of paganism and Christianity.

KANNAVIA (xxxvii)

The village church is of no interest. Close by lies the small Monastery of the B.V.M. Theotokos, which was built in the early eighteenth century. The contemporary iconostasis has unfortunately been repainted. The name of this village is derived from the *Cannabis sativa*, or hemp.

KANTARA (vii)

This is the third of the fortresses which protect the northern range of the Island. Although the least important, the view from the top is possibly even finer than that obtainable from St. Hilarion or Bouffavento.

You stand on the spine of a serrated limestone chain which, falling gradually on the right, runs out between two turquoise seas, and on the left bends northwards in a vast blue crescent, jagged like a crown. Two thousand feet below, to the north, lies a narrow strip of forest, and across a misty sea, crawling into innumerable tiny bays, you may descry the wild Taurus of Karamania, rising step by step to the snows. And commanding all this matchless prospect stands Kantara itself on a pillar of rock, its broken walls clinging to the lip of the precipice, and its great gate opening on a labyrinth of ruin, crowned by a little windy chapel. No painter has conceived a fairy castle more fantastic, no poet set his enchanted palace in a solitude more profound.[1]

[1] *Devia Cypria*, p. 101.

The castle was probably built in the closing years of the thirteenth century. It is situated on a large isolated mass of rock with steep precipices on three sides. The main entrance is on the east, and here the fortifications are well preserved. The main gate was defended by a small enclosure, now much destroyed, but at each end still stand small round towers with their battlements complete. Above this rises a high wall with two flanking towers; that on the north is provided with a turret of unusual form, with seven loopholes. A number of vaulted chambers still survive in the interior; they are in a good state of preservation, and some still retain their roofs. On one side of the main entrance is a guard-room, with an oubliette beneath.

The castle is mentioned but little in history. During the Genoese invasion it was held by the royalists, and provided a sanctuary for the unhappy Prince of Antioch, who was held prisoner in Famagusta. He escaped from there and reached Kantara, owing to the devotion of his faithful servant.

When the prince's cook Galeftira saw all this, that his lord the prince was in great straits (and fettered), and tormented to make him disclose his goods, and that he was a very long time in the castle, (he grew afraid that they would put him to death. And) he began to think how he could deliver him from prison: and even so it befell. And he says to him: "Sir, I am full of grief, to see the king and his mother (confined and guarded) in their lodgings, (and the knights in prison,) and you in prison (in the castle, as if you were a murderer or a robber). And it seems to me that they have evil intentions against you, for they hate you much; (because, if their intention was not bad, they would not have inprisoned you and put you in chains.) But, if you are willing to put yourself into bodily danger, (I have in my mind) by the power of God, how to bring you out from here." The prince said to him: "What you say pleases me, and I will do what you tell me, and let things be as God grants." And on the morrow he brought a kitchen boy with a pair of broad boots; and he brought the prince into the kitchen, and tied his irons high up his leg with a knot, and put the boots on him and fastened them in place, and dressed him in the boy's clothes; and he was covered with smuts. And he put a copper pot on his head and a little copper pot in his hand, and said to him, in case he were questioned by anyone: "Tell him that you are taking the pots to be tinned." And he brought him out of the castle, and out of the gate of Famagusta, and took him to his country estate at Kolota, and there he mounted him on the mare belonging to the captain of the castle and took him to Kantara.[1]

The castle was abandoned by the Venetians in 1525.

The Monastery of Kantara is of little importance, and the church is probably not older than the eighteenth century. The site, however, is ancient, and in the thirteenth century the monastery here was the centre of the resistance of the Orthodox Church to the Latin clergy. Two monks, John and Konon, from one of the monasteries on Mount Athos, who determined to come across and help their brethren in Cyprus against the Latin Church, settled at Kantara and collected round them a band of disciples. Soon the Latin clergy heard of this and decided to test the accuracy of the report. Two of them, therefore, went to Kantara, and began to question John and Konon about their religious beliefs. At first their answers proved satisfactory, but this did not last for long, and a division of opinion came over the use of leavened or unleavened bread by their respective Churches. The argument waxed fiercer, and at last one of the Latin monks, by name Andrew, put aside all pretence of friendship and summoned the two Orthodox monks to appear before the Archbishop of Nicosia to answer for the disrespectful way in which they had spoken of the Roman Mass. The news of this soon spread over the Island, and excited crowds met the monks outside Nicosia, kneeling in front of them and beseeching their prayers. The Latin Archbishop Eustorgius asked them if the reports that he had heard of their insubordination were true. John and Konon, beholding that their long-expected martyrdom for the Orthodox faith could not be far distant, answered boldly; hoping to shake their spirit, the Archbishop confined them in prison, where they were maltreated and tortured by their gaolers. In prison they remained for three years, till the

[1] *Chronicle of Makhairas*, p. 399.

Archbishop, despairing of ever being able to make them submit, sought instructions from Pope Gregory IX, who directed him to treat them as heretics. Eustorgius, therefore, handed them over to the tender mercies of their vindictive accuser, Andrew. They were brought before the King and were sentenced to death, the execution to be carried out with all the revolting cruelty of the Middle Ages. They were tied by the feet to the tails of horses and were dragged over the rough stones in the river beds till the very flesh was torn from their bones, and were finally burnt.

KAPEDHES (xxxix)

The Church of the B.V.M. was built in 1731, but in 1880 a fire damaged the interior and the mural paintings on its walls. The iconostasis was erected, according to an inscription on one of the lower panels, in 1753, during the time of Archbishop Philotheos. Philotheos (1734–1759) was born in the village of Galata. Kyprianos describes him as a man of generous disposition, a friend of the poor, and an ornament to the exalted office which he filled. He journeyed to Constantinople to implore the Grand Vizier to help the unfortunate peasant overwhelmed by the crushing burden of taxes imposed by the Turkish Government. Before he could lay his case before the Grand Vizier, complaints had reached the Sultan from Cyprus that the Archbishop himself had illegally exacted money from the Cypriotes. The Archbishop was arrested and sent back to Cyprus in chains and cast into prison, and the see was filled by a certain Neophytos, a youth of evil life and drunken habits. The people of Cyprus, however, refused to accept this intruder, who soon died, worn out by his vices, and Philotheos was restored to the throne.

KAPILIO (xlvii)

The village stands on a hill, and the stone-built houses with weathered tiles give it a certain air of antiquity. About a mile and a half from the village is the Church of the B.V.M. of the Vineyards, probably dating from the fifteenth century. The structure itself is in an excellent state of repair, and the interior was once completely painted, but most of this has now disappeared. The iconostasis is of the type of a mediaeval rood screen and still remains *in situ*. Near the church lie several ancient mills, a fragment of an aqueduct, and two chapels now in ruins. It would seem, therefore, as if a mediaeval village of some importance must have existed here.

KARAVAS (xi)

An important and rich village, famous for its fruit-trees. The Church of St. George was built in the last years of the eighteenth century and contains a charmingly decorated iconostasis and women's gallery, the panels of which are painted with flowers and conventional landscapes, etc. In this gallery is kept a large icon with a portrait of its donor priest, a certain Levrendi.

The Church of St. Irene was built in the early nineteenth century and is situated on a hill above the village; from here a superb view of the coast of Kyrenia and the distant hills of Asia Minor can be obtained. The church contains an attractive icon of five saints dated 1767.

KARAVOSTASI (xix)

At present Karavostasi is the port where the copper mined by the American Company at Skouriotissa is exported, and is nothing but a collection of hovels and shanties with the great crushing plant of the copper company rising in the centre. In the Middle Ages the port was known as St. Efxifios or St. Auxibios. According to Makhairas, it was here that Queen Helena Palaeologus landed on her arrival in Cyprus to marry King John II. This Queen Helena calls for more than passing notice: she was described by Pope Pius II as being "treacherous and sagacious, an adept in Greek treachery, hostile to the Latin religion, and an enemy of the Roman Church".[1] She was a strong and determined woman, who completely dominated her husband, and it was through her influence that the Greeks acquired a footing at Court at the expense of the Latins.

[1] Lusignan, *Chorograffia di Cipro*, Bologna, 1572, p. 60.

She was of a jealous disposition, and Etienne de Lusignan relates a story of how she quarrelled with her husband's mistress, Mary of Patras, and in a sudden access of jealousy bit off the end of her nose. This Mary was the mother of the bastard James II, the last King of Cyprus.

Near Karavostasi are the remains of the ruins of Soli. Little now remains of what was one of the most famous cities in Cyprus and capital of one of its nine kingdoms. It is said to have originally been called Oepea, and that the founder was Demophon son of Theseus. According to tradition, in 600 B.C. Philocyprus, then King of Oepea, transferred his capital to a more suitable site, on the advice of the famous philosopher Solon, in whose honour the king renamed it Soli.

The town probably reached the zenith of its importance during the Roman era; during early Christian times Soli gave its name to one of the Orthodox sees, and during the Latin domination it was the residence of the Orthodox Bishop of Nicosia. Little remains now but heaps of stones, though Pococke, who visited the ruins in 1738, speaks of the remains of temples, triumphal arches, and porticoes, all of which have long since disappeared. Their destruction can be explained by the fact that not only has Soli been used by the neighbouring villages as a stone quarry, but by the fact that sailing-boats came from Egypt to collect stone for the building of the quays at Port Said. In 1930 the Swedish Archaeological Expedition excavated a Roman theatre here of the first century A.D., which is now fenced in and is accessible to the public; and two years later they excavated the Temple of Isis, Aphrodite, and Serapis, the statuary from which is now on view in the Cyprus Museum. The site of the temple has again been filled up and nothing is now visible save ploughed fields.

KARPASIA (xi)

A Maronite village. The Church of the Holy Cross is an ancient structure which has recently been rebuilt. Outside the west door lies a marble cippus with a much-damaged inscription. The church contains a fine early seventeenth-century rood cross and two icons of the B.V.M. of the same period.

KATHIKAS (xxxv)

A large Church of the B.V.M. was built in 1870, to the south of which can still be traced the ground plan of an ancient chapel of St. Epatios. Nothing now remains save the altar slab which rests on a pile of stones. Those who are lame must walk or crawl three times round the altar invoking the name of the saint: the last recorded cure was in 1930.

KATODHRYS (xlix)

The ancient Church of the B.V.M. has recently been restored, and the interior painted a crude blue; only the apse and north wall remain from the former building. Fragments of sixteenth-century mural painting remain in the interior, more especially a St. George. In the church is preserved a large wooden cross with a smaller bronze one inset in the centre.

Half-way between this village and Vavlas lies the Monastery of St. Minas, a most delightful spot. The church is a large building with semi-vaulted cloisters round three sides of it, that on the north being supported by heavy flying buttresses. The monastery was rebuilt by Parthenios, Bishop of Kition, in 1754, and the icons, iconostasis, women's gallery, and chandeliers are untouched from the day they were placed here. On the north and south walls are paintings of St. George and St. Minas, dated 1757, which were done by a certain Philaritos of Amathus, who also, according to an inscription on its back, brought from Parsada the magnificent sixteenth-century icon of the Virgin and Child, which, alas, he or some other artist has touched up. In the church is kept a mediaeval plate, in the centre of which Adam and Eve are shown eating of the Tree of Knowledge, round which the serpent is twined. The gravestone in the centre of the church is supposed to mark the tomb of a certain Pasha, but why a Moslem should be buried in a Christian building the villagers are unable to explain. The monastic buildings entirely surround the church and on the north side are two storeys in height.

St. Minas the Glorious was an Egyptian martyr of the third century.

KATOKOPIA (xx)

The ancient Church of the B.V.M. was rebuilt in 1818; it contains some interesting late sixteenth-century wall paintings, unhappily restored, such as the Raising of Lazarus, and a fragment of a colossal painting of the Archangel Michael. The whole of the apse is covered with most interesting paintings of the Communion of the Apostles; to the left of the small window in the bema the giving of bread, to the right the giving of wine. Each painting measures about 6 feet by 4 feet, and is probably the work of some foreign artist. The disciples are ranged in a long line and look towards Our Lord, save Judas, who, in each painting, looks back over his shoulder.

KATYDHATA (xxviii)

The Church of St. John the Evangelist was rebuilt in 1870, and a few fragments from a former church are built into its walls, such as a panel of a cypress-tree between two lions. The ribs of the interior vaulting are supported on the north and south by two marble columns with Corinthian capitals, which probably came from the ruins of Soli.

Not far from the village is the small Monastery of Skouriotissa, dedicated to the B.V.M.; it was probably restored in 1845, which is also the date of the principal icon of Christ. Outside the church lie two large fragments of a marble frieze, one with a Byzantine cross cut on it. The church contains a few large and much damaged early icons, one of which has a fragment of a donor in the corner. The monastery takes its name from the slag heaps (scoriae) from the ancient mines which surround it. These copper mines have always been a source of wealth to the island and were at one time farmed by Herod the Great; they are now being worked by an American company.

KAZAPHANI (xii)

A corruption of the words Casal Epiphani or village of St. Epiphanius. It contains a small well-preserved mediaeval church dedicated to the Virgin of the River. On the north and west sides the church is enclosed with an unusual kind of narthex in the form of an aisle. At the west end of this narthex, added later, and against a south wall, is a well-preserved mediaeval wall tomb under a canopied arch; the tomb slab is engraved with a figure of a man in a civilian costume of the fourteenth century, but no inscription remains to give any clue to the person portrayed; a tradition still exists in the village that his three daughters are buried with him. It is possible that he was the founder of the church.

The whole church was once covered with frescoes, but they are now much damaged and decayed. The best preserved is a Day of Judgement, which fills the west wall.

There is also another church, dedicated to the Archangel Michael, in the village; a barrel-vaulted building of the late eighteenth century. In its churchyard lies a small classical sarcophagus of the same period and style as the much larger and better-known one at Bella Paise. Makhairas says:

> Also in the district of Casa Piphana there is a place lined with slabs full of relics, and these saints are called the Saints Manifested, and their relics dried up and came to be set hard like stone or something heavy as it were stone: and these are of the Three Hundred who fled from Syria.[1]

These relics are probably those at the Chapel of St. Phanourios, near Ayios Yeoryios.

KEDHARES (xlvi)

Outside the village is the Church of St. Anthony, a charming seventeenth-century building with a steeply pitched roof, which has recently been restored and now contains nothing of interest.

[1] *Chronicle of Makhairas*, p. 32.

In the modern village Church of St. John the Baptist are kept the icons which came from St. Anthony, including one of Christ, dated 1628, and another of SS. Cosmas and Damian, 1724.

KELLAKI (xlviii)

The Church of St. Marina was built in 1744, and was much restored in 1885 when a west front was added. It contains nothing of interest save a late eighteenth-century oil-painting on canvas of St. Paraskevi, an unusual relic to find in an Orthodox church, as nearly all icons are painted on wood.

About two miles from the village is the tiny Chapel of the B.V.M. Glossa, an ancient chapel recently rebuilt. It is supposed to take its name from a miraculous icon of the Madonna which cures dumbness.

KELLIA (xl)

The Church of St. Anthony is a cruciform building with a narthex on the west and south sides, and a curious sort of high transept which takes the place of the more usual dome. A number of fragments of sculpture of various periods lie outside, or have been built into the walls of this mediaeval church. On the west narthex is half the top of a white marble sarcophagus, with the face of a bearded man in relief, imitated from an Egyptian mummy case and dating from about 400 B.C. The marble is smoothly dressed but unpolished, and is probably from Syria. A complete specimen of this type of coffin-lid was found by Cesnola and is now in the Metropolitan Museum in New York.

Over the door of the east narthex is the coat of arms of the Gourri family, a sun displayed, while the door slab of the south door is possibly part of a Renaissance tomb. The interior was once completely decorated with paintings, but these have now all been whitewashed over. The lintel of the west door is formed of a stone with an inscription in the ancient Cypriote character, supposed to have come from the ancient Kition. Dr. Ross attempted in vain to remove this stone in 1850, with the idea of giving it to some

European museum. The iconostasis is early seventeenth century, but has an icon of the B.V.M. of 1695, which has been completely over-painted.

KELOKEDHARA (xlvi)

About three miles from the village is the Monastery of Santi. The church, dedicated to the B.V.M. Eleousa, is a large and carefully constructed building of about 1500. It consists of a single nave with a large and high hexagonal dome, and a square apse in the centre. What little remains of the iconostasis is in an excellent state of preservation; this finely carved and gilded work is probably contemporary with the building of the monastery. The icons are not nearly so well preserved; the best is a long sixteenth-century panel of the Transfiguration, and there is also a much damaged, but earlier, processional icon of St. George, with scenes from the Saint's life round the frame, in which the figures wear mediaeval vestments and armour. The monastic buildings, which form three sides of a square, have been rebuilt.

Across the river lies the ruins of a church dedicated to St. Paraskevi. According to a local legend this church was built by a craftsman who had as his apprentice a youth who showed great aptitude at his work. The pupil soon outstripped the master, and when quite young was given the responsible task of building the Monastery of Santi. When the work was finished, the young architect asked his former master to come and see it, taking him all over the building and even up on to the roof to admire the famous dome, of which he was inordinately proud. Standing there the master could look across to his own Church of St. Paraskevi, and suddenly realized how poor and mean it looked beside the magnificent building of his former pupil. Overcome by jealousy and in a sudden access of fury, he pushed the youth so that he fell onto the cobbles beneath and was instantly killed. It is curious how this story is common to nearly every country, perhaps the best-known variation being that of the master's apprentice of Rosslyn Chapel.

KHANDRIA (xxxvii)

The Church of St. George is a nineteenth-century building and contains an iconostasis from a former church. A curious feature of the building is that the roof of the south aisle is carried on wooden pillars, each formed from a single pine-tree. The church has no belfry, and the church bell is hung in the branches of a vast pine-tree which overshadows the west door of the church.

KHARCHA (xiii)

The Church of the Archangel was built in the middle of the nineteenth century, with a floor formed of rounded pebbles set closely together. In the gallery are two good icons, the first of Christ in Glory, with a male and female donor and the date 1521, and the other an Italian picture of the B.V.M. and Child, in an elaborate contemporary frame, the triangular top of which contains a painting of the Crucifixion. The icon is damaged, but is far above the usual wooden standard of Cypriote art, and is certainly not later than the early sixteenth century.

KHIROKITIA (xlix)

Below the village is the field of the Battle of Khirokitia, which proved so fatal to the people of Cyprus. It was on July 7, 1426, that the Saracens utterly defeated King Janus and his army, a blow from which the already tottering Kingdom of Cyprus never recovered. The King himself was taken prisoner, and his brother, the Prince of Galilee, and the flower of his army were slain. Janus himself was taken to Cairo and forced to ride through its streets "chained on a lame ass, with his banners carried before him reversed". Two accounts have come down to us of this battle, one written by Strambaldi, the other by Makhairas, who was actually present at the fight:

On the morning of Friday the fifth of July 1426 after Christ the king with all his army came to Kherokitia; and they lodged in the tower of Kherokitia with the knights, and the rest of the army pitched tents; others made themselves shelters (?). And they were spread over so much ground that when the herald had to give an order,—for they had no trumpet,—he would start out early and not have made the full rounds by midday; and if he had to publish another order, he would start out at midday and not have finished his round by nightfall.

The Saracens wrote a letter and sent it to the king; and they sent it to him by a villager. And it was as follows: "Valorous lord, we have come to this country, and you have not, as befits a son of our lord the sultan, sent any one of your people to receive us and to find out what are our desires and our demands. Now we send you this message, that you must come forth to us, that we may make a fresh bond together with stipulations of peace; and on these terms, that you do not allow the pirates and other freebooters to harass us, and that you do not give them the hospitality of your country, but that you take our friends as your friends and our enemies as your enemies, like good friends and neighbours. And our lord the sultan has given us his carpet which we are to spread out for you to sit upon. And when you come, we will speak together and you will be well pleased: and we will leave you in peace and go back again to our master. And know this, that if you do not come to us, we will come to you. And be very sure that Sunday will not pass by without our meeting one another." And when they were reading the letter, (the knights) laughed at them, because they were displeased with the style of the letter: and others muttered, and said: "They are beguiling and deceiving us." And they seized the envoy who had been brought by Picquigny, and put him to torture; and they treated him so cruelly that they brought him to his death, a wicked and treacherous act which had never been done to an envoy.

In the same way another envoy, who had been seized by Sir Thomas Provosto, they put into the Tower of the Arsenal at Lefkosia and kept him there. And the (numerous) Saracen slaves who had been baptized and were at Lefkosia, they forcibly prevented (from leaving the town on pain of death, for fear they should turn and) join the Saracens. And this was a foolish thing to be doing for there were many baptized Saracens who, (as soon as they heard of the king's defeat,) ran away (from fear) and hid themselves in the mountains, that they might not be caught by the Saracens. And among these were George of Damat, who made powdered sugar and Syrip, being a sugar-boiler; also Theotoki the king's builder, and Nicholas the son of the bathman, Michael the tax-gatherer, the Syrian freedman,

Paul the bishop's slave, the slave of the Makhaira monastery, and the slave called Stavrias of the monastery of Megalos Stavros, and many others who chose rather to die than to fall into the hands of the Saracens. But, since God chose to deprive the officers and the councillors of wisdom, they did everything perversely; thus too they dealt with the lives of the poor folk, to wit the poor envoy and the poor baptized Saracens as well.

Now we will return to the king and to his army which was lodged at Kherokitia. You must know that our scouts came in on Saturday the sixth of July 1426 and reported that the Saracens were making ready to attack our army. Then (the king) issued an order to all his men to come to bivouack round about the tower; and this was done. And at midnight there was a (great) portent: a great star was in the heaven, and fell down above the tower. And the people trembled and said: "O God, may this portent be against the prince, and not against our lord the king!" And all night they kept watch, to guard the king. And the wine ran out; there were no more than four loads. The king was angry with Podocataro, because he had not brought wine (for the army).

And when God's blessed Sunday dawned, the seventh of July 1426, the people came to get wine (for the army). And Messire Badin de Nores, the Marshal of Jerusalem, gave an order to me, Leontios Makhairas; "He must not give wine to any one in the field, until supplies are brought". The men were using violence to get the wine served out to them; so much so that one seized a full load, others a wine-skin; others seized upon heifers and animals. And there arose contention and a great riot in front of the tower where the wine was stored. When the said Messire Badin de Nores saw their violence and how they were carrying off all the wine, he came down the steps of the tower, and used the people so violently that a lad called Henry Scarama said to him: "Sir, will you drive us away with blows? Where are we to go to get wine to drink, that we may face our enemies?" The said marshal grew angry and hit him over the head, and the blow knocked off the said Henry's hood. Others went to the threshing-floor and carried off sheaves of corn as fodder for their horses; and they ate and filled their bellies as though they had been swine.

And when the king had finished eating, some men came with the news that the Saracens were "close at hand". And he, the king, put a steel cap on his head and went down to mount his horse; and Sistros Grellios who should have carried the standard was not there, and the king saw Peter David Fava and ordered him to take the standard, and carry it before him. And at the moment Sistros appeared, and was given the standard. And (before mounting) the king sent an order round by his herald that all (small and great should mount their horses and) arm themselves. And all round him the ground was level, and so he ordered the foot-soldiers to take their equipment and to stand each man close up to the next so as to be like a wall. And they had prepared a hundred large shields. And behold before them some of the advance guard wounded by the Saracens, and these were Scarmoutsa and Constantine, whose father was the priest, the brother of Sir Leon the bishop of the Armenians; and as soon as he came he fell dead. And twelve men of our army had captured a Saracen, and on their side they had killed three of our men; one was Dimitrios Lakkas, and two more with him; and they carried him to Togni. The king left his tent and advanced and found no one. He formed the men into squadrons of a hundred and of fifty to engage the enemy. This was done because of the lack of discipline in the army; for our good lord had appointed Sir John de Verni captain over one part of the army, (and he was a hard man,) and the people were afraid of him, and said: "Our desire is to be under the orders of our lord the king, and not of this man." And the rest too said the same, and they would not obey any one but the king alone, (and refused to have many commanders.)

The Saracens were advancing steadily, and they sent men forward who surrounded our army on the eastern side. And the Armenians and the freedmen went to one side, (and set up their shields as the king had arranged,) and were awaiting the onset of the Saracens. The king stood full in the midst of the army, and the prince was at his right hand, and Sir John de Grinier and Sir Badin de Nores (on the left), and all the army (stood in array) like a wall. And then the Saracens showed themselves at the top of the hill over against the plain. And when the Syrians and the rest of the foot-soldiers saw them, they shouted with loud and terrible cries and beat their drums; and the Saracens did the same. Then the king set his "lance" in rest, and all the army; and they advanced and attacked them, and came to close quarters at the top of the said hill. And they killed many Saracens, and the Saracens turned to retire, and the king turned to go back towards us. And a Turkish lad, (who had been baptized and) was kept by the king at a monthly wage, (—and he was a good man of his body,—) said to him:

"Sir, let us turn round and attack them once more and put them to rout," for the trumpet had sounded the retreat. And no one would turn back to renew the attack and (the most of our) foot-soldiers left their shields and their arms and ran off (this way and that, for they were men who had no experience of war.) And a man at arms on his horse saw this son of Takka and did not recognize him, and thought he was a Saracen; and he struck him with his lance (?) and with his sword pierced him right through and through; and he died. And Janot Castrisio and George and Ibrahim and Nicholas Chantelier overcame their enemies, but this was of no avail for the army was in flight. (And many of our army were killed, because they were ignorant of warfare and the command was bad.)

When the Saracens (saw that our army was in flight), they thought that the king had set an ambush at the tower of Kherokitia. "And (for this reason) they are making a show of flight, to make us pursue after them, and pass by the tower, and then they will run out and attack us from the front and these in the ambush from behind, and so they will slay us." And the Saracens pray God to send some one to make peace, and fortune would not have it so. And because they were afraid, they were advancing step by step, and they came upon our men who were tired out by the weight of their weapons and by the heat; and the Saracens made no effort to kill them.

The king was riding on his way and his horse stumbled two or three times, and after this he met a camel on the road which kept going on the road (in front of him); and his horse (was afraid and) refused to pass it. And the king dismounted, and took the horse which Antony Mari was riding. And the Saracens advanced to the gate of the lodging at Kherokitia, and found the Saracen envoy whom the prince had tortured to death and (on his return) had ordered to be burned. And (when they saw him,)—and the lodging they found deserted,—they became very angry, and came up with the prince and killed him. And they very nearly caught up with the king as well. And two Mamelukes couched their lances and attacked the king; and the king had no lance, but he had a sword and this he drew. And one (of the Saracens) struck him on the forehead with his lance; and the king warded off the blow and shouted out in Arabic, "Melek", which means "King". And the other Saracen achieved nothing. And this is as the constable of Cyprus told me. And they captured also a Catalan who was called Nicholas, who knew the Arabic language. Afterwards they turned back, and all the tired men whom they found they killed, and all those who stood in their way they put to the sword. Now there was a Saracen Mameluke, and also a young knight; the Mameluke threw the latter to the ground, and he remounted and rode on; the Mameluke fled from him in terror.

Now as for the king, as soon as the enemy heard him say that he was the king, they (fell upon him and) seized him, because he had not many men with him (to help him); and they took him to Aliki. And on that day before night fell they brought the news to the cardinal at Lefkosia.[1]

On the battle field can still be seen the remains of the tower of the Templars, including the fragmentary ruins of a large vaulted hall, called "Serai" by the villagers; it was near here that the King was taken prisoner. Close to the ruins of the commandery is a small mediaeval church dedicated to the B.V.M., and badly restored in 1920. A fragmentary painting with the date 1509 still remains on its walls, and there is a fine west doorway, with a Gothic dripstone which finishes in a finial in the shape of a human face.

KHLORAKAS (xlv)

The Church of the B.V.M. is probably mediaeval in date. The west door has a coat of arms above it; the interior is completely ruined, the dome and walls being covered with oil daubs, in the crudest style of workmanship, entirely hiding the original mediaeval wall paintings which must lie underneath. The church is now deserted, and near by rises its hideous supplanter, a fearsome modern building with a façade reminiscent of a continental railway station. The iconostasis contains some eighteenth-century icons from the older church, but they are of no special interest.

Outside the village lies the charming toy Byzantine Church of St. Nicholas with a later narthex, a church so tiny that hardly a dozen people could worship in it. Traces of painting survive on the north wall, showing St. Nicholas and his Martyrdom. The same coat of arms, as is on the Church of the B.V.M., is above the north door.

[1] *Chronicle of Makhairas*, p. 657.

KHOLI (xxxv)

The Church of the Archangel is unique in that the west end of the nave would seem to have been at some period the lower stages of a mediaeval watch-tower, the vaulted roof being added later. The body of the church is almost completely covered with mural paintings which are apparently the work of the early sixteenth century, mostly in an excellent state of preservation. The iconostasis is modern save for the holy doors. There are three early sixteenth-century icons of the Madonna and Child, one belonging to the church, the other two from the ruined Chapel of the B.V.M., Eleousa, and St. Ariston respectively. There is also an icon of St. Ariston of *c.* 1520, with a bearded donor in priestly brown vestments and a black hat, a gold cross suspended round his neck. In the west end of the church lies a curious relic which appears to be an iron Latin rood cross with bronze repoussé ornaments upon it.

Two churches lie in ruins near the village. That of the B.V.M. is a fifteenth-century building with remains of paintings in the vault, mostly scenes from the life of the Virgin; there are founders' tombs on the north and south sides. The Church of St. Ariston is entirely ruined and the saint is said to have been buried here. St. Ariston was a Cypriote saint supposed to have been martyred at Salamis in the third century.

KHOULOU (xlv)

The Church of the B.V.M. Platinassa has been much repaired at various times; the south door belongs to the original sixteenth-century church. On the interior north wall is a large three-arched recess, the centre compartment containing a much darkened painting of the Madonna supported by two Archangels; kneeling in one corner is a female donor in red with a black veil; nearer are two young men dressed in black doublets, the sleeves of which have gold buttons, and scarlet cloaks. On the opposite side is a portrait of a male donor; close by kneel two boys in black with scarlet cloaks, their golden hair is cut straight across the forehead but comes down thickly to the neck. From this fact, and from the type of dresses worn by these youths, it would seem that the painting is to be assigned to about 1510.

A number of churches and chapels in ruins surround the village. All show traces of painting; the best preserved is the small domed Church of St. George, which, according to an inscription, was built in 1480.

KHRYSIDHA (xxii)

The Church of the Holy Cross is an ancient building restored in 1836. From the former building survives the south door of mediaeval design. The iconostasis is a patchwork of various periods. Into the south wall is built a black marble base of a statue of the classical period; the inscription is much destroyed but seems to refer to a certain Jason. Another statue base is used as a mounting block outside the west door; probably both these relics come from the ruins of the ancient Cythera. According to the villagers a golden cross lies buried at a great depth beneath the floor of the church; frequent efforts have been made to find it, but they have all ended in failure.

KHRYSILIOU (xx)

A tiny decayed village surrounded by groves of ancient olive-trees. The village church, dedicated to Christ the Saviour, is built of carefully squared stones, but it is difficult to judge its age. It may only be work of the eighteenth century, although there is an elaborate west door in the mediaeval manner, with dog-tooth moulding. Several icons are dated 1748, which may, after all, be the date of the church.

KILANI (xlvii)

The Church of St. John was founded by Bishop Panaretos of Paphos (1769–1788), but the restorations in 1888 and 1903 have destroyed much of its interest. In the interior a picture in a recess in the south wall shows a portrait of the bishop offering a model of the church to Christ. Within the apse are kept several relics of Panaretos, his vestments, a covering for the chalice, a gospel dated 1711, and three icons; one of St. Paraskevi has two sixteenth-century kneeling donors. The iconostasis contains an icon of Christ dated 1722, while a small wooden cross cased in silver dates from 1712. There is also a modern church dedicated to the B.V.M., built on an ancient site, and from the earlier building comes a rood cross dated 1735 and a large early seventeenth-century icon of the Virgin. In the apse are two chairs, one with a leather back and seat, the other of carved and painted woodwork, the back formed by two serpents in the Italian manner of the early eighteenth century.

About two miles from the village is the Church of St. Mavra, a small late fifteenth-century monotholos, with a narthex added later. The whole of the original church is painted in a crude style. In the apse is the usual fresco of the Liturgy, the Apostles distinguished by the initial letter of their names above their heads, though the name of Judas is written in full. The church contains a few seventeenth-century icons; that of St. Mavra and St. Timotheos is said to cure colds.

According to a local legend St. Mavra was a Christian girl who wished to enter a convent, but her father forced her to marry a wealthy man. The night of her wedding she fled, when he and all the guests were busy eating and drinking, but her absence from the feast was soon noticed, and the bridegroom and her father pursued and caught up with her just as she reached the cliff where the church now stands. In despair she cried to the Madonna to save her, and in her anguish beat on the stone with her bare hands. The Virgin heard her prayer, and as the unhappy girl struck the rock the cliff opened and swallowed her up and she disappeared inside. Her husband and father tried to follow, but at that moment a spring of water suddenly gushed forth from the crevice into which the girl had disappeared. St. Mavra was seen no more, but the villagers built a church in her memory, and to those who fail to believe this legend show the marks on the rock where the saint struck it with the palms of her hands, and the spring of water which still issues forth from its face. Charming as this legend is, it has no foundation on fact; indeed, practically nothing is known of St. Mavra beyond that she is supposed to have been a niece of St. Barnabas and to have married St. Timothy.

KILANEMOS (iii)

About a mile north of the village and on a hill is the little Byzantine domed Church of St. George. Structurally perfect, it has recently undergone a restoration which has so garnished the interior that it now contains nothing of interest.

KISSONERGA (xlv)

The village church is modern and dedicated to the Transfiguration; it contains four icons from its predecessor dated 1775. Close by lie the ruins of a tiny chapel dedicated to SS. Zinies and Philonila. These two saints are said to have been close relatives of St. Paul, who accompanied him from Tarsus and came with him to Cyprus, where they died while St. Paul was at Paphos. The holy well beneath the church is in much request by the village women for curing various female diseases.

KITI (l)

The name of this village still records the name of Kition, one of the most ancient cities in the Island. It was said to have been founded by Kittim, the great-grandson of Noah, who colonized it after the Deluge. During the Middle Ages it belonged to a branch of the Royal House, and was known as the fief of Le Quid. Its last owner, Charles de Lusignan, was deprived of it by the usurper James II for his loyalty to the lawful Queen Charlotte. The Venetian Government sold it to the wealthy Cypriote family of Podocatoro, and the last of this family to possess it was killed at the siege of Nicosia in 1570.

Kiti contains the finest village church in the Island. It is dedicated to the "Angel built" Madonna, and has a central nave and transept of unusual height. But its chief glory is the mosaic in the central apse, which shows the B.V.M., a life-size figure, holding the Child. She stands on a footstool between the Archangels Michael and Gabriel. Smirnof[1] suggests that the fifth or sixth century is a possible date, and, indeed, the quality of the work is equal to anything at Ravenna, but the fabric of the church is not so ancient as this. It is possible, however, that the mosaic was reconstructed or that it dates from the second half of the ninth century, the period of Basil I.

Attached to the south side of the church is a Latin chapel which once belonged to the important mediaeval family of Gibelet. In it is preserved a gravestone with an effigy of a lady on it. According to the inscription which surrounds the stone, it is of the Lady Simone, daughter of Sir William Guers, and wife of Sir Renier de Gibelet, who died aged fifty on November 5, 1302. Built into the wall of the chapel are three coats of arms. They are: (1) A plain cross. (2) The royal quarterings of Cyprus and Jerusalem. (3) Three lions' heads, which is almost certainly the coat of arms of the family of Gibelet. On the north side of the church is a small dark chapel, which, according to Mr. Jeffery, was a small mortuary chapel.[2] It contains dim traces of frescoes on its walls, and a collection of ancient and decayed icons expelled from the church; they are, however, mostly too damaged to be of interest. The icons and iconostasis of the main church have been so repainted that they are now without interest, save for a gigantic icon of the Archangel Michael dating from the middle of the seventeenth century.

KIVIDHES (liii)

The village church dedicated to St. George is of the eighteenth century, and is doomed to destruction; indeed, at the present it is being pulled down and its stones used to erect a church in the hideous prevailing modern style.

Outside the village and close to the high-road is the fifteenth-century Church of the Holy Cross, now deserted

[1] *Christianskiya Mosiaki Kipra*, St. Petersburg, 1897.
[2] *Monuments of Cyprus*, p. 186.

and decaying, though the brick-built apse is in a good state of preservation. The interior was once painted, but the frescoes are rapidly flaking from the walls.

KIVISIL (l)

This Turkish hamlet contains a small domed church in the Byzantine style with a north aisle added at a later date. This was possibly once a Latin church, as one of the steps in front of the eighteenth-century iconostasis is formed by a mediaeval tombstone with an inscription in Gothic script beginning "Ici git", but the rest of the inscription is illegible.

KLAVDHIA (l)

The mosque is formed from the mediaeval church with additions on the north side. It is said that an inscription and date were visible just below the tympanum above the north door, but whitewash has covered this and the painting with which the interior of the church was once decorated.

KLEPINI (xiii)

The Church of St. Luke is an eighteenth-century building with a west end added during the present century. The south door of the original building has been blocked up at some period. Both the iconostasis and the icons are modern.

Near the village is a small Church of the B.V.M.; originally of Byzantine workmanship, it has been so completely rebuilt that nothing of interest now remains.

The village was once Maronite and is mentioned by Dandini in 1596 as such.

A curious local tradition records that not more than forty families can ever live in the village; should there be more, death will inevitably level the number before the end of the year.

KLIROU (xxxviii)

There must have been habitations here from a very early date, as the vast number of tombs which surround the village testify.

The large and modern Church of the B.V.M. stands in the centre of the village; the ground plan of its predecessor can still be seen to the north. The central portion of the iconostasis comes from this former building and is dated 1748. From the same source comes an early seventeenth-century icon of the Madonna. The icon of the Annunciation is covered with silver gilt, and is a rain-compelling icon, but woe betide the person who comes and prays to the icon, and after his wish has been granted fails to bring some offering to the church; for his crops will fail, his cattle die, and his children fall ill. This is a curious example of a vindictive icon.

A mile or so outside the village is the tiny monastery of the Virgin of Lakhni, a small, ancient, shed-like building surrounded by monastic ruins; it contains nothing of interest. The villagers relate that "many years ago the Turks came from the village of Aradhiou in mid-July, the hottest time of the year, and stole the beams from the roof of the church; but hardly had they left the building when the Virgin, in her wrath, sent hailstones so large that they immediately killed the animals bearing away the woodwork".

KLONARI (xlviii)

The Church of St. Nicholas is a small shed-like building with a west end added at a later date. Nearly all the walls of the earlier part are covered with paintings dating from the early sixteenth century. The iconostasis is a fine example of carved and painted woodwork of about 1620. The majority of the icons are contemporary, but have been repainted, except for one of St. John the Baptist. The original painted decoration of the tie beams and wooden roof remain. In a niche in the church lies a processional icon of St. Nicholas, and in the gallery is a mouldering collection of sixteenth-century service books.

KOCHATI (xxxix)

A poor Turkish village built on an ancient site, the ruins of which spread west and south of the modern hamlet. A large and carefully built mediaeval cistern lies 50 yards west of the village, and is about 50 feet deep.

KOKKINI TRIMITHIA (xx)

The principal church is modern, but outside the village lies the Chapel of the Archangel Michael, a carefully constructed stone building of the early sixteenth century; it was probably once a seigneurial chapel and it is still referred to by the villagers as "Venatico". There are a quantity of architectural details in the doors and narthex, and the base of a standard socket on the dome is in the form of a human head. The iconostasis is dated 1615, and there is a wall painting of the Archangel Angel, which is probably contemporary with the building of the chapel. A fine rood cross dated 1562 hangs in the narthex, but is full of dry rot and will soon crumble into dust.

The village undoubtedly takes its name from the fields of red earth which surround it.

KOLOSSI (lviii)

The Castle of Kolossi is a massive square keep erected by the Knights of St. John of Jerusalem in 1454. It is about 75 feet high, and the walls are 9 feet thick; it is divided into three storeys. The lowest floor was probably used for storage purposes, and beneath the stairs which lead to the middle stage is the castle well. The second storey consists of two rooms, one of which is the main hall; the entrance door into it was defended by a drawbridge; the small wheels on which the chains which lifted and lowered it are fitted are original, though the drawbridge is but a modern copy. To the right of this door is a large mural painting of the Crucifixion, with the coat of arms of Louis de Magnac, Grand Commander of Cyprus, and builder of the castle. The second room on this floor was probably the kitchen, as it contains a large open fireplace. A circular staircase in the corner leads to the upper storey, which was the actual residence of the Grand Master himself. It consists of two rooms, each measuring 45 feet by 20 feet, and in each are small windows, with window seats built *vis-à-vis* in the thickness of the wall. In the inner of these two rooms, and built in the thickness of the north wall, is the latrine. The chief glory of these rooms are the two superb fire-places, strangely reminiscent of those in the Châteaux of the Loire, both of them decorated with the badge of Louis de Magnac. A continuation of the circular staircase leads to the roof, which affords a superb view over the countryside and the salt lake of Limassol. Above the exterior of the north door is a beautiful and elaborate coat of arms. "Obviously the meaning of this achievement is to represent the year 1454, when Jacques de Milli was elected Grand Master of the Order of St. John in succession to Jean de Lastic, Louis de Magnac being Grand Commander of Cyprus. The two Grand Masters are represented by their shields, one on either side of the Cyprus royal arms, whilst the shield of Louis de Magnac occupies the lower division of the panel."[1] Surrounding the castle are the ruins of the enclosing courtyard, but little now remains save walls and foundations. Near the castle is the great vaulted barn of the knights; an inscription at the east end records that it was repaired by Murad Pasha, the second Turkish Governor of Cyprus, in 1591.

The Hospitallers, or Knights of St. John of Jerusalem, arrived in Cyprus soon after the Latin occupation of the Island, and in 1210 they were given the state of Kolossi by King Hugh I. In 1291, after the fall of Acre, Cyprus was the headquarters of the Order, and they, with the Templars, were placed by Henry II of Cyprus in joint occupation of Limassol. In 1310 Guy di Siverao became the first Grand Commander of the Order in Cyprus.

The next occasion on which the Order comes prominently into notice occurs during the unhappy struggle between Charlotte and her half-brother Jacques for the throne. Though it had previously given the usurper a hospitable reception on his flight to Rhodes in 1457, even to the extent of defraying the expenses of his maintenance while in that island, it plainly showed by its subsequent conduct on which side its sympathies

[1] Jeffery, *Report on Cyprus Monuments*, 1933, p. 16.

lay. Before recourse was had to arms, the Grand Master, Jacques de Milly, sent to Cairo Jean Dauphin, Commander of Nisyro, to effect if possible through the Sultan an accommodation between the disputants. But this emissary on his arrival in Egypt was handed over to Jacques, who after a while restored him to liberty. Even after hostilities had broken out he did not desist from his endeavours, but sent Louis de Magnac, Grand Commander of Cyprus, to bring about an agreement. The success of Jacques placed the Religion in a position of great difficulty. As it possessed numerous estates not only in Cyprus but also in the dominions of the Duke of Savoy, the father of Louis, Charlotte's second husband, it was anxious to maintain a good understanding with both the belligerents. To attain this object it was guilty of considerable duplicity. For, while professing to be actuated by good faith towards Jacques, it continued secretly to assist his foes. When the capitulation of Kyrenia rendered the usurper master of the whole island Pierre Raymond Zacosta, the successor of De Milly, made at the request of Pius II one final effort on behalf of the rightful sovereign. But the two knights, who were sent to Cyprus, failed in their mission as Jacques naturally would not consent to relinquish a throne of which he was in undisputed possession. Even after fortune had declared finally for her rival the Order did not abandon the cause of the dispossessed queen. Rhodes at all times offered her a safe retreat and a ready welcome. Indeed so touched were the brethren by her destitution and misfortunes that they allowed her out of their treasury a monthly sum of thirty florins to meet her pressing necessities when in their island. On the death of Jacques in 1473 the Religion once more came forward to champion the claims of this much-wronged princess. At her instance De Lignac, the Admiral of Rhodes, approached Pietro Mocenigo, the generalissimo of the Venetian fleet in the Levant, to request that he would assist in recovering the throne of Cyprus for the rightful occupant. But whatever hopes Charlotte and her partisans may have built upon the disappearance of the usurper from the scene were rudely dispelled by the reply of the Venetian commander. He declared that the Senate was resolved to maintain as queen its adopted daughter, the widowed Catarina, and to uphold her in possession of the kingdom, which her husband had bequeathed to her. At the same time, fearing that the vessels of the Order might be employed in enforcing Charlotte's pretensions, he wrote a strong letter of remonstrance to the Grand Master, Giovanni Orsini, requiring them immediately to rejoin the confederate fleet, which was operating against the Turks.[1]

Louis de Magnac was succeeded as Grand Commander by an Englishman, John Langstrother, who returned to England and was taken prisoner at the Battle of Tewkesbury, and was beheaded by King Edward IV. At the beginning of the sixteenth century Kolossi, with the consent of the Order, passed into possession of the Cornaro family. The first of these new owners was Cardinal Marco Cornaro, brother to Queen Catherine. After the Turkish conquest of 1570 the Cornaro family lost the property, but the title of Grand Cross still remained in the family. The House of Cornaro died out in 1799, but the title was claimed by the Count Mocenigo, who had married the heiress of the Cornaro house. The title still remains in this family.

Near the castle is the small double-aisled Chapel of St. Eustathios. This possibly served as a chapel of the knights, as the coat of arms of Louis de Magnac is still visible on the arch of the semi-vault of the apse. There are two periods of wall paintings remaining in the church, of which the best preserved is a spirited St. Eustathios on the north wall. The paintings in the dome are possibly contemporary with the building of the church in the middle of the fifteenth century. In the pendentives are the four Evangelists, each writing the opening words of his Gospel. In the floor of the south aisle are the fragments of a marble tombstone. The icons are without interest, save for one of the Madonna dated 1684.

Between the church and the Barn of the Knights is an aqueduct, in the middle of the central arch of which is the coat of arms and the badge of the Knights of St. John.

The knights spent their time cultivating corn, oil, vines, sugar-canes, and cotton. The wine made from these vines became the most famous of all Cyprus vintages, and from the place where it was grown was known as commanderia. Nor was the wine of only local fame, for it was exported all over Europe, and was even drunk by the Plantagenet kings

[1] Hackett, *Church of Cyprus*, p. 635.

in England. It is still obtainable in Cyprus and, like brandy, is kept in a cask which is added to as the wine is drawn out, and it is no unusual thing to find a barrel which has contained wine for more than a hundred years.

It was also the knights who introduced beccaficos to the gourmets of the world. This delicacy is a little bird, the black cap, which is caught on lime twigs, plucked and packed in jars filled with vinegar. The vinegar sinks into the flesh, which becomes slightly hardened, but softens the bones, so that the bird can be eaten whole.

An Englishman, John Locke, who visited Cyprus in 1553, gives the following description of these birds.

> They have also in the Island a certaine small bird much like unto a Wagtaile in fethers and making, these are so extreme fat that you can perceive nothing els in all their bodies: these birds are now in season. They take great quantitie of them, and they use to pickle them with vinegar and salt, and to put them in pots and send them to Venice and other places of Italy for present of great estimation. They say they send almost 1,200 jarres or pots to Venice, besides those which are consumed in the Island, which are a great number. These are so plentiful that when there is no shipping, you may buy them for 10 Carchies, which coine are 4 to a Venetian Soldo, which is peny farthing the dozen, and when there is store of shipping, 2 pence the dozen, after that rate of their money.[1]

KOMA TOU YIALOU (viii)

There appears to have been a considerable mediaeval village here, and Alexander Drummond, who visited it in 1745, says that it is "Prettily situated on the fields and well laid out near the sea; it was once so extensive as to contain fourteen churches; but now five-sixths of it lie in ruins, among which is the Church of Our Lady, where I found the following inscription on a stone accidentally laid on the four pillars of the altar table."[2] Drummond then goes on to give a copy of the inscription on the stone, which was apparently the tombstone of Margaret, the wife of Anthony d'Ibelin, who died in 1323. There are no longer

[1] *Excerpta Cypria*, p. 72.

[2] *Travels*, London, 1744, p. 279.

fourteen churches, but a number of chapels still surround the village, the principal church of which is that of the Archangel Michael, built in 1859.

About a mile west of the village lies the tiny Chapel of "Nikoloudi" (Little St. Nicholas), a building of the sixteenth century. There is also a Chapel of the B.V.M. of the seventeenth century, with remains of wall paintings, and a mediaeval Church of St. Nicholas with remains of mural painting of the sixteenth century. A partially destroyed inscription in the apse records the date of its building. On the flat table above the village is the small Church of St. Solomon, an untouched building of the fifteenth century, with considerable remains of crude but interesting paintings in the interior. Beneath the church is a large tomb, said to be that of the saint, the floor of which is covered with potsherds of the Byzantine period. This tomb beneath the church probably dates from the classical period, and is but one in a vast necropolis which surrounds the church.

Near the village is the Chapel of St. Anne. Hard by are the quarries which provided the stone for the rebuilding of the walls of Famagusta. On the face of the quarry is cut the date M.D. XXXIII, while on the wall of the chapel is the date M.D. XXXIII DIE XII MARZO.

KOMI KEBIR (vii)

The Church of St. Auxentios is an ancient building restored in 1859. A village legend relates that the body of this saint was discovered simultaneously by peasants from Komi Kebir and Ephtakomi in a cave near Davlos. At once a dispute arose as to which village should have the honour of caring for the body. To settle the question they decided to put the relics of the saint in a cart and see what the oxen who drew it would do; hardly had the body been placed in the vehicle than the oxen started off and crossed hills and dales till they stopped suddenly by the Chapel of St. Mavra near Komi Kebir. At once a fierce argument sprang up between the two rival parties, and they were nearly coming to blows when the saint, whose body had been miraculously preserved, raised himself and uttered the single word "Komi" (here). Not unnaturally the saint's intervention finished any discussion, and his body was placed in the Chapel of St. Mavra, which was rededicated to St. Auxentios; and the village which had, up to now, been called Kebir was given the additional name of Komi. The villagers built a special church in honour of the saint, whose body was placed in a small chamber in the roof above the central archway; this curious sepulchre is now blocked up and inaccessible, but the entrance is still visible. A part of the bridle supposed to have been used by the oxen hangs above his icon.

According to Sathas, Auxentios was a soldier, and so skilful was he in arms that he was soon raised to a position of great distinction. While still in the prime of life, the Virgin appeared to him in a vision, and he decided to give up the profession of arms. He made known his intentions to his comrades in arms, who, to the number of 300, decided to follow him. They journeyed to Cyprus, and on reaching land dispersed, each choosing for himself a hermitage or place of retreat. Auxentios himself went to Karpasos, and found a cave at a place called Iotion, where he lived in strict seclusion till the day of his death.

KOPHINOU (xlix)

Close to the village lies the Byzantine Church of the B.V.M. in the last stages of decay, although the dome still stands. There are considerable remains of frescoes of two periods, the first of which would seem to be fourteenth century, of this the best example is the Archangel Michael of colossal proportions, beneath the dome on the north wall; the second is of the late sixteenth century, and of this the best is a fairly complete figure of St. Theodoros on the north wall near the west door.

Above this church, on the hill side, lie the ruins of the Church of St. Heraklios; little now remains save a tomb chamber once painted, and said to have contained the body of the saint; this is borne out by fragments of a large marble sarcophagus which lie near by.

KORAKOU (xxviii)

There are several churches attached to the village, the principal of which is dedicated to the B.V.M., and is a large eighteenth-century building, the contemporary iconostasis ruined by repainting.

On an isolated hill stands the Church of St. Luke, an inscription over the north doorway of which reads, "This Holy Church of the Apostle Luke was founded on the 27th September in the year 1697 by the expenses of the priest Jacovos built by the hands of Constantine and Dimitri Gavriel."

There is also a church dedicated to St. Mamas, a small and untouched shed-like building of the seventeenth century. Acoustic vases are built into the apse. The church contains an icon of the B.V.M. dated 1749, and in the narthex is a collection of icons, which includes a sixteenth-century one of the Madonna.

KORMAKITI (xi)

The new Church of St. George is a good example of modern building and in excellent taste. Near by is the old Church of St. George, a fifteenth-century building, which still contains its belfry of two stages with openings for bells in the lower stage.

Kormakiti is the chief Maronite village in Cyprus. The Maronites are a branch of the Latin Church, and owe obedience to the Pope; originally they came from the Lebanon in Syria, and first came to Cyprus in the seventh century. Till 1840 they observed the Greek calendar, but in that year they adopted the Latin method of reckoning. They hold their church services in their native Syriac. There are at present about 1,300 of the sect in Cyprus.

Outside the village and near a ruined site, in the middle of which stands an oil press of uncertain age, is a tiny chapel dedicated to the B.V.M., with its barrel vaulting intact. Over the west door is a much destroyed coat of arms. The interior has been twice repainted; the later frescoes are of a good style.

KORNOS (xxxix)

The Church of St. John the Baptist was built in the early years of the nineteenth century, and contains an icon of that saint dated 1734.

The village is famous all over the Island for the huge red wine jars which it produces; these jars are not wheel made, but are built up by hand, and it is amazing how true they are in shape and form.

KOROVIA (iii)

Near here in 1929 the Swedish expedition excavated a fortress roughly rectangular in shape and dating from the Bronze Age. The fortress was thrice rebuilt after it had been destroyed either by fire or siege. The fortress was surrounded on all sides by ramparts; the entrance was guarded by two towers consisting of a covered passage with a right-angle turn to the left enclosed by an inner gate; along the north side of the courtyard lay a suite of three large rooms with a sun shelter along the façade; in front of this was a platform slightly raised above the courtyard, and reached by a short flight of steps; the kitchen lay in front of the barracks, and could be entered either from the platform or directly from the courtyard; along the west rampart there was apparently a suite of barracks similar to the northern rooms, but only one of them is preserved; the opposite side of the courtyard was flanked by a long storehouse, in the centre of which was the altar.

KOUKA (xlvii)

The Church of the Holy Cross is a cruciform Byzantine building with a dome over the transept. On the north side is a small square chamber probably built to contain the famous relic of the church, the dust from the suppedaneum of the Cross, when it was sawn in pieces by the order of St. Helena. There are considerable remains of painting on the roof and walls of the north transept. There is an unusual seventeenth-century icon of the B.V.M., with a bronze medallion of the Virgin and Child in the centre. The ruins of the monastic buildings still surround the church.

KOUKLIA, FAMAGUSTA (xxxii)

A Turkish village in which a colony of Jews have been settled for the past thirty years. During the Middle Ages there must have been a considerable village here, and the small bridge over the aqueduct is paved with fragments of mediaeval tomb slabs from some church which has long since vanished.

KOUKLIA, PAPHOS (li)

The history of Old Paphos, the site of the famous temple of Aphrodite, reaches far back into mythological times, the town being certainly as old as the late Mycenaean Age (*c.* 1200 B.C.). Pausanias is alone amongst ancient writers in ascribing the foundation of the temple to the Arcadian, Agapenor, the traditional founder of New Paphos, on his return from the Trojan War (*c.* 1180 B.C.). Tacitus (*Hist.* ii, 2 sqq.) quotes a vague tradition of the founder's name as "Aerias", together with a later story giving the name as Cinyras, a name mentioned in Homer (*Il.* xi, 19–23) as that of the Cypriote donor of a Breastplate to Agamemnon. The earliest historical reference to the town is on an Assyrian tablet now in the British Museum, on which a king of Paphos, whose name is variously read as Ithuander or Ittudagon, is recorded as having paid tribute to Esarhaddon (672 B.C.). Di Cesnola identified this name with that of Eteandros, whose gold armlets form part of the "Treasure of Curium". It is, in any case, certain that from very early times the priest-kings of Paphos were of the clan of Cinyras. The last of them, Nicocles, rebelled against Ptolemy I (295 B.C.), and from that time until the Roman occupation (58 B.C.) they retained the priesthood only.

In favour of the Phoenician foundation of the temple is the similarity noticed by the British excavators (1888) between its original plan and that of the earliest temple at Jerusalem, viz. a shrine and altar surrounded by colonnaded porticoes. Here the Cinyrad college of orgiastic priests presided over a nature-worship resembling that of the

Phoenician Astarte, whom the Greeks identified with Aphrodite, the legend of whose birth from the sea-foam was suitably localized in a spot remarkable for the masses of foam produced by winter storms. The goddess was worshipped under the form of a conical stone, with prayers, incense, and pure fire. The altar was carefully kept free not only from blood, but also from rain—although it was in the open—and only male victims were sacrificed. Many fragments of white marble cones were found on the site during the great excavations of 1888.

The primitive arrangements of the temple were, however, quite altered by later Roman changes and additions, notably under Augustus (in 15 B.C.) and again by Tiberius and Vespasian, when earthquake necessitated extensive repairs; and its appearance, as depicted on the famous Roman coinage of the first century, has never been satisfactorily explained.

On the foundation of Augusta Claudia (at New Paphos) by the Romans, and the extinction of the Cinyrad clan, the importance of Old Paphos rapidly declined. It received, however, as Tacitus informs us, a state visit in A.D. 79 from Titus, who was on his way to the war in Palestine, and who was much encouraged by the favourable omens attending his sacrifices. In the fourth century Jerome alludes to the site as ruinous and desolate; and in the Middle Ages it was exploited for the construction of a large sugar refinery, a part of which still survives towards the south. Finally, after a long period of oblivion, the ruins were identified by Francis Attar (*c.* 1540) and again by R. Pococke in the eighteenth century.

Little remains to-day of one of the most famous temples of antiquity. The excavations of 1888 add but little to the knowledge of the building, and the excellent description given by Dr. Ludwig Ross, nearly eighty years ago, still describes the temple.

With intense interest and like expectation I approached the famous temple of the goddess. The path swerves to the right up the low hills and brings one in a quarter of an hour to Kouklia (Palai-Paphos). But the site on which Phoenicians once estab-

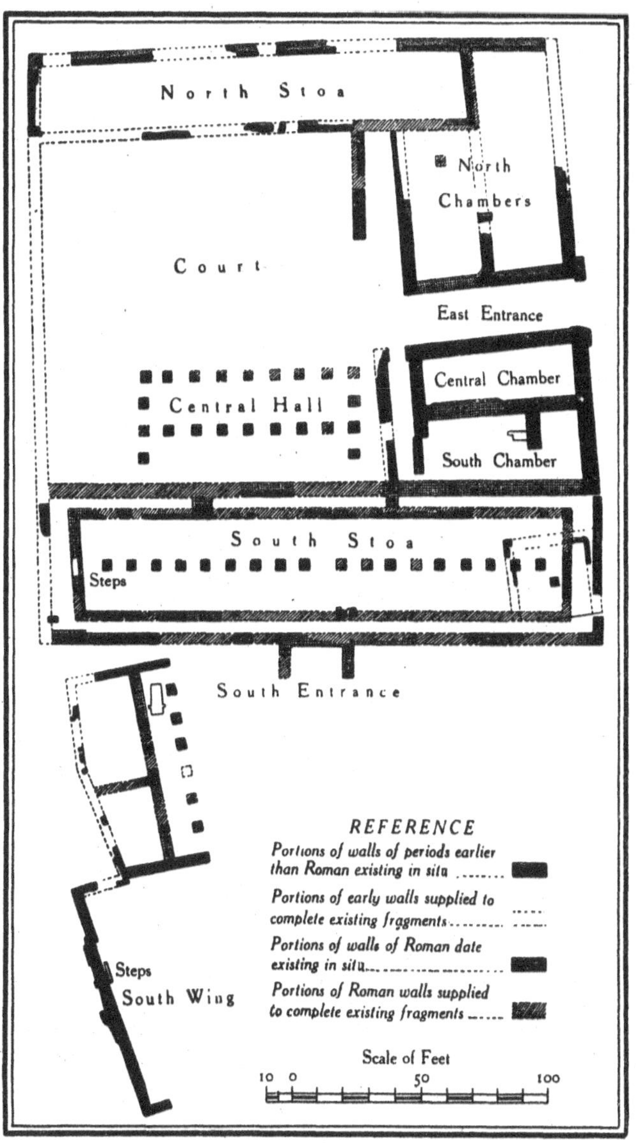

THE TEMPLE OF APHRODITE AT KOUKLIA

lished the throne of the Paphian goddess is now of sad aspect, a bare hill-shoulder with a few ruins, a mediaeval tower, and a wretched village. Near the parish church are a few bases of statues, but walled in so that their possible inscriptions are illegible.

The importance of the ruins of the supposed shrine of the Phoenician Aphrodite has been greatly overrated by earlier travellers: from their actual condition few conclusions can be drawn. All attempts to reconstruct the plan of the temple by comparison with the well-known Cypriot coins on which it is figured seem to me to rest on no solid ground. The blocks which compose the wall which is assumed to be the back-wall of the cella are of gigantic size, each of them is 2·11 m. high, 4·80 m. long, and 78 cm. thick, of soft sandstone somewhat blackened on the exposed side: on the inner surface they have notches and holes where the tools have gripped them as they were set in position; one sees just the same thing in the Sicilian temples. Hammer has a wonderful notion that these openings were a kind of sound-holes whence the oracles were delivered. But at the S.W. corner only are found in more or less good preservation five or six such blocks, the remaining sides of the quadrangle are destroyed to the very foundations. Nothing more is left of the materials of the temple, all has been dragged away and used over again.[1]

The ruins can be divided into two periods, Roman and pre-Roman. Of the latter the most interesting is the south wing built of huge blocks of stone.

It consists of a basement of polygonal blocks mostly of massive proportions brought to a fairly even face, and with a carefully wrought and levelled upper bed, on which rest a series of magnificent rectangular blocks, the largest of which measures 7 feet by over 15. These blocks are of limestone, and have been laid with their beds vertical so that they have suffered severely from the effects of weather. The stones both of the basement and upper parts of the wall are pierced with holes for the purpose of hauling them; the larger stones have two holes but some of the smaller ones in the basement are pierced with a single hole only.[2]

---

[1] Dr. Ludwig Ross, *Travels in Cyprus*.
[2] *Journal of Hellenic Studies*, vol. 9, p. 194.

The plan of the temple is unlike a Greek or Roman building, and with its covered and uncovered courts is more Phoenician in character.

As far then as we can gather from the plan, the earliest building consisted of a large square enclosure, with possibly some small shrine within its walls, though of this no evidence remains. To this, later, was added an important approach from the north, consisting of a long colonnade, probably of three parallel avenues, with chambers on either side, which underwent some alteration in Roman times; and there is no difficulty in assigning this work to Phoenician builders. It seems certain that the great quadrangle with its halls and chambers was designed and carried out at one fixed period, and from the character of the work it looks as though it was influenced by Greek methods of construction, though we cannot attribute it to Greek design. The careful work and fitting of the stones in the basement, and their comparatively small and uniform size, with the use of a course of extra depth as the commencement of the upper and visible portions of the wall, seem special marks of Greek methods of work.

It is a matter of some difficulty to identify the use and purpose of the various courts and chambers of this great block. It seems at least likely that, in its original state, the portion marked on the plan as south chamber was rectangular in form, and was the central one of three parallel chambers of the same size, or very nearly so; there is just sufficient room for two such chambers between the present central chamber and the small square one under the east end of the stoa; the cross wall at the back of the south chambers would then provide for an inner naos of special sanctity. This arrangement would agree well with the Roman coins, allowing for the middle chamber of these three being raised to a greater height than the others to denote its importance; but it cannot have existed in this condition at the time the coin was struck. It is quite conceivable that these coins may merely reproduce the design of older ones, and perhaps too much reliance must not be placed upon them as a record of the actual condition of the temple at any given time; but when we consider that the temple was actually restored by the Romans with very great splendour and magnificence, according to the records, it seems more likely that the coins should represent some portion of the building as it stood in Roman times. If this view of the case be accepted, then it seems most likely that the portion described as the east entrance forms the central feature of the design, the chambers on either hand being represented by the lower buildings. We should then be looking at the building from the open court, of which the boundary walls are represented as semicircular in order to get them on to the coin; the great cone stands in the foreground and behind the great piers, the foundations for which exist at the east end of the entrance, are seen towering up above the roof.[1]

A number of inscribed statue bases were found by the excavators, and the majority of these still remain in the ruins.

South of the temple lie the ruins of the château of Covocle, which was the headquarters of the sugar industry carried on during the Middle Ages under royal patronage. Little now remains save the eastern wing of the building.

The Church of Kouklia, known as Catholiki, is a mediaeval building, with a number of inscribed stones from the temple built into its walls. A number of frescoes still remain in the interior. In the dome is Christ Pantokrator, and at the west end are depicted the rivers Tigris and Euphrates as heads, with streams of water issuing from the mouths.

About two and a half miles from the village, and on the road to Arkhimandrita, is the rock-hewn church known as Enclistra. Here the river Kephalovriso runs through a narrow gorge. The cliffs of the left-hand bank rise sheer, and are at least a hundred feet high. In the face of these cliffs, where they are highest, three small caves have been cut from the sandstone. They are about 20 feet above the level of the river; the largest is about 13 feet square and about 7 feet high, and formed the cell of a hermit. The walls are covered with frescoes; on the roof are the Holy Trinity encircled by angels and archangels. On the left of the door is the tomb niche of the hermit, and on each side are paintings of SS. Cosmas and Damian. All the frescoes are in a good state of preservation, except that the eyes have been mutilated by the Turks. They probably date from

[1] *Journal of Hellenic Studies*, vol. 9, 1888, p. 201.

the fourteenth century, though the apple-green and brown in which most of the design is carried out is un-Cypriote in character. The other two caves are damaged and the frescoes are but fragmentary.

About half a mile above and on the other side of the river are the ruins of the Monastery of St. Constantine. The small Byzantine church is roofless, but the paintings on the walls are in a fairly good state of preservation. They are of two distinct periods, though it is only where the later paintings have fallen away that it is possible to see the first series. Of the second period is the painting of the B.V.M. in Glory, in the semi-apse; to her left can be seen the dim figure of a kneeling donor in a black cloak. The second series of paintings probably date from about 1500.

Close to the sea are two large monoliths, about 11 feet high, 3 feet broad at the top and 5 feet at the base, where they disappear into the soil. A number of ruined buildings lie round. These stones are still regarded as having magical properties, and are visited by barren women and girls who have lost their lovers.

KOURDHALI (xxxvii)

The Church of the B.V.M. is a most interesting building of the fifteenth century, although an unhappy restoration of 1921 destroyed the roof, and many of the paintings have been whitewashed. Over the west door is a Crucifixion, a well-painted and balanced composition; in the centre are the three crosses, that of Our Lord surrounded by a choir of angels; behind the cross is an embattled city, while the middle foreground is filled with a crowd of mounted soldiers bearing spears; to the right of the doorway are two donors with their wives, whilst between them is a model of the church; unhappily, the heads of these donors and most of the accompanying inscription has been destroyed. Farther along the wall are the remains of the Tree of Jesse. The paintings in the central apse are of the B.V.M. in Glory, while above the semi-dome is the Annunciation. The iconostasis is a superb example of early sixteenth-century work; on one of the upper panels is a delightful miniature painting of the Madonna and Child. The icons have mostly escaped restoration, and are contemporary with the iconostasis; the best are perhaps St. Sozomenos at the extreme left of the iconostasis, and the B.V.M., and St. John the Baptist below the rood cross; in all three icons the figures wear robes of Brusa embroidery, that of the B.V.M. being a lovely apple-green, powdered with golden flowers. There is also a noble but repainted icon of Christ seated on a throne, His feet resting on a long purple cushion.

As far as can now be seen, the original church consisted of a central apse with two most unusual chambers to left and right completely divided off from the bema by a wall formed of heavy beams of timber, between which is a filling of rubble; the faces have been plastered over to take frescoes. The chamber on the south still remains untouched; it measures seven feet by four. Three sides are frescoed: on the east the B.V.M. in Glory supported by Archangels, on the two side walls pictures of various saints; the fourth or west wall is formed by the iconostasis. In the church is kept a collection of service books, mostly printed in Venice in the last years of the sixteenth century; one has a leather binding with a bronze cross in the centre, while at the corners are gilt medallions of the four Evangelists; on the title page is written a list of benefactors to the church. There are also a number of MSS. of the early fifteenth century, one being bound up with a number of leaves from an Arabic MS. written in a clear hand and apparently of the same period as the rest of the book. This is most difficult to explain, but a curious sidelight is possibly thrown by a local tradition of the origin of the name of the village. The villagers declare that it was founded by a man from Kurdestan, and it is true that the termination "li" is the Turkish means of expressing from whence a man comes. Thus a villager from Galatia would describe himself Galatiali.

The church also contains a number of pews, whose carved arm-rests are formed by heraldic-looking beasts holding a stick in both paws, the top ending in their mouths. Just outside the church is a delightful single-arched humped bridge built of tiles, reminiscent of the Chinese bridge on a willow pattern plate.

KOUTRAPHAS, KATO (xxviii)

The Church of the B.V.M. was rebuilt in the eighteenth century; it is originally said to have been erected by that mysterious queen who figures so frequently but so vaguely in the folklore of Cyprus. Of this original building remain the west and north doors, the former with a white marble lintel and carved supports, while the latter has a lintel of black and white marble supported by two thin stone columns with elegant Gothic capitals. The iconostasis is modern, but fragments of its predecessor lie scattered about the church. The Gospel printed in Venice is dated 1604.

KOUTSOVENDIS (xii)

Between the village and the monastery lie the ruins of a large Byzantine church built in tiled brick, and dedicated to the Virgin of Koutsovendis. The dome has disappeared, and there are no signs of a narthex. On the south wall is a spirited painting of St. George on a white horse. To the south side of this church is a small building which may either have been a separate chapel or, perhaps, the original church; on the north wall is a beautiful fresco of the preparation of the Body of Christ for burial. Although it has been exposed to the rain and storm for numberless years, this painting is in an amazingly good state of preservation, and is one of the most lovely and beautiful things in the Island; it is hard to date, but probably belongs to the fourteenth century. It is like a perfect Italian primitive. On hot, dry days it may appear dull and flat; but in spring, when the rain beats on its unprotected surface, it lives and glows; the colours brighten once more, the bent, mourning figures come to life, the broken Madonna kisses the face of her dead Son in an agony of disbelief. St. John clasps the cold hand as if he, too, cannot realize that this is Death; at the head stand two women gazing with a look of mingled despair and hope on their faces, as if the whole scene were some ghastly dream, and that at any moment the dead Christ must rise; but the crouching figure which, in hopeless despair, embraces the feet of Christ, knows that the beloved Master has left them.

The Monastery of St. Chrysostomos belongs to the Orthodox See of Jerusalem. According to van Bruyn, who visited it in 1683:

> We returned to the convent, which I drew, as well as the mountain and its buildings. The former is fairly large, surrounded by a good wall, and contains some few rooms of modern style, rebuilt after the destruction, not long ago, of a great part of the edifice by fire. The church is in two parts, 48 feet long and 28 feet wide. Under a little dome is a large half-length painting of Christ, and all round other figures, nearly all faded. Eight columns built into the wall support the dome. The altar is adorned with much foliage and gilding, done five years ago. A princess is buried in the church, the same, they say, who built the edifice whose ruins we saw on the top of the mountain. Two of her slaves are buried with her, one on either side. Fourteen steps take one to the top of the church, and to a grotto in which it is said that the Turks found a large coffer full of gold. In the cloister is a small ruined chapel. The room used as a kitchen is thirty-six feet long and eighteen broad. The convent is ruled by a Father-Guardian, who has under him three priests and eleven monks. Within the cloister is a small garden with a few orange trees. I must not forget to say why the convent was built. The princess who is buried in it lived in the building on the summit of the mountain, for better protection against the violence of the Templars who, at that time, strove to be lords everywhere. Besides this source of disquiet it was her misfortune to be afflicted with a kind of ulcer, or mange. A little dog, which she loved passionately and which never left her, caught it; but as soon as it felt itself attacked by the disease, it went every day down the hill and remained away for an hour or two, and while doing so it got visibly better. It was watched, and seen to bathe in a spring close by. The princess, seeing the effect on her little dog, resolved to try the remedy for herself and with such success that, in a few days, she was freed from the disease and restored to her former health. To show her gratitude to God she caused this convent to be built for Greek monks, and

called it after S. Chrysostom, under whose protection she placed it. It still keeps the name, and the fountain its virtue, for every day several persons come to bathe there and, they say, find a cure.[1]

Another traveller, Pococke, who came to Cyprus in 1728, tells us:

Two leagues to the north-east of Nicosia, on the side of the mountains, is the rich convent of Chrysostom, to which we went on the twenty-third; it belongs to the Greek convent of the Holy Sepulchre at Jerusalem. Over it, towards the top of the mountain there is a place called the hundred and one chambers, which consists of several buildings, one over another; the highest is very difficult of access; they have a tradition that a queen of Cyprus, who had the leprosy, chose to live here for the benefit of the air, and that saint John Chrysostom advising her to build the convent below, she followed his counsel, and was cured of her leprosy; others add that she bathed in a water there, which is still resorted to by persons in that distemper, who find benefit by it. This monastery has been a very large building, though great part of it is ruined; there are two churches, one of which, called Saint Helena, is ruinous, the other is covered with a dome, and painted all over within; it is dedicated to Saint John Chrysostom. Before it is a handsome portico, from which there are three doors with fine marble door-cases, that do not seem to be very antient; two scepters were formerly deposited behind the folding doors, the figures of which are painted on the wall, and at the bottom there is a place where the crown was kept. All the account they can give is, that they belonged to some queen, and that they were taken away by a pasha of Cyprus. It is possible that the regalia of Cyprus were kept here.[2]

The present building consists of two churches side by side, one of which was fatally restored in 1891. Both churches were of the Byzantine period; the one still remaining unrestored has curious brick arcading round the central dome; the interior was once painted, but little now remains. The side marble columns of the iconostasis are still *in situ*, while two other columns with Byzantine capitals

[1] *Excerpta Cypria*, p. 237.

[2] Ibid., p. 260

serve as angle shafts at each side of the apse. There is no connection between the two churches save an iron grille. The rebuilding of the last century destroyed everything in the second church save the apse, which still retains its geometric marble floor; there also survives a superb door frame of marble, with a decoration of vine leaves, dating from the early sixteenth century. The wooden door of this same date is a most remarkable example of the carpenter's craft, for not only is it the most beautiful door still remaining in the Island, but it is made without a single nail being used. Both this door and its marble frame have been copied for the new Government House at Nicosia. The church contains an extremely interesting icon of about 1500, which shows Maria di Molino and her son being presented by St. Chrysostomos to the Virgin and Child; Maria wears a velvet dress with long sleeves edged with ermine, her low-cut neck covered with lace stiffened with whalebone, while her son, a youth of about twelve, wears a dress with long pointed sleeves, the front edged with fur. The other icons in the church are: St. John the Baptist with a male donor in the left-hand corner, much repainted; St. Sozomenos, with a coat of arms in the right-hand top corner of the frame (a cuttle fish gules), and a processional icon of the B.V.M., also sixteenth century, from the ruined Church of Abscithi.

The monastic buildings have been repaired and rebuilt at various periods, though the marble pillars and capitals which support the roof of the veranda on the first storey must come from the original building of the Middle Ages.

High above the monastery, and about two hours' walk from it, lies the Castle of Buffavento. Of the three castles which crown the Kyrenia range of mountains which run down the north coast of Cyprus, perhaps the least known is the Castle of Buffavento, called by the Greeks Koutsouvendis, or the Castle of a Hundred and One Houses, and in the mediaeval chronicles the "Castle of the Lion". Little enough is known of this castle; the ruins are still extensive, and there yet remains a roof over some of the rooms, but there are no architectural features which give any clue to the period when it was built. It is true that there are remains of Byzantine brickwork, but that may be but an accidental survival of an ancient method of building. We know that it was standing at the time of King Richard of England's capture of the Island in 1191, for Benedict of Peterborough in his account of the campaign in Cyprus says:

> After this (the King's marriage to Berengaria of Navarre at Limassol) the King of England, hearing that the Emperor's (Isaac Comnenus, Despot of Cyprus, 1184–1191) daughter was in a very strong castle went thither with his army. On his approach towards the fortress the Emperor's daughter came to meet him, and falling at his feet, did him obeisance, putting herself and the castle at his mercy. Thus was delivered to him the exceeding strong castle called Buffevent, and after that all the towns and fortresses of the Empire were surrendered.[1]

There is but little mention of the castle till the reign of King Peter I of Cyprus, which lasted from 1359 to 1369. Peter was one of those strange figures which flash across the pages of history and then die and are forgotten. There is no doubt that the genius of Peter was closely allied to insanity. He pictured himself the leader of Christendom against the Turks, and in his diseased mind saw himself the lineal descendant of St. Louis and Richard Cœur de Lion. He swore to slay all Moslems, and to remind him of this vow always wore a naked sword round his neck. As soon as he had received the double crown, that of Cyprus in the Cathedral in Nicosia and that of Jerusalem (but an empty honour) at Famagusta, Peter's knight-errantry burst forth. But the enchanted days of the Crusades were no more, and it was hard to raise the interest of Europe in the recapture of Jerusalem. One must suppose that it seemed as remote as the Kingdom of Hanover does to us, and even if Peter had been crowned King of Jerusalem, so was George III crowned King of France. Peter was only helped by the Knights of Rhodes, the Catalans (his wife was Eleanor of Aragon), and a few English knights under

[1] *Excerpta Cypria*, p. 6.

Robert of Toulouse. With these helpers he set sail for Adalia, which he captured without much difficulty, but he showed already that strain of cruelty which was to bring about his own death, and slew all within the city regardless of sex or age, for he regarded himself as the chosen of God to avenge the loss of Jerusalem. Europe was amazed that this young king of an almost unknown island should, at his first attempt, capture so notable a city from the Turks; perhaps they had the same rather uncomfortable feeling, that this youth must be taken seriously, as Charles of Sweden was to give Europe so many years later. However, Peter, having shown he was in earnest, decided to set out for the West, and to apply to all the Courts of Europe for arms and money to help him in his attempt to capture the Holy City. We need not follow him through his travels to the Pope at Avignon, to the Emperor Charles IV at Prague, and to Brussels and Bruges: but his visit to England is of more than ordinary interest. He was well received by our King Edward and Queen Philippa, both of whom gave him handsome presents and a ship called the *Catherine*. The Mayor of London, Henry Picard, entertained him in the Vintners' Hall at a state banquet, a banquet notable for the fact that four kings were present, for not only were there King Edward III of England and King Peter, but the Kings of Scotland and France. Even in 1816 only three sovereigns were entertained by the City of London. It is not quite so satisfactory to state that King Peter played games of chance after dinner and lost fifty marks . . . and his temper. Perhaps the Vintners' wine was too strong, or Peter could not afford so much money; in any case, he accused the mayor of unfair play, who, not wanting a dispute with so many kings present, handed Peter his money back. Peter must have left England with but a poor opinion of that country, for he was robbed by brigands on his journey to the coast.

The great Crusade started well, and Peter sailed from Venice with a considerable fleet. He captured Alexandria, and for a moment it really seemed as if the titular King of Jerusalem might enter his city as a conqueror. But the allies quarrelled, and most of them returned to their own countries, and the Venetians, whose commerce was suffering owing to these wars with the Moslems, prevailed on Peter to sign a peace.

Peter did but little more: a raid on Syria, a visit to Rome, and then he returned to his own Kingdom of Cyprus. Many troubles awaited him there. His loyal friend, Sir John Visconti, had written to the King during his absence and told him that his Queen, Eleanor of Aragon, had been unfaithful to him. Peter therefore held an inquiry, but the Court Party, for various reasons—the chief being fear of the Queen's country of Spain—conspired together to hoodwink the King, and led him to believe that Visconti had lied when he had accused the Queen. The King believed his courtiers, and Visconti was accused of slandering Eleanor. He was condemned without a hearing, and cast into the Castle of Kyrenia, where he lay for a year.

> And afterwards there comes a great French Lord from the West on his way to Jerusalem and the kinsman of Sir John Visconti begged him to ask the King to give him up, as is the custom of rulers. And he begged the King to take him out of the dungeon, and the King promised that he would take him out. As soon as this foreign Count had left he ordered them to take him from the dungeon at Kyrenia and sent him to the Castle of Buffavento: then they threw him into a dungeon, and there he stayed without food till he died—of this Knight I wish I could tell you how manly he was, and at jousting and in the use of all weapons he was indeed very valiant and manly. May our Lord God pardon him.[1]

So was one of the blackest pages in the history of the Castle of Buffavento and of Peter I written.

The end of Peter is tragic enough; the murder of Visconti was but a prelude to a reign of cruelty and torture of his nobility and people. Even his family were not safe, and at last, on January 16, 1369, he was assassinated by a body of nobles with the concurrence of his brother John, Prince of Antioch.

[1] *Chronicle of Makhairas*, p. 239.

The next mention of Buffavento in history is when it was held by the adherents of King Peter II against the Genoese, who had captured Famagusta, which they were to hold till the reign of James II of Cyprus.

The castle figured but once more before the end of the kingdom, and that during the reign of James I, 1382–1398. For political reasons, two brothers, Parot and Wilmot de Montolif, were imprisoned in Buffavento. Both brothers determined to escape from the cell which they shared. Parot, who was far the braver of the two, was able to bend the iron bars which guarded the window of his dungeon, and thus was able to make enough space between them for him to creep through. The window looked out on to the rocky and craggy hillside above Ayios Epiktitos, sparsely covered with pine-trees. Taking his courage in both hands, Parot leapt on to a pine-tree far below him, and was able to reach the ground with nothing worse than a sprained ankle. (His brother Wilmot, when he saw how difficult had been Parot's escape, preferred to remain in the comparative safety of his cell.) Parot meanwhile had found a small boy with a horse, which he commandeered and rode to Kyrenia, and took refuge in the chancel of the Church of St. Antony, but all to no avail, for he was apprehended by the Constable of the Kingdom and taken back to Buffavento, where he and his brother were confined with "two wooden beams across their feet, one to each of them".[1] Shortly afterwards both brothers were beheaded, and their bodies were put into a chest and taken to Cava (Leondari Vouno, above Athalassa) and buried there. There is a strange story how the mule which brought the chests containing the bodies fell dead as soon as it was eased of its grim burden.

The Venetians found they had not enough men to garrison the castle, and deliberately "slighted" it, removing not only its cannons and armaments, but also most of the roof.

During the Turkish rule of Cyprus the castle was visited by various serious travellers, one of whom, Cornelius van Bruyn, a native of The Hague, came in 1683. He visited

[1] *Chronicle of Makhairas*, p. 603.

Nicosia, and then went on first to Kythrea, where he found some fossil oyster shells, and then to Buffavento. He started the climb to the castle—

But we were obliged to rest and take breath a dozen times. The ascent is as difficult and dangerous as ever I made. The greater part of the time we had to climb with our hands as well as our feet, and whichever way we turned our gaze we saw only what made our hair stand on end. We took an hour and a half to reach the top. There one only sees the live rock, a number of ruined chambers, and large stone-built reservoirs. It must have been a huge building, with many rooms built at different levels.[1]

Another visitor was Ali Bey, and the castle has changed but little since he visited and described it in 1805.

At last, after much trouble, we reached the gate of the palace and took a few moments' rest. This singular edifice may be described as consisting of four separate blocks, some higher than the others. Let me call the first the guardrooms, the second the storerooms, the third the court or state apartment, and the fourth the sleeping quarters of the owners on the very highest point of the mountain. This last block was perhaps intended to serve also as a chapel or oratory. There are vaults below. I am told that no mention of it exists in any history worthy of credit, and on no part of it did I find any trace of an inscription or hieroglyphics.

The walls are built of stone quarried on the spot, cemented with lime. Several of the corners are of bricks, still red, and well burnt. Some which I measured were two feet long, one foot broad, and two fingers thick. The jambs of the doors and windows are of marble composed entirely of fossil shells of a thousand different kinds, quite well preserved. Some rooms still preserve their roof. When one thinks of the labour and cost involved in the building of such a palace, on such a site: when one reflects on its antiquity, one is astonished indeed. It was decorated with all the luxury known at the epoch of its construction. The window openings are well proportioned: the marble was certainly brought from a great distance, as well as the lime and bricks which could not have been made on the spot.

---

[1] *Excerpta Cypria*, p. 237.

The beauty, I might even say the magnificence, of the apartment probably used by the court, even the provision of water for a building so vast and situated on such a height, make one believe that the founder of the palace was a sovereign endowed at once with great talents, no ordinary spirit, and immense wealth.[1]

KYKKO (xxxvi)

The Monastery of Kykko is the most famous in the Island; it is, indeed, known all over the Orthodox world, for within its walls is sheltered one of the three icons attributed to St. Luke. The Russian and Greek Churches count only three icons as the work of the Evangelist: an icon formerly at Sumela, near Trebizond, and now preserved at Athens; one in the Monastery of Megaspelion, at the north of the Peloponnesus[2]; and the icon of Kykko.

The history of the foundation of the monastery in the twelfth century is given by Makhairas as follows:

Also there is in Marathasa at Kykko the picture of the very holy Mother of God. When the lord Manuel Voutoumitis came as duke to Cyprus, (as he was going to Marathasa towards Kykko, and had risen up one morning to go hunting), he fell in with a monk in the mountains of Marathasa; his name was Isaias. And because the monk stood in his way, he gave him a kick. And shortly afterwards he fell sick of the disease called sciatica, (and the very foot with which he had struck the monk was affected). And he saw in a vision (that he must go to the monk to ask his forgiveness, that he should pardon him, because no physician could cure him. And) he went back to the saint to get his blessing. And the Mother of God, (the Virgin of Trikoukkia,) revealed herself to the monk, telling him to seek the picture which is in the palace of the emperor in the City and that they should bring it here. (The duke went to the monk and burst into tears; and the monk pardoned him, and he was at once healed. And the monk asked him to let him have the picture; and he said to him: "The emperor has it in his palace." And when the said Manuel went to Constantinople, he found

[1] *Travels*, London, 1816, p. 280.

[2] It is said that this icon was rescued during the fire which completely destroyed the monastery in 1934.

the daughter of the emperor very sick even unto death, and no physician could cure her, and she was lying thus for a year. And when the duke considered the cure which the monk had done, he told the emperor of it. And he said to him: "Where is he?" "In Cyprus, at Marathasa." "And what is his name?" "Isaias." And at once the emperor sent a ship to Cyprus with orders that the monk should go to Constantinople. And when he saw the order he went: and as soon as he had stretched his hand out over the maiden, she was at once healed of her sickness, and rose up. And the emperor desired to give the monk great gifts; and he fell on his knees and asked him for the picture. And the emperor was loath to give it, but seeing the pains of the monk and the healing of his daughter, he was greatly moved and gave it to him. And he took it with him, and came to Cyprus: and men rejoiced much, and built a church and put monks there; and in time of drought it works marvels without end. And this is a work of the apostle Luke.)[1]

The monastery has been destroyed by fire several times, the first in 1365, being caused by a villager who, searching for wild honey, lit a fire in the forest to scare the bees, but the fire spread and enveloped not only the forest but the monastery, which was burned to the ground. It was rebuilt by Eleanor of Aragon, wife of Peter I, in 1365, who, although she was of the Latin faith, had been much impressed by the miracles performed by the famous icon. This erection, which was made of wood, was destroyed in 1542; rebuilt again, it was burned in 1751; finally in 1813 the church and monastery were burnt to the ground for the fourth time. Luckily on all four occasions it was possible to save the famous icon.

As we see it to-day, the monastery is a vast pile of irregular buildings erected round two courtyards; it is said to contain not less than seventy guest-rooms. The church itself is of little interest. The only fragment of the original building, destroyed in 1813, is part of the vaulting of the apse, which still shows dim traces of painting. Over the south door of the church is a marble panel with a Byzantine cross and two birds carved in relief on it. This may possibly be the only surviving relic of the first building.

[1] *Chronicle of Makhairas*, p. 37.

The famous icon of the B.V.M. is enclosed in a handsome shrine of tortoiseshell and mother-of-pearl approached by three semicircular marble steps. The icon is protected by a cloth decorated with a figure of the Virgin in silver and edged with seed pearls. The actual painting itself is covered with a silver gilt plate on which is stamped a representation of the painting beneath; this cover is said to date from 1776. It is regarded as the blackest of sins to attempt to gaze on the actual painting, which is said never to have been seen by a human eye since it was covered over in the sixteenth century. Strange and terrible is the fate of those who endeavour surreptitiously to get a glimpse of the painting. It is recorded that a certain learned monk, a native of Rhodes, John by name, came from Jerusalem in the year 1776 on a pilgrimage to the monastery.

He requested to be allowed to remain one night shut up alone in the church for the purposes of devotion. The brethren at first refused on the plea that it was not usual, but at length consented at his repeated request. Entering the church with some tapers in his hand he placed them in the chandelier opposite to the holy picture, and commenced his prayers to the Virgin. After being thus engaged for some time he at length approached the eikon and stretched out his hand to draw aside the covering, which concealed it from view. Suddenly from the aperture in the metal case there issued a hot blast, that striking him on the face caused him and the place, on which he was standing, to tremble. Turning his head in the direction of the chandelier, in which he had placed the tapers, he saw them take light of their own accord. Full of astonishment at the sight, and not knowing what to do, he cried out with a loud voice: "All-holy Theotokos," and then falling on his face lay speechless on the ground. Two men, who had been secretly posted by the Abbot to watch his proceedings and protect the church, on hearing the noise rushed to the spot, and seeing him lying there half-dead with fright carried him out of the building. After leaving him sufficient time to recover they inquired what had happened. John, who by this time had come to his senses, looked fixedly at them, but was unable to reply, and again entering the church lay at full length before the eikon. The brethren so far knew nothing of this strange occurrence, as it had happened during the fourth hour of the night. But on the conclusion of matins they closely questioned him, when he related what had befallen him.[1]

The icon has always enjoyed a great reputation among the islanders as a bringer of rain. Van Bruyn, who visited Cyprus in 1693, says:

They carried, too, in procession a certain picture of the Virgin Mary with the Child Jesus in her arms, said to be the work of St. Luke. This picture is generally kept in a convent called Chicho, to which belong some 400 caloyers, part of whom are sent to Muscovy and elsewhere on various duties. The convent is built on Mount Olympus, the highest mountain in the island. In times of drought the picture is brought with great ceremony out of the convent, and placed on a stage about twenty steps high, with the face turned to the quarter from which they may expect rain. Now it happened that the same ceremony had been observed on account of the locusts, and as soon as the picture had been set on the stage there appeared forthwith certain birds not unlike plovers, which swooped upon the locusts and devoured a great quantity.

To the right of the icon are hung two curious relics, a bronze arm and the "saw" of a sword fish. The story of the former is that an impious Turk tried to light his cigarette at one of the lamps in front of the icon, and the outraged Virgin at once withered the offending member, turning it into bronze. Of the latter, it is said a sailor gave it in gratitude to the Virgin of Kykko, to whom he prayed, and who saved him when in danger of drowning.

The rest of the icons in the church are unimportant, though there is one painting by Cornaro, the famous Cretan icon painter of the end of the eighteenth century. The treasury is a small room south of the apse, and guarded by an iron door. It contains a collection of relics and church furniture of various periods, no doubt quite meritorious, though nearly everything of value was carried off by the Turks when they sacked the monastery in 1821. There is a large collection of carved wooden crosses with gilt and

[1] Hackett, *Church of Cyprus*, p. 341.

cloisonne settings, adorned with seed pearls and flawed emeralds. There are about a dozen Gospels, including one larger than the rest, its gilt cover decorated with enamel plaques of the Evangelists in frames of brilliants. This is Russian work of the nineteenth century, for till the Russian revolution the Monastery of Kykko held not only great property in Cyprus, but lands in Russia, Roumania, and Asia Minor; indeed, many pilgrims used to journey from Russia to visit Kykko, and left behind valuable presents. It was said that before the war the revenue of the monastery from its lands in Cyprus and abroad was more than £10,000 annually.

Of the remaining relics only a few call for special attention: an antimission of 1653, a box of relics of various martyrs, in the centre a carved ivory plaque of a saint of much earlier workmanship. There is also a large circular gilt plaque with a reliquary containing a wooden cross in the centre, and with a pendant formed by a large misshapen baroque pearl; there are the usual endless silver boxes containing fragments of the bones of saints, all of which are regarded as miracle working.

KYPEROUNDA (xxxvii)

The Church of St. Marina is a late eighteenth-century building with a modern iconostasis; the carved front of the women's gallery is pleasant rustic work. The church contains five processional icons, but all are so damaged that it is difficult even to distinguish which saint they represent.

On a tiny hill close by is the Church of the Holy Cross. In the interior of the north and south walls are two arched recesses. One of these contains a painting of the Cross itself, between the arms of which are scenes from the life of St. Helena, and the story of the finding of the three crosses; below kneels a male donor in a black robe, and an inscription dated 1521, which is probably also the date of the church itself. In the other, to the south, is a painting of the Archangel with St. John the Divine. The base of the proskenetarion is well carved, and has what would seem to be a coat of arms in it: a lion crowned rampant regardant.

Outside the village and by the edge of the river is the early eighteenth-century Church of the B.V.M. It contains nothing save an over-painted processional icon of St. John the Baptist. The name of the village probably comes from the Greek word for the cypress-tree.

KYRA (xx)

The Church of the B.V.M. Chryseleoussa was restored in 1879. Originally a sixteenth-century church, little remains of that period save two buttresses and a fragment of a wall on the north-east side of the modern church. The church is built over a spring, the waters of which run into a vast tank, and are the property of the Evkaf. Outside the west door lie two very fine spirally fluted columns, said to come from the ruined Church of St. Stephen.

Three miles to the north, and situated on a barren ridge, is the small Monastery and Church of St. George. Originally built in the fifteenth century, the church has been much repaired. The vaulting of the roof is supported by marble columns, which still retain traces of painting; a Byzantine marble capital lies in the bema, and various fragments of the same period are scattered in the yard. Behind the church and across the plateau is a vast cemetery, the tombs appear to belong to the late geometric and early classical period, and are all robbed; some have standing stones erected above the dromoi.

On the spur to the south are the ruins of some mediaeval building, called by the villagers the "Castle of the King". It is possible that it may have been a watch-tower or blockhouse.

The Monastery of St. George is never kept locked, for it is so sacred that no thieves would ever enter in and steal.

KYTHREA (xxii)

The former settlement at Kythrea, called by the ancients Cythera, was sacred to Venus, and lies east of the present village and near the ruins of the Church of St. Dimitrianos.

Here in 1928 was found the superb heroicbronze statue of the Emperor Septimius Severus now in the Nicosia museum.

Kythrea is really four villages all joined together, and lies each side of the river, which issues forth from the side of a hill at a place called Kephalovryso. The stream is supposed to come across from Asia Minor under the sea, and this is firmly believed by the villagers; for, many years ago, an old woman came from Anatolia to stay with her daughter who had married a man of Kythrea. The old dame went up to the spring-head one day with her daughter to wash clothes, and while so engaged saw a silver vessel borne by the stream issuing from the mouth of the tunnel; the old dame seized it and at once recognized it as one that she had dropped a year before, in the stream that ran near her house in Asia Minor. Thus it was proved that a river which disappears into the ground in Asia Minor reappears in Cyprus. Unfortunately geologists have a far better and more convincing reason for the appearance of this river from the hillside. During the Middle Ages this spring supplied the flour mills which ground the corn for the capital, and also, according to Lusignano, watered the cotton plantations which surrounded the village.

In 1220 Queen Alice granted the Archbishop of Nicosia the free use of the mills of Kythrea for the redemption of the soul of her husband King Hugh.

Kythrea's greatest claim to fame is that in the cultivated fields below the village was grown the cauliflower, and it is from here that it was introduced into Europe in 1604.

Starting from the spring-head, near which, in 1934, the writer picked up the fossil tooth of a pigmy elephant, the principal churches are: St. Andronicos, a small ancient chapel belonging to the Maronites; it contains an icon of St. Andronicos with a long inscription in Arabic, dated 1681: one of the B.V.M. Galataga, a good example of an untouched sixteenth-century icon, and one of St. Macarios supported by two saints dated 1692. The Church of St. Anna, an ancient vaulted building on the side of a hill, which is rapidly disappearing; indeed, the north wall has recently fallen owing to a landslide. The church probably dates from the early sixteenth century, and from its style of building may possibly have been a Latin church. On the other side of the stream is the modern Church of St. Anna, which contains a seventeenth-century iconostasis probably removed from the ancient church; in the gallery lies an icon of the B.V.M. and Child, dated 1675. The Church of the B.V.M. is a modern building on an ancient site; in the gallery are various icons from its predecessor, most important of which are St. John the Baptist, 1673, the B.V.M. in Glory, 1671, and a panel from the former iconostasis of 1714. In the body of the church is kept a large and curious icon of St. George, measuring 6 feet square, but so destroyed that it is almost impossible to make out anything of the various scenes depicting the life of the saint, which surround the central figure. Further down the valley is the Chapel of the Archangel Michael, a poor and mean building, into the base of the belfry of which has been built a marble Byzantine slab with a cross and foliage in relief, probably of the twelfth century. It may possibly once have formed the lower panel of the iconostasis. Close to the chapel Mr. Jeffery discovered, lying at the side of the road, a curious block of stone:

> Intended to form a standard of measures, similar to the measure standards frequently found remaining in front of the Palazzo Publico of a small Italian town. This is said to have been brought from the ancient site of Ag. Dimitrianos, where it no doubt was used by the millers of mediaeval times to check their corn measures. It consists of a cubical block of stone with carefully cut sinkings of the following dimensions: 1, 24 cm. square, 12 cm. deep; 2, a circle, 16 cm. diameter, 25 cm. deep; 3, a circle, 12 cm. diameter, 25 cm. deep; 4, a circle, 10 cm. diameter, 15 cm. deep; 5, a circle, 7 cm. diameter, 8 cm. deep.[1]

The Church of St. George is modern; the interior in the worst possible taste is a glaring example of how not to decorate a church. The walls are painted to represent veined marble, and the windows filled with the brightest and

[1] *Monuments of Cyprus*, p. 270.

crudest colours. It is probably the ugliest church in Cyprus. The Church of St. Andronicos has been almost completely rebuilt, and only the south wall remains from the earlier building. The mural paintings in the interior probably date from *c.* 1720. In the apse is kept an icon of the B.V.M. supported by two saints, dated 1742; here, too, lies the tombstone of a Greek lady, a certain Avlina Merlin, dated 1556. Also in the church is a Byzantine marble slab, the pair to the one already described above.

The Church of St. Marina was built in 1734. The small marble pillars and capitals in the south arcade came from some older building; the wall paintings are contemporary with the church, though the iconostasis is dated 1634, and doubtless comes from some former church on this site. In the centre of the floor is inset a Byzantine marble panel with an intricate design, and two others are placed in front of the iconostasis. The only icon of interest is one of Christ dated 1681, that has been touched up by a later and inferior hand.

At the far end of the village and close to the high-road lies the Monastery of the Virgin, the property of the Archbishopric. According to an inscription the church was rebuilt by Archbishop Chrysanthos in 1771. The iconostasis is a superb and unrepaired example of baroque woodcarving; time has dulled the bright colours and gilding, but the twisted pillars and fanciful animals intertwined amongst the vines are reminiscent of the façade of an eighteenth-century Neapolitan church. The icons also are of interest, the earliest being St. Mavra dated 1561; the saint has a head-dress like the Holbein portrait of Queen Katherine; it is true that the face of the saint has been touched up, but her gold and blue cloak are original and show no signs of over-painting. There are two icons of Christ and the B.V.M. dated 1680. In the gallery lies a small and rather wooden painting of the Madonna and Child, enclosed in a remarkable Italian frame with elaborate festoons ending in human masks down each side. Slightly damaged by fire as it is, it is a fine thing, and it is difficult not to believe that this frame dates from the Venetian era.

In the bema is kept a wooden chest with a Byzantine eagle carved on the front panel.

LAGOUDHERA (xxxviii)

The Church of St. George is a small shed-like building of the mid-nineteenth century, though part of the iconostasis, including three of the lower panels, probably date from the last quarter of the sixteenth century. The church contains some interesting icons: (1) B.V.M. and Child, *c.* 1560, in an excellent state of preservation, and apparently not repainted or touched up. It is curious to note for how long the Byzantine method of painting lasted, as the face of Our Lady is in the true tradition, although the elaborate folds of her robes show Western influence. (2) A triptych, in the centre the Deisis, namely Christ, between B.V.M. and St. John the Baptist, on the wings SS. Nicholas and Athanasios, dated 1593. (3) Christ, with the remains of an inscription, and dated at the bottom 1620.

The monastery of the B.V.M. Aranou, a domed twelfth-century Byzantine building, was in the eighteenth century entirely covered with a shed-like roof, while verandas with lattice work were added round three sides. There are still remains of painting on the exterior north wall of the church, and a rudely carved plaque of the Crucifixion is fixed above the north door. The whole of the interior of the church, save the narthex, which was added later, is covered with mural paintings of the late twelfth and early thirteenth centuries. The paintings are in an excellent state of preservation, and, after those in the Church of Asinou, are the earliest in the Island. A majestic figure of Christ Pantokrator fills the dome, and the walls are covered with the figures of various saints. The most beautiful of all the paintings is a Dormition of the Virgin with superb dawn-blue background and long attenuated figures. The iconostasis dates from 1673, and contains the icon of Christ painted on both sides. In the bema is a curious early sixteenth-century icon of the B.V.M. and Child, painted on coarse canvas; the figures have raised and decorated haloes; this picture has been stuck, at some period, on to a far older icon, but all that is visible of the latter is a silvered background. In the church is kept a silver orb about the size of a tennis ball. The story goes that many years ago a Turk came to deface the paintings in the church, but the Virgin, jealous for her monastery, sent hailstones of so large a size that they killed the Turk before he reached the monastery. One of these hailstones was picked up, and the silver orb, of exactly the same size, was made in commemoration of the event.

LAKATAMIA (xxx)

About a mile and a half from the village, on the other side of the river, is the Monastery of the Archangel Gabriel. The church, with its incomplete monastic enclosure, was built in 1636 by the Archbishop Nicephoros. The appearance of the church with its carefully cut stones and richly moulded doors and windows, shows that not only was the Cypriote stonemason still as adept as he had been in the Venetian era, but that the Orthodox Church, even so soon after the Turkish conquest, was rich and powerful enough to erect such a building. The interior is plain and unplastered. There is, however, a vast fresco of the Archangel, holding a bust of the Child, on the south wall. The iconostasis dates from 1650, and contains some interesting icons; those of the B.V.M. and Child, 1650, and the Archangel, 1652, have donor portraits of the Archbishop in full regalia. There is also a large icon of the Archangel Gabriel, 1785, which has a portrait of the donor priest on it. In the narthex is a founder's tomb, with an elaborate moulded arch and dripstone, but the gravestone has disappeared; it is possible that the Archbishop himself was buried here. When the rain-compelling icon of Kykko was brought down to the plains to work miracles, it was given shelter in this monastery, and *graffiti* on the right of the north door record its visits in 1683, 1813, and 1816.

LANIA (xlvii)

The Church of the B.V.M. is a late nineteenth-century building, which has replaced the ancient tiled structure.

From the former building, however, survives a mediaeval plate with the figures of Adam and Eve in relief in the centre. In the apse is preserved an early sixteenth-century icon of the B.V.M., but much damaged. The early eighteenth century iconostasis is in a good state of preservation, and also comes from the older church.

LAPATHOS (xiv)

The tableland between this village and Gypsos is a vast necropolis of the Iron Age (1000–500 B.C.) period, but the majority of tombs have long since been opened and robbed. The Church of St. John the Baptist is a double-aisled building, and dates from the early eighteenth century, though the north door may be earlier. The aisles are divided by clumsy arches supported by heavy round pillars. The iconostasis in the north aisle is of unpainted woodwork, and may well be early; above the holy doors is carved a coat of arms, a lion rampant holding a flower in the dexter paw; a coat not unlike this was borne by the Venetian family of Pisani.

LAPITHOS (xi)

This is one of the most beautiful villages in Cyprus, entirely surrounded as it is by orange and other fruit trees. It is lucky in that it has a perpetual stream of water which issues forth from the hillside above the village. According to Strabo,[1] it was founded by a colony of Lacedaemonians under Praxander, although another account describes its origin to the Phoenicians, under Belus King of Tyre. Poracchi says:

> Lapethos, two leagues from Cerines, was also an ancient capital, its last king being Pisistratus, a companion of Alexander the Great. Now it is a village of the same name, wonderfully fertile, and quite famous for its excellent lemons. They say that in the earliest ages Cinaras, son of Agrippa, here first discovered the art, still practised, of making earthen vessels.[2]

Pococke, who also visited it in 1728, writes:

[1] *Excerpta Cypria*, p. 2.

[2] *L'isole piu famose*, Venice, 1576.

We set forward towards the west, and travelled about two leagues to the ruins of antient Lapithos, which I suppose to be the capital of another kingdom. Here, I saw several walls that were cut out of the rock, and one entire room over the sea; there are also remains of some towers and walls, but the old name is translated to a village near called Lapta, where there are some sources of very fine water, which seem to be those of the antient river Lapithos. I lay here at the rich convent called Acropede.[1]

During the Byzantine times it was the seat of an Orthodox Bishop, but was with many others suppressed in 1222. The village contains a number of churches; the principal ones are: (1) St. Luke, a nineteenth-century building; a number of florid Corinthian capitals from the ruins of Lambousa lie in the churchyard; they were brought here with a view to being used in the building of the church. (2) St. John the Baptist, an eighteenth-century building with an elaborate north doorway decorated with dog-tooth moulding. There is a well-preserved icon of St. John with two female donors in the costume of 1680; one wears a green dress with wide white sleeves embroidered with needlework, the other is robed in scarlet. The icons in the screen are dated 1793, which may well be the date of the church itself. (3) St. Theodoros, built in 1834. In the yard lie two large white marble columns with Byzantine crosses cut in relief on them. The church is devoid of interest, save for a pair of well-painted late seventeenth-century holy doors, which lie coated with dust in the gallery. (4) St. Anastasia, a modern church with an extremely ugly and overloaded iconostasis. From a previous church come three large icons dated 1772. In the bema is kept a well-preserved limestone cippus, the gravestone of a certain Seleukion, with a delightful design of bunches of grapes and vine leaves carved in high relief on it; this is probably the most elaborate Roman sepulchral monument still existing in Cyprus. (4) St. Paraskevi, a large ugly building of 1892, built on the side of a more ancient church; it contains many icons from its predecessor, of which the most

[1] *Travels*, London, 1743, p. 223.

interesting is a long panel of St. Paraskevi, given in 1701 by a certain Michael. Among the others may be noted a roundel of St. Pantelemon in an elaborate rococo frame of the late eighteenth century, and a triptych of the B.V.M. with pictures of SS. George, Demetrios, etc., on the wings, *c.* 1720. (5) St. Minas, a curious double-aisled building of 1843, with arches on heavy pillars dividing the aisles; it contains a large early eighteenth-century icon of St. Minas riding on his horse.

About a mile and a half north of the village and close to the sea lie the ruins of the city of Lambousa. Nothing now remains save shapeless heaps of stones. Lambousa was probably founded about the eighth century B.C., and reached the height of its power and importance during the Roman and Byzantine periods. From the latter period date the ruins of the lighthouse, a number of mosaic floors, and also the large artificial fish-pond and its channels, cut in the rock on the sea-shore. At the west end of the city, running inland from this fish-pond, can be seen traces of the original city wall. Lambousa was sacked by the Arabs in the seventh century A.D., but revived during the Middle Ages, when it was known as "La Fief de la Pison". The two churches which still remain date from that time. The principal monument is the Monastery of Akhiropietos, or "Built without hands", for, according to a legend, the whole building was brought over in a single night by the Virgin from Asia Minor, where it was in danger of being destroyed and defiled by the heathen. The church is dedicated to a wonder-working icon of the Holy Handkerchief of St. Veronica, though according to an old Cypriote legend the shroud of Christ was once kept here, and carried off by a Princess of the House of Savoy, and given to the Cathedral at Turin, where it is to this day. Whatever the dedication may be, the church is certainly one of the oldest foundations in the country.

As we see it to-day, the building is of several periods, the oldest portion being the central cruciform church with two domes over the transept, probably dating from the thirteenth century. The marble columns in the side aisles come from some Byzantine building. At the end of the fifteenth or the beginning of the sixteenth century, the apse was destroyed and a vast new one was built out of all proportion to the rest of the church; it seems probable that a complete rebuilding was contemplated, though only the apse was erected. It is seven-sided externally, and semicircular inside. The mural paintings of the Fathers of the Church are contemporary, but much destroyed by the sea air. About 1550 the west end of the church was lengthened by the addition of a narthex with elaborate stone carving and decoration. According to tradition the cost of this was borne by a certain Alessandro Flatros, whose tomb lies in the west end of the church. The tombstone is of gypsum, and shows the deceased in civilian costume. In the middle of the last century part of the inscription and the date 1563 were visible, but the feet of the villagers have worn all signs of this away. The iconostasis is mostly seventeenth century; in the centre are four white marble columns, two of which have Corinthian capitals; the pillar to the left of the holy doors has a painting on it, in the Byzantine manner, of a saint holding a book, the face carefully painted and probably dating from the fourteenth century; to the right of the holy doors the lower panel of the iconostasis is formed of a portion of a large marble Byzantine plaque, with crosses in relief upon it. The icons are mostly eighteenth century; two of them, choir of angels and Christ, were painted by Philotheos, a monk of the monastery, in 1761. The famous icon of the Holy Handkerchief was covered with silver gilt in 1814, and nothing of the painting can now be seen. The floor of the church is formed of coloured marbles in a geometric pattern, but is rather a patchwork and probably comes from an earlier building on this site. In the centre of the floor is a delightful floral design carried out in small and differently shaped pieces of black, red, yellow, and white marble. In the apse lies a pair of holy doors, painted in 1692 by the monk Leontios. In a cupboard is kept an ebigonation or a painted square worn by a bishop or priest on the right side, suspended by a cord round the neck; this example is in an excellent state of repair, and is painted with the Resurrection, in oils in the manner of the Italian eighteenth century, with gilded putti in relief at the corners. The proskenetarion is a perfect example of baroque woodwork. Outside the north door lies the large square base of a statue with a long inscription to the Emperor Tiberius Caesar in A.D. 30.

The monastic buildings are of two storeys, all of various periods. A number of marble capitals and columns, several of them Byzantine, are reused up in the building.

Amid the ruins of Lambousa stands the Church of St. Evlalios, one of the early occupants of the See of Lapithos. The church is deserted, but it is in a good state of preservation, and probably dates from the fifteenth century.

The most interesting feature of the interior is, however, the treatment of the side walls of the nave in the form of arcades carried on four ancient columns in grey cipollino marble. Three of these columns have been carefully and ingeniously pared down to match the diameter of the fourth, and on the surface thus treated a large Byzantine cross had been left in relief.[1]

There are remains of the original floor formed by square hexagonal and octagonal pieces of yellow marble, and the altar stone, with five incised consecration crosses, is *in situ*. To the east and south of the church are traces of a former building, and the remains of a mosaic pavement. All round can be picked up tiny tessera of coloured glass, remains of some perished Byzantine mosaic.

Between the monastery and the church just described is the Chapel of St. Evlambios. This curious monument is a mass of rock in the centre of a quarry, which has been worked down to the floor-level, leaving this singular building detached. The walls are about three feet thick, but are pierced on all sides with tomb niches like the Roman catacombs. There is an apse cut in the rock, but the narthex has disappeared. Faint traces of painting can still be observed, but there are no other architectural details. Two most interesting finds of silver treasure of the sixth century A.D. were made here in the early years of

[1] Jeffery, *Monuments of Cyprus*, p. 321.

the present century; the treasure has been divided up, part bought by Mr. Pierpont Morgan is now in the Metropolitan Museum, New York, while the remainder was shared between the British Museum and Cyprus. The silver dishes in the Cyprus Museum show the Marriage of David, and are interesting as having on the back what appears to be the earliest known hallmarks, or whatever corresponded to them at that period.

LARNAKA TIS LAPITHOU (xi)

Not far from the village lies a small monastery of the B.V.M. Kathari. It is difficult to judge at what period this building was erected; the only date, 1707, is over the west door, and must refer to a rebuilding. Both the north and west door, especially the latter, which is a good example of the richly moulded pointed arch with a square drip-stone are early sixteenth century. The steps opposite the north door are formed of architectural fragments from the original church. Above the north door is a curious stone carving like a mediaeval helm, with two lines of inscription in Gothic script, too weathered to be deciphered.

The village is supposed to be built on the site of the ancient town of Lacedaemon, which contained a Temple of Poseidon erected by Ptolemy Soter, *c.* 312 B.C.

Escorted by two mounted priests we started for a little cluster of stone houses high up in the mountains, called Larnaca of Lapethus. The place is so named from the large quantity of rock-cut tombs by which it is surrounded. The ancient city of Lapethus was just on the other side of the range of mountains at the foot of the northern slope, and there is no doubt that these rock-cut tombs must have belonged to it. On the slope of a conical rock, which at a distance seems to be artificial, ten or fifteen minutes' walk from this "Larnaca", there is a bilingual inscription in Greek and Phoenician of the Ptolemaic period, which has been considerably damaged by a tourist who copied it some years ago. In its vicinity I discovered the ruins of a small oblong temple, and the ground is strewn with many fragments of terra-cotta statuettes and stone statues, mostly life-size, and of Cypriote workmanship. I dug here for five days in 1872, and laid bare several large granite pedestals, with Greek inscriptions engraved on them.[1]

LASA (xxxv)

The Church of the B.V.M. is late nineteenth century; it contains a tiny icon of the B.V.M. dated 1580. The priest's maniple has the date 1786 woven into it, and the two mother-of-pearl buckles of the same period have figures of SS. George and Dimitrianos on them. The church contains a silver Venetian spoon of the sixteenth century, probably the only piece of plate of that period still existing in the island.

LAXIA (xxx)

Although this village is marked in the mediaeval maps, there are no signs of an ancient church. Close to the village, where the main road crosses the river of The Ten Men, by an iron bridge, and on the right-hand side of the road, is a vast deposit of fossil sea-shells. Though they must have been here for thirty thousand years or more, they are as fresh as if they had just been washed up by the sea, except for the fact that they have lost all traces of colour. Some of the species found here are of shells which are now extinct in the Mediterranean.

LAYIA (xlix)

The Church of the Dormition of the Virgin is only late eighteenth century, but it contains some interesting icons which come from some former building. They are: (1) An early sixteenth-century palimpsest icon of the B.V.M., in a poor state of preservation, the frame decorated with paintings of various saints and martyrs. In the right-hand corner of the icon is a small hinged door, which once covered a relic, on the reverse of the icon is a painting of St. John the Divine. (2) A large icon of Christ, with robes of Brousa embroidery, *c.* 1620. (3) A large and perfect icon of the B.V.M. and Child, dated 1559, and, according to an inscription at the foot, given by Jacobus and Constan-

[1] *Cyprus: its Cities, Tombs and Temples.*

tine. The heads of both the Mother and Child are unusually well painted and show strong Italian feeling.

LAZANIA (xxxviii)

A most attractive village with magnificent views of the Monastery of Makhaeras and the Messoria. Most of the houses are of the late eighteenth and early nineteenth centuries, and have carved doors, window-frames, locks, etc. Being far away from any direct communication with the outside world, this village has escaped the hand of the modern builder, and gives an excellent idea of a Cypriote village before the British occupation.

The Church of St. George, built in the eighteenth century, was restored in 1855; it contains a well-preserved icon of the saint of about 1700.

LEFKA (xxviii)

This town is one of the centres of orange growing in Cyprus, and the whole village is surrounded by orange groves and date palms. During the Middle Ages it was one of the principal baronies of the kingdom of Cyprus. There is a simple but clean hotel here, where visitors who wish to see Soli and Vouni and the churches of the Solea and Marathassa valleys can stay.

Both the mosques have been rebuilt, and are supposed to stand on the sites of ancient Christian churches. In the graveyard is a large rococo tomb, of about 1820, of some Pasha, and a number of inscribed cippi; these cippi come from the vast Hellenistic and Roman necropolis which surrounds the town, and date from the period when the famous copper mines were being worked by the Romans. These tombs have produced a number of glass objects which, according to Professor Myres,[1] are "of quite unusual variety and beauty, especially needle-like toilet pencils and finger rings of variegated glass".

LEFKARA PANO AND KATO (xlix)

The town is one of the richest in Cyprus, and is the centre of the lace industry, which is made by the women,

[1] *Catalogue of Cyprus Museum.*

whose menfolk travel all over the world selling it. Leonardo da Vinci when he visited the Island in 1481, purchased lace made at Lefkara for the altar-cloth at Milan Cathedral.

The principal church of Pano Lefkara is dedicated to the Holy Cross, a large well-built church of the mid-nineteenth century, which replaced an ancient and interesting Byzantine building. According to Constantius, this contained a fragment of the True Cross: "Which exhales a strange yet unspeakably pleasant odour, and works many miracles for its devout worshippers."[1] The iconostasis and icons date from the eighteenth century; a door in the former, painted with the emblems of the Passion and dated 1749, leads into a tiny chamber which contains a large wooden cross covered with silver plates depicting scenes from the life of Christ. This relic, which is held in great veneration, probably only dates from the early eighteenth century.

There is also a Chapel of St. Mamas, a tiny Byzantine building, but an unhappy restoration has destroyed its painting and robbed it of all interest. A few fragments of ancient woodwork still remain in the iconostasis. According to the villagers, the paintings, before they were whitewashed over, had an inscription giving the date of the building of the church as A.D. 900.

There is also a small church dedicated to St. George Xorinos, or the Exiler. The origin of this name is that any person who has a grudge against another goes into the church and collects a little dust from the floor, this is then taken away, placed in a small rag and cast into the sea in the belief that the person will thus exile his enemy from the island.

In Kato Lefkara are three churches. (1) The principal one is dedicated to the B.V.M., and was built in 1847. It contains an icon of the Madonna covered with silver repoussé, and said to have been painted by St. Luke. (2) St. Timotheos, a well-preserved example of a mediaeval domed church. The inevitable whitewash covers any mural painting there may have been, but two founders' tombs and an icon of the

[1] *Excerpta Cypria*, p. 317.

saint in a late eighteenth-century carved frame remain. (3) The Archangel Michael, a small Byzantine building with a modern narthex; there are still considerable remains of painting on the walls. While repairs were being carried out to the church about 1865 a bishop's crown and other relics were found under the floor. These were sold to one of the foreign consuls at Larnaca, probably General Cesnola.

Lusignan has a story that owing to the hatred of the Venetians by the Orthodox, when the Turks landed, a Greek priest guided the Moslem forces to this village, which was occupied by the Turks without any serious opposition on the part of the local inhabitants, who readily changed their allegiance from the Doge to the Sultan. To check the serious consequences of this disloyal example, the Venetians at once despatched a body of troops from Nicosia with orders to raze Lefkara to the ground and to kill all the inhabitants regardless of age or sex.

"In 1570, during the siege of Levcosia the Levkarites sided with the Turks against the Venetians, and up to a few years ago were on that account exempted from the poll-tax. In the oil-trade they are reckoned very fraudulent, for they mix their produce with mallow-water."[1]

The fields round Kato Lefkara in the spring are a mass of *Fritillaria libonatica*. Here according to van Bruyn was collected in the eighteenth century *Ladanum*.

Lefkara is at the foot of Mount Olympus, quite close to the sea. The mountain begins from this point to rise gently, and stretching always inland attains at last a great height. There is nothing to see at Lefkara except a river which rises in the mountain, and waters in its course several pleasant villages. It is here that is collected the famous *Ladanum*, which is produced by a dew falling on the leaves of a little plant about half a foot high, not unlike the smaller sage. To gather the *Ladanum* the peasants drive their goats to the fields before sunrise that they may browse on this herb, and as the *Ladanum* is soft and sticky it adheres to their beards, which are cut once a year and the gum is extracted by the use of fire. This is the best, or virgin

---

[1] Ross, op. cit.

Ladanum. There is a second kind which is caught on a little tuft of hair on the goat's shanks. A third way of gathering it is with a coarse rope made of cow's hair, which two men drag across the plants. There is yet a fourth way, to tie several little cords to a short stick and to rub them about the plants every morning as long as there is any gum on them. But the last two methods only give a coarser and inferior quality, because sand gets mixed with it and spoils it. *Ladanum* is black, has a strong odour, and is of great service in time of plague and has other uses in medicine.[1]

Van Bruyn is referring to the rock cistus, called by Hasselquist, the Swedish botanist, who visited Cyprus in 1749, *Cistus Ladanifera*. *Ladanum* is chiefly used as an external stimulant, and is not to be confused with laudanum, which is a kind of opium.

LEFKONIKO (XIV)

This is one of the largest villages in the Messoria. The principal church is dedicated to the Archangel Michael, and is an ancient building, which was completely remodelled in the early nineteenth century. It contains a diptych icon of scenes from our Lord's life, of the late seventeenth century. There is also a tiny fragment of what is probably a late thirteenth-century icon, measuring 42 cm. by 19·5 cm., and showing three male figures with tonsured heads. The writer found this early and most interesting relic in use as a support to a shelf.

The Church of St. Theodoros contains a well-painted icon of the B.V.M. dated 1700, but much blistered from candles being burnt in front of it.

The Church of the Holy Cross contains a pair of holy doors dated 1680, and an icon of the B.V.M. of the same period, which are said to come from a destroyed church at Platani.

Outside the village club is a large headless Roman statue which comes from a much-plundered temple site about a mile and a half south of the village.

[1] *Travels*, London, 1702, p. 272.

LEMITHOU (xxxvii)

The church of the B.V.M. is modern, but the iconostasis and some of the icons of the former building lie in the gallery, and include a processional seventeenth-century one of the B.V.M. The principal icon was covered with silver-gilt in 1798. The church also contains an elaborate carved and gilded baroque proskenetarion.

At the top of the village lies a tiny early sixteenth-century church, dedicated to St. Theodoros. The west wall is covered with mural paintings in a good state of preservation, and there is a fine painted head of a saint with a gilded plaster nimbus in relief on the north wall. In the church is kept an icon of St. Theodoros, dated 1718, and one of the B.V.M., repainted 1710.

St. Theodoros was the patron saint of Venice before the body of St. Mark was brought from the East in A.D. 827.

He was a general in the army of the Emperor Licinius, but was converted to Christianity. Like a great many other converts, he was at once seized with a great zeal to do something to prove his earnestness and devotion, and decided to burn the Temple of Cybele. He succeeded, but was captured, and was sentenced to be burnt alive.

In the Greek legends there are two saints of the same name—St. Theodoros Tyro and St. Theodoros of Heraclia, but it is the former who destroyed the temple, and he is generally depicted on icons on horseback and armed with a lance.

In the famous statue on the top of the column in St. Mark's Square in Venice, the saint is shown standing on a crocodile, or dragon—it is difficult to decide which—but whatever it may be the monster is exactly like a plaster-cast of one of those prehistoric animals that stand in the South Kensington Museum.

In the village is the Mitsis Commercial School, founded in 1912 by a Mr. D. Mitsis, a native of the village, with a gift of £16,000. The school buildings, which are a prominent landmark, have accommodation for about eighty boys.

LEMONA (xlv)

The Church of the Archangel Michael is modern. In it, above the icon of the saint, there hangs an iron chain formed of twelve hollow links, which is in great request by the women of the district, for it is believed that those who wear it during childbirth will be ensured an easy delivery. The icon is also held in much repute as a curer of insanity.

About three miles from the village is a grove of olive-trees sacred to the Archangel, which must never be cut down or injured in any way.

In the vicinity of the village lie ruins of two mediaeval chapels dedicated to SS. Barbara and George.

LEONARISSO (viii)

Neither of the churches in the village is of any interest. One of the largest fairs in the Island is held in the yard of one of them—St. Dimitrios—on October 26th.

For many years two colossal statues, more than 9 feet high, have lain in the village: the writer has recently erected them outside the police station, on the left of the main road. Their provenance is unknown, but they probably date from the third century B.C.

LETIMBOU (xlv)

The Church of St. Kyriakos contains some of the most beautiful frescoes in the Island, but they were irreparably damaged by a restoration in 1919, which covered them with whitewash. At the same time the seventeenth-century iconostasis was swept away and replaced by a vile modern one of stone. Hogarth, who visited the church in 1888, has left an excellent account of the frescoes before they were tampered with. He writes:[1]

> The most interesting is that of St. Kyriakos, whose frescoes are of truly remarkable beauty in such a land of daubs as Cyprus; those on the transept-roof represent scenes from the life of our Lord, those on the roof of the nave and choir a legend,

[1] *Devia Cypria*, p. 29.

probably of St. Kyriakos; and in all there is a freedom of attitude, beauty of expression, and richness of colouring which I have seen nowhere else in Cyprus. I could only regret that there was not with me someone with greater knowledge of fresco painting, who might have said with authority that which I suspected, namely, that this church has been decorated by Italian artists, and was a Latin edifice.

So far as can be seen the background of the frescoes is of gold, which in places appears as bright and fresh as the day when it was put on. St. Kyriakos was probably an early bishop of Paphos, and his skull was preserved there at one period as a relic.

There is also a Church of St. Theodoros, which contains two palimpsest icons, one bearing Christ, 1778, and on the reverse a painting of the Prophet Elijah, the other the B.V.M., much repainted, with a Transfiguration, of the seventeenth century, on the other side.

Four tiny chapels, all of them once frescoed, surround the village, but they are now in ruins.

LIMNIA (xxiv)

The Church of St. George was built in 1862, and has an elaborate narthex on the south side. The north wall is supported by three flying buttresses. A large fragment of a marble frieze, with an acanthus leaf design, from one of the temples at Salamis, is built above the window of the apse. The church contains an icon of St. James dated 1718. There is also a small modern chapel dedicated to St. Nicholas, which replaces an ancient Byzantine structure. In the gallery lie the rood cross and iconostasis screen from the former building, which date from about 1710.

LIOPETRI (xlii)

The village church, dedicated to the B.V.M., is a small mediaeval building with a dome; the west end has been lengthened at some later period.

Close to the village lies the Church of St. Andronicos, which possibly was originally a chapel of the Latin faith.

It has a large octagonal dome, and a poor modern narthex added recently which masks the west door; over this is a lintel with three plain shields, the coats of arms on these either having been destroyed or never cut. Remains of painting of a superior style can still be seen in the apse; at the west end are two arched niches, one in the south and the other in the north wall, which were probably founders' tombs; in the former is a life-sized painting of a saint with three donors, an old man in a red dress and two women, but the figures are much damaged. The style of costume is that characteristic of the end of the fifteenth century, and this may probably also be the date of the erection of the church.

At one period this village was a stronghold of the Linobambaki.

Cesnola speaks of the village as follows:

> Leo-Petro is a mere agglomeration of huts. The inhabitants are very poor, and eke out a scanty living by trafficking in poultry, which they buy in the mountain villages of Carpass and sell in the bazaars of Nicosia and Larnaca. They are nick-named "Linobambaki", that is, *linen* and *cotton*, a figurative expression which means a combination of Christian and Mussulman. While to outward appearance they are Turks, and are so recognized by the local authorities, in reality they are Christians whose ancestors, at the time of the Turkish conquest, were forced to declare themselves Mussulmans and to embrace Islamism in order to save their lives and property. Many, if not all of them, had been adherents of the Latin Church, though it is still frequently a matter of dispute between the Greek bishops and the Latin priests as to which Church they rightfully belong to, each Church being desirous of claiming them as its adherents. The marriage and baptismal ceremonies of the Linobambaki are performed in secret by a priest of their choice.
>
> On the birth of a male child the rite of circumcision is evaded by means of a present of money to the Hodja. They adopt such names for their sons as are common to both Christian and Moslem, such as Ibrahim (Abraham), Moussa (Moses), Yusuf (Joseph), etc.[1]

---

[1] *Cyprus: its Cities, Tombs and Temples.*

LIVADHIA (KARPAS) (vii)

About half a mile from the village lies the tiny Church of the B.V.M. Kyra, a small early Byzantine building with narthex and south porch added at a later date. In the semi-vault of the apse are the remains of a mosaic of the B.V.M. with a gold background. Unhappily a local superstition has it that a mosaic cube carried in the pocket will cure and prevent pimples and diseases of the blood; such a superstition is apt to militate against the survival of the mosaic, and, indeed, so little is left to-day that it is difficult to judge to what period it belongs; it is probably to be assigned to the ninth or tenth century. There is a good seventeenth-century iconostasis and icons of the B.V.M. and Christ dated 1702 and 1708. A small Byzantine marble column is built into the north wall above the iconostasis, and another lies in the narthex.

LIVADHIA (LARNACA) (xl)

The Church of St. Paraskeva is an early nineteenth-century building on an ancient site. Above the west door is a finely preserved fragment of mediaeval sculpture, a shield with a coat of arms (three martlets), while above is God the Father in Glory, to His right an angel, to the left the B.V.M. beneath a canopy.

The church contains a number of icons from the former building. The principal ones are St. Paraskeva dated 1735, Christ the Saviour, a well-painted icon in a good condition, and the B.V.M., with portraits of various saints in painted roundels encircling the frame; the two latter icons should be dated *c.* 1740.

In the bema lies a triptych bearing the Deisis, Christ, with the B.V.M. on one side and St. John the Baptist on the other; it has an elaborately carved frame, and is dated 1642.

LIVERAS (v)

The village church, dedicated to SS. Constantine and Helena, is a poor mud-brick building of 1894, on an ancient site. Near the village are the remains of a square building which was once a mediaeval or Venetian watch-tower. About five miles from the village, by the sea-shore, lie a number of marble columns, while two or three more can be seen lying in the sea. This is all that remains of a Roman temple which is said to have existed on this site.

LOPHOS (xlvii)

The Church of the B.V.M. Evangelismos is a large and extremely ugly late nineteenth-century building, and contains nothing of interest save two wooden exapteriga.[1] These are probably the only pair not of silver in the Island. They are of gilded wood with carving in relief in the centre of the six-winged angel of the Book of Revelation. In the bema is kept a much-damaged sixteenth-century icon of the B.V.M. The legend concerning this icon is unique; the villagers say that a painter once wished to repaint it, but the Virgin appeared to him and forbade him to touch it; the artist persisted, and hardly had he taken up his paint brush when the Virgin struck him dead. How often has one wished that the idea had appealed to the Madonna more frequently, and that she had more often been roused to anger on those numerous occasions when charlatan restorers have defaced and destroyed with the idea of restoration!

The village with its steep and narrow cobbled streets and stone-built houses has a great charm; it is in a way reminiscent of Clovelly.

About a mile outside the village lies the small Chapel of the Prophet Elijah. The icon of the prophet is unusual in that it has the power of preventing rain, and is much resorted to by the villagers in the early summer when a storm would ruin the corn lying out on the threshing floor.

LOUROUJINA (xl)

On a hillock above the village is built the small fifteenth-century Church of St. Epiphanios, which was unhappily restored in 1864, when the painted interior was white-

[1] Silver roundels carried by acolytes on long poles in front of the officiating priest.

washed. On the dome can still be seen the four equidistant standard sockets.

The Church of St. Andronicos was built in 1831, and contains a late sixteenth-century icon of the B.V.M.

About two miles from the village and close to the main Larnaca road lies the small ruined Byzantine Church of St. Catherine. The dome still stands, and there are a number of paintings still to be seen on the walls.

The village was the centre of the Linobambaki, for description of whom see Liopetri.

LOUVARAS (xlviii)

The Church of St. John the Baptist was built in 1863. In the bema is kept a collection of seventeenth- and eighteenth-century icons from some earlier building. One of these is unusual in that it depicts St. Spyridon in his tomb; his head is bent in exactly the same way as on the corpse preserved in a silver coffin in Corfu, which can be still seen.

Close by is the tiny chapel of St. Mamas. According to an inscription in the interior, it was founded by the chief priest Constantine in 1454, and the paintings were done at the cost of John Cromides and George Pelekanos in 1495. The portraits of these later donors and their wives are still visible above the west door. The completely painted interior is in a good state of preservation, except for some clumsy filling of cracks with whitewash which has been slashed on in a slapdash and careless manner, unnecessarily covering the frescoes in various places. The iconostasis is possibly contemporary, and is of the open type, like a Latin rood screen. There are two good icons, the B.V.M., late sixteenth century, and Christ, early seventeenth. The tie beam which runs across the church is beautifully carved and painted.

LYSI (xxxii)

The Church of the B.V.M. is a vast edifice covered with misapplied Gothic details clumsily copied from the Cathedrals of Nicosia and Famagusta, and dating from the closing years of the nineteenth century. Beneath the floor of the church is a large holy well, and in this was found an icon of the B.V.M. dated 1560, which is kept in the apse.

About two miles south-west of the village is the Church of St. Ephimianos, a well-preserved building of the fourteenth century. The interior was once completely painted, but has now been whitewashed, and nothing remains save the paintings in the dome and apse, which are of Christ Pantakrator and B.V.M. in Glory; both are superbly painted and in a marvellous state of preservation.

LYSO (XXXV)

The Church of the B.V.M. Chryseleousa is an ancient edifice, which has been restored; originally it was probably a Latin church, and still has Gothic capitals and arcading on the south walls. The north and south doorway are decorated with panels containing coats of arms. Of these Mr. Jeffery writes:[1]

Each panel contains two shields of arms with well-known Cypriote bearings. In one panel is a plain shield charged p.p.p. dexter, a six-pointed sun, sinister, a plain cross. Side by side is a shield couché beneath a helmet with wreath, but no crest, charged with a seven-pointed sun. This is doubtless the cognizance repeated twice over of some member of the once powerful family of the Gourri or Urri. The second panel contains two shields side by side, one of which is charged p.p. fess six fleurs-de-lys, three above and three below; the second shield is charged p.p. fess six crosses patee, three above and three below. The first of these two coats of arms occurs on the tombstone of Dame Alice de Nevilles in the Armenian Church, Nicosia, and elsewhere in Cyprus.

The iconostasis contains some fragments of ancient woodwork, and there are some late sixteenth-century icons, including one of St. John the Baptist with two donors, a man and his wife; the former is dressed in a white shirt with a blue collar, while the woman wears a red dress with a white veil. Unhappily this icon has been repainted, as has the large processional icon of the B.V.M. of the same date. Inset in the back of the priest's throne is an early eighteenth-

[1] *Monuments of Cyprus*, p. 410.

century icon of St. Nicholas, with a charmingly carved frame. The altar of the prothesis is supported by a semi-column with a Gothic capital. The window in the east wall of the church, with remains of Gothic tracery, has been blocked up, and now forms a cupboard for the communion plate. The background is painted with the B.V.M., with angels holding a chalice on each side of her. In the bema is kept a curious Venetian glass flask.

LYTHRANGOMI (viii)

Close to the village is the famous Monastery of the B.V.M. Kanakaria. The church consists of three naves with semicircular apses, covered with barrel-vaulting, and probably dates from the eleventh or twelfth century. The chief glory is the mosaic in the apse, which represents the Virgin seated with the Child upon her knees; the Infant is dressed in a white robe, and holds a parchment scroll tied with a ribbon, the Virgin is surrounded by a dark blue "glory": around the group are small medallions of saints with a gold background, but they are much damaged. On each side of the Madonna are remains of two angels. Like the better preserved example at Kiti, this mosaic probably dates from the ninth century. Of the original church contemporary with this mosaic little remains save a number of marble columns and Corinthian capitals built up into the western narthex and south porch, or else lying scattered around the monastic buildings. There are remains of wall paintings of the sixteenth century in the body of the church, but a restoration in 1779, when the narthex was added, and a more disastrous one in 1920, has not improved them; nor has the local belief that glass cubes cure skin diseases, which we also saw at Livadhia, been of much assistance to the mosaic.

THE MONASTERY OF MAKHAERAS (xxxviii)

The Monastery of Makhaeras, or the Sword, is situated at the head of a valley on the slopes of Mount Kinonia, and is supposed to derive its name either from the icy cutting wind which blows down the valley, or from the fact that the miracle-working icon of the B.V.M. which the monastery possesses was originally discovered in a cave with a sword buried in front of it. According to an old legend, the monastery was founded by an aged hermit called Neophytos, who was expelled from Syria in the twelfth century. He came to Cyprus, and with his faithful disciple Ignatios built a cell on Mount Aoos, where he resided till his death. Ignatios was then joined by another hermit, Prokopios.

Being unable through want of funds to realize their project of building a monastery, they determined to proceed to Constantinople and appeal in person for assistance to Manuel Komnenos (1143–1180). The Emperor in answer to their petition bestowed upon them an annual donation of fifty pieces of money from the imperial treasury, besides making them a grant of the mountain and surrounding district, and pronouncing the absolute independence of the community from all external interference. . . . On their return from this successful mission they at once commenced to erect an oratory in honour of the Theotokos, as well as a few cells for the reception of the inmates of their proposed community. In the midst of these labours Prokopios died, but Ignatios was not left alone on the death of his associate, his fame for sanctity having so spread that he now found himself at the head of a small band of some five or six followers. Among those thus attracted to him was Nilos, the real founder of the establishment, who appears upon the scene in 1172. He seems to have been a foreigner and was led, as he himself tells us, to Cyprus by the advantages which it offered for a solitary life. From the very first he was distinguished by the special favour of Ignatios, whose intimate friend and assistant he became. During the prevalence of a severe drought and famine in the island he was sent on a mission to the neighbouring coasts of Cilicia, to seek there the means of subsistence for the brethren. Feeling at last the approach of death Ignatios designated Nilos as his successor, a position which the latter only consented to accept after much reluctance. The new hegoumenos had not been long in office when the community was again reduced to great straits by another drought, which continued for three years. It was during this period that the church was erected and other additions made to the monastic buildings. At the consecration of Nilos the privilege of independence, which had already been secured by imperial decree, was formally recognized by the then diocesan, Niketas Hagiostephanites, Bishop of Tamasos. A deputation of the monks subsequently sent to Constantinople succeeded in obtaining from Isaac (II) Angelos (1185–1195) a confirmation of the previous charters, together with the grant of one of the imperial gardens at Nikosia and a donation of twelve pieces of money. Alexios (III) Angelos (1195–1203) was another of its imperial patrons. In addition to ratifying the benefactions of his predecessors he bestowed upon it a gift of twenty-four serfs, with perpetual exemption from taxation.[1]

In 1393 James I and his Court took refuge here during the period of the Great Plague.

Now when the king saw the greatness of the plague, he took his wife and all his servants and went to Makhaira to keep safe. And he passed some days there; and the plague was growing worse, and the deaths were many. And the king and queen said: "If they all die, what profit have we in the island, when the men themselves are dead? Let us go and die too with them." And the king and queen and all who were with them left Makhaira, and in a great procession they came to Lefkosia. And the queen was barefoot, and all those who were with her, with much weeping. And they sent word to the bishop, and he made a great procession and went to meet the king as far as Strovilos. Now, (as soon as they came up with the king,) the procession turned back, and little by little the plague was stayed.[2]

It was in this monastery that the imperious and self-willed Alix d'Ibelin, wife of Hugh IV, had an unpleasant adventure; being herself of the Latin faith, she treated the Orthodox with but scant respect, and once when visiting the monastery insisted on forcing her way into the church, which was forbidden to women; but this effrontery was more than the B.V.M. of Makhaeras could allow, and the Queen had hardly set foot across the threshold when she was struck dumb.

In 1892 the church and monastery were completely destroyed by fire, but both have since been rebuilt; luckily the famous icon of the Theotokos was rescued. This is covered

[1] Hackett, *Church of Cyprus*, p. 613. [2] *Chronicle of Makhairas*, p. 69.

with late eighteenth-century repoussé, and it is, therefore, impossible to form any idea of how old the relic may be. Above the icon hangs a tiny gilt and enamel knife, which is said to cure wounds. The usual proceeding is for the priest to take the wounded person up to the icon, there to say a few prayers, and at the end make the sign of the cross above the wound with the knife. Here, too, hangs a pair of enamel buckles decorated with seed pearls, which are in great request by the village women, who wear them during childbirth. The only other icon of interest is an early eighteenth-century one of SS. Joachim and Anna. The treasury contains amongst the usual collection a silver-gilt cross of 1804 containing a tiny fragment of the True Cross. There are the usual number of the small carved church crosses encased in silver gilt, decorated with flawed emeralds and misshapen pearls, all of the seventeenth and eighteenth centuries; the only dated one is of 1729. There are two large silver-gilt boxes containing relics of nearly every known saint, Basil, Barbara, Barnabas, Cosmas, Damian, etc., said to have been brought by the Archbishop Kyprianos from Moldavia when he went there in 1795 to raise funds to reconstruct the monastery. There is also a magnificent pair of green cuffs sewn with silver thread and seed pearls, which are said to come from Akhiropietos; it is possible that they date from the sixteenth century. The gospels are mostly without interest, save one printed in Venice in 1588.

In the modern monastic buildings hang portraits of the Archbishop Kyprianos and his Archdeacon Haralambos, which were painted by a Moldavian artist during their visit there towards the end of the eighteenth century.

Two miles below the monastery is the Church of St. Onouphrios, but a recent fire has destroyed all of interest in this fourteenth-century domed building.

St. Onouphrios was a monk of Thebes, who retired to the desert, far from the sight of men, and dwelt there in a cave for sixty years, and during all that time never beheld one human being, or uttered one word of his mother-tongue except in prayer. He was unclothed, except by some leaves twisted round his body, and his beard and hair had become like the face of a wild beast. In this state he was discovered by a holy man whose name was Paphnutius, who, seeing him crawling on the ground, knew not at first what live thing it might be.[1]

MAKRASYKA (xxxii)

During the Middle Ages this was apparently a village of some importance. A number of ruined churches remain. In the centre of the village are the remains of a large sixteenth-century double-aisled church dedicated to St. George. There is also a church dedicated to St. Eustathios; the remains of paintings on the north walls include three saints with raised haloes. The Church of the B.V.M. is a double-aisled building containing a few eighteenth-century icons and a curious small wooden one with carving of the Crucifixion, Presentation, etc., in relief; it is probably eighteenth-century work.

MALOUNDA (xxix)

The Church of the B.V.M. Chrysopantanitissa was built in 1763. The iconostasis is dated 1853, but much of the woodwork used up in it is far earlier. The church contains an icon of St. Panicrios dated 1708. In the gallery is kept a large icon of the Archangel Michael dated 1723. A carved wooden box contains the skull and bones of St. Eliophotos, one of the "German" saints of Cyprus (see Eliophotes); he is said to have been buried in a church near the village, which is now destroyed.

Below the village a large repaired mediaeval bridge crosses the river; between the arches is a defaced shield with a Lusignan coat of arms on it.

MANDRIA (KILANI) (xlvii)

The Church of St. George is a recent construction, but it contains an icon of that saint dated 1775. The front panel of the women's gallery is brightly painted with scenes from Old Testament history, interspersed with the signs of the zodiac. In this gallery lies a large gilded frame for the icon of St. George, given by Meletios Bishop

[1] Augustus Hare, *Walks in Rome.*

of Kition in 1819. The Bishop was martyred by the Turks in 1821 in Nicosia.

MANDRIA (PAPHOS) (li)

The Church of St. Andronicos is modern. Above the west door is a most curious marble capital between the two volutes: a female head wrapped in a wimple; it probably dates from the fourteenth century, but it is difficult to explain how it came to its present position; it may possibly have once formed part of some Latin convent.

Close to the sea is the Chapel of St. Evresis, built on ancient foundations of old material; a number of marble columns are embedded in its walls. The altar is formed of an "Oil Stone" of coarse pinkish marble.

Between this church and the sea is a wall, once plastered, and hard by large squared blocks. To the west is an ancient quarry of considerable extent, and to the east a tumulus, and a curious mass of rock pierced in all directions by tunnels, roughly hewn and vaulted. One such tunnel is as much as 150 feet in length, and all are now used to stable flocks at night; and I can only suggest that in former days they served the purposes of warehouses or of a covered bazaar, and had been excavated to this end: in any case they are not natural, and are clear proof of ancient settlement at this point.[1]

MANSOURA (xviii)

A tiny Turkish hamlet on the road to Polis, near which a few years ago, when the road was being constructed, were found the foundations of a Byzantine villa. The mosaic floors were still preserved, and were removed to the Nicosia Museum. The most charming shows a sporting dog with his foot on a partridge, and looking up at his master, who is not shown; the partridge has obviously just been shot down by the master, and the dog is looking up with an expression in his face which seems to ask whether he himself shall kill the bird or wait for his owner to wring its neck.

[1] Hogarth, *Devia Cypria*, p. 42.

MARGO (xxxi)

The complete village and its lands were sold to a Jewish syndicate in 1885. The Jews continued to reside here till 1927, when the estate was sold to an Englishman.

Above the village is a small graveyard, containing about twenty tombs with inscriptions in Hebrew. When the property was sold the Greek villagers migrated, and their houses have already disappeared or fallen into ruins, but the church still stands in an excellent state of repair. It is dedicated to St. Thecla, who was one of the most famous of the early saints of the Church.

The legends relate that when St. Paul came to Anconium he preached in the great square; and there was a certain Virgin called Thecla who sat at her window and listened to the word of God and, believing, was converted.

Now Thecla was betrothed to a certain youth called Thamyris, who loved her much, and when she could not be prevailed to move from the window her mother sent for Thamyris, saying, "What shall I do? My daughter will not move, but sits and listens to this preacher of a strange religion, and will take neither food nor drink!" So Thamyris came in haste and chid her, saying: "Beloved, what is this? Who is this stranger who has so stolen your mind?" But Thecla did not even turn her head to hear the words of her mother and lover.

Thamyris went to the Governor and complained that Paul had seduced the mind of his betrothed with his strange doctrines. The Governor at once threw Paul into a dungeon, but Thecla came by night and, taking off her gold ear-rings, gave them to the turnkey, and bribed Paul's jailer with a silver looking-glass. He allowed her to enter the cell in which Paul was confined, and in the dungeon she was baptized. Together they fled from the city and came to Antioch, but she was arrested by the orders of the Governor of that city and condemned to be thrown to the beasts.

The lions and bears in the pit, when they saw Thecla, touched her not; instead they came and lay at her feet as if they had been lap-dogs.

When the Governor saw this he was amazed, and said

to her: "Who art thou, that wild beasts will not touch thee?" And Thecla replied: "I am a servant of Christ."

Then the Governor ordered that she should be set free, and allowed to depart from the city.

St. Thecla spent the rest of her life preaching the Gospel of Christ, and healing the sick at Seleucia, so that all the doctors of that town had no work, and lost their profits.

The physicians took counsel what they should do, and at last came to the conclusion that if she lost her chastity then would her power depart from her.

So they hired certain lewd fellows to go to the mountain where the saint lived. When they came to the place Thecla walked to meet them, thinking they were poor, sick people who wanted her help; but they laid hands on her. Frightened, she turned and fled towards the mountain, which opened and swallowed her up—and all that remained behind was her veil.

Thus ended the life of Thecla, after seventy-two years of Christian work; so that she was more than ninety years old when the Lord translated her.

The walls of the church are covered with frescoes, which are well preserved. This is all the more wonderful, for a local supersitition holds that fragments of frescoed plaster from this church are an infallible cure for bleeding from the nose. The best preserved of the paintings are the Giving of the Bread and Wine, in the apse, and the Crucifixion and Betrayal, on the west wall. Part of the iconostasis is seventeenth century, and contained an icon of the B.V.M. and Child, dated 1672, and another of St. John the Baptist dated 1738. On the north wall hangs a curious sixteenth-century icon of the Virgin and Child; the Madonna is seated on a throne, one of the legs of which is formed by a female figure, after the manner of a Caryatid. A portion of a good seventeenth-century icon of Christ has been cut in halves and used to patch one of the lower panels of the iconostasis. The unusually heavy stone supports for the rain gutter still remain on the exterior south wall. The church contains a number of mildewed gospels, printed in Venice towards the end of the sixteenth century.

MARI (lv)

In the middle of this Turkish village stands a large mediaeval church dedicated to St. Marina. It is now roofless and used as a sheep-fold, but during the sixteenth century must have been a building of very considerable pretensions. The two windows on the south wall have arched dripstones, after the Gothic style, and the apse contains the remains of mural paintings. From the general style of this building it is possible that it was once a Latin church.

MARONI (lv)

The cemetery chapel is dedicated to St. George, and is an ancient building which has been restored. The original western door remains, but has been blocked up. The iconostasis and all the icons are eighteenth century; the icons must all have been painted by the same hand; the work is not good, but it has a marked and individual style of its own. From its name it would appear that this village once belonged to the Maronites.

MASARI (xx)

The Church of St. Antony is a small ancient barrel-vaulted structure, but it has been repaired and its once frescoed walls whitewashed. A large and fine ilex grows in the yard of the church. Fragments of painting are still to be seen above the west doorway.

The village is small and poor, but has a charming situation on the bank of the river.

MATHIATI (xxxix)

The principal church of the village is dedicated to St. Paraşkeva, and was built in the eighteenth century; the south door is in the sixteenth-century style, and the interior vault of the church is decorated with porcelain plates.

Outside the village lies the early eighteenth-century Church of the B.V.M. Galatoussa. The iconostasis, dated 1715, is unusual, in that it is painted but shows no carving; it contains an icon of the B.V.M. of the same date.

Half-way between this village and Sha lies the round Byzantine Church of St. Eftikios, which still retains fragments of painting in its dome.

In 1878, when the British troops first landed, a camp was formed here, but was soon removed owing to the unhealthy nature of the site. The only memorial remaining is a small churchyard which contains three graves, two of which have monuments: Charles Richards, Drum-major 1st Battalion A Regiment, 1878, and J. Browne, R.E., 1879.

MAZOTOS (l)

The Church of St. George is modern, but contains a good eighteenth-century rood cross. There are also chapels dedicated to S. Xenophon and the B.V.M. Near the latter, and close to the sea, are remains of a Roman town, the tombs of which lie behind. It was off here that Constantine Kopronymos defeated the fleet of the Calif Yezid III, capturing and destroying the complete fleet of 1,000 ships, except for three which were allowed to escape so that they might carry the news of the disaster to their country.

In the Middle Ages Mazotos gave its name to one of the principal baronies of the kingdom, and during the Venetian era it became the capital of one of the twelve districts into which the Island was divided.

MELANDRA (xxxv)

A small Turkish village which contains two deserted mediaeval chapels dedicated to St. Luke and St. John the Baptist. The latter contains remains of wall paintings. St. Theosetios was born in this village; during his lifetime he was credited with many miracles, making the blind to see and the deaf to hear. He built a church which was famous all over the countryside. An entertaining legend is concerned with the origin of the church. One morning the saint left the sheep he was looking after and disappeared, nor could he be found, until after three days' searching his father found his son's body in a cave, uncorrupted. The cave was enlarged and made into a church. The saint is a friend to the farmer, and those whose crops are devoured by crows pray to him; and he answers the prayers by blinding the crows, so that they cannot see to steal.

MELINI (xlviii)

The Church of the B.V.M. was built in 1721, as is shown by an inscription of a beam above the west door. It is a shed-like building with carved tie beams. The iconostasis is modern, but the original rood cross of the church lies in the women's gallery.

MELOUSHA (xxxi)

About a mile south of the village are the ruins of a large domed church called Kirhoulouir Monastir, or St. Photios, by the Greeks. Only the north and west walls now remain; they show traces of painting. It is possible that this village was the site of the early Orthodox See of Chytri, which was suppressed by the Latins in 1222. It was always obscure, and John, the biographer of Epiphanios, describes it as being a "miserable little village twenty-five miles distant from Salamis".[1]

According to Hackett, its bishops included Spyridon, who was present at the second Council of Nicaea in 787, while Germanos was present at the eighth General Council in A.D. 869.[2]

MENIKO (xxix)

The principal church is dedicated to St. Kyprianos; it was of considerable importance during the Middle Ages, but the present church was only constructed in 1818; the north aisle probably dates from the mediaeval building. The iconostasis is contemporary with the rebuilding.

Further there are in Cyprus the two heads of St. Cyprian and Justina [covered with silver]: they were martyred at Antioch and when Syria fell into evil plight, they were brought to Cyprus and put into a little church at Meniko. And at the side of the chancel towards the south there is a trough, [and men come

[1] *Vita Epiphanii.*

[2] Hackett, *Church of Cyprus*, p. 321.

there and take a draught]; it works great cures for rheum in the eyes and for fevers. And in the time of King Peter the Great,—he had a quartan fever and could not be cured,—certain men told him about St. Cyprian and Justina at Meniko near Akaki; and he came and drank and was at once cured. It is true that the water is very brackish and ill to drink, but it is marvellous for healing. And he [immediately] ordered [the church to be destroyed], and another church was built new from the foundations. And he covered the two heads with silver, and in the crown he left a space with lids that opened, so that men might do their reverence to the relics.[1]

MESA KHORIO (xlv)

The church is a modern building dedicated to St. Marina, and a ruined chapel of the same name lies south of the village. Of this chapel the villagers relate that their forefathers wished to dedicate the church to St. Nicholas, and twice it was built and twice it fell down by itself without human agency. One night St. Marina appeared to the principal villager, saying: "Dedicate the church to me and it will stand." This was done, and the church has existed to this day. A local superstition is that if a man quarrels with his wife and she drives him out of the house with her constant nagging, he goes to the church and collects a little dust from the floor, and on his return sprinkles it in the house, and at once he and his wife are reconciled.

MESANA (xlvi)

The village church is dedicated to St. Tychikos, a disciple of St. Paul, who was deacon of Paphos. It contains nothing of interest save a large mediaeval plate with a raised central boss.

About two miles from the village is the Monastery of St. George, built in the late fifteenth century. It is in a good state of preservation, and the west door is ornamented with a well-cut cable pattern. There are remains of paintings in the interior, especially a gigantic St. George and an Archangel Michael, but they are probably a hundred years later than the rest of the building. Portions of the late

[1] *Chronicle of Makhairas*, p. 39.

sixteenth-century iconostasis remain, and there are half a dozen or so fine, untouched icons of the same date. Of these some are in the iconostasis, notably Christ, St. John the Baptist, and the B.V.M., while in a separate frame on the north wall hangs a noble painting of the B.V.M. and Child, perhaps dating from about 1550. This is a wonder-working icon, and many are the stories told of its power. A great many years ago a man came to pray to this icon, which was kept on a stand outside the church, and promised two oxen if his son was cured. He brought the oxen with him, and tied them up to a tree which stood near the monastery, but in the evening his son was so much better that he came to steal back his own oxen; the Abbot, knowing the man and his selfish character too well, had covered the icon with honey; this had got all over the coats of the beasts as they licked it off, so that it was easy for him to identify what had been dedicated to the monastery and to recover it. History is silent as to whether or not the child paid for his father's parsimonious action with his life.

MESAYITONIA (liv)

The Church of St. John the Baptist was built in 1846. The west and north doors have a curious architectural motive of interlaced links around the arch.

There is much malaria in this village, and the inhabitants, instead of going to a doctor, prefer to walk three times round the church and then tear off a fragment of their clothing, which they tie to the iron grill outside the north window.

MIA MILEA (xxi)

The Church of St. John the Divine was built in 1894 with crude Gothic details copied from Nicosia Cathedral. In the gallery lies a panel of an iconostasis painted by a certain Philotheos in 1757; below are donor portraits of a priest and his wife.

Near the village is a tiny mud-brick Chapel of St. George,

which contains a vast eighteenth-century rood cross propped up in a corner, almost as big as the chapel itself.

The village derives its name from the fact that it is one Greek mile—three English miles—from Nicosia.

MILEA (xxiii)

The principal church is dedicated to St. Andronicos, and is an early nineteenth-century building. Marble Corinthian capitals and columns lie near it.

About a mile from the village is a mediaeval Church of St. George, with ruins of a former settlement round it. An unhappy restoration has destroyed all the paintings, and added a loathsome sky-blue iconostasis.

In a house in the village is a most elegant square well-head, probably formerly the marble base of some Roman statue; on the four sides are heavy floral swags, while at the corner dolphins are carved in high relief.

MILIKOURI (xxxvi)

The village contains a large and ancient church dedicated to St. George, which was rebuilt, according to an inscription above the west door, in 1811. There is a fine late seventeenth-century iconostasis, but the extremely interesting icons have been utterly ruined. About twenty-five years since a person from Greece offered to restore the icons, which he did, with the most disastrous and distressing results. This is all the more tragic as several of the icons are early; the oldest is a curious icon of the B.V.M., dated 1523, partially covered with gilt repoussé, and so holy that the face of the Madonna can never be seen, but must always be covered up with an embroidered cloth. There is also an icon of the B.V.M. Eleousa, dated 1612. On a lower panel of the iconostasis, which mercifully escaped both the restorer's eye and hand, is a picture of St. Spyridon with a kneeling donor in sixteenth-century costume.

MILIOU (xxxv)

Near the village lies the small Monastery of SS. Cosmas and Damian. The tiny church was built in 1649; over the west door is a small carved plaque of two panels, on one of which is depicted the Deposition and on the other the Crucifixion. The iconostasis contains two repainted icons of the B.V.M. and Christ, dated 1670. A medicinal spring near the church is much resorted to by those who suffer from rheumatism.

Near the monastery is a neolithic site, the surface covered with axe heads, pieces of pottery, arrow heads, etc.

MITSERO (xxix)

The Church of the Archangel Michael is a modern building replacing an ancient structure, of which only the apse remains. The iconostasis is from this former building, and according to an inscription was renovated and regilded in 1796, during the time of Archbishop Chrysanthos, by a certain Christodoulos and his wife, who, at the same time, added the charming lower panels painted with various flowers.

There are many signs of ancient mining round the village.

MONAGRI (xlvii)

The Church of St. George is an ancient building that was much repaired in 1872. There are considerable remains of paintings of the late sixteenth century in the vault, including some curious ones of the Day of Judgement and an altogether delightful one of Daniel in the Lions' Den. The church contains a large processional icon of the B.V.M. and Child, damaged at the top; at the bottom left-hand corner there is a kneeling male donor and the date 1566. In the apse lies the almost completely destroyed icon of the B.V.M. Essobyra, possibly a work of the late fifteenth century; it comes from a church of the same name, which has long since disappeared.

About two miles from the village and near the river lies the Monastery of the Madonna of Damascus. The church was probably built in the early sixteenth century. The iconostasis contains three most interesting icons in an excellent state of repair. They are St. John the Baptist with a donor, dated 1529; an icon painted on both sides, on one side the B.V.M., and on the reverse the Crucifixion, dated 1569; and, thirdly, an icon of Christ, undated, but undoubtedly of the mid-sixteenth century. The monastic buildings which surround the church are now in ruins.

On the other side of the village is a small monastery dedicated to the Archangel Michael. It is said to have been a Latin convent during the Middle Ages, but was rebuilt in 1740 by Macarios, Bishop of Kition. The porch outside the west door is supported by two marble pillars with Corinthian capitals. These pillars have been painted at some time with figures in the Byzantine manner. In the tympanum of the west door is a portrait of the Bishop himself; the inscription below gives the name of the painter of the portrait as a certain Philaritos, Deacon of Amathus. The interior has a number of wall paintings, and a panel in the iconostasis bears a portrait of the Bishop with a model of the church, and an inscription giving the name of the painter, a certain Savva Nicolaou. The contemporary iconostasis contains three processional icons, all repainted. A hole in the great west door is said to have been caused by a Turkish soldier, who fired at a former Abbot when he was holding service here.

MONI (liv)

The church, built in 1858, is dedicated to the Holy Girdle of the Virgin. In the apse are kept six late seventeenth-century icons with raised gilt plaster haloes, which have been brought from another church in the vicinity now in ruins. They are in a good state of repair, and seem to have been but little repainted. The church contains a fine carved wooden cross which may be of the fifteenth century, but the silver setting does not seem to be earlier than the late seventeenth century.

MORA (xxii)

The mosque of this Turkish village is modern, but in the courtyard of a house survive the foundations of the ancient church, while in another courtyard can be seen the outlines of a large building with the remains of a red brick-tiled floor of a herring-bone pattern. A local tradition maintains that this building was once a monastery. A large number of tombs surround the village; indeed, many of the houses are built on the site of a Hellenistic necropolis.

In the Middle Ages the village was known as Mores. The Seigneur de Laumont, who visited Cyprus in 1419, says: "From the Castle of Chastran Franc, without a halt, I pushed on four leagues to a place belonging to the Hospice of Rhodes, called Mores, and there I slept the night."[1]

MORONERO (xlv)

Near the village is the ruined Church of St. Yennatios, Patriarch of Constantinople during the reign of Emperor Leo the Great, in the fifth century. While on a voyage from Jerusalem to Constantinople with his deacon, he landed at Paphos and went by himself on a pilgrimage to the cave of St. Hilarion near the village of Episkopi. It was in the middle of winter, and when the Archbishop reached Kissotera he knocked at the door of a widow to ask his way, but owing to the cold the door and shutters were fast closed and the woman did not hear him. After vainly knocking, the Archbishop fainted from cold in the street, and in the morning his body was found frozen to death. As soon as the Bishop of Paphos heard of this he at once went with the Archdeacon to the place, and it was decided to transport the corpse to Paphos for burial. But the body was so heavy and the roads so bad that they could only get as far as Moronero, and the body was buried and the church erected over it. Not unnaturally, perhaps, the saint has a great local reputation for curing colds.

MORPHOU (xix)

Morphou is one of the principal towns in the Nicosia district, and during the Middle Ages gave its name to one of the baronies into which the Island is divided. The principal monument of the town is the Monastery of St. Mamas; the original church was Byzantine, but at some period it was rebuilt, and during the Middle Ages a building of con-

[1] *Excerpta Cypria*, p. 30.

siderable importance in the Gothic style was erected. This was again almost completely reconstructed in 1725, when a large central dome was added. From the Gothic building a number of details survive: the north and south doorways, the nave columns, the two marble columns in the west window, and the shrine of the saint himself, all of them in the flamboyant style of the late fifteenth century. The superb iconostasis is a mixture of the two periods and styles; the four marble columns with Gothic capitals and the lower panels of marble probably dating from about 1500. These marble panels call for more than passing notice: they are, perhaps, the finest example of the Minor Arts of the Venetian era still remaining in the Island. They are decorated with figs, grapes, acorns, etc., carved in high relief, with Venetian heraldic shields at the corners; the latter were once painted with coats of arms, but these have long since disappeared. The woodwork in the iconostasis is a magnificent example of late sixteenth-century carving, painted dark blue and gold. Of the same period are the two small holy doors at the extreme left of the iconostasis, and the painted baldachino above the altar. The altar itself is supported by five marble columns, two of which have Byzantine capitals. The only old icon remaining is one of the B.V.M., dated 1745. The painted pulpit dates from 1761. The shrine of St. Mamas is an arched recess in the north side of the church; the Gothic stonework of this arch has unhappily been painted with oil-colours carelessly applied. The Byzantine sarcophagus of the saint lies beneath this arch, and is built into the thickness of the wall, so that it shows both inside and outside. It is of white marble, and almost certainly dates from a very early period. The west door is covered with a number of graffiti, including the name of M. Porey, who was French consul in 1738, and an inscription recording the visit and cure of a man from Moscow in 1753.

The monastic buildings were erected in 1779, but a number of capitals and columns come from the former church.

St. Mamas is one of the most famous of the saints of

Cyprus. In his icon he is shown riding on a lion with a lamb in his arms. According to a local legend, St. Mamas was a poor and humble hermit who lived in a cave near Morphou. The Byzantine duke of the period issued a decree that everyone in the Island, irrespective of what they did, must contribute his share to the taxes. St. Mamas felt that as he lived in an obscure cave and did not use the public high-roads, or take any part in the communal life, he should not be forced to pay: the Duke came to hear of this, and sent two soldiers to arrest the saint, and bring him to Nicosia to be tried and punished.

The soldiers duly arrived at the cave and arrested the unfortunate hermit, and started back to Nicosia. As they were passing through a wood, without any warning, a lion—an animal which had never been seen in Cyprus before—sprang out and made as if to devour a small and woolly lamb which was gambolling in the path in front of the saint. St. Mamas held up his hand; the lion stopped, the saint gathered up the lamb and, presumably being tired with his long walk, mounted on the ferocious lion as if he had been an ordinary mule. He rode thus with the lamb in his arms, not only to Nicosia, but up the steps of the palace into the actual throne-room of the Duke. The Duke was so amazed at the sight that he at once announced that St. Mamas need never pay taxes for the rest of his life.

The income-tax payers of England have, so far as I am aware, no patron saint, and St. Mamas, who seems one of the few people who have got the better of a tax collector, should at once be adopted.

Makhairas has, however, a different reason why St. Mamas is depicted on his icons riding a lion. He writes:

Also St. Mamas from Alaya, and in his lifetime he used to catch lions and milk them, and made cheese and fed the poor. And the Turks ran after him, and he tripped, and the vessel of milk was broken and the milk was spilled, and the place where the milk fell can be seen in the village of Alaya to this day. And he was martyred, and his parents put him into a coffin, and by the grace of the Lord it reached Cyprus at the beach of Morphou. And it was revealed to a worthy man that he should take his yoke of oxen and his four sons; and he went there, and they put a rope round it and lifted it up as though it had been some small thing, although it was very heavy, so that many men would have had great toil to carry it. And when he came to the place where it is to-day, it stood still and no one could budge it. And they built a church, and a fragrant oil wells from it, and it works great marvels for all the world, for wounds that cannot be cured. And wherever they set up his picture there is an abundance of cures.[1]

MOSPHILOTI (xl)

The Church of St. Paraskeva is a nineteenth-century building containing a pleasant late sixteenth-century icon of the B.V.M., and one of St. Triophone, dated 1684. Near the village lies the Monastery of St. Thekla; the church is dated 1741, but contains nothing of interest. A large holy well lies beneath the church, and runs back in the form of a tunnel for some distance; the lime which is formed by the water in this tunnel is considered a certain remedy for boils.

The name of the village is derived from the Greek word for the white hawthorn.

MOUSOULITA (xxiii)

The Church of St. Luke is modern, but a curious corbel in the shape of a man's head is built into the south wall, and must come from some former building. The few early icons the church possesses have been so completely and vilely repainted that they no longer have any interest.

MOUTOULLAS (xxxvii)

The principal church of the village is dedicated to St. Paraskeva, and was built in the middle of the nineteenth century. It contains two seventeenth-century icons of Christ and St. Nicholas from the ruined Church of St. Basil.

Near by is the small Chapel of St. Mamas, with a collection of much decayed icons, the best preserved being a seventeenth-century one of the saint himself. Above the

[1] *Chronicle of Makhairas*, p. 33.

iconostasis is a long panel with ten scenes from the life of Our Lord, probably dating from the late sixteenth century. The church contains a carved wooden candlestick in the Italian manner.

High above the village is a tiny Chapel of the B.V.M.; in the apse on the north wall are pictures of John Moudoulas and his wife Irene, who built this chapel in 1279. The lower portion of this fresco is damaged, but the extremely interesting costume worn by Irene is well preserved. The whole church is frescoed, including the wall of the north narthex. A musaraby niche shelters the icon of the B.V.M., dated 1659. The well-carved contemporary wooden doors should be noticed.

MYRTOU (xi)

The Monastery of St. Panteleemon is the principal monument of the village. St. Panteleemon was born at Nicomedia in Bithynia, the son of a heathen father and a Christian mother. He became the favourite physician of the Emperor Galerius Maximianus.

During his residence at the heathen Court he was converted by an aged priest called Hermolaus. When the persecution broke out, he realized that he could not hope to escape martyrdom.

He was seized by his enemies and bound to an olive-tree and then beheaded. Although it was winter, no sooner had his blood bathed the roots of the tree than it burst forth into leaves.

St. Panteleemon is the patron saint of physicians, and there is a church in Venice dedicated to him, with an altar-piece by Paolo Veronese showing the saint healing a boy.

The extremely interesting church has recently been restored, with the usual fatal results.

The loggia, pointed arches, and vaulting have been torn down, and the floor of the church re-done with glazed and slippery tiles.

The iconostasis is dated 1743. The chief icon is of St. Panteleemon, with the Bishop Chrysanthos kneeling in the left corner, and God the Father in the right-hand top corner; each figure holds a scroll with a long inscription recording the restoration of the monastery; the icon is dated 1770.

An ancient icon of the same saint is also preserved; it was covered with silver-gilt repoussé in 1798, so that it is impossible to guess the age of the painting which lies beneath.

Another icon of the saint was also covered in the same way in 1763. In the screen is hung a curious needlework portrait of the saint, carried out in coloured silks, with a background of gold thread; it is dated 1804, but has the appearance of far greater antiquity. On the south wall hangs a large icon of the Martyrdom of the Saint, dated 1743.

The throne dates from 1772, and the well-carved women's gallery was erected in 1780. The treasury contains two Gospels covered with silver gilt, dated 1780 and 1801, and a curious reliquary made in Venice, the top copied from the dome of St. Maria della Salute. There is also a small collection of crosses; the processional one is dated 1789, and there is a small standing one dated 1718. The communion plate was made in 1801, and is one of the few dated examples in the Island.

About a mile distant are the ruins of a Byzantine village and church, at a locality called Margi. The modern Maronite Church, which lies hard by, is of no interest.

NEOKHORIO (KHRYSOKHOU) (xxii)

The name Neokhorio, or the new village, shows that the village is but a recent growth, and it contains nothing of interest. About a mile south lie the ruins of the mediaeval village of Potanios. Little now remains save the half-destroyed Church of St. Minas, with traces of painting on its walls. A vast number of Roman tombs lie round this village; they are of unusual size, and besides pottery and glass generally contain a certain amount of gold jewellery.

NETA (viii)

East of the village are the ruins of a large temple; remains of walls can still be seen, and two headless life-sized statues, one seated on a throne, lie on the hillside. About 200 yards south of this site is a small hillock covered with potsherds and fragments of terra-cotta figurines. Close to the school, also, is another site where terra-cotta statuettes can be picked up.

The Church of the B.V.M. was built in the eighteenth century; it contains little except a fine, but damaged, sixteenth-century icon of the Virgin and Child. By the belfry a trap door leads down a worn flight of steps to a curious subterranean chamber with a vaulted roof; at the end of this is a holy well. This chamber is much earlier than the present church, and is doubtless a part of some former building.

Two miles from the village is the fourteenth-century domed Church of St. Sergios; it was once completely painted, but the frescoes have been defaced by the Turks and damaged by wandering shepherds.

NIKITARI (xxviii)

The Church of St. John the Baptist is modern. It contains a number of late seventeenth-century icons and a fine pair of holy doors, all of which come from the famous Church of Asinou. The doors are untouched, and are a delightful example of Cypriote painting of about 1680. A Gospel of 1570 has a contemporary repoussé bronze plaque of the Crucifixion on its cover.

The road ends at Nikitari, and those who wish to visit the perfect Byzantine Church of Asinou, already described, can hire donkeys in the village to take them three miles uphill to the church.

NIKOKLIA (lii)

The Church of St. Dimitrianos was built in 1768, and contains a number of icons contemporary with its construction. A marble Corinthian capital and pillar, probably from Kouklia, lie outside the church.

The name of the village is supposed to preserve that of Nikokles, an early King of Paphos.

NIKOS (xxxvii)

The Church of St. Barbara was rebuilt in 1906, but contains a number of early icons from the former building, slightly repainted. They are (1) A processional icon of the B.V.M. Agniotissa, dated 1584. (2) A triptych, dated 1688, in the centre the Deisis; on the wings, patriarchs, saints, etc.; while on the exterior of the wings a St. George and St. Demetrios. (3) The Dormition of the Virgin, 1748.

NISOU (xxxix)

The Church of St. Paraskevi dates from the eighteenth century. It contains a good late sixteenth-century icon of the B.V.M. Hodegetria, and a small silver plate with the date 1815 scratched on it, but obviously of earlier workmanship. There is also an icon of the saint of the church dated 1678, and a number of early printed books of the offices for various months, viz. September 1545, April, June, and December 1689.

A mile or so distant from the village lies the tomb of St. Epaphras, a Hellenistic tomb turned into a burial chapel for the saint. A modern flight of steps leads down into this tomb, which contains a marble sarcophagus in which the saint is said to lie, with a large Byzantine cross cut in relief on the lid. At the head is a small inscribed Roman cippus. Past this sarcophagus is an inner shrine which contains an altar, and on the rough-hewn walls are fragments of mural paintings. St. Epaphras is supposed to be one of the seventy Apostles, and to have been Bishop of Adriake, where he suffered martyrdom. He is also said to have been sent by St. Paul to Cyprus, where he was consecrated Bishop of Paphos by the Bishop Heraklides. He is commemorated on December 9th.

ODHOU (xlviii)

One of the prettiest villages in Cyprus, situated at the head of a valley with the mountains rising behind it. It is surrounded by walnut- and mulberry-trees, and far beneath can be seen the distant sea.

The Church of St. Marina was built in 1777, and has

contemporary tie beams elaborately carved and painted. The iconostasis is older than the church, but has unhappily been repainted.

During the summer the woods round the village are full of nightingales.

OMODHOS (xlvii)

The famous Monastery of the Holy Cross stands in the middle of the village. The church has recently been rebuilt on a vast scale. Into the north wall of the church is built an extremely interesting gravestone of an Englishman who died here, with the following inscription:

> Under this marble are deposited / the remains of Henry Rooke Esq. formerly Major in the / Hundredth Regiment of Foot with brevet rank of Lieu / tenant-Colonel in the service of His Britannic Majesty / King George the Third. After quitting the Army he travelled / thro' various parts of Europe, and being in Italy / in the year 1799, joined the Russian Army before Ancona / as a volunteer officer and for his services and / assistance in reducing that fortress his late Imperial / Majesty of all the Russias Paul conferred upon him the / Order of S. Anne of Holstein 2nd class. He died in this / Convent the 7th day of July in the year of our Lord and Saviour / 1811 and was interred by the Holy Fathers under / neath this stone with their consent and that of / the most Reverend the Bishop of the Greek Church in the island of Cyprus. His only surviving brother W. / Rooke as a last tribute of fraternal regard and affection / hath caused this memorial to be conveyed and / placed over his grave.

The iconostasis dates from 1817, and was erected by the Bishop Chrysanthos. It contains an icon of St. Philip dated 1773, with a kneeling priestly donor, who holds a reliquary containing the skull of St. Philip; this relic is still preserved in the church; it was kept originally in the Church of Arsos, but was brought here for better security. The relic was well authenticated by the Imperial seals of the Byzantine Emperor who had presented it, which were attached to the reliquary. The skull is at present kept in the apse, but the silver-gilt reliquary, though ancient, is not of the Byzantine period. In a niche in the iconostasis, with an inscription stating it was built by Chrysanthos, Bishop of Paphos in 1813, are two large crosses covered with silver-gilt repoussé work; one contains a fragment of the True Cross, the other the "Bonds of Christ", or the ropes with which the hands of Our Lord were tied behind His back before the Crucifixion. History is silent how these most interesting relics came to Omodhos, but they have certainly been here for centuries. In the gallery are kept two donor icons: St. Philip with a lady in a red dress decorated with gold embroidery, and dated 1528, and St. John the Baptist with a male donor, *c.* 1570.

The treasury contains besides the usual Gospels a wooden cross, with a beautiful silver-gilt setting decorated with emeralds and pearls, and late eighteenth-century communion plate given by the former Abbot.

The buildings of the monastic enclosure are on a large scale, and of two storeys. The wood carving of the synod hall is a remarkable example of rococo work; this also was erected in 1812 by Chrysanthos, who was Bishop of Paphos from 1801 till he was martyred by the Turks in 1821.

OMORPHITA (xxi)

The Church of St. Dimitrianos was built in 1902. In the gallery lie the eighteenth-century icons and rood cross from a former building; here, too, is preserved a large icon of St. Paraskevi, *c.* 1560, with a female donor in a red dress and a pearl necklace, in the right-hand bottom corner.

ORMIDHIA (xli)

The Church of St. Constantine is modern, and had replaced an earlier building of which nothing remains except the seventeenth-century rood cross, which is preserved in the west end of the modern church.

About a mile from the village are the ruins of the village of Angona, now but heaps of tumbled stone. Amid them still stands the fourteenth-century Church of St. George, with a small dome above the narthex. There are considerable remains of paintings on the walls, of which the best is the Annunciation, above the semi-vault of the apse. The reverse of an icon of the B.V.M., dated 1880, has on it a much-damaged painting of the B.V.M. and Child, dated 1655; only the head of the donor remains, but the dedication is complete.

Ormidhia was, during the eighteenth century, the summer resort of the foreign consuls and merchants of Larnaca. There must have been a regular colony here, and an Englishman who visited the Island in 1779, during July, tells us that he stayed ten days at the villa of the Venetian consul, where "His time was spent in one continuous scene of gaiety and amusement at the different villas of the European gentlemen".[1]

At the beginning of the nineteenth century these villas seem to have been deserted, and Captain Kinneir, who passed through Omidhia in 1818, gives a very different account:

Thoroughly drenched to the skin I took shelter in a Greek house in the valley of Ormidia, and as it was now nearly dark, and the storm continued to rage with increased violence, I resigned all thought of reaching Larnica that night. In the house where I halted, several Greek mariners were making merry round a large fire in the middle of the hall, and on our entering opened their ring to afford room for us near the fire; but as this apartment was the only accommodation the house afforded I inquired whether or not it were possible to hire a room in some other part of the village, which consisted of a number of scattered huts built along a range of heights overlooking a bay of the sea. I was informed that there was at some distance, close to the seashore, an old house belonging to the English dragoman, where the Greek believed I might be accommodated, as it was only inhabited by a man and his wife, who had the care of it. I sent for this man, who said I was welcome to pass the night in the house, and that he would show me the way. It was excessively dark, but after following him for about a quarter of a mile, through pools of water and over hedges and ditches, we entered the hall of a large and ruinous building, filled with broken chairs and tables, worm-eaten couches, and shattered

[1] *Excerpta Cypria*, p. 324.

looking-glasses. In this uncomfortable place I settled myself for the night, and notwithstanding my carpet, as well as my clothes, was quite wet, lay down to rest, and slept soundly until break of day.[1]

ORNITHI (xxii)

The village has completely disappeared, but the fifteenth-century church remains in a good state of preservation; it is dedicated to St. Artemios. Everything of interest has been removed from the interior, and the church is now disused. In a gable over the apse is a mediaeval coat of arms—an eagle displayed. St. Artemios was an early Archbishop of Salamis.

OROUNDA (xxix)

The village church is dedicated to St. Luke, and is a large and ill-constructed modern building. The ruins of its predecessor are near at hand.

Across the river lies the small Monastery of St. Nicholas. The church is a domed building, possibly dating from the late sixteenth century. The stone is well cut, and the building shows signs of careful construction. The church was repaired in 1733. Above the west door is a crude stone carving of the lion of St. Mark, native imitation of Venetian work. The interior is devoid of interest save for an eighteenth-century icon of St. George.

The village takes its name from the ancient Greek word for vetches, which are to this day much cultivated in the vicinity.

ORTA KEUY (xxi)

A miserable Turkish hamlet. Close to the village is a mediaeval bridge which is in extremely good repair. It was once on the high-road between Nicosia and Kyrenia, but since the British occupation the road has fallen into disuse and a new one has been built.

[1] *Excerpta Cypria*, p. 413.

PAKHNA (liii)

The principal church of the village is dedicated to the B.V.M., and was erected in 1849 on an ancient site. Two arches from the former building still stand near the west door. The church contains a damaged sixteenth-century icon on canvas of the B.V.M.

In and near the village lie a number of chapels, all in ruins and all once painted. They are dedicated respectively to the Apostles, St. Andronicos, St. George, St. Marina, and St. Epiphanios.

Two miles south of the village is the small Chapel of St. Stephen, surrounded by the ruins of a long-vanished village. Two large monoliths rise near by. These monoliths, or standing stones, occur frequently all over Cyprus; sometimes they rise as much as 12 feet above the surface of the ground, and taper upwards from a square base; there is generally a slit driven right through the stone of about 2 feet in length, by 1 foot broad. Many and various have been the reasons set forth to explain them. Cesnola sought to prove that they had a religious explanation like Jachin and Boaz in Solomon's Temple. Hogarth, however, has a far more prosaic theory: that they are the remains of ancient oil presses, whose use the modern Cypriote has forgotten.[1]

PALEKYTHRO (xxii)

As its name implies, this village was probably the site of the ancient bishopric of Chytroi. Nothing remains except the ruined mediaeval church dedicated to St. Katherine. It may have been in this church that the icon was kept which stopped the plague of locusts in 1344.

Also Ignatios the patriarch of Antioch, hearing of the great damage done by the locust [in Cyprus in the time of King Hugh], told King Hugh to give orders for a picture to be painted of St. Christopher the Martyr and St. Tarasios, Patriarch of Constantinople, and St. Tryphon the Martyr, and the said patriarch [being here in Cyprus] consecrated it; and they sent

[1] *Devia Cypria*, p. 47.

it to Palokythro, where the plague was. And he told them that when the locust hatched they should carry the picture in procession and say mass, and the Lord will protect the crops. [And they were delivered from the locust.][1]

Mr. Consul Drummond visited the village in 1750.

This night I lodged at Palaecitraea, about three miles from Citraea. It had been one of the ancient Cytheras or Cythereas, of which there were several in the island; but I saw no vestige of antiquity: indeed I was conducted to a place where the foundation of a temple, sacred to the queen of love, remained about a foot high some years ago; but the cadi, in order to save the expense of working a quarry, ordered the stones to be removed and employed in building an house for his women. I should not be sorry to hear they had tumbled down upon this barbarous Goth, and crushed him in the embraces of his favourite concubine, provided the innocent girl could escape unhurt.[2]

PALEOKHORIO (xxxviii)

The Church of St. George is the usual double-aisled building of the hill district and was rebuilt in 1864. The iconostasis contains a good deal of ancient woodwork, and a fine rood cross of the seventeenth century lies in the apse; the holy doors are dated 1720.

The beautiful Church of St. Luke, with its extremely interesting frescoes, has recently been torn down and nothing remains but a belfry. According to Mr. Jeffery, these frescoes were of more than usual merit, and included "the representation of 'Dives' Feast' with, in the foreground, Lazarus and the dogs, and a spirited group of musicians blowing long trumpets and dressed in doublets and trunk-hose, with long curling hair, irresistibly reminds one of Italian painting".[3] Nothing remains from the ancient church except the belfry, a few seventeenth-century icons unhappily restored in 1854, and the altar table.

The Church of the B.V.M. lies the other side of a little stream which runs through the middle of the village.

[1] *Chronicle of Makhairas*, p. 41.

[2] *Travels*, London, 1744, p. 274.

[3] *Monuments of Cyprus*, p. 304.

Originally a sixteenth-century church, it was restored in 1863, and fragments of a portion of the door, in the Gothic style, lie scattered in the church. A number of early seventeenth-century paintings survive on the arches and pillars of the two aisles. Much the best is the Invention of the Cross, which is superior in composition, grouping, and painting to the rest of the frescoes. In the apse is preserved a fine icon of the B.V.M. dated 1560, with a female donor in a black dress in the left bottom corner; her hair is confined by a veil, which hangs down behind her head. There is also an icon of the Body of Christ after the Deposition, *c.* 1600; at each side are five small panels containing pictures of various saints. On the altar is kept a mediaeval plate with the Annunciation, in relief, in the centre. In the body of the church hangs an extremely fine brass chandelier, probably early eighteenth-century work. A few curious stamped terra-cotta tiles remain on the floor in the west end.

The Church of the Saviour is a tiny chapel placed high above the village. The interior was completely painted in 1612, though a series of saints on the north and south wall are probably slightly later. In the apse is the B.V.M. in Glory. The church has a narthex on the south as well as the west side, and fragments of painting are still visible on the exterior wall. The iconostasis is probably contemporary.

A mile or so from the village lies the Church of SS. Cosmas and Damian. It consists of a nave and a south aisle, and probably dates from the first quarter of the sixteenth century. There are considerable remains of paintings on the north wall, in the usual rather wooden manner of the period. In the floor of the church is a terra-cotta slab stamped with a crude figure of some saint.

As its name implies, this village is one of the most ancient in Cyprus; indeed, even in the thirteenth century it was known as the old village. It is extremely picturesque in its situation, with houses built on each side of the steep hills which form the valley, and the stream shaded by tall poplars running between. So far corrugated iron has not reached the village, and the roofs are still covered with the home-made earth brown tiles.

PALEOMYLOS (xxxvii)

The Church of the Holy Cross is a small shed-like building, with considerable remains of paintings of the seventeenth century on the north wall in the apse. The beams and woodwork of the church are also painted, and the central tie beam has a bust of Christ Pantokrator in the centre of it. There is an unusual icon of Christ and the Twelve Apostles, painted on a single piece of wood which runs the whole length of the iconostasis screen beneath the rood cross.

PALEOSOPHOS (xi)

The Church of St. Paraskevi has the date 1857 on the iconostasis, which may well be also the date of the erection of the church.

The village is one of the most charming in Cyprus; below it wild pink antirrhinums grow in profusion, while all the edges of the small fields are planted with the large purple iris, so that they form hedges. In the middle of April the whole place is a glorious mass of colour.

PALIOURIOTISSA (xxi)

The Church of the B.V.M. was completely rebuilt in 1887. It contains a large over-painted icon of Christ dated 1693, and one of the Resurrection dated 1830, with a donor in the bottom corner; this is interesting as showing how late the mediaeval custom of donors lingered. In the women's gallery are the iconostasis and icons of the former church. In the present iconostasis screen, a barbaric piece of work, is a well-painted icon of the B.V.M. and Child, with scenes from the Virgin's life round the frame; it has the appearance of a double-sided processional icon, but owing to the fact that it is screwed into a wooden case it is difficult to determine if this is so or not.

In the churchyard lies part of a door lintel, with two defaced coats of arms on it; and part of the tracery of a Gothic window and a marble slab with the arms of Mocenigo: this is all that remains of the important mediaeval church that once stood here.

PALODHIA (liv)

The Church of St. Nicholas is a small barrel-vaulted building erected in 1801. There are flying buttresses on the north and south sides; between the buttresses on the south side is an open arcade of two arches. The church contains a large early seventeenth-century processional icon of the B.V.M. Valheriotissa, with a smaller painting of the Madonna and Child inset. This icon comes from a ruined church about two miles distant, and on the Tuesday after Easter the icon is taken back in solemn procession to its original home. The icon is famous all over the countryside for the miracles it has worked; and, indeed, does still work, for it is only four years since a man came from Limassol to pray to the icon, and was cured of a withered foot. The icon is covered with silver eyes, for the Madonna is famed far and wide for the cures of ophthalmia which she makes. Nor is she neglectful of the interests of the village. A few years ago, it is recorded, the villagers of Polemedia came to the church by night and tried to divert the spring which runs near there to their own fields, but hardly had they begun their evil work when the Virgin herself appeared, and the water began to boil, so that clouds of steam arose, and the robbers threw down their spades and fled, frightened out of their lives. The icon is probably unique in that it owns several fields. The story goes that one Easter Tuesday it was being taken out in procession when a Turk mocked it, saying: "What power has a piece of painted wood? I have a golden bell, I will leave it in the village church; if the icon can remove it and take it to the old church, then shall I believe." That night the Turk put the bell in the church, the doors were locked, and he lay down to sleep outside the west entrance, but he soon heard the noise of a bell ringing down the village street and across the fields, supported by no visible agency. In the morning the golden bell was found in the old church. The Turk was so impressed that he gave the fields in perpetuity to the icon, and the bell was sold in Limassol and with the money thus obtained the present communion plate was purchased.

PANO PANAYIA (xxxvi)

The village church is dedicated to St. George, and is a small building of the seventeenth century. A vast new temple built in a bastard Byzantine style rears its ugly head above the roofs of the village, but is as yet unfinished. The old church contains an extremely interesting collection of icons, mercifully untouched by the hand of the restorer. They are: (1) St. George, *c.* 1520, with three female donors in the corner. (2) St. Dimitrianos, of the same period and by the same hand; in the corner is a shield with a coat of arms, an eagle displayed sable. (3) B.V.M. and Child, damaged, but probably the work of the late fifteenth century. Superimposed on the Madonna's head is a gold crown set with semi-precious stones; on the crown itself are etched St. Nicholas, the B.V.M., and the Crucifixion. The crown of the Child has a hatched design with a simple cross rising from the centre. The neck and hand of the B.V.M. are also covered with bronze. This is a most unusual and interesting icon. (4) A large and well-preserved processional icon of St. George, *c.* 1500. (5) The principal icon of the church, the B.V.M. Eleousa, dated 1733, and covered with votive offerings, as it is supposed to cure the diseases of children. There are also three small icons, all by the same artist, and work of the mid-sixteenth century. They are the Baptism, the Raising of Lazarus, and the Pentecost. All show Italian influence. In the foreground of the Baptism is the River Jordan; in it are reclining two Triton-like figures, the allegories of the river and sea, who look as if they had come straight from a Renaissance fountain in Rome. The church also contains a bronze plate of the fifteenth century, with remains of a mediaeval inscription running round the edge, but now too worn to be legible.

About a mile from the village lies the important Monastery of Chrysorrhogiatissa, said to have been founded by a monk named Ignatios. It was at one time one of the most important in the Island. After the Turkish conquest it fell on difficult times, and in the eighteenth century was almost completely deserted. In 1770 it was repaired by Panaretos, Bishop of Paphos. The monastery possesses an icon supposed to have been painted by St. Luke. The story goes that the icon was originally kept in Isauria, but when the iconoclastic wars broke out it was saved by being thrown into the sea by a woman, and it drifted across the water to Cyprus. A monk Ignatios was directed to where it lay washed up on the beach by a vision and he brought it back into the hills, where a shrine was built for it; around this rose the monastery. The present monastic church is a large building of the end of the eighteenth century. The iconostasis was erected in 1790 by the Abbot Kalinikos and his successor Chrysanthos, and is an excellent example of the florid carving of the period. It contains two icons of the Archangels and St. John the Baptist, painted and presented by the Abbot Kalinikos himself in 1743. There is also a large late sixteenth-century icon of Christ, said to have come from the ruined Monastery of Chrysolakkourna. The gilt hand on the icon was added in 1848 by the priest Polycarpos, who was cured of leprosy by it. The famous icon of the B.V.M. is inset in a heavy and elaborate frame made in 1786; the icon itself was covered with silver gilt in 1762, the money for this being subscribed by all the inhabitants of the Paphos district. The icon is held in great veneration by criminals and persons condemned by law; the families of those sentenced to death come from miles round to invoke the Virgin's aid to save their loved ones from the hangman's noose, while even the youth who has stolen goods worth but a few piastres from his master will pray to this icon that he shall not be found out. Against the north wall hangs a large wooden cross covered with silver gilt plaques, which were made at the expense of the dragoman Haji Georghiou in 1803; the cross itself was lost for many years, but its hiding-place was revealed by the Virgin to some shepherds. The treasury is without interest; there is a heavy gilt and silver processional cross of 1793 and there are some cuffs dating from the late eighteenth century, thickly sewn with seed pearls. The large women's gallery was added in 1802 by the Abbot Joachim, who also, according to an inscription, erected the huge monastic buildings which surround the church. In the monastery is kept the original copper plate made by the Cretan painter Cornaro in 1801, which depicts the icon of the Virgin, while surrounding it is a series of tableaux and legends of the history of the icon and the cures it has worked.

About two miles from Chrysorrhogiatissa is the small Monastery of Moni, the property of the Abbot of Kykko. The monastery is almost certainly built on the site of a Temple of Hera. When the church was restored in 1885, two inscriptions in Cypriote characters were found, while a third in ordinary Greek characters was built into the west wall on either side of the doorway. The principal Cypriote inscription refers to a King Nicocles, who perhaps was the prince dethroned by Ptolemy Lagus in 310 B.C. The entrance to the monastery is through a high arched doorway. On each side of this entrance are two small windows, now blocked up, with stone frames with a leaf design; above these windows are two others with frames and heavy stone sills in the late sixteenth-century manner. According to an inscription on the doorway, the monastery was rebuilt by the Abbot Nikephorus in 1696, but these windows must almost certainly come from an earlier building. The monastic buildings form three sides of a square, the fourth side being filled by a church. An open arcade lies on the south side built by that Abbot of Kykko who was hanged in 1821 by the Turks. The church consists of a main aisle and a small north aisle, separated by arches carried on plain columns. According to an inscription on the west door, the church was built in 1638, but the age of the superb apse must be earlier. It is built of beautifully cut blocks of white stone with a boldly carved acanthus leaf design below the semi-dome. The icons are without interest and are repainted, the earliest being Christ 1641 and the B.V.M. exactly a hundred years later.

A few yards north of the church lies a small cruciform chapel. It has no architectural features and the Abbot informed the writer that a tradition had always been handed down that it was once a Latin building, but the curious thing is that it is orientated north and south, not east and west, and this would seem to make it open to doubt, in spite of its form and apse, whether it was ever a church at all.

A number of drums and fragments of columns—all that remains of the Temple of Hera—surround the monastery.

The importance of this shrine may be inferred from the royal dedications, and the size of the columns. It was situated in one of the most favoured spots in Cyprus: the cliffs of the Eagles Eyrie close round it in a half moon, averting every wind but the west, and from their foot gushes a perennial spring, famous throughout the district for its purity; as it flows down the slope its course is marked by orchards and olive-groves, and the flowering shrubs give forth a scent almost overpoweringly sweet on the June evening on which I first rode into this happy valley. Lying nearly 3,000 feet above the sea, it enjoys cool airs in the hottest summer, and the view over the Papho ridges to the Bay of Poli and the Akamas, and up the Ezuza valley to the shaggy heights of the Forest, is of singular beauty. Claudian might have seen such a spot, and made of it his "Venusberg".

The ascription to Hera is of great interest in a part of the island devoted to Aphrodite. So essentially Hellenic a goddess must have come late to Cyprus, and perhaps this temple was only erected in the fourth century B.C. by this King Nicocles, whose name appears in all its inscriptions; even Apollo ought to be her senior in the island, for the settlement of Curium gives a definite period and reason for his introduction, and, as I have conjectured, his easy assimilation with Asiatic divinities would tend to spread his cult. But Hera had no such sponsors, and probably was not known in Cyprus until the Hellenizing period which followed the introduction of Athenian influences in the middle of the fifth century, and culminated under the rule of Evagoras at Salamis in the early part of the fourth. Her individual cult was never popular; indeed we have further evidence of it only at Old Paphos and Amathus: in a fragmentary inscription built into the church of the Panagia Chrysopolitissa at the former her name appears after Zeus and Aphrodite, and at the latter another inscription makes mention of a Heraeum.[1]

---

[1] *Devia Cypria*, p. 34.

PARAKKLISHA (liv)

The Church of the Archangel Michael is an ancient building with a narthex added later. The north door survives from an even earlier building and has fragments of an inscription in Gothic script on it. The church was once painted, but frescoes only remain on the founders' tombs in the north and south walls. The church contains a large icon of St. John the Baptist, dating from the late seventeenth century.

The Church of the Holy Cross is probably of Byzantine foundation, and the apse, with its typical Byzantine window, is of the twelfth or thirteenth century; the large west end is a recent addition; above the small north window is a curious stone carving of a hand holding a standard, but only a portion of the staff now remains. The apse is completely frescoed; in the semi-dome is the B.V.M. and Child, with the kneeling figure of a donor holding a scroll; the costume indicates the sixteenth century.

Just outside the village lies the tiny cemetery Chapel of the B.V.M. Nerophorousa, completely rebuilt save for a portion of the north wall, which still retains fragments of mural painting. This small chapel contains a magnificent early sixteenth-century icon of the B.V.M., with female donors, *c.* 1520.

PARALIMNI (xxxiii)

The Church of the B.V.M. was originally a small domed church, but a south aisle has been added later. It contains late eighteenth-century paintings. The vaulting of the church is decorated with porcelain plates, some of which are above the usual standard, and it is possible to discern Italian, Dutch, and Rhodian ware, mostly of the early eighteenth century. There is a good seventeenth-century iconostasis and rood cross.

The large lake which existed near the village has recently been drained. Between the village and the sea lies the site of the ancient Leucolla. Cesnola dug here in 1875 and found a fine colossal head of Cybele with a mural crown.

After digging a few days at random, I came upon the foundations of a building, from which I brought out some large heads and fragments of stone sculpture, all bearing a decidedly Greek character. From the geographical situation of these ruins they can be no other than those of Leucolla, a town which was in a flourishing condition at the time of Alexander the Great, and gave its name to the famous naval battle fought in its neighbourhood between Demetrius Poliorcetes and Ptolemy. Its harbour, some 130 feet below the level of the city, was reached by a road cut in the rock, still partially visible. From the small extent of these ruins, Leucolla must have been a town of no great importance.[1]

PARAMALI (liii)

A Turkish village. About a mile south lies a church dedicated to the B.V.M., and the remains of a mediaeval settlement. Except that the roof of the semi-vault has collapsed, the church is in a very tolerable state of repair. The west end is built of carefully cut stone, and above the tympanum of the arch is a small round window. The keystone of the door has the remains of an illegible inscription on it. The interior was once painted, but time has destroyed nearly all the frescoes.

PATRIKI (xv)

The principal church of the village dedicated to the Archangel Michael is without interest. Near by lies a small Chapel of St. George, with a few fragments of early woodwork built into the miserable iconostasis, which is otherwise formed of boards from packing-cases. The poor and late seventeenth-century holy doors from some destroyed church are kept in a coffee-shop.

One of the most curious local customs still remaining in the Island is practised every Easter Monday in this village; all the married persons gather into the churchyard, and the men, without taking off their coats, have to crawl through a hole in a large stone which stands here. If the man is unable to crawl through this stone it means that his wife is unfaithful to him, for it shows that he has antlers

[1] *Cyprus: Its Cities, Tombs and Temples.*

which prevent him from passing through. In 1935 only one man stuck, and he, on his return home, beat his wife and has since started divorce proceedings, the fact that he was unable to pass through the stone being considered by him and his co-villagers as ample evidence.

PEDHOULAS (xxxvii)

The most interesting monument in the village is the tiny Church of the Archangel Michael, which was built in 1472 by Basil Chamades. The walls of the interior are completely covered with contemporary frescoes. Above the north door is a painting of the donor, his wife, and two daughters, presenting a model of the church to the Archangel. The costume of the portraits is interesting, and the long linen veils they wear are edged at the bottom with a design in coloured wools, exactly like the work still done by the women in some of the Paphos villages. The iconostasis is the best-preserved example of a type of which a dozen or so still exist in the Island. It is more like a European rood screen in that it does not completely hide the altar from the view of the worshippers. It is almost certain that till the sixteenth century all iconostasis screens were more or less open, but in the late sixteenth century the Orthodox Church found they were losing their hold on the peasants, who were becoming more educated. As a result there came into general use in the churches a screen which completely hid the priest from his congregation, causing an air of mystery to surround the clergy, who seemed to communicate alone with their God, so that to the peasant the priest seemed a man apart, and one to be treated with reverence and looked up to as a leader. This iconostasis is unusual in that on its "ceiling" and above the holy doors is painted the royal Lusignan coat of arms, while to left and right are coats of other noble Cypriote families; it is probable that the builder Basil caused the royal arms to be painted here out of respect to, and in honour of, the reigning king.

There are a number of other chapels in the village, of which the most important is St. George, with a superb carved west door. The repainted iconostasis is of the same date and style as that of the Archangel. The church contains a seventeenth-century icon of St. Onouphrios.

PELATHOUSA (xxvi)

The mosque was originally a mediaeval Church of St. Katherine. About a mile and a half below the village, and at the locality Horteni, stands the Church of the B.V.M., a domed Byzantine building with founders' tombs and a small south aisle added at a later date. The frescoes which remain include a bust of Christ Pantokrator in the dome.

The name of the village is said to be derived from the local Greek name for the genista, or wild broom.

PELENDRIA (xlvii)

The Church of the Archangel Michael was rebuilt in the early nineteenth century and contains late seventeenth-century icons of SS. Peter and Paul and the B.V.M.

The fourteenth-century Church of the Holy Cross is one of the most interesting remaining in the Island. It has recently been carefully restored by the local inhabitants. In the tympanum above the west door is a bust of Christ with donors and inscriptions. Practically the whole interior of the church is painted, the most interesting work being in the north aisle, where there is a painting of Christ and the Doubting Thomas, with two kneeling donors, who are in all probability Jean de Lusignan and his wife. Pelendria was a fief of Prince Jean, and close to this painting is the royal Lusignan coat of arms, with a bend for a difference and with two partridges as supporters. These two facts make it almost certain that the two personages represented here are the Prince and his wife. Jean was born about 1331, and was the son of Hugh IV and brother to Peter I. He married a daughter of the House of d'Ibelin, and became Constable of the kingdom and Prince of Antioch, and during the minority of his nephew, Peter II, he was regent of the kingdom. He was beloved by his people, but his sister-in-law, the Queen Eleanor of Aragon, was jealous of him and encompassed his death.

The queen Eleanor saw that her husband's brother the prince Jean had many Bulgarians with him at St. Hilarion. Now she was seeking to 'put him to death'. And before she left Kerynia, she sent word to him to come to Kerynia, and he came with a great host. And she was afraid that he might seize her in the Defile, and so she had a Mass said, and each of them swore to the other on the Body of Christ that they would be at peace. And then he went back to St. Hilarion, and the queen went with him as far as the Defile, and there they said farewell to one another, and the queen came to Lefkosia, and the prince with his men went up to St. Hilarion.

And when the queen reached Lefkosia, she sent a letter to the prince: "My beloved brother, be on your guard to take the castle of St. Hilarion, and be careful for your own life. And because I love you, I tell you this." The good lord believed this letter of his enemy, she who was more poisonous than poison, and so he fell into great sin, for he murderously took their lives[1] without cause. [For when the prince read the letter] he brought them up to the castle one by one. And at his orders they were thrown down from the window, and such was the height that they were killed. And the last one of all escaped, by the will of the Lord; they threw him down, but he was not killed, that it might thus be made known how unjustly they had been killed. And the man lived a long time after this.

Because of the oath which she had taken and because of all that she had written to him, the prince thought that the queen's heart had melted towards him, and so he left St. Hilarion and came to Lefkosia. The queen's mood was very high and much set against him, and she was seeking how she might set her son the king to kill him, as being the man to blame for the killing of his father. After dinner she sent word to him to come to the king, and in the arches at the back she concealed Sir Francis de Marin, a Genoese who had remained in Cyprus in the king's employ as his squire, and Sir Francis Saturno, a Catalan who was their squire, and Neapolitans and Lombards also, and Louis Bon the king's squire, and certain knights of Cyprus.

And as soon as he heard the king's order, the said prince came down to mount his horse. The people who loved him said: "Do not go: if you do, they will kill you." And he did not believe them, and went down to the terrace. And they said

---

[1] The Bulgarian guard.

it again, and he would not believe them, but said: "Are the oaths [which we have taken] things to play with?" And when he sat on his horse, the horse slipped and came to the ground. And with this he went off to the court. And before he dismounted, the knights signed to him: "Go back again." And he refused to believe them, that what was to be should be accomplished. Well and good: he dismounted and went into the king's room, the room hung with gold,—what is called the Chambre de parement. There he found the king and his mother sitting on the bench. And the prince greeted them. And the table was set for them to sit down to eat. And the queen said to the prince: "My lord and brother, come to the table and let us eat." And he, to show no ill will, said to her: "As you wish." And they sat at the table. And she had arranged that, when they took off the napkin, the shirt of the king her husband, whom they had killed, should be there in the dish; and she said to the men whom she had put in hiding: "As soon as I show him the shirt, you must be ready to kill him." And so it was done. The prince was sitting at the table, and his heart was as spellbound. They said to him: "Sir, eat." And he said to them: "Oh, my heart, my heart! I do not know why, but it is as bound; I do not know what is upon me." But when they had finished eating, she put the shirt on the table, and said to him: "Sir Prince, do you know whose is this shirt?" And they leaped out at once and killed the good prince in the room where they had killed King Peter. And there was great weeping and great sorrow. And they carried him away dead into his house, and buried him in St. Dominic's.[1]

On the walls of the church are a number of donors and their wives, who may possibly have belonged to the household of the prince. The church contains a large wooden cross, with a smaller bronze cross inset, the whole covered with square silver plates with scenes from the life of Christ. It stands in the iconostasis in a shrine of Coptic musharaby work. The icons include a large processional one of St. George, dated 1716, and a sixteenth-century one of the B.V.M. A modern icon of the B.V.M. has on the reverse a most unusual painting of the Preparation of the Cross, possibly work of the early sixteenth century: on the left

[1] *Chronicle of Makhairas*, p. 547.

stands Christ, behind Him soldiers with curious peaked head-dresses; next comes a figure, possibly the executioner, and on the right St. John and the Virgin—St. John appears to comfort the Virgin, who wears a look of deep horror on her face. This icon is unusual, perhaps, in that all the figures show far more expression than is usual in the average wooden painting of the period. A large stone in the shape of a rough cross is let into the top of the altar.

The Church of the Madonna is a large seventeenth-century building with a contemporary iconostasis, which has unhappily been repainted. The church contains an interesting collection of processional icons, alas! mostly restored, of which the best is one of 1673, with the B.V.M. on one side and the Crucifixion on the other. There is also a rain-compelling icon of the B.V.M., dated 1640. In the screen is a charming and spirited painting of St. Mamas; the saint's cloak flies behind him in the wind, and the lion turns round and gazes up at the rider with a most engaging smile. St. Mamas is one of the few Cypriote saints who were well known to the European world during the Middle Ages, and was often painted by the Italian artists of that period. He appears in the large altar-piece by Pesellino in the National Gallery in London.

The Church of St. John Lampadistes was destroyed by a flood, and a vast formless church has risen from the ruins.

PENDALIA (xlvi)

The Church of St. George is modern but contains an older icon of the patron saint hung round with silver coins, the gifts of those who have lost their animals and have found them again through the intercession of the saint. In the apse is kept an extremely interesting processional icon of the sixteenth century, on one side the Madonna and Child, with her halo, veil, and sleeve in relief, on the other the Prophet Elijah being fed by the ravens. Unhappily this icon has been restored in the usual fatal manner, and its dark green background is certainly not original.

PENDAYIA (xix)

The large Monastery of Xeropotamo is the property of Kykko, and has a church dedicated to SS. Cosmas and Damian, an unimportant building of the eighteenth century. In the iconostasis are a number of fragments of early woodwork. In the churchyard of the monastery lie marble Corinthian capitals and granite columns from the ruins of Soli.

About a mile and a half from the village are the ruins of the Church of St. George. A number of Roman tombs surround it. During the Middle Ages Pendayia was one of the twelve baronies into which the Island was divided.

PERA (xxx)

The Church of the Archangel Michael was built in the seventeenth century and restored in 1890. A fine brass chandelier hangs from the central dome. The iconostasis has been damaged by fire, and a huge seventeenth-century icon of the Archangel, which was also partially burnt, lies in the apse.

The Church of the B.V.M. Hodegetria has a black granite column standing outside the north door, while the lintel of the west door is a fine marble slab; both of these come from the ruins of Tamassos. The church contains a number of icons from the deserted Church of St. Dimitrianos. They are: Christ, dated 1609; B.V.M., 1734; and St. Nicholas, 1743. The iconostasis is dated 1773.

PERAKHORIO (xxxix)

The principal church of the village is dedicated to St. Marina, and was built in 1853. It contains an unusual icon of a saint with a group of Orthodox priests standing at his feet, probably work of the eighteenth century.

Close to the village and on a small hill stands the interesting church dedicated to the Twelve Apostles. The interior still contains the remains of superb mural paintings, probably dating from the twelfth or thirteenth centuries. In the dome is Christ, while below is a decorated frieze of winged angels carrying gifts. The figures of these angels are of supreme beauty, and the perfectly painted hands are in the true Byzantine style. Though the frieze is damaged it still remains one of the most lovely and satisfying things in Cyprus. In the semi-dome are the B.V.M. supported by Peter and Paul, while below are the Fathers of the church. The paintings on the south wall are probably later.

PERAPEDHI (xlvii)

The village is the centre of the wine industry, and a large modern factory has recently been erected here.

The Church of St. Nicholas was built in 1796; it contains a very fine sixteenth-century icon of the B.V.M., and also one of St. John the Evangelist, dated 1550. A wooden box contains relics of SS. Spyridon, Neophytos, and Philip, set in a silver gilt repoussé case, which is apparently of the seventeenth century.

Maura (3rd May), and Timothy, her husband, are generally mentioned together. Lusignan claims the village of Perapedi at the foot of Troodos as their birthplace, and says they were martyred on the banks of the Kurias near the town of Kilanion. According to his account, on the spot where their blood fell a spring of water gushed out. The stains, so he affirms, still remained to his day, and were visible on the earth and rocks beneath the water. The accuracy of this statement he vouches for by personal experiment. The legend doubtless owes its origin to the presence of some reddish rocks on the supposed site of the execution, the colouring of which is due to certain minerals.[1]

PERISTERONA (FAMAGUSTA) (xxiii)

The Church of St. Anastasis is a late eighteenth-century building, with a small tomb-chapel of the saint on the north side. Round the church are columns and capitals from some former building. A small fragment of a marble frieze of the Roman era is built into the west wall of the chapel. The iconostasis is dated 1779, and contains an icon of St. George of 1723. From the attached chapel steps lead down

[1] Hackett, *Church of Cyprus*, p. 397.

to the tomb of the saint, the roof of which is supported by a highly polished marble column. On the grave of the saint lie the shuttle and other implements of the weaver's craft, for such was the saint's profession during his lifetime. Those who have pains in any part of their bodies come here, and after praying to the saint beat the afflicted portion of their person with the shuttle and are immediately cured.

PERISTERONA (KHRYSOKHOU) (XXXV)

The Church of St. Mamas is a hideous modern building, but in it are preserved icons from some former church, including an unusually large one of St. Mamas, measuring 9 feet by 3½ feet; this icon was unhappily completely repainted in 1889. There is also an icon of Christ given by the priest George in 1551, and a curious late fifteenth-century icon of the B.V.M. and Child; her halo, veil, the neck of her dress and her sleeves are in relief in the manner of a picture by Crivelli; a long inscription runs round the Virgin's veil, which apparently reads, "Give praise to those who praise me." Alas, this interesting relic has suffered the usual fate with the additional horror that a pale blue background has been added. The church also contains a fine mediaeval plate of St. Christopher, staff in hand, with the Infant Christ on his shoulder. As this saint and legend are unknown to the Orthodox church, the plate must come from some Latin building.

PERISTERONA (MORPHOU) (XXIX)

The Church of SS. Barnabas and Hilarion is one of the most charming in Cyprus, situated on the edge of a river and close to the main road to Troodos. It is a large mediaeval building with five domes. The narthex has been added more recently, but the large and well-carved west doors are probably contemporary. The restored iconostasis is dated 1549 and contains a sixteenth-century icon of the Presentation in the Temple, which has a kneeling donor in a red dress with a white belt, green collar, and a black cloak. During the building of the narthex a gypsum tomb slab of a man in civilian costume, dating from about 1520, was discovered. It was unfortunately broken by the workmen, but the writer has recently placed it against one of the piers at the west end of the church. In the apse is kept an ancient chest; the interior of the lid has been painted with a scene representing a siege of a castle, a banner flying on the right of the attackers bearing the arms of St. John of Jerusalem. It is possible that the painting on this ancient piece of furniture may depict the siege of Rhodes in 1522.

The Church of St. Barbara has been repaired but still contains a considerable number of mural paintings; on the south wall is St. George with three kneeling donors dressed in black, on the west an Evangelist with a donor in a black dress. The apse contains the B.V.M. and the Fathers of the church. There is a sixteenth-century icon of the B.V.M., and a large board which runs along the top of the iconostasis has portraits of saints in painted circles.

PERIVOLIA (l)

The Church of St. Leontios is a late eighteenth-century building with a south aisle added later. The church contains a fine icon of the saint, *c.* 1720. In the gallery is a large dower chest full of icons, but they are all too decayed to be of interest. St. Leontios lived during the reign of the Emperor Maurice (582–602) and was the author of a *Life of St. John the Almoner*.

Close to the village is a Venetian blockhouse in a very good state of repair, standing on a small eminence and overlooking the sea; the only entrance is by a door about 12 feet above the ground. On the lintel of this door are three coats of arms: in the centre the lion of St. Mark, while to the left is a shield bearing a chevron between three crescents, to the right a shield bearing a bend dexter. Perhaps these arms may belong to the builder or to the Venetian Governor of Cyprus.

PETRA (xxviii)

The Church of the Transfiguration has recently been entirely rebuilt. It contains, however, six ancient icons, including two of Christ and the B.V.M., dated 1765 and given by the Abbot of Kykko to the church at Asinou, from whence they were stolen by a Turk, who presented them to the village of Petra. There is a large and beautiful icon of the B.V.M. and Child, *c.* 1500. The B.V.M. wears a claret-coloured cloak over a dark blue robe; the cloak is fastened by a circular gold brooch, which the Infant Christ clasps in His tiny hand. The icon has apparently never been repainted, and is an excellent example of the Italian Cypriote style.

The mosque is a former Church of St. Basil, a small domed mediaeval building. It is said that frescoes are still on the walls, under the whitewash.

PETROPHANI (xxxi)

A poor Turkish hamlet. Near the village is Malloura, the site of a temple, but it has been so ransacked by Lang[1] and the villagers that little is left. A fragment of the floor can still be seen, and near by the ruins of a church, which was erected, as was so often the case, on the site of the heathen temple; a number of broken and defaced limestone statues have even been built into its walls.

PEYIA (xlv)

The Church of the B.V.M. is a large modern building without the slightest interest. About two miles from the village are the ruins of the monastery of the B.V.M. Zalagiotissa, which is much frequented by those who suffer from varicose veins.

Five miles from the B.V.M. Zalagiotissa are the remains of the large and important Roman town of Drepanum. The ruins are about a quarter of a mile square, but nothing of architectural interest remains save a few pillars and Corinthian capitals.

Near by is a small Byzantine Church of St. George, with a curious altar formed of two Byzantine capitals on top of each other, so that they look like an hour-glass. Many are

[1] Sir Hamilton Lang, British consul, 1871–1877.

the superstitions and legends connected with this little church. It is much frequented by youths who are in love, for they come to the church and light a small candle and repeat three times the name of the girl they love; the boy then holds the candle downwards; if the flame burns, the girl returns his love; but if it goes out, she cares for someone else. It is also much resorted to by both Turks and Greeks who lose their animals. It is credulously told that quite recently a Turk lost his mule. He at once came to this little church and left an offering for St. George and then sat down outside to eat his meal. As he finished he lifted up his eye and, lo and behold, there was his mule swimming in from the sea. A story still told in the village is that during the sixteenth century pirates landed at Peyia and stole the son of one of the leading villagers. The distracted father came to the church and offered St. George a great gift if only his son could return. That evening the boy suddenly appeared in the village dressed in barbaric apparel, still clasping in his hand the basin of soup which he had been handing to the pirate chief and which, even more wonderful to relate, was still steaming hot.

Opposite the Cape of Drepano is the small Island of St. George rising sheer from the sea and distant about three hundred yards from the shore. It is about two hundred yards long and sixty across in the broadest part; the cliffs are about a hundred feet high. On the southern side are considerable remains of a neolithic settlement, and flints and fragments of pottery lie scattered about. At the west point of the island is the base of a Roman building, possibly a lighthouse, and the remains of defensive walls, a cistern, millstones, etc., all dating from the Roman time. The north cliff has been supported at some period by a sea wall, formed of well-cut stones. The island is the haunt of innumerable wild pigeons, but is difficult of access except in calm weather.

From the ruins of Drepanum to Cape Arnauti is a large uninhabited tract of land known as the Akamas; for thirteen miles there is no human habitation save a custom house at Cape Lara.

A line drawn from the latter cape to the mouth of the Poli river begins the wild forest-tract of the Akamas, so-called from the ancient name of its extreme northern point, which, except for two or three villages on the summit and east of the central ridge, and hardly to be included in the district at all, is devoid of human habitation other than isolated tchifliks or huts inhabited only in summer. It is a sterile corner of Cyprus, thickly covered with scrub, abounding in deep gullies and bold rock formations, the central spine being broken into bold peaks or miniature table mountains; here and there in a tiny valley is a cultivated patch, but nine-tenths of the district produces nothing but game.[1]

There is no doubt, however, that this district was once much more thickly inhabited. At Agios Konon are the ruins of a large town about a mile and a half inland from the sea; an area of about half a square mile is covered with ruins. In the middle stands a Byzantine church dedicated to St. George, in the interior of which to the south of the altar a built tomb with an arch at the head was recently found in the floor; it is said to have contained a number of gold Byzantine objects. Behind the village and in the thick scrub is a vast Hellenistic-Roman necropolis; many of the tombs have been opened, but a number must still be unexplored.

The harbour of this ancient town can still be traced, and several black marble mooring pillars remain *in situ*.

PHASOULA (LIMASSOL) (liv)

Outside the village lie the ruins of the ancient Church of St. Rheginos. Hardly anything is left of the walls, but in a tomb chamber beneath, and approached by a flight of steps, lies the sarcophagus of the saint, cut from a single block of lime-stone, and with remains of a domed lid. It is empty and measures 2·20 metres in length, 1·16 metres in width, and 0·84 metres in height. The sides are 10 centimetres thick. In each corner of the interior are half-columns to support the lid. The north side panel is decorated with a spirited relief of a hunting scene, with a frieze above and

[1] *Devia Cypria*, p. 10.

beneath. The upper frieze contains grapes and vine-leaves, with a fish, an early Christian symbol, in the centre. The lower frieze has various birds, such as peacocks, etc. The main or central scene shows the mounted hunters armed with spears, while hounds are attacking a stag. The edge of the tomb is much worn by the elbows and knees of those suffering from rheumatism. For it is believed to be a certain cure to place the elbows or to kneel on the edge of the sarcophagus. There can be no doubt that this Byzantine sarcophagus dates from the fifth century, and that it once contained the body of St. Rheginos, Archbishop of the Island, who was present at the Council of Ephesus in 431. On a ruined wall of the church grows a fig-tree, and though it is covered with excellent fruit, no one will pluck the figs, for it is certain that he who eats them at once finds that his face swells and breaks out in boils. When Lord Kitchener was making his survey of the Island in 1882, he wished to cut down this tree as it interfered with the making of some observations, but he was prevailed on by the villagers to spare it, and they built him a special platform so that he could see above its branches.

In the village is the Church of the B.V.M., a mediaeval building restored in 1859 and again in 1884, when a portion of the south aisle was destroyed, but two well-built arches were allowed to remain which have been bricked up and are now used as an oil store. The interior was once painted, but all that remains is an angel's head with a raised halo. A number of inscribed cippi are built into the wall of the church.

On the top of a high isolated hill called Castra, a mile or so from the village, are the remains of a large Roman fort. The ground plan is quite clear, and huge stones, some of them 6 feet square, lie about. There are remains too of the paved road which led up the hill. In the centre of the fort lie a number of life-sized statues, all headless. The writer saw some of the heads, which are kept by a villager, and they would appear to be about the fourth century A.D. The best preserved, that of a youth, had the typical cork-screw curls of that period at the back of the head. On the

Tuesday after Easter a small icon of the B.V.M., in a carved frame, is solemnly taken to the top of Castra, where a short service is held. The icon is then restored to the church. In this custom may possibly linger some memory of a heathen festival.

PHIKARDHOU (xxxviii)

The Church of the Twelve Apostles is an attractive building of 1787. It contains a fine icon of Peter and Paul in an excellent state of preservation, and dated 1741. The village has an almost unique example of a rectory built at the same time and erected by the same priest who built the church.

PHILOUSA (KELOKEDHRA (xlvi)

The Church of St. Mamas dates from the seventeenth century, and contains a very fine early sixteenth-century icon, inscribed St. George of Cappadocia.

About a mile from the village is the Chapel of St. Nicholas, which contains a large and well-painted icon of that saint, dated 1520; round the frame are scenes from his life, while to the left of his head is Christ holding a Gospel, and to the right the B.V.M. holding a napkin. In the iconostasis is a late fifteenth-century fragment of a holy door, with busts of three saints; the background and haloes are in relief. The altar of prothesis has a fragment of a dedication stone built into it.

PHINI (xlvii)

About two miles from the village lies the deserted Monastery of St. Cosmas and Damian. The monastic buildings have long since disappeared, but the church is in a good state of preservation. The west doorway is decorated with a fine dog-tooth moulding, and is possibly work of the late fifteenth century. In the interior on the north wall are paintings of St. George and the Archangel Michael. The iconostasis is dated 1697, and there is an icon of the B.V.M. of 1635, and one of St. John the Baptist dated 1705. There is also a processional icon of Cosmas and

Damian of the early eighteenth century. There are some charming wooden candlesticks, probably of the Venetian era. On the walls various visitors have cut their names, including Porry, the French consul of the eighteenth century, and Rohr, the German traveller. The villagers relate that at dusk every Saturday night the figure of a dark-complexioned youth, mounted on a horse, is seen to issue from the great west door and ride away into the night. About five years since a girl from the village, who went early one summer morning to the fields to work, saw a priest in bygone vestments standing outside the door. So terrified was she by this vision that she sank into a decline and shortly afterwards died.

PHRENAROS (xxxiii)

The Church of the Archangel Michael is a charming mediaeval building with two domes, and, except for a new door and a window added during a restoration of 1883, is little changed from its original state. Built into the exterior north wall is a Venetian coat of arms, possibly a fragment of a tombstone. The restoration, alas, has not spared the interior, for a local artist has perpetrated a wall painting in the crudest style, and the original frescoes have been hidden by coats of whitewash. Nor has the iconostasis been spared, and with the icons has been daubed over with oil paint. One of these icons, the B.V.M. and Child, was, according to an inscription, painted by a certain Dimitri of Moscow in 1721. In the apse lie two icons which have escaped the vandalistic hand of the restorer; they represent the B.V.M. and Christ, and date from about 1550. In the bottom left-hand corner of the former is a donor with his wife and child.

About one mile south of the village lie the remains of a vanished town of considerable size. All domestic buildings have long ago disappeared, but three churches remain, "occupying the chief place still, and dropping now and then a stone as it were a monumental tear for their glorious past".[1]

[1] Mahaffy, *Rambles and Studies in Greece*.

The largest church is dedicated to St. George. The central nave and two aisles may be work of the twelfth century. At a later period the church was considerably enlarged by building on an elongated narthex, but the façade of the west end remains untouched, so that the original west door is now the centre of the building, and two later side aisles end against the blank façade of the old church. This is a curious and rather clumsy method of construction. Below the tympanum of the old west door is a lintel with five crosses cut on it. Considerable remains of mural painting still adhere to the walls and dome. Near the church are the remains of walls or fences formed of large unhewn boulders of considerable weight and size.

Slightly south lies the Monastery of the B.V.M. Kourdhali. The church is intact, and would seem to be work of the early sixteenth century. A recent restoration has been carried out in a most haphazard manner, and the interior has been slashed with mortar and whitewash, thus covering and obscuring what few paintings remain. The iconostasis is formed of packing-cases and painted a peculiarly vile post-card blue. Two seventeenth-century icons, however, of the B.V.M. and Christ still remain. Round the church lie the ruins of the monastic buildings, and various marble pillars which must have once been used in their construction. To the west is an ancient cistern excavated in the solid rock, and measuring 13 metres by 2½ metres and about 16½ metres in depth. Close to this is the third of the churches, that of St. Theodoros. It is the most destroyed of all, and little remains save the domed narthex; in the body and ruined apse of the church lie drums of stone columns and plain capitals, which show that it must have been a building of a certain elegance of construction.

About a mile north-east of Phrenaros lie two churches, St. Andronicos and St. Marina. St. Andronicos is a tiny Byzantine chapel, in a perfect state of preservation, untouched and unrestored. To left and right of the west door are two curious semicircular recesses not unlike the tympanum above a lintel; this is an unusual architectural motive and unknown in any other church in the Island;

they may once have contained frescoes. The paintings that decorated the interior have disappeared.

The Church of St. Marina is now disused, but is a barrel-vaulted building of the fifteenth century. Above the west door is a shield with a coat of arms of a cross. This was the badge both of St. John of Jerusalem and also of a Cypriote family, and the same coat appears on a lintel which lies in the Armenian cemetery near Nicosia. The interior is decorated with wall paintings of two periods. Of the first and best period all that remains is a Crucifixion that fills the entire west wall; it is damaged, but well enough preserved to show that the artist was undoubtedly skilled in design and technique.

PHTERYKOUDHI (xxxviii)

The Church of St. Avvagoun was built in 1818. The contemporary woodwork, iconostasis, and gallery have a certain attraction with their faded gilding and paint. St. Avvagoun was a poor youth who lived in Syria. One day, while taking food to his master, who was working in the fields, an angel appeared to him and told him that the Prophet Daniel had need of the food. So saying the angel seized the boy by his hair and, carrying him thus, duly deposited him in the lions' den where Daniel was confined. St. Avvagoun handed the dish to Daniel, which, miraculous to relate, was still warm, and having done so was transferred by the angel back to the field from whence he had been—like Ganymede—so suddenly removed. The legend neglects to tell us exactly what the saint's master said when his luncheon was not forthcoming.

PILERI (xii)

A Turkish hamlet. Close by is a large and well-built cistern, the conduit of which is quarried for some distance into the hill behind. This tunnel is some eight feet high, with pointed arches of cut stone. Above, a wall is built across a wide depression in the face of the cliff and forms a large room. These ruins are known as the House of the

Princess, and the villagers have various legends to account for them. They are probably of mediaeval date.

Close by is the ruined village of Bilesha. The remains of the church is easily identified and traces of wall paintings still remain.

PISSOURI (lvii)

Perched at the top of a sheer cliff, the village commands superb views of surrounding country. The principal church, dedicated to St. Andrea, was built in 1882.

About a mile and a half west of the village is a tiny chapel dedicated to St. Elias, hollowed out from the face of the cliff. It contains considerable remains of mural paintings on its rough-hewn walls. A small cave near by is shown as the burial-place of the saint's mother.

Far below Pissouri are the ruins of the Church of St. Mavrikios, which possibly may originally have been a Latin chapel, dedicated to St. Maurice. Portion of an inscription lies in the church; it would seem to refer to a certain Dimitrianos but it is so damaged as to be nearly illegible.

PIYENIA (xviii)

A small hamlet with a church dedicated to St. Charalambos. It contains a late eighteenth-century icon of St. Marina, which is taken out in times of drought and carried round the village, frequent pauses being made so that prayers for rain can be offered by the priest.

PLATANISTASA (xxxviii)

The Church of the Archangel Michael was built in the early years of the nineteenth century but was restored in 1916. It contains a not unpleasant rustically carved and gilded iconostasis. Plates decorated the walls, some of which seem to be of a certain antiquity. This curious practice of ornamenting the walls of a church by building in coloured pottery is said to have suggested the Venetian practice of inserting roundels of marble; in any case it was familiar in the Byzantine world at an early date, and even in the ninth century special plates were made for the purpose. The villagers are very proud of a large eighteenth-century blue-and-white Delft plate, which in some curious manner has found its way into this obscure hill village.

The Church of St. John the Baptist was rebuilt in 1740. Two interesting objects survive from some former building: (1) A small bronze circular plaque, behind the door-handle of the west door, which has six shields with a coat of arms of three bends on each shield. (2) An icon of the Archangel Michael supported by SS. Parakesvi and Marina. Each side of the feet of the Archangel are the donors, a man and his wife; the latter is robed in a red dress, with a large gold and pearl brooch, a black veil covers her hair, and she wears gold and pearl earrings. This icon dates from the first years of the sixteenth century.

About four miles from the village is the monastery of the Holy Cross, a curious double building completely covered with a shed-like roof with gable ends. The outer wall of the inner church has considerable remains of paintings on it; the best being the Day of Judgement, over the west door. The interior is completely painted, and the frescoes are in a good state of preservation. An inscription over the south door apparently records the erection and painting of this church in 1436. In a niche on the north wall hangs a large painted wooden cross, possibly contemporary with the building. The iconostasis is sixteenth century, but the icons have been repainted. The cornice above is divided into eleven squares, each decorated with a painted circular medallion of a saint. There are charmingly carved pew ends, and some of the terra-cotta floor slabs are decorated.

PLATRES (xlvii)

This village is the chief summer resort of the wealthy Cypriotes and visitors from abroad. It first became known as a convalescent hospital for English soldiers after the Egyptian campaign, and the present police station was originally built as a military chapel.

About seven miles down and in the middle of the forest,

is the Monastery of Mesopotamos. Deserted for many years, it has lately come into prominence as a health resort, and the monastic buildings have been largely rebuilt for the accommodation of visitors. The tiny shed-like church has also been repaired and contains a few icons, all of which have unhappily been repainted. The oldest is one of St. John the Baptist, dated 1581, and given by the Abbot Sophronios. There is another smaller one of the same subject, given in 1775 by the Priest Lorentios, and also an icon of the Annunciation presented by a certain Marios and his children in 1751. Here is supposed to have lived and died and been buried Theophanes, a monk and native of Nicosia, who was the last of the Cypriote saints, having died in 1550. He was Bishop of Soli, a post he was undesirous of accepting, for he was of a gentle and humble nature. While Bishop, he had on occasion to reprove his deacon. The latter, a saucy knave, answered by boxing his superior's ear soundly. The meek Bishop perceived the scanty respect with which he was regarded, and requested the Venetian Government to relieve him of his high office, and retired to the lonely monastery, where after many years he died. Lusignan says that his grave, which he declares that he has seen, was open five or six years after the decease of the Bishop. The remains were uncorrupted and presented an appearance quite unlike that of a corpse.[1]

POLEMI (xlv)

The Church of the Nativity was originally a Byzantine church, but was much enlarged in 1723, when a south aisle and narthex were added. The fine capital which supports the dividing arches is mediaeval. The repainted iconostasis is late sixteenth century. A remarkable panel survives to the right and left of the holy doors, and is painted in the style of the Italian Renaissance: in the centre is an angel holding a scroll in either hand; on each side are portraits of Christ and St. John the Baptist. The background of the panel is filled with an elaborate design of flowers, birds, masks, festoons, and figures holding shields,

[1] *Chorograffia*, p. 24.

and, except for the repainting of the two angels in the corners, is untouched. This painting is reminiscent of the decoration of some sixteenth-century Venetian palace, and one is tempted to speculate what wealthy Italian ordered it, and if it perhaps once formed part of the screen of a Latin chapel. The icons are mostly seventeenth century, though none are dated.

One and a half miles from Polemi is the ruined Chapel of St. Nipios, with a mineral spring.

POLEMIDHIA (KATO) (liii)

The Church of St. George is an ancient building much repaired. In the yard lies a boss and fragments of vaulting of some Gothic building.

About a mile from the village is the small Monastery of St. George, recently rebuilt. There must have been a Byzantine church here at one time, as the marble pillars which lie scattered about outside testify. In 1927 a limestone slab was found here bearing a peacock in relief, possibly Byzantine work of the eleventh century; it is now in the museum at Nicosia.

In the fourteenth century Polemidhia was granted to Janot, Lord of Beyrouth, an illegitimate son of John, Prince of Antioch, who was himself the second son of King Hugh IV.

From Makhairas we learn that Janot's mother was the Lady Alice de Giblet, the wife of Sir Philip de Costa, "and to prevent the said Sir Philip de Costa from knowing that the boy was the Prince's bastard, she called him Janot, which was the Prince's name".[1]

The reason for this was that in Cyprus boys do not bear their father's names, so that by calling the boy Janot, or John, after him, Lady Alice would keep people from suspecting the truth of the child's parentage.

POLEMIDHIA (PANO) (liii)

The Church of St. Anastasia is a delightful Byzantine mediaeval building of the fourteenth century, with two

[1] *Chronicle of Makhairas*, p. 523.

domes crowning the roof. There are a number of wall paintings in the interior, the best of which is the Deposition, which is above the usual level of mural decoration. An unusual feature is a man who stands at the foot of a cross, and with a large pair of pincers pulls out the nail which holds Our Lord's feet to the cross.

Not far from the village lie the ruins of the Latin church of Karmi, where the Carmelites possessed a convent in the fourteenth century. The convent has long since disappeared, but the church is in a fair state of repair. The east end is square, and the original Latin altar still remains *in situ*. At the west end are the traces of an open porch, on one of the corbels of which is sculptured a little figure of a Carmelite monk, in his cloak and hood. Near the church is a holy well, the shrubs that surround it being covered with fragments of clothing, left by those who come here to wash and be cured.

POLIS (xxvi)

According to Lusignan it was said to have been founded by Acamanthus the Athenian, who fled from Troy.

> The city was on the north coast where there is now a large Casale called Crusoccho, because specially in this place are veins and mines of gold, and near by is a well from which they draw water, which, placed in receptacles for the purpose, congeals, and becomes what the Greeks call "Crusoccola", and the Latins vitriol. This water issues from the veins of gold, and also with the vitriol gold is extracted. The sea which borders this district is called the Gulf of Crusocco, and there was formerly a fine harbour here, which is now entirely ruined; nevertheless ships which are forced to take shelter from storms anchor here. A river runs down to the port, and near by is still found the spring, which, the Poets say, whosoever drinks from, falls in love; and so the Latins call it "Fontana Amorosa". There is also another spring which makes one forget love.[1]

Its ancient name was Arsinoe Marion. The inhabitants were transferred to Paphos after the rebellion of their king, by Ptolemy Lagus.

[1] *Chorograffia*, p. 14.

The whole village is surrounded by a vast necropolis, which has been excavated by various expeditions since the British occupation.

The necropolis is of great extent, and very richly furnished, particularly with imported pottery of Attic types. MARION was the headquarters of the copper trade with the West; which helps to account for the abundant Hellenic imports. The necropolis lies in two main divisions, one near ARSINOE, and south of Poli village; the other about a mile further east, probably more closely associated with MARION, for it appears to contain a larger proportion of sixth-, fifth-, and fourth-century tombs, whereas Hellenistic tombs are characteristic of the other; but a number of types are certainly common to both.[1]

During the Venetian period the town was of considerable size and importance, and was known as Crosoccho. The principal church of the village is dedicated to the B.V.M. Chrysolpolitissa, and dates from 1742, but the marble south doorway must come from a mediaeval or Venetian church. The altar is supported by a finely carved Corinthian capital.

About six miles from the village, and best approached by a rowing-boat, is the Fontana Amorosa.

On this side of the Akamas we enter a land of classical and mediaeval romance; for here, according to Cypriote tradition, was the Fontana Amorosa of Ariosto, and a distinct and far more beautiful Fount of Love, where the natives say that Aphrodite wedded Acamas. The latter rises at the foot of the cliff in a tiny bay half-an-hour's ride north of Agios Nicola, and is a prosaic little fount enough; but the former, three and a half miles to the south, near the Potami tchiflik, has no rival in Cyprus. Approaching from the sea the traveller follows a rushing stream up a densely wooded ravine, barred at last by sombre cliffs, whose top can scarcely be discerned through the arch of boughs; spreading and shimmering over the slanting face of the rock falls a mountain stream, until near the base the cliff slopes inwards and the water falls from a forest of maidenhair ferns in a thousand silver threads to the pool below: across the

[1] Myres, *Catalogue of Cyprus Museum*.

threads here and there shoot stray shafts of sunlight, penetrating the dense shade of a gigantic fig-tree, and three separate springs rise on either side under the cliff and gurgle down to join the pool. The traveller, whose eyes have seen only the rock and scrub of waterless Cyprus, seems in an enchanted spot, not seeing from whence the water comes, and he ceases to wonder that native fancy has peopled the spot with legendary loves, and sailors carried westward vague reports of its beauties to the ears of Ariosto.[1]

It was near the Fontana Amorosa that Rizzo di Marino was captured in 1488. He was a member of the so-called Spanish party, members of which James II had raised to the highest positions in the kingdom, and which was bitterly hostile to Catherine Cornaro. After the death of James, the Spanish party supported the candidature of Alphonso, natural son of Ferdinand, King of Naples, who wished to marry the natural daughter of James. In this he was assisted by his father, King Ferdinand, who hated Venice, and was also anxious to remove Alphonso from Naples. To help this Rizzo organized a plot, and assassinated the two uncles of the Queen, Andrea Cornaro and Marco Bembo, in the Palace of Famagusta on November 15, 1473. In spite of the murders, the plot was a failure, and Rizzo had to fly from the Island. The justly outraged Venetians placed a price of ten thousand ducats on his head, and he was captured here when visiting Cyprus. He was taken to Venice, where he was secretly strangled.

Prodhromos is now but a suburb of Polis. It is marked on the old maps as Podrinio. About a mile from the village is the tiny Chapel of the B.V.M. Venetiotissa, which has recently been completely rebuilt by a wealthy caroub merchant. The name, however, suggests that a mediaeval chapel once stood here.

POLITIKO (XXX)

Here was the original capital of Cyprus, the ancient town of Tamassos. The district was once famed for its inexhaustible supply of copper. According to a legend, the

[1] *Devia Cypria*, p. 14.

town was sacred to Venus, who had a temple here, wherein grew the tree which produced the three golden apples she presented to Hippomenes.

> The Cyprian lands, though rich, in richness yield
> To that surnam'd the Tamasenian field.
> That field of old was added to my shrine
> And its choice products consecrated mine.
> A tree there stands, full glorious to behold,
> Gold are the leaves, the crackling branches gold.
>
> Ovid

The legend has it that there were two fountains here.

> Hence flow two fountains, sweet of taste the one
> The other bitter, and of poisonous taint,
> Whence Cupid ting'd, as fame reports, his darts.
>
> Claudian

Of the ancient city little remains except two extremely interesting royal tombs of the fifth century B.C. They are built in the form of wooden houses with gables. The larger contains two chambers, with an outer entrance and dromos; the entrances are flanked with pillars with Ionic capitals, and the interior imitates a wooden building, even down to such details as the bolts on the doors. The pitched roof is formed of two vast slabs of limestone cut to represent the rounded side of a tree-trunk. The inner doorway, over which is a panel containing a conventional floral pattern in the Assyrian manner (which is also repeated above the inside of the outer door), leads into an inner chamber, which contains an immense sarcophagus, of which the lid has long since disappeared. Above this, in the roof, may be seen the hole through which, at some period, robbers entered and ransacked the tomb of its treasures. The tombs, like others in Cyprus, are constructed within the earth, though not at a great depth.

Not far from the village was the temple of Apollo, but nothing now remains, though it was here that about a hundred years ago the life-size bronze statue of the god was found.

It was between the two that in 1836, while digging for water in the dry river bed, the peasants found a bronze statue of life size, another account makes it somewhat larger, and perfectly preserved. I asked the villagers all I could about this treasure, without being able to frame from their confused recollection and vague description an intelligible notion. The main traits were these: the head was shaved, this might describe a flat and close arrangement of the hair, as in the Apollo of Thera, which would remind orientals of their own custom of shaving the head, but might point also to the close-fitting headdress, common to the Egyptians and the figurines of Idalion: but it had curl or plats on the temples and behind the ears; the figure was entirely naked, the privities bare, but it had something tied round the hips, which they likened to their own cartouche-box, or small silver case which Eastern men wear on a strap round their loins and let hang on their back. The left foot was a little advanced, the arms, as well as I could understand, hanging along the sides. The head, arms and legs were cast in separate pieces and soldered to the trunk, but as the statue was dragged over the gravel of the river-bed they came easily apart.

And what became of this incomparable find? Partly from ignorance, partly from fear of the Turks, who when they hear of a discovery always dream of a treasure, and squeeze the unhappy finders, the peasants hacked the statue to bits and sold it gradually as old copper, about 80 okes of it, at 5 piastres the oke, making scarcely 40 gulden.[1]

Near the village lies the historical Monastery of St. Herakleides, which was rebuilt by Bishop Chrysanthos in 1759. The iconostasis dates from 1774, though earlier fragments survive in it. The icons are mostly eighteenth century, save a fine St. John the Baptist of 1611. The principal icon of the church was covered with silver gilt in 1799. The skull of St. Herakleides is kept in a wooden box on the altar. Adjoining the church is a most interesting mediaeval chapel, with a very unusual iconostasis, formed of four large stone slabs carved with a Byzantine geometric pattern; these have been covered at a later date with plaster, to take paintings of the portraits of the four saints, whose sarcophagi lie in a row beneath. The sarcophagi are said

[1] L. Ross, *Reisen nach der Insel Cypern*, Halle, 1846.

to have once contained the bones of SS. Theodoros, Macedonios, Heracleidiana, sister to St. Herakleides, and St. Myron. Against the north and south walls are two other large sarcophagi, with coped lids, which are supposed to be the resting-places of St. Herakleides and St. Mnason. The floor is composed of hexagonal marble tiles. There is a gaping hole in the centre, which leads down to a cave said to have been the original burial-place of St. Herakleides, but in all probability a Hellenistic tomb. To the south of this chapel is the ground plan of the first and earlier Byzantine church, while to the east are the remains of a fine mosaic pavement.

Tamassos was the earliest centre of Christianity in Cyprus, and St. Herakleides was the first Bishop, being appointed by St. Barnabas himself. He is said to have been the son of a heathen priest, and to have met the two Apostles Paul and Barnabas when they came to Cyprus.

During his career as a bishop he is reported to have built churches, cured diseases, raised the dead, cast out devils, and worked innumerable other wonders. He was burnt at last by the idolaters together with Myron, his successor in the See of Tamassos. Even so late as 1769 his miraculous powers do not seem to have entirely deserted him, as the following well-attested story proves: A certain Haji Savas, an inhabitant of the Phaneromene quarter of Nikosia, had a son named John, the victim of demoniacal possession. During a festival held in honour of Herakleides the parents brought the child to the saint's shrine in hopes that the latter might do something to alleviate his sufferings. While the Holy Mysteries were being celebrated a most strange occurrence took place. The boy suddenly falling to the ground in convulsions began to vomit, when to the astonishment of the beholders, his ghostly tormentor issued forth in the shape of a snake, a span long, and two crabs. These reptiles were afterwards hung up publicly in the church to confirm the faith of the credulous and to silence the cavils of the unbelievers.[1]

To the south-west of the village are the ruins of the Monastery of St. Mnason, a friend of St. Paul.

[1] Hackett, *Church of Cyprus*, p. 377.

There went with us also certain of the disciples of Caesarea, and brought with them one Mnason of Cyprus, an old disciple, with whom we should lodge.[1]

Mnason (19th Oct.), at whose house St. Paul lodged during his last visit to Jerusalem, was a Cypriot by birth. Local tradition represents him to have been one of the Seventy. He is reported to have suffered a martyr's death. Cypriot sources supply further information concerning him which is not to be found elsewhere. According to the legends he was a native of Tamassos and the child of idolaters. While on a visit to Jerusalem with a friend named Theonas the two met with John the Divine who, after instructing them in the doctrines of Christianity, counselled them to return, as Paul and Barnabas were in Cyprus. On reaching Tamassos they found the two Apostles engaged in missionary work there, as he had said. Mnason they ordained a monk for his knowledge of Scripture, while his companion, Theonas, they appointed a reader. The story goes that one day Mnason, leaving the cave near the city in which the little congregation of Christians used to meet for worship, walked through the streets of Tamassos until he came to a temple dedicated to Asklepios (Aesculapius). Moved with indignation at the sight of the heathen shrine he ordered it in the name of Jesus Christ to come down. The idols at his word immediately fell shattered to the ground. The heathen priests seeing what had been done ran off to tell the people, who rushed upon the saint to kill him. But Mnason breathing upon his assailants, blinded them, nor would he consent to restore their sight until they had promised to become believers. As a result of this adventure 300 of them received the rite of baptism. Many stories, as usual, are related of the wonderful things he is said to have done. A woman named Trophime having lost her son from the bite of a snake besought the saint to restore the child to life, whereupon Herakleides, who seems to have been present also on the occasion, by his prayers raised him from the dead. Overcome with joy the mother herself next expired, but at the intercession of Mnason the same miracle was wrought in her case too. In consequence of these marvels 400 more were added to the Church. At another time he intervened to protect a poor Christian from the ill-usage of a heathen money-lender, in whose debt he was. The usurer, resenting the interference of the saint, abused him and threatened to strike him, when

[1] Acts xxi. 16.

his uplifted arm suddenly became withered and immovable. But upon his promising to forgive his debtor, Mnason restored the use of it to him, upon which he was at once baptized with all his household.[1]

The church was rebuilt in 1774, but it is a poor construction and without interest. A Cypriote capital of the fifth century B.C. is built into the north wall.

POMOS (xvii)

A small hamlet, no more than a collection of mud hovels. About three miles from the village is the Monastery of Chrysopateritissa, or the golden crozier. Of the monastic buildings nothing remains. The church is a simple barrel-vaulted building of the early sixteenth century, with an unusual narthex raised about three feet above the floor-level of the church, and added in 1816. There are three arched enclosures in the exterior south wall, which may possibly be founders' tombs. The church contains remains of a fine contemporary iconostasis, with a ceiling like that in the Church of Pedhoulas. There is an icon of the B.V.M. Chrysopateritissa, given in 1524 by the priest Nicholas, his wife and children, and a processional icon of about the same period, of the three Patriarchs, given by the priest Thomas and his family. On the south wall is a large painting of St. John the Divine.

POTAMI (xxix)

The Church of St. George is a carefully constructed building, and probably dates from the Venetian period. An elaborate architectural frieze runs round the top of the church, broken only above the north door by a lion's mask. A bell tower has been added at a later date, but for once detracts but little from the appearance of the building. There is a tiny window at the east end, with heavy stone tracery, while to the right is a standard socket.

The local legend is that the church was built by a queen, and it is true that the building is almost certainly contemporary with the reign of Catherine Cornaro. The interior,

[1] Hackett, *Church of Cyprus*, p. 379.

modern iconostasis, is void of interest, save for three large seventeenth-century icons, on walnut panels; the finest is of the B.V.M., but the wood is so eaten by dry-rot that only a thin film of paint remains.

POTAMIA (xxxi)

Here, during the Middle Ages, was the famous royal castle built by King Peter II (1369–1382). It was destroyed by the Saracens in 1426, and little now remains except for a portion of the walls of well-cut stone, and a large room with a vaulted roof, and dim fragments of frescoes on its walls.

Potamia was a royal residence of the Lusignan dynasty, and inhabited by Catherine Cornaro. It was fortified, and when the Venetians took possession of the island it was dismantled by order of the Venetian Senator, and Governor-General of the island, Francesco Prioli, together with the other royal castles of Saint Hilarion, Buffavento, Dio d'Amore, Cava, and Kantara. The Palace of Potamia now belongs to three notable Turks. In returning their visit I was served coffee and sweetmeat as is the custom in the East, and to my surprise I remarked that the silver tea-spoon I used had the lion of St. Mark and a royal crown engraved upon it. I asked Mehemet Effendi if he would part with that and the other spoons which I supposed he possessed, but he declined, though as a Turkish compliment he offered me as a present the spoon I had used, which of course I declined. I had heard rumoured that in digging in their garden these three Turks had found an iron coffer with gold and silver objects. That tea-spoon might have belonged to the treasure. I repeated my visits there at other times, but the tea-spoons with the royal crown had disappeared.[1]

Close to these ruins are the foundations of a church still called, by the villagers, Santa Catherina. North of the château, at a locality known as Elinos, was an important temple site. The villagers ploughing here frequently unearth fragments of statuary. In 1933 a small excavation was carried out by the Cyprus Museum in these fields; the principal find was a life-size limestone head of Apollo, now exhibited in the museum.

[1] Cesnola, *Cyprus: Its Cities, Tombs and Temples.*

POTAMIOU (xlvii)

The Church of St. Marina was, according to an inscription over the south door, built in 1551, and has remained unchanged since that date. There are a certain number of architectural details in the building, including an unusual double-light window over the west door, and the arch of the tympanum above the south door has dog-tooth moulding. The whole building is crowned with a central octagonal dome. The interior has two carved corbels supporting the ribs of the vault at the west end. Both the iconostasis and icons are modern.

Close to the village is the ruined Church of St. Jason. At the west end a flight of steps leads down to a passage, which runs beneath the church for the length of the whole building. In the middle of the north side is a Gothic arched recess, which was probably the tomb of the saint. On the south side of the church are the foundations of a small chapel, which possibly contained the relics of St. Jason. Little is known of this saint, save that Eudes de Château Roux, when Cardinal Legate in the East, ordered that special honour should be paid by the Latin clergy to certain of the Cypriote saints, whom he mentions by name; the list included St. Jason.

POTAMITISSA (xxxvii)

A charming village situated on the steep bank of the Stremmata river. One would have thought that a village so obscure, tucked away as it is in a valley far removed from the main road, would have spared its ancient church. But the craze for erecting a modern temple, larger and newer and more imposing than that of the neighbouring villages, has reached this hamlet. Only a few years since, the ancient building, which had served their forefathers for generations, was ruthlessly pulled down, and a hideous modern structure substituted, with windows filled with the harshest of lodging-house-landing stained glass. It is a mercy that owing to lack of funds the villagers had to be content with the ancient furnishings, so that the original iconostasis and icons have been placed bodily in this new erection. According to an inscription on a lower panel, this screen was gilded at the expense of the Exarch Chrysanthos, in 1803; while the two neighbouring panels show portraits of the priest Nicholas, and a wealthy farmer from Dymes, called Haji Michael, at whose charge the iconostasis was carved and erected. These two portraits are interesting as giving a representation of the village costume of the period. The icons are devoid of interest, save for two processional ones of the B.V.M. of the seventeenth and eighteenth centuries respectively.

In spring all the fields surrounding the village are covered with the scented wild violet.

PRASTIO (EVDHIMOU) (lii)

The principal church of the village is modern. Not far away, in a secluded valley, lies the curious Church of the B.V.M. It appears to be an early eighteenth-century barrel-vaulted building, with two small fourteenth-century, or earlier, domed chapels at the north-east and south-east corners. Over the main west door is a fragment of carved mediaeval stone-work, while the step is formed by a marble column. In the apse of the south-east chapel is a hole which leads to a holy well, while a deep-cut channel sunk in the rock encircles the apse for the overflow from the well. There is a painting, over an older one, of the B.V.M., in the semi-vault. The north-east chapel is far more difficult to explain. There is no trace of an apse, but merely alcoves at each of the four corners; it is possible that this was a tomb chapel, or built to house the reliquary of some forgotten local saint.

In the fields belonging to the village are the ruins of two mediaeval chapels dedicated to the Archangel Michael and St. Helena respectively.

PRASTIO (KELOKEDHARA) (lii)

A small Turkish hamlet. Close by lies the large deserted Church of the Archangel Michael, a late fifteenth-century building. The walls are formed of unhewn rocks from the river-bed, though the doorways and window-frames are of well-cut stone. At some period the north and west doors have been blocked up. The interior is bare, save for the remains of a gigantic painting of the Archangel on the north wall, and the altar slab, with a consecration cross, supported on two marble columns. Considering that this building has almost certainly been deserted since the arrival of the Moslems in the sixteenth century, it is in a very good state of preservation.

About two miles from the village is the charming Monastery of St. Savvas. According to an inscription over the west door, the church was rebuilt in 1501, and again restored in 1724. The inscription referring to the sixteenth-century rebuilding is as follows:

> It must be that a king first built this monastery, which time has so damaged. May God on the awful Day of Judgement remember the Exarch of this monastery, who in 1501 repaired and beautified this church.

At the north and south corners of the west end, and indeed in several other places on the western façade, are curious fragments of zigzag moulding, with words or fragments of words cut on the stone. They appear to have formed the doorway of the earliest building, with an inscription running round the semicircle of the arch, but so many words are missing that it is impossible to decipher it or understand what it means. The letters are well formed and deeply cut. Above the tympanum is the central support of a rain gutter, which has long since disappeared, and which was carried on a corbel carved with a human mask. Above this again is a tiny round window, filled with delicate stone tracery. Both the north and west doors show Gothic influence, and are excellent examples of the period. The former is approached by a flight of five semicircular steps. The interior is unfrescoed, and the plain carved iconostasis, which probably dates from the restoration of 1742, is unpainted. The collection of icons is of deep interest, and they are, considering their age, in an amazing state of preservation. Nor has the hand of the modern restorer blighted them, for such slight restoration or touching up as they have received dates from the early eighteenth century. In the iconostasis itself are placed three icons: to the right of the holy doors are St. John the Baptist and Christ, both of the early sixteenth century. St. John is robed in golden drapery, powdered with red flowers, while Christ wears a red robe with a golden and blue cloak; both are strongly reminiscent of Brusa embroidery. To the left of the holy doors is the B.V.M. Eleousa, dated 1521. On a north wall is hung a processional icon of the Virgin and Child, damaged in the right-hand corner, but otherwise an excellent example of untouched work of the late fifteenth century; on the back are painted the emblems of the passion. Next to this icon hangs one of St. Savvas. This painting is curious in that it shows none of the usual emblems associated with the saint, who wears an Elizabethan ruff of blue and gold; this painting probably dates from the middle of the sixteenth century. There are considerable remains of monastic buildings, which show in a staircase north of the church and in the well-cut door and window frames more artistic feeling and elegance than one is apt to associate with the haphazard collection of rooms which usually surround an Orthodox monastery. Outside a tiny spring of water falls into a large marble basin, with a child's head carved in relief on it. This may have been the original font; in its present position it is supported by a florid Corinthian marble capital. In a cupboard in the church are kept three pewter chalices. It is possible that the first monastery here was of the Latin faith, as in 1234 Baldwin de Morpho gave a donation of a thousand bezants a year to the cathedral at Nicosia from the revenues of St. Savva, Paphos, which he held by royal grant. There is still in existence a letter of the Abbot Gerasimos to King James II of Cyprus in 1486.

Thrice noble and thrice magnificent and great king of Cyprus, Jerusalem and Armenia. May Christ Our Lord multiply the years of your reign. I, Gerasimos, Abbot of St. Savva and humble servant of your Majesty, who for ever prays that your Majesty may ever reign, submit that in this monastery of your kingdom a calamity took place on December 7th, that is the day following the feast of St. Nicholas. For during the night the monastery was struck by lightning and devoured by fire, so that all the monastery, save the church, was destroyed, all the upstairs and downstairs rooms, our clothes, wheat, and barley, all were burnt, and so great a damage was caused to us that we are utterly ruined. Therefore, as this monastery has a property called Lacrida which pays to your revenue nine bushels of wheat and sixteen of barley yearly, I do most humbly pray and beseech your Majesty that your kindness will reach our monastery, and I apply for your permission that this wheat and barley, before mentioned, shall be given free to the monastery for our help. So that we can rebuild and renew all those buildings destroyed. And I pray this in the memory of the Lord your father now deceased, and may your Majesty reign for many years.[1]

It is pleasant to be able to record that the King remitted the tithe of wheat and barley in perpetuity, on the condition that Masses were ever said for his soul.

PRASTIO (MORPHOU) (xix)

The Church of St. George is a barrel-vaulted building of the late eighteenth century. Outside the church is a large Corinthian capital with five crosses on it, which possibly may have formed the altar-stone of some earlier church.

About a mile distant is the Monastery of St. Nicholas, built in 1828, but both the church and the monastic buildings are of the poorest construction, and without interest.

PRETORI (xlvi)

The Church of the B.V.M. is a large modern building, and contains a much-venerated icon of the Virgin, which appears to be sixteenth century. Most of it is covered with silver gilt repoussé work, but this is older than the usual coverings of such icons, and may possibly date from the closing years of the seventeenth century. The icon is supposed to cure blindness. It is said to have been in the original church, which was destroyed many years ago by fire, and to have been saved by a Turk who rushed through the flames and snatched it from the screen and bore it to

[1] I am indebted to M. Loizou Philippou, of Ktima, for calling my attention to this letter, which I believe was discovered in Europe by M. de Mas. Latrie.

safety. In the gallery is kept a late sixteenth-century icon of Christ, with a sad and thoughtful face.

PSEMATISMENOS (lv)

The Church of St. Marina was almost completely rebuilt in 1886, except for the apse, which still has considerable remains of painting in a fair state of repair, probably dating from the sixteenth century. The iconostasis, which is dated 1850, and icons are without interest.

PSOMOLOPHOU (xxx)

The Church of the B.V.M. was almost completely rebuilt in 1847, and of the earlier building little remains, except part of the south wall, which contains late mural paintings of the forty martyrs. A large icon frame on the north wall is made from the fragments of a sixteenth-century iconostasis, and contains an eighteenth-century icon of SS. Cosmas and Damian. In the women's gallery is preserved an early seventeenth-century icon of the B.V.M., with a dedicatory inscription.

A large number of small chapels surround the village, but nothing but tradition or heaps of stone survives to mark where they once stood.

PYLA (xli)

In June 1934 a very fine tomb of the fourth century B.C. was discovered by a workman digging for stone. It is a stone-built tomb, with an arched roof, and contains four chambers, the doors formed by huge gypsum slabs. Over the doorway of the main hall, which leads into the room in which the three built sarcophagi are placed, were three plaques, in the centre a grotesque mask, to left and right winged sphinxes. After excavation a fine flight of steps was revealed, leading down to the chamber, and traces of an enclosure above. The tomb has since been fitted with an iron door, the key of which is kept at the local police station.

The principal church of the village is dedicated to the Archangel Michael, and is probably of mediaeval origin. On the north wall is a fragment of a painting of the Archangel, and some late fifteenth-century woodwork is built up into the iconostasis screen.

About a mile from the village is the Church of the B.V.M. of the White Hill, a modern building, but it contains a magnificent wooden cross, with scenes from Our Lord's life carved in relief on it. The silver base is dated 1758, but the cross must almost certainly be at least two hundred years earlier. Above the icon of the B.V.M. hangs a silver model of an eye, which is in much request by those who suffer from ophthalmia, who take it from the church and, after wearing it for two or three days, are completely cured.

There is also a small ruined Chapel of St. George. Here is kept a stone with a footprint of the saint's horse on it.

The principal relic of the village is a large mediaeval tower, which rises close to the Church of the Archangel. The tower is now without roof or floors, but stands to a height of three storeys. The original entrance was by means of a drawbridge, which led to the first floor, about 14 feet from the ground. On the outside of the south wall of the upper storey is a curious little balcony with stone walls and roof, which must have been the mediaeval latrine. The casale of Pyla belonged in the fourteenth century to John de Brie, Prince of Galilee, but afterwards passed into the hands of the family of Gibilet.

PYRGA (xl)

The little Latin Chapel of St. Catherine is one of the most interesting relics of the Lusignan kingdom still remaining in Cyprus. It has a barrel-vault, and three doorways, two now blocked up. The door on the south has a small catherine-wheel badge on a lintel, while above is a fragment of stone with a French name, Bazoges, carved on it. Till the last century an inscription in French survived under the east window, recording the building of the church in 1421: "In honour of God and the Passion of Our Saviour." A number of paintings still remain in the vault and on the walls; underneath some of them can still be seen the titles in French, such as "La Pentecouste", etc. The most remarkable fresco still remaining is the Crucifixion, at the west end: at the foot of the cross kneel two crowned figures, who are without doubt King Janus and his wife, Charlotte de Bourbon. The King wears a heavy crown on his head, and a grey cloak over his shoulder; his consort is also crowned, and wears the French costume of the period. The ribs of the vaulting are painted with the royal badges of the House of Lusignan.

Five hundred years nearly have come and gone since a King and Queen of Cyprus knelt with trembling hearts within this little sanctuary, their miniature realm reduced to bankruptcy by the exactions of the powerful Genoese Republic, whilst the terrors of an Arab invasion loomed upon the southern horizon. But for all these trials and sufferings—and they were many—"good King Janus" (as he was known to his subjects) and his unfortunate Queen maintained their position and their rank until the end. In spite of the King's long imprisonments in Genoa as a youth, and in Cairo in later years, the tumults and disasters of his long reign, and his last days of lingering sickness, he left the world regretted by his friends, respected by his enemies (June 28, 1432). His only surviving monument—and almost the only surviving memorial of the later Lusignan dynasty in what was once a flourishing kingdom—is this little chapel built not far from the scene of perhaps the finishing stroke of vengeful fate in the history of mediaeval Cyprus.[1]

M. Enlart found some curious invectives scratched on the west wall, against the Orthodox, who would affix yarn round the bells as a charm against illness.[2] Curiously enough this custom is still adhered to, and in the remoter villages the women frequently wind lengths of cotton round the church in the belief that it keeps sickness away from the village.

The village Church of St. Marina is a domed building of the fifteenth century. There are traces of a north aisle, which has vanished, but the narthex is modern. On the south-east corner by the apse are various graffiti, including an inscrip-

[1] Jeffery, *Monuments of Cyprus*, p. 342.
[2] Enlart, *Art Gothique*, p. 437.

tion and the date 1508, and a heraldic beast. Fragments of a painting of St. Marina survive in the tympanum, above the north door. The interior contains considerable remains of paintings on the dome, arches of founders' tombs, etc. There is an icon of St. Marina dated 1712.

The mosque is about a hundred years old, though the west wall may be a portion of some mediaeval building.

About five miles from Pyrga is the ruined Latin Monastery of Stazousa, standing on a cliff above the bed of the river. The building may possibly have been a Cistercian abbey, and was probably built in the fifteenth century.

The monastery had the general plan of Oriental convents: the church isolated in the centre of a rectangular enclosure surrounded by buildings. A fine entrance gateway with a richly moulded pointed arch gave access to the monastery on its west side. All the buildings are well constructed of rubble masonry, with cut stone for the architectural features. The church consists of a nave of two bays, a semicircular apse, and a small narthex. Above the apse and the narthex, which are considerably lower than the nave, a circular window occupies the wall space. A small window lighting the semicircular apse was closed with a wooden shutter, of which traces remain.[1]

PYRGOS (LEFKA) (xviii)

This village is the centre of the district known as the Tylliria, which consists of the sea-shore between the villages of Polis and Lefka, and the hinterland of forest and hill country. The soil is poor and but little cultivated, and the tiny scattered villages of no interest. According to a legend, this part of the Island was colonized by St. Helena after a great drought, which ended in A.D. 327. Many of these newcomers came from the Island of Delos, and gave their name to their new home. In the whole district the only church of interest is about a mile and a half from Pyrgos. Dedicated to the B.V.M., it is a tiny Byzantine building divided in the middle by a heavy and clumsy arch, and with a dome over the west end. It measures but 24 feet from the west door to the iconostasis, and 12 feet across. (The

[1] Enlart, *Art Gothique*, p. 424.

walls are of the unusual thickness of 4 feet.) The interior was once painted, but has, at some period, been whitewashed. According to a local legend, milk instead of mortar was used in the construction of the building. There is a damaged early processional icon of the B.V.M., which is much resorted to by expectant mothers.

PYROI (xxxi)

The Church of St. Antipas is a delightful small Byzantine structure with a central nave, and two aisles; the latter measuring only 4 feet in width. The exterior west door has a small Gothic rose window above it. St. Antipas cures toothache, and his icon is much resorted to by those who are unable to find a dentist. St. Antipas is an obscure saint, who was martyred at Pergamos.

A mile or so distant from the village lies the B.V.M. Pallouriotissa. There are fragments of frescoes of two periods on the walls, and the interesting carved gutter supports remain *in situ* on the north wall.

In the village of Pyroi was born in 1833 Kiamil Pasha, afterwards four times Grand Vizier of Turkey.

Till recently the River Yalias, near the village, was crossed by a mediaeval bridge of several arches, but this has been destroyed and replaced by an ugly iron structure.

RIZOKARPASO (i)

The ancient city of Karpasia lies two miles below the modern village and close to the sea. It was the seat of a bishop from a very early period. Its legendary founder is supposed to be Pygmalion, King of Cyprus, and it is said to have contained a temple dedicated to Sarpedon, son of Zeus. During the Latin period it belonged to the Nores family.

The principal church of the village is dedicated to St. Synesios, one of the early bishops, and was during the Middle Ages the cathedral of the Orthodox See. The reason for the Bishop of Famagusta living so far from his cathedral is as follows:

Meanwhile, Rizo-Karpaso had obtained the doubtful distinction of becoming the residency of the Greek bishop of Famagusta; this anomalous arrangement was the result of the Concordia, brought about at Famagusta in 1222 by the legate Pelagius, sent expressly to Cyprus to settle the difficult questions which had arisen during the last thirty years from the simultaneous presence of bishops and clergy of both the Western and Eastern Churches. It was probably to minimize the chance of further collisions that Pelagius, while sanctioning the presence of four Orthodox bishops for the future, contrived that each should take up his residence as far as possible from the old See, and, indeed, from the centres of civilization. Thus were banished—the bishop of Nicosia to the valley in the Forest Range, a long day's journey from his metropolis; the bishop of Paphos to Arsos in the recesses of the western hills; the bishop of Limassol to Lefkara among the foothills of Machaeras; and the bishop of Famagusta to the extreme eastern end of the island, where thirty miles up the peninsula lies Rizo-Karpaso. Needless to say, the Orthodox bishops were not satisfied with these arrangements, and 250 years later Pope Sixtus IV on hearing of continual offences against the Concordia, despatched a Bull, once more defining the bounds which must not be exceeded.[1]

The church consists of a nave and two side aisles. The east end of the church probably dates from the twelfth century. The southern apse was destroyed when the campanile was built, but the two remaining apses still retain their Byzantine arcading on the exterior. The whole of the western end of the church and the octagonal dome date from the eighteenth century, when the church was enlarged. The façade is a poor copy of Gothic work with details copied from the cathedrals of Nicosia and Famagusta.

Drummond, who visited the village in 1745, says:

Here is an ancient church built after a mean and vulgar form, though the wooden carved work and the choir is better than what I have observed in any Greek church, and must have belonged to some other, for it is very old.[2]

A recent restoration has swept away this woodwork, and the present iconostasis and icons are of the poorest workmanship.

[1] *Devia Cypria*, p. 59. [2] *Travels*, p. 303.

The village and its surroundings contain a large number of churches and chapels. They are: (1) The Holy Trinity.—According to a date on the south wall, the original church was built in 1730, but the whole building has recently been reconstructed, and now contains nothing of interest. At the corner of the wall which surrounds the church is a large stone lion, which must have come from a tomb in ancient Karpasia. (2) St. George.—Only the north wall and apse of this mediaeval chapel now survive. On the former are paintings of St. Paraskevi and Christ. The original altar remains *in situ*, a square block of black marble, possibly the base of a Roman statue; it stands on a stone Corinthian capital. (3) St. Mavra.—A most interesting thirteenth-century chapel, and, except for a gaping hole in the apse, in a good state of preservation. Over the west door is chevron pattern carried out in thin red bricks. The north and south walls are divided into three bays, and the interior was once completely painted In the first bay on the south side is a noble and well-preserved life-size painting of St. Demetrius. The saint wears a brown-and-white cloak, which flies behind him in the wind, and bestrides a spirited white horse which has a cross painted on its forehead. The other paintings, which are not so well preserved, are: on the north wall, the Archangel Michael; in the roof, the Transfiguration; in the apse, the B.V.M., supported by SS. Michael and George. In the apse are remains of the original floor, a mosaic pavement of white and yellow marble, cut to geometric patterns. (4) St. Marina.—A small chapel, with fragments of paintings on the south wall. There are several curious features about this building, for there are no windows save a tiny arrow-slit high up on the south wall, and the roof is formed of large slabs of stone. In the interior can still be seen a fragment of the original stone iconostasis, and in the apse lies a fluted Roman column of black basalt. (5) The B.V.M. Eleousa.—A small monastery belonging to St. Catherine of Sinai, is about two miles distant from the village. The church is an early sixteenth-century building of two naves divided by arches carried on heavy round pillars with plain capitals. The richly decorated south door is ornamented with dog-tooth moulding. The church contains three small icons, *c.* 1520: the B.V.M., Christ, and St. John the Baptist. The icon of Christ has a kneeling middle-aged donor, who wears a black robe and red hose; he has long auburn hair which is receding on the forehead, and a beard of the same hue. There is also a well-painted long narrow panel of St. Thomas of the same, or possibly even earlier, date. The church was once completely painted, but, as usual, the frescoes are hidden by whitewash. The holy doors date from the seventeenth century, and there is an eighteenth-century chalice with an inscription on the foot.

Down by the sea, near the ancient ruins of Karpasia, is the Church of St. Philos, possibly at one period the cathedral of the early bishops of the See of Karpasia. Fragments from the ancient city are used up in its walls. Constantius, Archbishop of Sinai, says of St. Philos:

> Then Carpasia, one of the most notable cities of the island where Philo, the commentator of the Scriptures, was bishop. As a deacon he was at Rome, in the train of Pulcheria, the sister of Arcadius and Honorius. There she fell sick, and learning that God healed the sick by the hand of Epiphanios, bishop of Constantia, Philo was sent to bring the saint to Rome. He came to Cyprus, and, following a revelation from above, Epiphanios about A.D. 401 consecrated him bishop of Carpasia, and being himself about to sail for Rome, left Philo in charge of the church of Constantia.[1]

A much earlier building has been discovered to the south of this church, which is almost certainly the earliest church of all. Little has been uncovered so far, save a superb circular floor carried out in mosaics of yellow, red, black, and white marble. All round lie ruins of the ancient city, but they are covered with drifted sand brought down from above.

The two most remarkable features remaining are the harbour and the tombs. Of the former very considerable traces can still be seen of the two moles; that on the eastern side can be followed for 370 feet from its starting-place on

[1] *Excerpta Cypria*, p. 316.

the shore, and is formed of large square blocks riveted to each other by clamps of metal. Of the latter a number survive about a mile distant in the cliffs of Tsambres. Some have Christian symbols cut on the walls and were doubtless re-used during the early Byzantine period.

Two more churches yet remain to be noticed in the neighbourhood of Rizokarpaso. South of the village lies the ruined Church of St. Pappos, only interesting from its dedication to the first bishop of the See of Chrytri, who distinguished himself by forcibly consecrating the famous Epiphanios, Bishop of Salamis.

It happened to be the season when the grape harvest was approaching maturity. Before sailing, Epiphanios proposed to his companions that they should go into the market and buy grapes. He had just chosen two very fine bunches, and was in the act of paying for them, when the saintly Pappos drew near, his tottering form supported by two deacons and attended by three bishops. Addressing Epiphanios, he invited him to leave the fruit with the merchant and accompany them to the church. The latter accepting the invitation, Pappos on their entrance requested him to offer prayer, when he excused himself on the plea that he was not in orders. The words had scarcely left his lips before one of the deacons, by main force, dragged him to the altar, where, after rapidly passing through the grades of deacon and priest, he was consecrated bishop.[1]

About five miles from Rizokarpaso and on an abandoned southern road is Sykhada. Here is a large ruined church in the Romanesque architecture of the twelfth century. The church measures 78 feet by 45 feet, but only fragments of the vaulting and arcade remain over the two side aisles. This church is of the same style as those at Aphrendrika, already described.

ST. HILARION (xii)

This is the principal fortress, and the most incredible example of the architecture of the Middle Ages still existing in Cyprus. The ancient name of the site was Didymos, from

[1] Hackett, *Church of Cyprus*, p. 404.

the twin peaks which rise from the Kyrenia hills. This name was confused by the Latins with the worship of Venus, and in their ignorance they thought it to be Dieu d'Amour, and it was from this fact that the mediaeval legend arose that the castle was once the habitation of Cupid. According to another legend, the hill was the hermitage of St. Hilarion, who passed the evening of his days here. The saint's first hermitage was in a desert in Egypt, but he was so distracted by the importunities of his many visitors that he came to Cyprus in search of peace and rest. He landed at Paphos.

But he had not been there twenty days when the local demons, through their victims, announced his presence in the island. After a residence of two years he had determined in consequence to return to Egypt, when Hesychios persuaded him to retire instead into a more secluded part of the country. The faithful disciple visited every region of the island, and at last hit upon what seemed a likely spot, to which he at once led his master. The new retreat was situated in a most inaccessible place among the lofty and precipitous mountains of the northern range, overlooking Kyrenia. The property of a heathen, it was surrounded by trees and supplied with an abundance of water, containing besides a house and garden with fruit trees and the ruins of an ancient temple. Previous to the saint's arrival it had been the habitation of evil spirits, who, perceiving that they could no longer remain with him for their companion, raised on his approach a terrible uproar to scare him away. The holy man, nothing daunted by the din, merely acknowledged their efforts by remarking that he had at last come to a place where he was welcomed with music. Such a specimen of ascetic humour proved too much for his ghostly serenaders, who retired in despair, leaving the facetious anchorite in sole possession. Here he passed the last five years of his life, rarely, if ever, disturbed in his meditations save by the faithful Hesychios, who frequently visited him in his mountain retreat. At length, in his eightieth year, feeling the approach of death, he wrote with his own hand a short letter, bequeathing to Hesychios all his worldly possessions—consisting of a copy of the Gospels, a hair-shirt, cowl, and cloak. His closing hours were soothed by the presence of some pious Christians, who came from Paphos to be with him at the last, and by a lady named Constantia, whose daughter and son-in-law he had once miraculously snatched from death. These he charged, as soon as all was over, to bury his body in the garden without delay in the clothes he was wearing.[1]

The castle was almost certainly standing when King Richard conquered the Island in 1191, but the first actual reference to it is in 1228, when the Emperor Frederick II was trying to force his suzerainty on the youthful King Henry I of Cyprus. It was then that Jean d'Ibelin, Regent of the kingdom, converted the Orthodox monastery into a fortified castle. Two years later the imperial troops gained possession of the castle and the Regent was forced to lay siege to his own building. Among the garrison on this occasion was Philip Chinard, who afterwards became chief engineer to Frederick II, and built many of his castles for him. On the royalist side in this siege was the famous Philipo di Novarra, soldier and poet, and it was on this occasion that the incident occurred, recorded in his own book, *The Gestes de Chyprios*, of his lying wounded by an arrow on the rocks facing the castle, and improvising satires and verses, much to the annoyance of the imperial troops on the walls. In 1232 the castle was secured by the royalists, but was again besieged by the imperial troops. Within the castle were the sisters of the young King Henry I, who had just attained his majority and was absent in Syria. He hurriedly returned and with an army marched to raise the siege. He fell on the imperial troops at the entrance of the pass which leads to Kyrenia and cut them to pieces on June 15, 1232. Thus was ended once and for all the pretensions of the Emperor Frederick to be Overlord of the Kingdom of Cyprus.

A century and a half passed without further incident in the history of the castle, and it was embellished and restored so that it became like Windsor, half palace, half fortress. During the summer months the king and his court resided there and passed their time in tourneys and pageants. In 1733, during the Genoese invasion, John of Antioch, uncle to the young King Peter II, took refuge there with his wild but

[1] Hackett, *Church of Cyprus*, p. 409.

faithful Bulgarian mercenaries, whom in a fit of insanity he killed. (See Pelendria.)

With the arrival of Venice the days of the castle were numbered, for the Venetians looked on the Island merely as a military post, and not having enough men to defend St. Hilarion it was dismantled in 1489, lest it should fall into the hands of the enemy from the opposite coast. To-day it is but a vast and confused ruin, where junipers grow in the crevices and climbing plants cover the grey stone walls, showing here a Gothic arch and there a fragment of moulding.

The castle composes three distinct sections, and they were all built in the early thirteenth century. The outer barbican encloses a large area, which forms the bailey of the castle. It has a small outwork, and above the doorway remain four brackets of the machicoulis, one of the few architectural features still remaining, for each bracket is decorated with sculpture, including a woman with a horned head-dress. The enceinte encloses the whole top of the mountain, and the wall is about a quarter of a mile long and has nine towers spaced along its length.

The second section consists of a confused collection of buildings, including a chapel, barracks, and magazines, connected by passages. The chapel is a Byzantine building, and is the original church of the Orthodox Monastery of St. Hilarion, which stood here. It is built of bricks, and once had a dome supported on four columns. At the north-east of the chapel is a tiny chamber which may have been either an oratory or the tomb chamber of the saint.

The floors of the rooms of this part of the castle are of different levels, and are linked by small staircases. At the south-east of one of the great rooms the abrupt angle of rock ends under a square platform, on which has been built a belvedere or view. Two of its sides lead to the apartments, while the others are open arches giving extensive views of the plain and tilting-ground which lie far beneath. Near here is a vast cistern which could have contained the entire water supply for the garrison.

The third section is approached by a very long and steep

flight of steps, and contains what were evidently the royal apartments. On the west side stands the chief architectural feature of the whole castle, a long and narrow building of two storeys. Only two windows remain, earthquakes and time having destroyed the rest. But these two examples give an idea of the charm and luxury which this royal residence undoubtedly possessed.

The highest portion of all terminates in a line of wall with three bastion-like towers, and it was probably from here that the Prince of Antioch threw the unhappy Bulgarians.

SALAMIOU (xlvi)

A mile or so from the village and in the middle of the vineyards lies the little Church of the B.V.M. Eleousa, built in the sixteenth century and repaired in 1916. Of the iconostasis only a fragment remains. Most of the icons are early seventeenth century, damaged, but apparently never repainted, and there is also a sixteenth-century processional icon of the B.V.M. Round the church grow some magnificent oak-trees; they are sacred to the Virgin and must never be cut. Some ten years since, a man from the village determined to cut down one of these trees. Thrice the Virgin appeared to him in a dream, warning him not to do so, but the man hardened his heart, and one morning went with his two sons and felled one of the largest of the oaks. Towards evening the father and his sons loaded their beasts with the wood and started back towards the village, but hardly had they gone a few paces when two large snakes appeared from the grass and attacked the eldest son, so that he died that night. Within a year the other son was dead of a mysterious and wasting disease.

Below the church is a field as fertile as those that surround it, but no vines will ever grow on it, though the villagers have often planted them there. This curious phenomenon is the subject of much discussion in the village. Near the village are pointed out some ancient olive-trees. It is said that St. Paul and St. Barnabas, while journeying from Salamis to Paphos, rested here in the middle of the day and took food. The olive stones which they threw away grew and became these ancient trees.

SALAMIS (xxiv)

Ancient writers are unanimous in asserting that Salamis was founded by Teucer, the son of Telamon, King of the famous Island of Salamis, in Greece, on his return from the Trojan War (*c.* 1180 B.C.). Excavations have, however, shown the existence of an important Mycenaean colony of somewhat earlier date; while there seems also to have been an ancient Phoenician settlement on the hillock now known as "Toumba" about a mile away to the south. In any case Salamis appears to have always been a characteristically Hellenic town with a predominantly Greek population; and from the earliest times until the transfer of the capital to New Paphos by the Romans, the principal city of Cyprus.

The earliest historical reference appears to be on an Assyrian clay tablet mentioning, among a list of tributaries to Assur-bani-pal (668 B.C.), King Kisu of Silua, a name probably to be identified with that of Salamis. The first certainly known ruler was Evelthon (560–525 B.C.), who is mentioned by Herodotus, and under whom Salamis seems already to have become the most powerful city on the Island. In the fifth century B.C. the town was the centre of more than one revolt against the Persians and the scene of several battles, until its independence, together with that of the whole Island, was finally secured by the famous patriot-king Evagoras (410–374 B.C.), whose reign was not only a time of great local power and glory, but also marked an epoch in the struggle between the Hellenic and Oriental powers.

With its large trade and good harbour, the town continued to flourish under the Ptolemaic viceroys (294–58 B.C.), as also under the Romans, though no longer the capital of the whole Island. A Christian community was founded here in A.D. 45–46 by the Apostles Paul and Barnabas, of whom the latter was a native of the place, and suffered martyrdom here at the hands of the Jewish mob. His reputed tomb, near the monastery of Ag. Barnabas, was discovered in A.D. 477.

The ensuing centuries saw a rapid decay. The large Jewish colony made it a centre of the great Jewish revolt of A.D. 116–117, when, according to Orosius (vii, 12), "it was utterly destroyed". Repeated earthquakes completed the ruin, until the Emperor Constantius (A.D. 337–361) rebuilt a smaller, but beautiful, city named Constantia, which was finally destroyed by the Arab conqueror Mu'âwiya (A.D. 648), the site being subsequently used as a quarry for the construction of Famagusta.

The site of the great city of Salamis is now almost entirely covered with sand, which has since the British occupation been anchored down by planting trees on it. This, though it prevents the sand from spreading, makes it almost impossible to see the few monuments which still remain, and part of the ruins are covered with thick impenetrable scrub.

The most remarkable monument of the Roman city is the Agora or Market Place. It measured about 700 feet by 200 feet and was bordered by a peristyle of limestone Corinthian columns nearly 27 feet high. All have been thrown down by an earthquake, and the majority of the drums and capitals have been taken away and re-used in the construction of the Byzantine city; but one complete column which still lies as it fell at the north end gives some idea of the size and the magnificence of the market-place, which probably was the largest in the Roman Colonial Empire. At the southern end are the remains of a temple, on an artificial hill. This was excavated at the end of the last century by the British Museum, but nothing was found save a colossal bull-headed capital, which is now in the British Museum.

At the opposite end to the temple are the ruins of the great cistern, which was apparently in a good state of preservation in 1394, when it was seen by Martoni.

> In the middle where the castle stood is a certain ancient cistern, no bigger one I think is found in the world, with a vault raised on thirty-six columns and with apertures above whence the water was drawn. Into this tank water flowed continuously from a certain mountain, along a conduit built

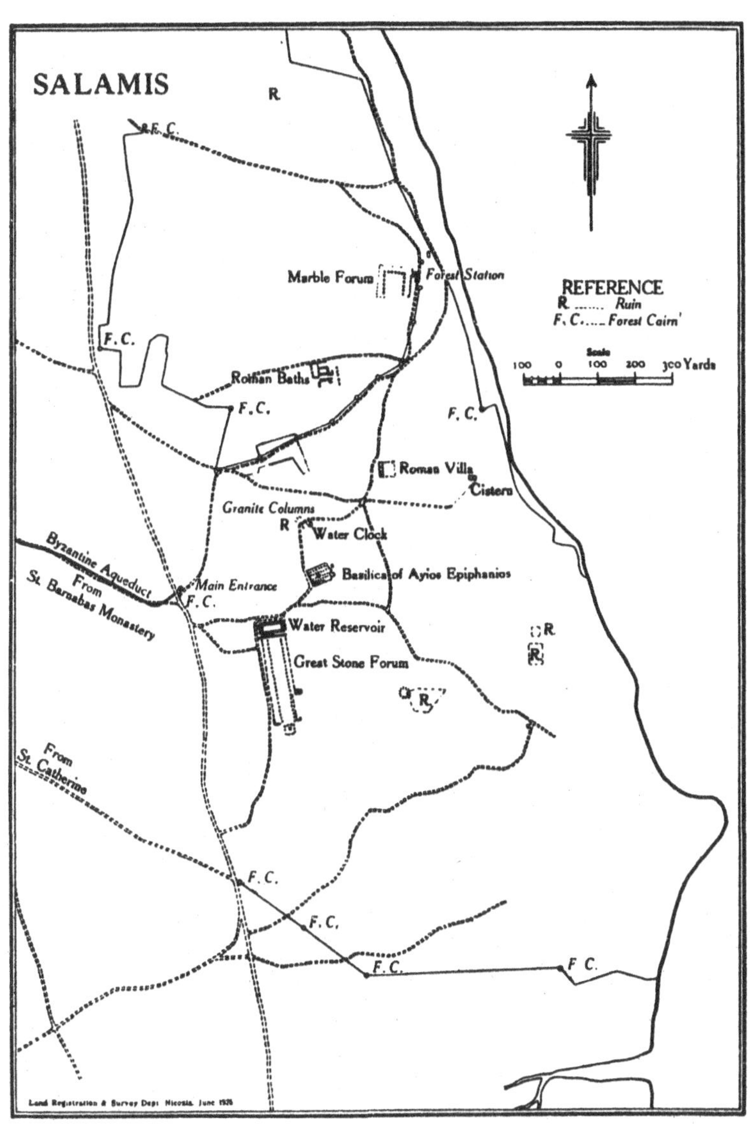

SALAMIS
R
F. C.
Marble Forum
Forest Station
REFERENCE
R .... Ruin
F. C...... Forest Cairn'
Scale
100 0 100 200 300 Yards
F. C.
Roman Baths
F. C.
F. C.
Roman Villa
Cistern
Granite Columns
R
Water Clock
Basilica of Ayios Epiphanios
Byzantine Aqueduct
From
St. Barnabas Monastery
Main Entrance
F. C.
Water Reservoir
Great Stone Forum
R
R
R
From
St. Catherine
F. C.
F. C.
F. C.
F C.
Land Registration & Survey Dept. Nicosia. June 1926

with pillars and arches, just as at Scolo, an appurtenance of the castle of Trajetto or Garigliano.[1]

This cistern was filled by the great aqueduct which brought water from Kythrea, thirty-five miles distant. Only a few arches of this remarkable monument remain, about two miles from Salamis, between the Monastery of St. Barnabas and the village of Ag. Sergios. It was probably built by the Emperor Justinian, though Pococke in 1738 states that many arches were standing and that on one "there is an inscription in Greek, which makes mention of an Archbishop".[2] This has long since disappeared and more likely than not referred to some restoration.

Near the forest hut is the small marble forum, which possibly dates from the second century A.D. This, too, has been ruined by an earthquake, but a number of columns and capitals still remain. The marble is of a beautiful white colour and the capitals are carefully carved. Near the flight of modern steps which leads down to it is a fragment of the remains of the original pavement. When this forum was excavated a number of marble statues were found, and are now in the Nicosia Museum. They are clumsy work of little artistic merit, and are reminiscent of the Nollekens, heathen goddesses who so surprisingly decorate the heavy eighteenth-century tombs of obscure statesmen in St. Paul's.

Between these two monuments are the remains of the great Basilica or Cathedral of Constantia, the city which was built by the Emperor Constantius II about A.D. 345; it must have been at the time of its erection the largest Christian church in the Levant, if not in the world, and the importance of the building can still be judged by the size of the fragments of the columns of the central aisle. The roof and walls were doubtless covered with mosaic work, as when the ruins were cleaned a few years since thousands of golden and coloured mosaic cubes were found in the débris.

Not far distant is an interesting water cistern which was discovered in 1933 and contains the remains of Byzantine

[1] *Excerpta Cypria*, p. 25. [2] Ibid., p. 256.

paintings, of which the most remarkable is a medallion of Christ, probably dating from the fourth century.

Scattered over the whole area are remains of other ruins, but all are so damaged and destroyed that they call for little attention. They include a Roman villa, the base of a water-clock, and the Roman baths. Salamis is one of the most disappointing sites in the Near East, if we remember the size and importance of both the Roman and Byzantine cities which stood here. Nothing more is likely to be learnt of the city or its monuments till some of the vast sand-dunes which bury it are removed. Yet I know of few things more lovely than to stand in late spring on some hillock in Salamis and look across the sea of yellow fennel and gold mimosa, broken here and there by a heap of stones that was once a temple or a Byzantine church (beyond is the sea, blue as the Madonna's robe, while to the right lies Famagusta with its towering cathedral, which in the haze seems as perfect as when it was built, for distance is so much kinder than time); then to descend and to force a way through the undergrowth, finding here and there marble columns half buried in the ground, whiter from their background of brown branches and the black-green of the cyclamen leaves growing beneath.

Few can resist the lure of picking up fragments from the ground, those unconsidered débris of an ancient town, and of all the ruins in Cyprus it is in Salamis that one can best indulge this passion. The whole vast area is covered with trifles: fragments of Samian pottery red as holly-berries; Roman glass iridescent as a shell; marble tiles from the floor of a palace, yellow, green or red; verde-antico, breccia, or sienna travertine; tiny mosaics which once glittered in the dim apse of a Byzantine church; little squares which formed the dark blue wings of an archangel; the scarlet footstool of Christ; the bright golden background of the Mother and Child; or the apple-green of a saint's robe. There is always the chance that it may be something more rare: the handle of an amphora with the maker's name stamped on it, or a worn coin on which it is still just possible to discern an Emperor's head.

No one who has looked can ever have left Salamis without a heavy and dragging pocket, for when the ruins are finished there is always the seashore; more shells seem to get washed up on the narrow beach of Salamis than anywhere else: Venus's ears, bright as pearls; purple murex, looking like crystallized violets on the hard white sand; shells pink as a woman's finger-nails; sea-urchins as green as olives or round and white like a prehistoric bird's egg.

All of us have the love of collecting, perhaps so buried as to be hardly realized, but few who come to Salamis will fail to bend down and pick up, at first surreptitiously, some fragment which was once Rome or Byzantium.

SANDALARIS (xxiii)

About a mile from the village lies the monastery of Avgasida. A small double-aisled church with strongly marked Gothic influence in the doors. In the dome are remains of a fine and well-preserved painting of Christ Pantokrator. The iconostasis is seventeenth century and contains a number of eighteenth-century icons, that of Christ being dated 1729. The columns which support the porch of the monastic building are of marble and a number of fragments, bases, capitals, and pillars lie scattered about, including some fine Byzantine capitals with crosses in relief on them, showing that an ancient monastery must once have stood on this site. Into the buttresses of the north wall of the church is built a mediaeval tombstone on which is shown in bas-relief a man in a short slashed jerkin, full breeches, and a cap on his head. The Greek inscription is much damaged, but seems to be in memory of a certain George (his surname destroyed) who died in 1482.

SARANDI (xxxvii)

This is one of the most picturesque of the hill villages. The Church of St. Constantine has been repaired and most of the wall paintings are damaged; they are not very early, almost certainly dating from the seventeenth century. The most interesting is one of the Last Supper, in which all the disciples are seated on the ground in Eastern fashion.

SHA (xxxix)

The Church of the B.V.M. was built in 1886 and contains little of interest, save an icon of St. John the Baptist dated 1735, and an icon of the B.V.M. painted on the front panel of a dower chest.

Close to the village lies a curious building, with several small plastered chambers and a complicated system of pipes, which was possibly once a Turkish bath-house.

About a mile and a half north of the village are the ruins of a Roman village site, with traces of water channels in the valley to the east. To the west is a rock-cut tomb of the same date, plastered inside, and several more lie farther up the valley.

SILIKOU (xlvii)

The Church of St. George is modern. A number of ruined chapels lie round the village, one of which is dedicated to St. John the Baptist. A curious custom connected with this building is that any child suffering from malaria is taken and rolled three times up and down on the floor in front of the ruined altar.

SINDA (xxxiii)

This is a small Moslem hamlet. Near by is a large stone enclosure of the late Bronze Age, *c.* 1500 B.C. The main enclosure is an irregular rectangle some 100 yards by 40 yards, and on the next hill to the north-west is a stone circle about 40 yards in diameter. The larger of these two enclosures is probably a Mycenaean acropolis. On the west side is a well-defined doorway, and on the north what may have been a block-house. The stones which form the wall of this enclosure are of great size—some, indeed, must weigh as much as ten tons—and it is difficult to imagine how they could possibly have been moved.

This was during the Middle Ages a Christian village and there was a Church and Cult of St. Therapon here.

It was here, too, the Genoese rested after they had sacked Nicosia. They had a vast booty of gold, silver, gems, ducats, and pieces of camlet, and imagined they were safe from attack, but a little boy, who had been forced to help the Genoese load the wagons with plunder, escaped and came to the Constable of the Kingdom, James de Lusignan, who was holding the Castle of Kyrenia; and he told the Constable all:

> "And I am one of the boys who carry the treasure for them to take away: and they are five hundred men, and because I am a Cypriote I have come to tell you." The Constable thanked him and gave him a good reward and a place in the service of his chamber. And he at once ordered five hundred men-at-arms to mount and ride after them."[1]

The Constable came up with the Genoese at Sinda and attacked them, killing all save six men, whom he took captive to Kyrenia.

SKILLOURA (xx)

The Church of the B.V.M. Skillouriotissa is a large restored mediaeval building. Originally three-aisled, only the centre one now remains; several Gothic details survive in the exterior walls. According to an ancient legend, a certain nobleman had a dog suffering from the mange, which was healed after its owner had, by chance, washed it with water from a sulphur spring in the village. This fountain is supposed to be the holy well which exists in the church to this day, and the name of the village is supposed to be derived from the Greek word for dog, though it is more likely that the real derivation of this name is from the Greek word for the Irginea Maritima, perhaps best known for its bulbs, which are the squills of medicine and childhood.

SOTIRA (liii)

Between the village of Kandou is an excellent example of a standing stone. The church is dedicated to the Transfiguration, and is a small seventeenth-century building in the usual style, with faint attempts of architectural decoration in the west doorway. The iconostasis is of the commonest and crudest painted woodwork, and most of the

[1] *Makhairas Chronicles*, p. 43

icons are of the same type; two of them are, however, of more than passing interest:

(1) A seventeenth-century icon of St. George, recently miraculously discovered buried in the sand in a ruined chapel of that name. (2) A much damaged early sixteenth-century icon of the B.V.M. Eleousa. The two angels each side of the Virgin's head are delightful examples of the art of the period.

SOTIRA (FAMAGUSTA) (xxxiii)

The Church of the Transfiguration was at one time a much larger building, but the north and south aisles were torn down at some subsequent period. Their columns and capitals lie scattered in the churchyard. An inscription over the south door of the church records a rebuilding or restoration by a certain Theodore Contarino of Placatou in 1553. The church contains an interesting wooden antimission, or covering for the chalice, of the seventeenth century.

Close to the village lies the fifteenth-century Church of St. Mamas. The narthex and north and south aisles have been destroyed; a founder's tomb remains in the south wall, and on the north-west buttress are two coats of arms, the lower a lion rampant regardant and a fish. In the interior a considerable number of frescoes remain; they are mostly the work of the late sixteenth century.

SOUSKIOU (lii)

The modern Church of St. Marina contains nothing of interest, save a large and important icon of Christ, *c.* 1520. In the lower corner is a kneeling donor priest in a white alb with a red cassock; he wears a black cap and from underneath this falls his long auburn hair; in his hand he holds a scroll. To the right is a figure of his wife, but only her head and hands remain.

SPATHARIKO (xxiv)

The Church of St. George is a tiny shed-like building, but the lower courses of its walls are formed of well-cut stone and would appear to be mediaeval.

There is also a church dedicated to the Apostle Luke, the south doorway of which is decorated with dog-tooth moulding.

Two miles distant lie the ruins of the village of Paradisa. Only the church survives, a sixteenth-century building with remains of paintings on the walls. A number of classical columns and capitals from the ruins of Salamis are built into the south narthex. The iconostasis is late seventeenth century, and in the body of the church is a finely carved proskenetarion. During the Middle Ages there was a royal residence here, and it was from this château that Queen Isabella, wife of King Amaury, was carried off with her children by a Greek pirate from Cilicia, then making a raid in Famagusta Bay. They were eventually ransomed and restored by King Leo of Armenia.

SPITALI (liv)

The Church of St. Anna, except for the north wall, is a modern rebuilding. A large number of inscribed Roman cippi lie in the churchyard, and many more are built into the wall of the church itself. Close to the church lies a curious stone, roughly hewn into the shape of a man, and with an oblong hole in the centre. It is in much request by sufferers from malaria, who walk seven times round the church and then crawl through the hole in this stone, and are immediately cured.

Near the village well lies the lid of a Roman sarcophagus turned upside down, and used as a cattle trough.

The name of this village may possibly come from the number of "small houses", or Roman tombs in the vicinity.

STAVROVOUNI (l)

The Monastery of Stavrovouni was one of the most famous in the Island. Perched on a hill 2,260 feet above sea-level, it commands superb and unrivalled views of the Island. In classical times the hill then called Olympos was crowned by a temple of Aphrodite. The famous Monastery of Stavrovouni owes its inception to St. Helena, who when she was in Jerusalem found not only the True Cross, but also the crosses of the two thieves. She unnailed these crosses and joined the long piece of the cross of the good thief with the short piece of the cross of the bad thief and thus made one cross; and she did likewise with the upright and foot rest of the bad and good thief, which remained.

And when they had arrived and cast anchor by the land, she brought out the chest and the two crosses, and ate meat at Vasilopotamos. And when she had finished eating, she lay down, being wearied by the sea, and fell asleep; and she saw a dream, that a young man said to her: "My lady Helena, as you did at Jerusalem, building many churches, so do here also, for it is commanded that in this same land men shall dwell until the end of all things, and it shall not be destroyed for all ages. And build a church in the name of the Venerable and Lifegiving Cross, and put in it of the Holy Wood which you have with you." And she awoke and rose up from her sleep and sought for the chest and the big crosses. And lo the miracle! one of the big crosses was gone. And she sent to search for it, and it was found on the mountain called Olympia, because of the Cross of Olympas, the name of the good thief. And she built a church of the Holy Cross, and set in the heart of the cross a fragment of the Holy Wood.[1]

The monastery is mentioned by nearly all the mediaeval travellers, the earliest being Abbot Daniel of Russia, who visited the Island in 1106.

There is a very high mountain here, on the summit of which is a cross of cypress-wood (erected) by the Empress St. Helena to drive away evil spirits and heal all sorts of diseases; she put into this cross one of the sacred nails of Christ. Manifestations and great miracles are worked at this spot, and near this cross, even at the present day. This cross is suspended in the air without being attached by anything to the ground: it is the Holy Spirit which sustains it in space. I, the unworthy, worshipped this holy and miraculous thing, and saw with my sinful eyes the Divine favour which rests upon this place.[2]

Another visitor was Oger, Seigneur d'Anglure, who visited the monastery in 1396.

[1] *Chronicle of Makhairas*, p. 7. [2] Hackett, *Church of Cyprus*, p. 441.

We shaped our course to go on pilgrimage direct to Holy Cross, which is in Cyprus. It is the cross on which the good thief was suspended at the right of our Saviour Jesus Christ. . . . Know that St. Helena, the mother of Constantine, brought that holy cross, on which the good thief was suspended, and placed it on the highest mountain in all the kingdom of Cyprus, which indeed is very high and difficult to climb. On the extreme top is a beautiful church with fine dwellings around it. In that church there are two altars, viz. the high altar and another in a chapel behind it. In the choir of the church we were shown one of the nails with which our Saviour, Jesus Christ, was fastened to the True Cross. Behind the said chapel is another small one, in which is the said holy cross of the good thief. Know that that holy cross presents a very strange sight, for though it is large and heavy it hangs in the air without any visible support, and when touched shakes violently.[1]

The best description is that given by Felix Faber, a Dominican monk, who visited the Island in 1480.

When we reached the top we knelt in prayer before the church, and sat down in the breeze before entering it, to recover our breath, to wipe off our sweat and get cool. Then, as was fitting, I hurried on before the rest, entered the church and pulled the bell to warn the sacristan. There appeared at once a clerk who knew no Latin. He brought out some very old Latin books, with what else was necessary for the Mass. The bell was rung, and I read the Mass of the Holy Cross, with the collects for the holy martyrs John and Paul, and for travellers. After Mass I returned to my brethren and preached to them on the fitting veneration of the Holy Cross, and explained the difference between the cross we were going to see, and that of our Lord, and the respect to be shown to each. I exhorted them also not to pry too curiously, nor crave to see a miracle, for not even in Jerusalem, in the most holy sepulchre of our Lord, were we going to see a miracle, much less should we expect one here. This, I said, because we heard about that cross strange and wonderful things which were to be seen there. I then took a lighted candle, and passed over to where the cross was: my brother pilgrims followed me, and the chaplain accompanied me. When we came to the place the chaplain opened it, so that

[1] Hackett, *Church of Cyprus*, p. 444.

we had the holy cross before our eyes. I first went up and kissed the cross, and observed it carefully before and behind. Then my companions approached and did it reverence, one after the other looking at it carefully. The cross is fairly large, covered in front with silver-gilt plates, but on the side to the wall it is bare, of a fair and sound wood like cypress. They say it is the cross of Dysmas, the thief on the right hand to whom Jesus on the cross promised Paradise. For S. Helen when she found under Mount Calvary three crosses, threw away one, namely, that of Gesmas, the thief on the left. The second, that of Dysmas, she kept for herself. The third, the cross of Christ, she exposed to the veneration of the whole world. But her own cross, that of Dysmas, she carried whole from Jerusalem to this mountain, and here she built a large monastery of monks, and a church, in which she left this cross as a relic of rare value, and caused to be built for it near the altar a niche or shrine, and set it therein. And there is still remains, untouched, though long since the monastery was utterly destroyed by the Turks and Saracens, and the monks of S. Benedict, who served the church, are scattered.

Wonderful is the position or location of this cross in its place. It is in a niche dimly lighted, both its arms are sunk in recesses made in the wall, and its foot is sunk in a recess in the floor. But the recesses of the arms and the foot are large, disproportionately so to what they hold, yet does not the cross touch the wall, but is absolutely free from any contact with it; and this is the wonderful story about the cross that it hangs in the air without support, and yet it stands as firmly as though it were attached by the strongest nails, or bonded to the wall, which it is not, for all these recesses are large, so that a man can put in his hand and feel that there is no fixture in the back or the head of the cross. I might have examined it more curiously than I did, but I feared God, and what I forbade others to do I ought not to do myself. For I ascend this mountain to do honour to this cross, not to find a miracle or to tempt God.[1]

All these travellers, and many more, assert that like the coffin of Mahomet, the cross was able to sustain itself in the air unsupported, but a Moslem writer, Khalid, the vizier of the Mamluk Sultan, has remorselessly exposed the fraud. He reports:

[1] *Excerpta Cypria*, p. 39.

That after the fatal battle of Chierochitia (July 7, 1426), the Egyptian general, Tangrivirdi, despatched a body of troops to destroy the church of Stavro Vouni and carry off the treasures which it contained. Among the booty captured was a cross of massive gold, examination of which conclusively proved that the miracle was not due to any inherent sanctity it possessed, but to the presence of cunningly devised springs concealed within it.[1]

After the Turkish invasion the monastery remained deserted till occupied by Orthodox monks in the seventeenth century. The present buildings are mostly modern, but the basement storey remains from a very early building.

The church contains nothing of interest, save a large and magnificent wooden cross on an octagonal base, the whole minutely carved with various scenes from Our Lord's life and Bible history. It was made in 1476, and was framed in silver in 1702. There is also a tiny fragment of the True Cross enclosed in a gold cover, which may be early seventeenth-century work. Into the south wall of one of the corridors of the monastery is built an inscription, partially destroyed, which records the supplication of a certain monk, Philotheos, of the eleventh century.

STENI (XXXV)

About two miles from the village lie the ruins of the rich and important Monastery of Chrysolakhourna. The original thirteenth-century church consists of a central nave and two side aisles ending in a semicircular apse. Over the west door was a small lancet window of two lights. In the sixteenth century, owing to an earthquake, the church was much remodelled. The west front was covered with a heavy buttress wall four feet thick at the base, which blocked the two entrances into the side aisle. The north wall was rebuilt, and the windows in the west and east end of the church were blocked up. All the paintings which remain are of the period of the rebuilding, save a figure of St. John the Baptist in the west end, and even this has been chipped to form a key for the later series of frescoes. The monastic

[1] Hackett, *Church of Cyprus*, p. 450.

buildings are of considerable size, but are now much ruined.

A number of Hellenistic tombs surround the monastery, and the scattered marble columns and pillars suggest that there was perhaps a heathen temple here at some period.

Just below the church is a tiny valley shaded by giant oaks, and from a cleft in the rock trickles a holy spring, which is frequented by those who suffer from ophthalmia. According to a local tradition, this monastery was once the residence of a bishop, and it is possible that during the Latin domination the Orthodox Bishop of Paphos was forced to reside here. The last Abbot is said to have been hanged by the Turks in 1821.

Near Steni are the Turkish hamlets of St. Isidoros and Myrimikoph; each still contains the ruins of a mediaeval church dating from before the time of the Turkish conquest.

STROVOLOS (xxi)

The Church of the B.V.M. was rebuilt in 1817, but the apse and the dome are from a former building of the Byzantine period. The dome is decorated with a figure of Christ Pantokrator. In the apse is kept a charming chair of the French Empire period. On the south side of the church is a small chapel, and on the outside is a curious column of stone with a capital in the form of an archiepiscopal crown. This column may commemorate Archbishop Kyprianos, who was born in the village and martyred in 1821. (See Phaneromeni Nicosia.) Here, too, was the favourite château of King Henry II, where he died in 1324, after a troubled reign.

Henry II of Cyprus reigned nominally from 1285 to 1324; but during great part of the time he was superseded by one or other of his brothers: his quarrels with them form the whole history of his reign; at one time he was a prisoner in Armenia, whither his brother, Amalric, the prince of Tyre, had sent him; another brother, Guy, the constable of Cyprus, was put to death by his orders for a conspiracy against him. The Popes were much exercised by this fraternal strife; but it was not until after the death of Guy that Henry had peace. As so often happens after an unquiet reign, he outlived all his enemies, and died rather regretted than not. This was in 1324: he was buried in the church of the Franciscans at Nicosia. When he had been able to exercise independent authority he had used it well; he had welcomed the refugees from Acre and fortified Famagosta; he contributed largely to the judicial decisions which form the supplement to the Assizes, and he established a strong judicature in Cyprus. But he was an epileptic, which perhaps accounts for his incapacity to retain the rule; and he left no children.[1]

SYKHARI (xii)

About a mile north of the village are the remains of the ruined Monastery of Apsidhiotissa, the property of the Orthodox See of Jerusalem, and known in the Middle Ages as the Abbey of Abscithi. The church is much ruined; the best preserved portion is the narthex, with curious apses in the north and south ends. This part of the church was Byzantine, but was restored in the Gothic style in the fifteenth century, and the rib vaulting carried on short wall shafts, and the bosses date from that period. There are fragments of paintings in the church of both periods, and in the apse of the north aisle is the broken tombstone of a woman in fifteenth-century costume.

Little is known about the history of the monastery, except that Leontios, Abbot in 1222, was one of the delegates to Patriarch Germanos II at Nicaea, after the expulsion of the Archbishop Neophytos of Cyprus by the Latins.

SYNGRASI (xv)

The Church of St. Procopios is a large thirteenth-century cruciform building, with remains of paintings on the walls. The apse retains its original coloured marble floor, and the seats in the bema are reminiscent of the arrangement of an eleventh-century basilica. In the apse, too, are kept a small portion of a well-cut inscription of the Byzantine period, and two Corinthian capitals; a large cippus with a hollow top is used as a font. The church is much resorted to by those who suffer from blains and boils. There is a hole in the wall of the church, from this the priest takes a little

[1] Stubbs, *Lectures on Mediaeval and Modern History*, p. 214.

earth and mixes it with oil from the lamp which burns in front of the icon of the saint. This concoction is then rubbed on the sufferer.

On a hill overlooking the village is a small early eighteenth-century chapel dedicated to the B.V.M. Aphendrika. Near the south door lie two marble columns, with elaborate Byzantine floriated crosses cut on them, and the remains of an illegible inscription. Youths who suffer from any infectious disease stand outside the west door, and, taking off all their clothes, smear themselves with oil from the lamps. They then completely redress in new clothing, leaving their infected garments behind. That this custom is still carried on can be seen by the number of shirts and trousers which lie outside the west door.

Near the school are the ruins of the double-aisled sixteenth-century church of St. Nicholas. Little remains save part of the north aisle, and two arches which divided the north and south aisles; these arches are in a perfect state of preservation, and are carried on thick squat columns, with plain moulding. A large Roman cippus lies in the apse, and probably once supported the altar. Round the school, which is nearby, lie fragments of architectural details from the church, including the south door, with an elaborate zigzag design, and dog-tooth moulding; two corbels with human faces and, most curious of all, a large stone with a carving of a male figure, his right hand across his stomach, and his left hand on his knee. This unusual fragment may have once formed a respond of a door.

TALA (xlv)

The Church of St. Catherine is a large and well-built edifice in the Byzantine style, with a central dome. The narthex has been added later. A year or so ago two completely unnecessary doors were pierced in the south wall. There are considerable remains of frescoes on the west wall, more especially the Judgement, and also three heads of animals with water gushing from their mouths, representing the sources of three rivers, perhaps the Jordan, Tigris, and Euphrates. The Gospels and church plate are Russian.

About a mile from the village are the ruins of a large church dedicated to St. George. Founders' tombs remain on the north and south walls, with traces of painting in their arches.

TEMBLOS (xii)

This is now a small Moslem hamlet, though from the name it is almost certain that in the Middle Ages there was a commandery of the Templars here.

About two and a half miles from the village is a small Chapel of the Phaneromeni, much resorted to by Greek and Turkish women whose daughters have remained unmarried and neglected by the youths of the neighbouring village. They offer prayers to the Virgin, who reveals to them in a dream the name of a likely and suitable son-in-law.

TERRA (xxxv)

The mosque was built about 1840. A number of ancient churches lie round the village, all now in ruins. The best preserved are St. George and St. John the Baptist, and both still show traces of their ancient mural decoration.

In a house in the village a large Roman milestone is used as a support for a veranda; it still retains its inscription, but it is too destroyed to be read.

About two miles from the village lies the large and interesting, but decayed, Church of St. Catherine, a building of three aisles. There are considerable remains of paintings, of which the best is a fine and exceptionally large fresco of St. Catherine, which covers the whole of the southern wall of the narthex. This narthex is unusual in that it is crowned with three domes, one at the north and south ends, and a larger central one. The church is known as the "Seven Domed", and it is possible that there were two at the end of each aisle, one above the main apse and one at the central crossing; these, with the three over the narthex, would make up the requisite number.

The abundance of water surrounding the village makes it one of the prettiest and most charming in Cyprus.

TERSEPHANOU (1)

In the village is the seventeenth-century Church of St. Marina, now alas threatened with destruction. Within it lies a marble slab with a coat of arms and two angels as supporters. It records the building of some church by a certain Sir Peter Podocatharo, who, according to the inscription, held the curious and unusual title of "Auditor of Jerusalem". Over the east window of the apse is a marble lintel with a much-damaged coat of arms within a Renaissance wreath. In the churchyard, too, are a black marble column, Corinthian capitals, and the carved marble jamb of a door; all these relics must come from the Latin church that was once in the village, perhaps that built by Sir Peter.

About a mile and a half from the village is the deserted Church of St. George of Apera. The reason of its foundation is said to be as follows: A certain Christofakis Constantinou, while journeying to Larnaca, lost from his saddle-bags a large sum of money. He prayed to St. George to help him, and promised that wheresoever he found his treasure there would he build a church and dedicate it to the saint. That night St. George revealed to him in a dream the spot where his money lay, and here in 1747 Christofakis built the church.

There are a certain number of paintings in the interior of the church; the most interesting is above the north door, and depicts the donor and his family of eight persons presenting a model of the church to an angel. Christofakis wears a rich robe edged with fur and a kalpack on his head; his wife has a green brocade dress, trimmed with ermine. All the dresses show marked Turkish influence, and the picture is extremely interesting as giving in great detail the costume worn by a wealthy Cypriote and his family in the middle of the eighteenth century. The iconostasis, decorated with paintings of flowers, birds, etc., is contemporary. There is an unusual icon of St. Christopher with a dog's head. According to a local legend, St. Christopher was a youth of such beauty that he was for ever being worried by the girls of his village when he wished to lead a life of prayer and retirement; in his trouble he prayed to the Virgin to help him, and she granted his wish by giving him a dog's head, so that no woman could ever bear to look on him again.

Close by stands the tiny mediaeval Chapel of St. Andronicos, with fragments of paintings on its walls.

Distant about two miles from the village is the Church of St. George of the River, a deserted building of the sixteenth century, but in a good state of preservation. An unusual feature is a heavily decorated window at the east end of the apse in the shape of a cross.

THELETRA (xxxv)

The village, difficult of access, is built on the side of a steep ravine with the River Lithini running far below. The Church of the B.V.M. Chryseleoussa is a handsome stone building erected in 1755. The iconostasis and the holy doors come from some former building, and date from the closing years of the seventeenth century. They were repaired and regilded in 1768. There is an icon of Christ of 1528, with two donors, a certain Vasilios and his wife, in black robes; the husband holds an open scroll in his hand. On the other side of the holy doors is a large and noble icon of the B.V.M. Theletrophilatria, or Protectress of Theletra. The Madonna wears a gilt crown set with turquoises; an inscription, a quotation from the Gospel, runs round the edge of the frame. According to another inscription at the foot, this icon was painted by the priest Dimitrios. It is undated, but the style and the writing and the general technique of the painting is in the manner of the last years of the sixteenth century.

THERMIA (xii)

The Church of the B.V.M. is built in an ancient style, and probably dates from the seventeenth century. Two English sailors were buried here in 1882.

A curious custom still surviving in the village is that any child who suffers from malaria is carried three times round the church and then rolled thrice backwards and forwards on the ground in front of the west door.

A number of the village houses are built of well-cut stone,

and while most of them date from the early years of the nineteenth century one house is earlier, and would seem to date from about 1740.

TIMI (li)

The Byzantine Church of St. Sofia has now been turned into a mosque. It is in a good state of repair, and is said to have been once completely painted, but innumerable layers of whitewash conceal any remains of frescoes that may still survive on the walls.

TOKHNI (lv)

The village of Tokhni is connected with one of the most interesting mediaeval legends still remaining in Cyprus. St. Helena, on her return from Jerusalem, was driven ashore at Zygi, near the mouth of the river which to this day is known as the River of the Queen. While resting on the shore, an angel appeared to her in a dream and commanded her to build a church to shelter the cross of the Penitent Thief, which she had brought from Jerusalem with her, and at the same time to build a smaller church, in which was to be placed a fragment of the True Cross. The Empress carried out the angel's command and built the Monastery of Stavrovouni to shelter the cross of the Penitent Thief, while near where she landed she built the Church of Tokhni to receive the fragment of the True Cross.

In 1318 a Latin priest, a certain Sir John Santamarin, went to Tokhni and in the night stole the cross, hiding it in his cloak, and went down to the shore to a boat which was waiting to take him away from the Island; but hardly had he set foot on the boat when a great storm arose and they were forced to land again. The priest, therefore, stripped off the jewels and gold and pearls with which the cross was decorated, and threw the relic itself into the centre of a hollow carob-tree, where it remained for twenty-two years. One day a shepherd boy, called George, while guarding his master's flock, fell asleep. In a dream an angel appeared to him, and told him that in the tree beneath which he slept was the missing cross of Tokhni. Thrice the angel appeared to the boy, and twice he took no notice, for he thought it was but a dream, but the third time the angel was angered, and the boy, in terror, ran to the village, and at last persuaded some of his companions to come back to the tree. When they got back the tree was burning, but though the flames licked the wood and leaves, the tree was not consumed. As they stood waiting and watching in amazement the fire died down, and one of the boys, bolder than the others, climbed up into the tree and down its hollow centre, and there found the cross, whose loss had been so mourned by the villagers. The cross was taken back to the village, and at once miraculous cures were performed, cripples, paralytics, and others recovering their health. The Latin Bishop of Famagusta, as soon as he heard these stories, was jealous, and declared the cross to be a fraud put forward by the Orthodox Church. The whole Island was rent in twain, the Orthodox maintaining that the cross was the genuine relic of St. Helena, the Latins declaring that it was an impudent forgery. At last King Hugh IV was appealed to, in order that the matter might be settled finally one way or the other. Now there was only one way to prove whether it was of the wood of the Cross of Christ or not, for the wood of the True Cross can never be destroyed by fire. At last the day of the trial came, and the cross was brought to Nicosia and into the great audience chamber of the palace. On one side stood the proud prelates and nobles of the Latin faith, on the other the humble and untidy villagers of Tokhni, with their priest in his sombre robes. The great royal brazier with four corners was brought in and filled with charcoal and set alight. Then the cross was laid on it and soon became red hot, so that many said "it is burnt". Now Queen Alice, the wife of King Hugh, had been struck dumb for insisting on entering the Church of Makhaeras, which was forbidden to women, and her tongue had remained tied for three years. After an hour, the cross was taken off with a pair of tongs, and it came out just as it had been put on the fire. When the Queen saw that the cross was unharmed, she cried out aloud, "I believe that this cross here is of the wood of the cross upon which Christ the Son of God was crucified." Then all realized the miracle, for these were the first words the Queen had uttered for three years.

The subsequent history of this cross is obscure. Lady Mary d'Ibelin, mother of the Queen, who was present at the trial, was so amazed at the miracle and the recovery of her daughter that she obtained permission from the King to build a church for the cross. The church was built between Nicosia and Agios Dometios, but nothing now remains of this building, and its very site is forgotten.

The present Church of Tokhni is, of course, dedicated to the Holy Cross. It was completely rebuilt in the nineteenth century, and is situated, like its predecessor, in the middle of the bridge over the river, which divides the village into two parts. The reason given for this curious site is that at one period Tokhni was infested by forty devils, to the distress and mortification of the inhabitants, who were mocked by all the neighbouring villages as being unclean and unwholesome. In their distress they obtained the services of a priest noted for his success in dealing with evil spirits. The priest advised them to dig a pit at the far end of the bridge, and when it was ready the priest was able, by various incantations, to entice the devils into it. Hardly were the devils inside than masons, who were standing ready, clapped a cover over the hole, and at once built the church; and so long as the church stands the devils must remain bottled up.

Close to the Holy Cross stand the ruins of a mediaeval church, built in the Gothic style, and dating from the fourteenth century. Little remains now, as the church has obviously been destroyed by fire, and the ornamental details are calcined.

About 400 yards from the church on a cliff in the river valley is an inscription cut in deep letters coloured red; many persons have seen it, but what it signifies, whether it is a date or a magical formula, or, indeed, in what alphabet it is inscribed, no one has ever been able to determine.

TRAKHONAS (xxi)

The Church of the B.V.M. was completely rebuilt in 1916, when the extremely interesting mediaeval church was destroyed. Carved capitals, stones, and fragments of architectural details from the former church lie scattered round, while above the south door of the present building is an early sixteenth-century marble coat of arms barry of three with a plumed helm above. The interior contains a few eighteenth-century icons, and in the women's gallery lies a curious fragment of what appears to be a plaster reredos, with the Crucifixion and the B.V.M. carved on it.

TRAKHONI (NICOSIA) (xxii)

The Church of the B.V.M. is a pleasing and attractive domed building of the seventeenth century. It contains an icon of the Virgin much repainted, with a priestly donor in rich robes kneeling at the foot. It is dated 1670, which would also seem to be the date of the iconostasis. The narthex has two fine early Gothic capitals.

Close by is the little Chapel of St. Nicholas, which was originally a mediaeval Latin chapel, and later became a mosque. It was built in the fifteenth century, and is in a fair state of repair. The south doorway is of elegant construction. Till recently this building had suffered a further transformation by being used as a stable, but it has now been rescued, and the entrances walled up.

TRAKHONI (LIMASSOL) (lviii)

The Church of St. Mamas was built in 1792 on the site of an earlier building. It contains nothing of interest.

Near the village is the small mediaeval Chapel of the B.V.M. It has recently been re-roofed, but the corbels and fragments of the ribs of the original vault still remain. A Latin cross is carved on the north-west angle of the exterior wall. The interior shows remains of paintings, including a fresco of St. George, on the north wall, and there is a founder's tomb in the south wall.

TREMETHOUSHA (xxxi)

The Monastery of St. Spyridon is one of the most ancient in Cyprus, but the church was rebuilt in the eighteenth century. It is a large building, with four vast buttresses against the south wall. Above the south door of the church is a painting of the saint, with a priest kneeling at his feet, and the date 1739. The fine interior contains a plain marble sarcophagus, once the resting-place of the saint. The iconostasis is dated 1684, and built into it in addition to the usual woodwork are three marble columns from the original Byzantine structure. A delightful hexagonal baroque lantern of the early eighteenth century hangs above the sarcophagus of the saint. Those who suffer from earache come to the church and lay the afflicted member against a hole in the tomb of the saint, and then light a candle in front of his icon.

The straggling monastic buildings have a number of Byzantine and Gothic details built into the walls, including large marble fragments of the ambo, or pulpit, of the Byzantine church, and probably dating from the seventh century. The capitals on the north side of the arcade, by the main entrance to the monastery, are Gothic work of the fifteenth century. It therefore seems almost certain that there must have been three or four buildings on this site.

St. Spyridon, Bishop of Trimythus, is one of the most famous of the early saints of the Cypriote Church. As a youth he was a shepherd, but his knowledge and piety being noised abroad, he was early in life consecrated a bishop. He attended the great Council at Nicaea in 325. When he was about to leave Cyprus for this conference, eleven Arian bishops were also bound for the same place, and, fearing Spyridon's eloquence, persuaded the Governor, who was of their party, to forbid any ship to take him. Trifles like this could not defeat the saint, and a few days after the eleven bishops had departed he went down to the sea-shore, and taking off his cloak placed half of it on the water and tied the other half to his staff to form a sail. Committing himself to this strange barque, he reached his destination long before his rivals, much to their surprise and astonishment. After his death his body remained for some centuries at Tremethousha, but was carried for safety to Constantinople during one of the Arab invasions. Here it remained till 1460, when the priest George Kalochairetos, shortly before the great siege, carried the body of St. Spyridon and that of the Empress Theodora to Corfu, where he became the patron saint of the island; it was, indeed, owing to the saint's intervention that the Turks were defeated in their attack on that island in 1710. So sensible was the Signory of Venice of the great service rendered by the saint, that it dedicated a large silver candlestick to his church, and decreed that his body should each year be carried in solemn procession round the city walls on August 11th, the date of the day of deliverance.

Tremethousha was also the scene of the decisive battle between Richard Cœur de Lion and Isaac Comnenos, in which the latter was defeated and taken prisoner in 1191.

TRIKOMO (XV)

The Church of the B.V.M. was built in the twelfth century, but the north aisle was added later, and the whole church was repaired in 1804. A magnificent twelfth-century Byzantine marble slab is built into the belfry, and a number of paintings survive in the interior, which appear to be work of the late fifteenth century.

The tiny little chapel of St. James is one of the most charming miniature churches in Cyprus. The interior has porcelain plates in the vaulting, but the icons and iconostasis are without interest. An exact model of the church has been erected by the Queen of Roumania, at her palace on the Black Sea, to serve as her private chapel.

About seven miles north-west of the village is the small Monastery of the B.V.M. Tochni. The domed church was probably built in the fourteenth century. There are fragments of painting in the dome and in the founder's tomb in the north wall. The unpainted iconostasis and baldachino were gifts of a pious woman in 1751. There are a few ancient icons; one of St. Panteleemon is dated 1651. The marble font is formed from a mediaeval capital.

The monastic buildings are poor and unimportant; a number of marble pillars and capitals are built into them, or lie scattered about; they are Roman or Byzantine, and possibly come from Salamis.

TRIMIKLINI (xlvii)

The Church of the B.V.M. was built in 1744, and the iconostasis was placed in the church in 1755; it contains nothing save a fine but over-cleaned icon of Christ.

A mile and a half north-east of the village lie the ruins of the Church of the B.V.M. Saittiotissa. Many years ago a dragon inhabited this spot, the curse of the surrounding villages, for it devoured all their sheep and other animals; nor was it above eating a small child, if it could find one that had strayed from its mother's side. In despair the villagers prayed to the B.V.M., who at last took pity on them, and appeared suddenly from the sky, mounted on a magnificent white horse, and armed with nothing but a bow and a single arrow. As soon as the dragon saw the Madonna, it rushed towards her, but the Virgin, taking aim, loosed her single arrow, which transfixed the dragon so that it died on the spot. The delighted villagers built a church there in memory of the event.

TRIMITHI (xii)

The Church of St. Charalambos, originally a well-built and interesting mediaeval church, has been damaged by a restoration of twenty-five years ago. Nothing remains save fine Renaissance doorways and windows. The interior is without interest.

About a mile below the village lies the Church of the B.V.M. Originally a tiny Byzantine church stood here, but at some period the west end was elongated, so that the original chapel forms the apse of the present building. The Byzantine church must have been so small, that it is difficult to see how it ever contained any congregation.

TRIS ELIES (xxxvii)

The Church of the Archangel Michael was, according to an inscription below the east window, built in 1731. The icons are mostly eighteenth century, and include one of St. John the Baptist, given by the priest Yerasimos, also in 1731; so that it is possible that this priest was the founder of the church. In the apse is kept a Gospel of 1590.

The Church of the B.V.M. Eleousa is a modern building on an ancient site, but retains the iconostasis from the former church. All the icons are unhappily repainted. The church contains a circular bronze reliquary, with a roughly etched picture of a king on it, and contains the bones of the saint Charalambos.

St. Charalambos was martyred in A.D. 198, during the persecution of the Emperor Severus.

This curious and unusual object may possibly be mediaeval. The marble altar slab has a long inscription referring to the Bishop Nikephoros, of Kyrenia, and the date 1741.

TROODHITISSA MONASTERY (xxxvii)

The large and picturesque monastic buildings date from the eighteenth century. Unhappily corrugated iron has started to replace the delightful local brown tiles. The present three-aisled church was built in 1731, but both an earlier structure of the thirteenth century and its predecessor were destroyed by fire, so that the present church is the third on the same site. In the apse are a few damaged but well-painted icons of the sixteenth century, showing marked Italian influence in their design and technique. The principal icon of the church is the B.V.M., which was covered with silver in 1799. Above it are kept a pair of buckles; any woman who desires a son must wear them and her wish will be granted, on the condition that the child is dedicated to the service of the monastery. Many years ago, a woman from Paphos wished deeply for a son, and came to the monastery to wear the buckles. In the course of time her wish was granted, and when the child was ten years old his mother brought him to the monastery and left him there as she had promised. But he was an only son, and she sorrowed for him. One day she came back to the monastery and induced the child to come away with her. They fled down the hill together, but a priest, missing the boy, guessed what had happened and followed. He shouted at them, but they would not stop. A large boulder stood on the hillside, and the priest pushed it, and in rolling down it struck the boy, who lay like one dead. The body was brought back to the monastery, and for three days the Abbot and his priests prayed over it. At last the child suddenly sat up and was well, and remained in the monastery ever afterwards. In commemoration of this the Abbot ordered a fragment of the rock to be cut off, and it can be seen to this day fixed to the back of the icon.

Between Troodhitissa and Prodhromos is the small monastery of Trikkoukia, which was rebuilt in 1761. The shutters of the windows are excellent examples of the carved woodwork of the period. There are two curious cells north and south of the apse, which demand explanation; they may have something to do with the rain-compelling icon of the B.V.M., which is still sheltered in the church, and appears to be a work of the early seventeenth century. This icon is venerated by Greek and Turk alike.

TROODOS (xxxvii)

Here is the summer seat of the Government, situated nearly 6,000 feet above sea-level. Except for the beauty of the scenery it has but little to recommend it.

The summit of Troodos is known as Mt. Olympos. According to Constantius:

> The highest and most remarkable of the mountains whose chain extends from west to east, and divides the island into two parts, is the breast-shaped Olympus, called Troodos. On its crest was once a temple dedicated to Aphrodite Acraea. By a law strange indeed in a country so devoted to this goddess, this temple might not be approached, nor even seen, by women. There are found upon this mountain, according to Aristotle and other later writers on physics, many varieties of plants useful in the healing art. About its slopes are situated the gold mines, at a place called Boucaisa, looking to the north. When Titus was Emperor, one of the peaks of this range burst forth at the top with such a fierce fire that many cities and villages lying near it were consumed.[1]

[1] *Excerpta Cypria*, p. 312.

Another legend is that there was a Church of St. Michael here, and hard by a great stone on which the ignorant and credulous peasants believed the ark to have rested. In times of drought the villagers were wont to come here and lift up this stone with wooden beams, singing hymns to God, and soon after they had started their prayers rain would come.

The Venetians built a fort here, but little can be seen now save remains of the breastworks.

Apparently no effort was made to defend it against the Turks, for, according to Calepio, "Pietro Paolo Sinclitico, captain of the hill troops, Scipion Caraffa, Gioane Sinclitico came in at once from the mountains to surrender, and Mustafa clothed them from top to toe in brocade."[1]

During the Turkish period, Troodos remained unvisited, save for the peasant who came to collect the snow, which was taken to Nicosia to be sold.

On the arrival of the English in 1878, Lord Wolseley decided to make a summer camp for the troops here, and three years later a residence for the Governor was erected. This curious house, exactly like a Scotch shooting lodge in the wilds of Caithness, was built under the directions of Jean Arthur Rimbaud. Of all the people connected with Cyprus, this French poet and adventurer is surely the strangest; born in 1854 at Charleville, he spent the life of a vagabond. In 1875 he disappeared from Europe and enlisted as a Dutch soldier, and was drafted to the Sunda Isles, but he soon deserted and lived in the wilds of a forest in Java. Later he came to Cyprus, and while in the Island is supposed to have built Government Cottage at Troodos and the Commissioner's House at Limassol. But he soon tired of the life and went to Abyssinia, where he became a semi-independent chieftain, living in a palace at Harrar.

Meanwhile, his friend Verlaine, believing Rimbaud to be dead, had, in 1886, published his poems under the title of *Les Illuminations*. Their success was instantaneous, and they caused a great sensation in Paris.

In March 1891 a tumour on the knee forced Rimbaud to

[1] *Excerpta Cypria*, p. 141.

go to Europe. He reached Marseilles, but his case was hopeless, and he died in the hospital.

His poems, his friendship with Verlaine, his tumultuous existence, and the veil of mystery which still shrouds most of his life has made him one of the most fascinating figures of the nineteenth century.

A thousand feet or so beneath Troodos is Amiandos, where there is a large and important asbestos mine. Asbestos is mentioned by a number of ancient writers.

Signor Cicach gave me a piece of Amianthus, the stone which can be spun into thread, and from which the ancients made a cloth said to be incombustible, which was cleaned by fire like other cloth by water. Of it they made the shrouds in which they burned dead bodies, so that the human ashes should not be mixed with those of the fuel, but remain by themselves within the cloth, which was not consumed. No one knows now how to make the cloth or the thread; still you can clearly see a white substance like cotton detach itself from the stone, and this might be spun. The stone itself, while intact, is a darkish green, or nearly black, but lustrous, almost like talc: when it is broken the filaments come out white. In the laboratory of Ferrante Imperato of Naples, a man of most curious learning, among the innumerable simples and strange things he had collected I remember seeing both the stone and the cloth woven from it.[1]

Of recent years, as much as two million tons of rock are quarried in a year, and the company working here has given employment to as many as six thousand workers in the summer.

TROULLI (xxxi)

The Church of St. Mamas is a sixteenth-century barrel-vaulted building, with an open arcade on the south side. Unhappily the extremely interesting sixteenth-century iconostasis and icons have been restored in the usual fatal manner, and the restorer, not content with revarnishing five of the largest, has added a border of green and red paint, thereby covering any inscription or date which may have existed on the lower edge. There is a large icon of

[1] Della Valle, *Excerpta Cypria*, p. 214.

the Archangel Michael of 1580, with two donors in the corner, the priest Eleftheros and his wife. He wears a white cassock with a green stole, ornamented with black and white crosses, and carries a Gospel bound in red in his hands. His wife has a black dress, square cut and laced in front, and a white veil covers her head. The remainder of the large icons already referred to are sixteenth century, though one of the B.V.M. may be as early as 1500. In the solea platform lies a large Renaissance tombstone, much worn by the feet of the devout villagers, who walk in front of the iconostasis kissing the icons, so that only that portion of the inscription which lies beneath the screen is still legible; the few words that remain give no clue to the name of the person buried beneath. In the centre is carved a wreath, with a shield and a coat of arms (three cockle-shells). Against the north wall hangs a large icon of St. Mamas, which was, according to an inscription, painted for the priest John in 1708; this picture has the peculiar power of curing sore throats, and is hung round with the offerings of those who have benefited from the saint's powers. In the churchyard is a marble column, with carved on it a Byzantine cross surrounded by a wreath, with two smaller crosses to left and right. The top of this column is hollowed out, and may once have been a font in some primitive church. A later font, with a simple arcaded design on it, also lies near by.

The fields round the village are much quarried for terra-umbra, and all the surrounding hills have great splashes of coloured earth, red, brown, pink, yellow, or black, as if some giant's child had spilled his paint-box over the landscape. It is from this that the Monastery of St. George of the Black Hill receives its name. It lies about two miles from the village, and consists of a barrel-vaulted church, largely rebuilt in 1722. The original church was undoubtedly Byzantine, but nothing remains of this period, save fragments of the flooring, carried out in a geometric design in coloured marbles. Unhappily a local carpenter was allowed to restore the iconostasis, and at the same time destroyed the fine sixteenth-century altar. The ceiling of its baldachino lies against the north wall of the church, and has a painting of Christ the Saviour surrounded by angels and the emblems of the four Evangelists; at the edge are golden stars in high relief against a blue background. The icons are much damaged, but there is a fragment of a noble head of Christ, cut up by this unspeakable carpenter and used to patch the iconostasis, and there is also a St. Nicholas with remains of a lovely gold background; both these icons are work of the sixteenth century. Of a later period are St. John the Baptist, given in 1702 by Eleni and her child, and an icon of the Virgin, given in memory of the priest Yerasimos, who lived in the monastery and died there in 1782.

Of the monastic buildings little remains, save a few fragments which are now used as cattle byres; the roof of the largest of these is supported by three pillars with capitals exactly like those in the Cistercian convent at Nicosia. Nor is it utterly improbable that this building was, during the Middle Ages, a convent, for the tiny hill to the south is to this day called by the villagers the Hill of the Nuns.

In the tangled undergrowth near by are various marble pillars from the original Byzantine building. The most interesting of these is square, eight feet long, and of white marble, with an elaborate Byzantine pattern at the top; it may once have formed one of the supports of the iconostasis.

A curious local custom still survives in the village. It is said that when the monks lived here they kept so many hens that every morning it was possible to fill a large basket with eggs, and now when the hens of the village fall ill or fail to lay, the finest bird of the flock is picked out and sold, and the money thus obtained is spent in providing oil for the lamp which burns in front of the icon of St. George, and at once the remaining birds lay more eggs than they ever did before.

TRYPIMENI (xiii)

The Church of the B.V.M. Eleousa has recently been rebuilt, but contains a few icons from the former building, including a St. Nicholas, Archangel Michael, and Madonna, all painted in 1679, and a Transfiguration dated 1718.

There is also a Chapel of St. Andronicos, with fragments of a fine seventeenth-century iconostasis, above which is placed a small bronze repoussé cross of the same date. In a corner lie a large rood cross and two pairs of holy doors of the early eighteenth century from some vanished building. The church contains a sixteenth-century Gospel, and a few manuscript leaves in vellum are bound up in it.

TSADHA (xlv)

The Church of the B.V.M. was rebuilt in 1908, but it contains an interesting icon of the B.V.M. with two kneeling donors, the priest Gideon and his wife. According to an inscription the icon was "Painted at the expense of and by the sinner Titus". This icon probably dates from about 1540.

About two miles from the village lies the small Monastery of the Holy Cross, at one time the residence of the Bishop of Paphos. The doorway into the monastery shows Gothic influence, and the south doorway of the church appears to be work of the early sixteenth century. The iconostasis is dated 1740, and contains nothing of interest save a large cross, which was covered in silver in 1834. This cross has a great reputation in the neighbourhood, for one day, about a hundred years ago, the threshing floor of the monastery caught fire; at once the Abbot seized the cross and flung it into the flames, which were miraculously extinguished; and to prove this, faint signs of burning can be seen on the cross to this day.

TYMBOU (xxxi)

The Church of St. George was built in 1858, but contains icons from some former building, including a St. John the Baptist painted by the priest Joannidou in 1713. In the gallery lie two unusual large seventeenth-century icons, repainted in 1849, and measuring 4 feet by 5 feet. They represent Christ and the B.V.M.; round the edge of the former are scenes from our Lord's life, while the icon of the Madonna is decorated with portraits of the Old Testament prophets.

Across the river lies the Turkish shrine of Kirklar, or the Holy Forty. This is one of the most strange monuments still remaining in the Island. The little mosque is dated 1816. From it steps lead down into a vast cave consisting of a central nave and two side aisles, the dividing walls pierced by rounded arches. It is of the size and plan of a large church, the central nave ending in an apse, while the side aisles terminate in square chambers; small apertures in the roof admit the light. In these side aisles are buried forty saints, each tomb covered with a green cloth, but who these forty were and from whence they came, whether they were Christian or Moslem, nobody now knows. The number forty frequently appears in Moslem and Christian folklore alike; there are thus forty martyrs, saints, ogres, or djinns. The shrine is equally holy to Moslem and Christian, but ill will happen to the man who disbelieves, for there is still kept here the sword which, wielded by an unseen hand, decapitated an Orthodox priest who mocked these holy men. A spear shaft is driven into the wall of the small chamber at the end of the north aisle, and whoever grasps it in full belief, wishes, and repeats the name of Allah three times, shall have his desire granted.

About a mile from here is the small Chapel of the Prophet Elijah, which contains an icon of St. John the Divine, painted in 1711, and a fine pair of holy doors, painted by the priest Nicholas in 1702.

VAROSHA (xxxiii)

This is really a suburb of Famagusta, actually quite a large town surrounded by orange groves which straggles for about a mile parallel to the coast. The most interesting church is that of the Chrysospiliotissa, which is entirely underground, but can easily be identified by the fact that a tall campanile rises from the ground, with no apparent church attached. A wide flight of steps leads down to the church. Undoubtedly at one time it must have been a pagan tomb. There are remains of paintings on the walls, but they are much damaged. The iconostasis is curious in that instead of being carried across the east end of the church, it forms three sides of a square. The north side is formed by a vast icon nearly eight feet square representing the Baptism. Though much obscured by dirt and damp, this icon has, apart from its size, a certain nobleness of feeling. It is true that the main figures in the composition are ill-drawn and that the painting is crude, but the smaller figures in the corner seem to show a true Italian manner. During the Middle Ages this church was known as the Madonna della Carva, and it is mentioned by most of the mediaeval travellers who visited Famagusta.

We anchored in the harbour of Famagusta, a city of Cyprus, on Friday, the last day of June, 1335; and on the following day we all, merchants and pilgrims, sailors and crew, went to the church of St. Maria della Cava, which is about two bowshots outside the town, and there in most devout fashion I celebrated Mass, and we offered one large, or double, candle to the glorious Virgin who delivered us from so many dangers, for while we were yet at sea we had thus made our vow. The church is worthy to be visited devoutly and often: it is in a cavern, and you descend to it by thirty-six steps. Everyone who lands goes there forthwith. There are three chaplains who remain there continually, and celebrate daily for the crowd of visitors. For at sea, when the sailors at even sing *Salve Regina*, one of them always invokes the help first of the Holy Cross of Mount Calvary, then that of the B.V.M. of the Cave, and the worshippers respond *Deus exaudiat*.[1]

At the other end of the town is the Church of the Holy Cross, a building of the mid-nineteenth century. A large number of fragments from classical and Byzantine buildings are used in its construction. The vaulting is supported on the north and south sides by white marble columns with Corinthian capitals, though one column bears a Byzantine cross cut in relief. The church contains icons from some former building, which include SS. Constantine and Helena dated 1725, and there is also a curious icon of the B.V.M. and Child in a chalice, within a florid rococo

[1] Jacobus de Verona, 1335, *Rev. de l'Orient Latin*, 1895, p. 175.

frame. The church contains three ancient rood crosses. One of unusually large dimensions hangs on the north wall, it is 7 feet in height, and appears to be work of the late seventeenth century; according to local tradition, it came from a church in Famagusta. Of the other two rood crosses, one is dated 1773 and the other is of about the same age.

Close to the church is a tiny private cemetery containing a single grave on which rests a Roman marble sarcophagus. This sarcophagus was known as the Tomb of Venus, and for many centuries had stood in front of the cathedral at Famagusta. During the Moslem period it was covered with a mediaeval tomb slab torn up from the floor of the cathedral and used as a bier for the bodies of dead Turks. In 1880 the first English Commissioner of Famagusta took his own life, and it was suggested that this Roman sarcophagus might be used as a tombstone for the unfortunate man. It was, therefore, removed and placed in the little cemetery, where it remains to this day. It closely resembles in design the sarcophagus used as a lavabo in the cloister of Bella Paise, and is decorated in the same way with swags and garlands of foliage and fruit.

The remaining churches of Varosha are without interest, except for St. Paraskevi, the only ancient part of which is the apse, possibly of the sixteenth century. In the floor in front of the iconostasis lies a large defaced Venetian tombstone.

VASA (xlvii)

Outside the village is a small domed church of the fifteenth century, dedicated to St. George; the narthex was apparently added at a later date. There are considerable remains of paintings on the walls, but they are of a crude nature and seem to date from the late sixteenth century. Apparently there was once a Venetian watch-tower on the hillock in the middle of the village, and the foundations of a square building can still be seen there. When the writer was in this village in 1933 he was given a collection of Venetian swords, one with a basket handle, which were found by villagers cutting stone on the supposed site of this watch-tower. The swords are at present in the Nicosia Museum.

VATHYLAKKAS (viii)

The principal church of the village is dedicated to St. George and was built in the seventeenth century, with an open colonnade on the south side. There are considerable traces of wall paintings in the interior, and the vault is decorated with plates, some of which appear to be of some antiquity; they may be Persian.

Close by is the little ruined Church of St. Theodoros, of the fourteenth century. Only the north wall and apse remain. It was once completely painted, but little can now be seen; the best preserved figures are three Fathers of the church in the semi-apse. The church is completely hidden and overgrown by trees and shrubs, but the villagers firmly believe that sickness, if not death, will visit the man rash enough to cut wood here.

VATILI (xxxii)

The Church of St. George was so completely restored in 1856 that only a fragment of the original mediaeval structure survives in the south wall and in the Gothic west door. Within the church is kept a most interesting icon of Italian workmanship. It depicts the B.V.M. supported by St. Nicholas and St. George; at its foot are the heads of six people, an old man, his wife, and four sons; between them is painted a book open in the middle, on the pages of which are written the names of the various members of the family and the dates of their deaths, which occurred between 1532 and 1604. According to a local legend this picture was brought back by a priest who visited Italy, and the portraits beneath are of himself and his family. The southern end of the iconostasis is formed by a colossal early nineteenth-century painting of St. George, but it appears to be repainted over a much earlier picture. The ceiling of the iconostasis above it is late sixteenth century.

VITSADHA (xxiii)

The church of the village is dedicated to St. Mamas; near by lie the ruins of its mediaeval predecessor. The present building contains icons from the earlier one, including one of St. John the Baptist, *c.* 1540, with a kneeling donor, in a black robe with a white collar, holding a string of beads. The inscription at the foot of the icon gives his name as a certain Bernard Katla. Outside the church lies a large grey marble slab, with a finely cut Roman inscription, which is said to have come from the neighbouring village of Knodhara. It may have been an altar—perhaps the one referred to by Ross, who visited Cyprus in 1844.

Walled in on the N. side of the church at Knodhara is a stout pillar of bluish limestone with a Latin inscription, from which it appears that a Roman castle stood here in which was quartered the seventh cohort of the Breuchi: the old name of the place is unknown.[1]

VIZAKIA (xxix)

Close to the village lies a little Chapel of the Archangel Michael, a tiny building with a shed-like roof and a semi-open narthex. It is of poor construction, mud-brick and unshaped stone, and was built about 1500. In the interior are still preserved paintings on the west and south walls, but the technique and workmanship are crude, even for Cypriote wall paintings. A large composition of the Crucifixion above the west door is, however, curiously effective from the very distortion of the figures; the artist has introduced into his painting some charmingly naïve effects, including octopus in the River Jordan in his picture of the Baptism, and Venetian swords and helmets in that of the Betrayal. The iconostasis is of the open rood type and contains a damaged processional icon of Christ. In the apse lies a large sixteenth-century wooden cross painted with a Crucifixion, which is said to come from a Chapel of the Holy Cross, long since destroyed.

[1] Ludwig Ross, *Reisen nach der Insel Cypern.*

VOKOLIDHA (viii)

The village is surrounded by tombs of various periods. Close to the sea-shore can still be seen the remains of an Austrian steamer wrecked here about 1860. According to the villagers, the ship was conveying emigrants to America, but on the voyage they mutinied and the captain deliberately ran his ship on to the rocks; in the ensuing confusion the majority of the emigrants were drowned, but the captain and crew managed to reach the shore in safety.

VONI (xxii)

North of the village a large temple site was excavated in 1883, but nothing can now be seen except the large stones which mark the temple enclosure. A number of statues found here are now in the Cyprus Museum.

The Church of St. George is modern, but in the churchyard lie a number of damaged statues, which the excavators of 1883 did not think worth the trouble of transporting to Nicosia.

VOUNI (xviii)

The Palace of Vouni, excavated by an expedition sponsored by the Crown Prince of Sweden, is at once one of the most important and one of the most unusual sites in the Island. The site comprises a small township grouped on the steep slopes of a conical hill a few miles west of the ancient City of Soli, a Temple of Athena perched on the precipitous edge of the hill on the land side, and a superb palace site on the summit of the hill facing the sea and the north, looking at Asia Minor. Only the palace site and the temple site have been fully excavated and both remain now well-tended and open to visitors, with a resident custodian.

The whole site belongs to a period not earlier than the late sixth century and not later than the end of the fifth or early fourth century B.C. It has not yet been fully established what was the name of this settlement in antiquity. What is certain is that it represents the palace and dependencies of one of the local kings of Cyprus built at a time when the Island was torn by dissension between the pro-Greek and the pro-Persian factions. The palace was evidently a building of great wealth and luxury, and there were found not only a group of sculptures and works of art, some imported from the Greek mainland, but also a treasure consisting of silver coins of Cypriote cities and two superb gold bracelets which can rank among the finest known examples of Persian goldwork. The palace contained elaborate baths supplied with a hot-water system and numerous deep and efficient wells. The living-rooms of the palace were grouped round a central atrium which was surrounded by a colonnade. A "royal road" led from the lower township into the palace.

The king or prince who lived in this palace may have been a local Cypriote of nationalist sympathies or else a nominee of the Persian overlords of Cyprus. It is impossible as yet to decide on such historical problems, since nothing except architectural and artistic data are available. But from these it is clear that we are here in the presence of a settlement which is typical of Cypriote life in the most interesting century of its existence, the period roughly between 500 B.C. and 400 B.C. The palace is of a type which is unlike the usual type of Hellenic living-house and has qualities which connect it with a more Oriental world. The bath is equally un-Hellenic in type and the central colonnade, while a feature of most Hellenic private houses, was probably derived by Greeks and Cypriotes alike from Oriental origins. The social organization implied by the whole complex of buildings is not that of the typical Hellenic city-state, but rather that of Homeric times. It is certainly not that of the ordinary Oriental despot, for in that case the palace would have been larger and more elaborate. It represents, in short, the typical Cypriote local kingship, of which the origin goes back to the days of Achaean colonization in the fourteenth century B.C., and which never died out in Cyprus until Ptolemaic days. As such Vouni is the first site to illustrate this typical and peculiar social organization of Cyprus. There should be several other similar sites, but so far none has been found. There is a possible parallel in the case of a similar building in the Carpass; but this site is already too ruinous for excavation to tell us much about it.

The palace was only occupied for a short time, possibly as an administrative headquarters in the neighbourhood of Soli. It appears to have been commenced about 480 B.C., and was finally destroyed by fire in 400 B.C. Even in this short time a number of alterations and additions were made to the original building and its surrounding shrines; these can be divided into four principal periods:

Period I

The palace, when first planned, consisted of a building with a grand entrance, [1–2][1] to the south supported by columns, with a series of lateral rooms [3–4] on either side: this entrance communicated by a flight of steps with a central court [5] to the north. In the centre of this was an open cistern [6] in which the water from the roofs was collected (the court itself was drained to the north under [14*a*]). Around the court were living-rooms [7–14], of which [8] was the largest; [12–13] in the north-east corner communicated with one another and were the baths; [12] was the caldarium, in which the groove for the bench may still be seen along the south wall. Traces, too, can be seen on the floor where the tubs for hot water stood; the water appears to have been brought by hand from the kitchen; [13] was the frigidarium.

The kitchens consisted of a series of rooms [14–16]; [15] was the kitchen proper with the hearth; the other two rooms were later pulled down. Communication with the main building was through [3]. At this time there was a cistern in [46], which was later disused.

The south-west wing consisted of an open court [17] and passage [18] surrounded by living rooms [19–22], a group of store-rooms [23–26, 28], in which some of the stores and provisions were found *in situ*; [27] were cold baths and latrines. In [18] was another cistern taking drainage from the adjoining roofs. Communication with the main building was through [19] and [14] and also by steps in [22, 29, and 30].

[1] The numbers refer to the plan of the palace.

THE PALACE OF VOUNI

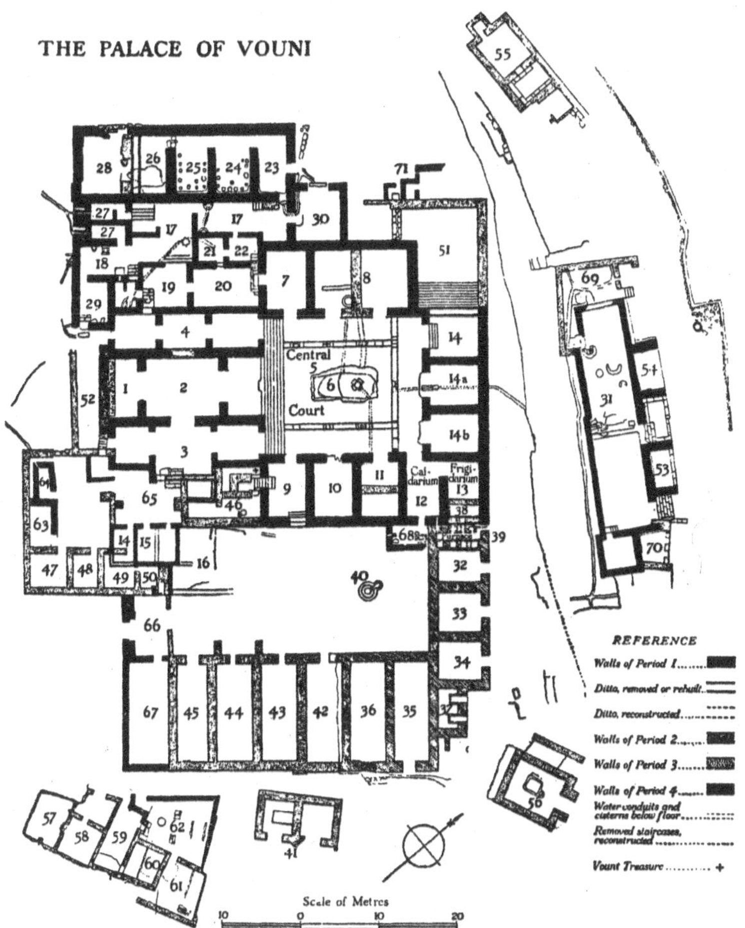

At this period there was no second storey to the building.

The north-west temenos [31] consisting of a cellar, entrance court with flight of steps flanked by statues, a priest's room, was also constructed at this period.

Period II

The main plan of the palace was not altered, but several additions and alterations were made. Large store-rooms [32–36] were added to the north-east, together with the latrines [37].

A sudatorium was constructed over the large furnace [39]; it was reached by a wooden stair, and heated by hot air from the furnace; only the furnace now remains. Part of [13] was partitioned off for a fuel room [38].

Another large bottle-necked cistern 25 metres deep [40] was constructed in the court formed by the new store-rooms. The kitchen [15] was divided in half at this time, and a new shrine [41] was built on the east side.

Period III

Great changes were now made in the whole plan of the palace: the entrance was made to the north-west through the ante-room [51 and 14]. The earlier entrance [1] was closed, and the series of room [1–4] receded into the background. Room [8] was divided: and the open cistern [6] in the central court was filled and replaced by the bottle-neck cistern, over which a small wooden windlass was erected to raise the water.

Outside, store-rooms [42–45] were added, enclosing the east court; room [16] was demolished and the entrance to the court made near the kitchen. Store [36] was disused and filled with rubble, also the cistern near the kitchen.

In the kitchen quarters rooms [47–50] were added, and the court [65] enclosed. The passage [53] was made behind [1] to communicate with the south-west wing. Rooms [49 and 50] contained cement "sinks" full of broken pottery, and appear to have been the pantries.

At this time a second storey of timber and mud brick was added over the original main building, and the store-rooms [32–36]. These were reached by wooden stairs; the principal staircase was constructed in [46] and consisted of two flights on a rubble base. Beneath this the Vouni Hoard, consisting of four gold bangles, eleven silver bangles, three silver bowls, and some 350 silver staters, was found and can now be seen in the Cyprus Museum.

The stairs for the north-west wing lead from [17] to over [23] and also to room [26].

Two open porticoes [53–54] supported by columns were added to the north-west temenos, and a new road of approach made along the north side.

The two shrines [55–56] were built, and also the large irregular building [57–61], the use of which is uncertain.

Period IV

Minor alterations only were made at this time, and were in some cases never completed, for the palace was destroyed by a widespread conflagration, and never again inhabited.

Work on the cistern in the central court was continued, and two stone stelai prepared to replace the wooden windlass, but never completed. One is *in situ*, the other in the Cyprus Museum.

Room [11] was divided and another stair added there. Rooms [63–64] were added in the kitchen court, [64] with a large drain.

Store [67] was added to the main court with a new entrance [66].

A new furnace [68] was added to the caldarium in the north-west corner of the main court, probably for heating water.

Two rooms [69–70] were also added to the main temenos and another [62] to the south-east building.

Little is at present known of the history of this palace. It must have been a building of some importance, for it was well finished. Many small private buildings apparently covered the surrounding slopes, but remain unexcavated. The original approach was from Soli, up the eastern slope. On the lower ground a large open space may be seen, which marked the stopping-place for vehicles or animals;

from thence the visitor in ancient times approached the palace by flights of steps cut in the rock, some of which may still be seen among the bushes on the north-east slope.

Of the temple on the top of the hill little remains. It is known to have been dedicated to Athena, and the bronze cow and other objects in the Cyprus Museum were found there.

VOUNO (xii)

This is one of the Maronite villages and their church is dedicated to St. Romanos. It contains some interesting icons: St. George, dated 1698; B.V.M. and Christ, both by the same painter, dated 1690; St. Romanos, sixteenth century; and the Body of Christ after the Deposition, with a kneeling donor, *c.* 1520. St. Romanos was born in Palestine, the son of Christian parents of the town of Antioch. He was martyred in the year 310, during one of the Christian persecutions.

Near the village is a cave with a number of fossil bones in it, believed by the villagers to be the remains of early martyrs. It was visited in 1683 by van Bruyn.

While I was at Larnaca the Consul had strongly recommended me to go to see his place, and as I expected to find something important I had brought with us hammers and scissors. I partly accomplished my purpose, for I extracted some of these bones from the rock. The chief was a bone which I took to be the radius of a man's arm. It was imbedded so firmly in the rock that it took us two hours to get it out, and despite all our efforts to preserve it whole, the rock itself broke and the bone with it. This after all was an advantage, for the fracture allowed us to see the marrow plainly defined. I carried it off carefully wrapped in cotton. On the same spot I found plenty of fragments just hidden by the earth; some were human bones, others those of beasts, and some teeth of surprising size. All round the rock were candle-ends. I guessed the place was held in veneration, and found indeed that the Greeks came there occasionally to pray, believing perhaps that some of their saints may be buried there.[1]

[1] Van Bruyn, *Travels.*

XYLOPHAGHOU (xlii)

The Church of St. George is a sixteenth-century building. According to a local tradition, the interior was burnt by the Turks, and it is true that such of the original paintings as still remain show signs of blackening. Of these sixteenth-century paintings, the best preserved are the Tree of Jesse, above the north door, and scenes from the Life of Our Lord, in the vaulting; the rest of the paintings in the church, for the whole interior is thus decorated, are dated 1772 and 1805, and are of poor and ordinary style.

About three miles east of the village lies the mediaeval Chapel of St. George. All the frescoes are whitewashed. A stone with a dim coat of arms lies in the ruined narthex, and to the south is a curious square stone pillar, exactly like a sundial.

At Cape Pyla is a large cave known as the Cave of the Forty Martyrs. The entrance, difficult to find, is in the cliff which rises sheer from the sea. The cave itself is of considerable size and runs back for some distance. The sides, roof, and floor at the west end are full of the petrified bones of animals, probably pigmy hippopotami, though they are regarded by the villagers as being the remains of early Christian martyrs who were massacred here. This is the cave referred to by Cesnola.

> My guide, who was the nephew of the Greek priest, told me with religious awe that they were the bones of "forty saints," and that to within a few years ago it had been the custom of the peasants of Ormidia, Afgoro, and other neighbouring villages to make a pilgrimage to this cave, accompanied by their priests, on the anniversary of the 9th of March, but that the Greek Archbishop of Cyprus, who happened to be Ormidia collecting his church dues at the time of one of these pilgrimages, had ordered them to be discontinued.[1]

Between the cape and the village is the base of a circular Venetian watch-tower; the walls still stand 12 feet high, but there are no signs of an entrance, which probably was considerably above this level.

[1] *Cyprus: Its Cities, Tombs and Temples*, p. 208.

XYLOTYMBOU (xli)

Near the village lie two small chapels, dedicated to St. Basil and St. Marina, both of them recently repaired. Both contain considerable remains of paintings, but the frescoes in St. Marina are much the best preserved, and those in the vault show faint foreign influence. These churches were probably built in the late fifteenth century.

Close to St. Marina is a Hellenistic necropolis with large tombs cut in the solid rock.

YENAGRA (xxiii)

Outside the village lies the mediaeval Byzantine Church of St. George, with a small central dome. This is a most unusual building, as most of the church is 7 or 8 feet beneath the ground-level. The apse itself is formed of a pagan tomb. There are remains of paintings, possibly work of the early fifteenth century, including Christ Pantokrator in the dome. A number of marble columns lie both inside and outside the church, including a curious double one in the apse, which may have formed part of an early Byzantine iconostasis.

YERI (xxx)

The Church of the B.V.M. was rebuilt in 1814. Little remains from the former church, which would seem to have been a sixteenth-century building with painted walls, save the apse and fragments of frescoes by the west door. A fleur-de-lis finial, on the roof, must also come from the mediaeval church. In the women's gallery is preserved a much damaged icon of the B.V.M.; in the bottom corner is a male donor, and the date 1542. The church is built on a plateau above the village, and near by is a small hillock completely composed of fossil oyster shells.

YEROSKIPOS (li)

The name of the village is evidently a survival of the Hieroskepos, or the Sacred Garden of Venus, who was regarded as the goddess of springtime and flowers. The principal church of the village is dedicated to St.

Paraskevi, and is a very interesting Byzantine building. The original church was of cruciform plan, covered with five domes, and there was a small chapel at the south-east corner. It was considerably enlarged in the nineteenth century by the addition of a nave and aisles at the west end. The little chapel at the south-east corner is difficult to explain, and may possibly have been a chantry chapel, as an ancient tomb is built into it on the outside. There are remains of extremely fine frescoes in the church, probably early fifteenth century; the best is a fragment of the Betrayal, beneath the dome, and the armour and weapons of the soldiers are most interesting and curious. There is also an icon painted on both sides, and probably dating from the last years of the fifteenth century. The group at the foot of the cross is reminiscent of the mediaeval Spanish or Burgundian school. In the village is still pointed out the house of Haji Smith, who was British Vice-Consul. In 1800 Sir Sydney Smith anchored off Paphos with Marshal Junot as prisoner. Sir Sydney visited Yeroskipos one day, was much struck by the intelligence of one of the village youths, a certain Zimboulaki, and appointed him Vice-Consul for Great Britain. So delighted was the youth with the kindness of the Admiral that he took his protector's name and called himself Haji Smith.

Near the church are the remains of a small Roman temple, and a number of marble capitals and Corinthian columns lie scattered about. According to a mediaeval legend the vineyard of Engadi was situated near here. Rudolf von Suchen, who visited Paphos in 1340, gives the following description of it:

Concerning the vineyard of Engadi.—In this same province of Paphus is the vineyard of Engadi; its like is nowhere found. It is situated in a very high mountain, and measures two miles in length and in breadth, girt on all sides with a lofty rock and a wall; on one side it has a very narrow entrance, and within it is quite level. In this vineyard grow vines and clusters of many different kinds, some of which produce grapes of the bigness of plums, others small grapes like peas, others again grapes without stones, or grapes in shape like an acorn, all transparent, and grapes and clusters of many other kinds are seen therein. It belonged to the Templars, and more than a hundred Saracen captives were daily therein, whose only task was to clean and watch that vineyard, and indeed I have heard from many of experience that God had made for the use of men no fairer or nobler ornament under the sun. And so we read of it in the Song of Songs "my beloved is unto me as a cluster (of Cyprus) in the vineyard of Engadi".

Concerning the little Engadi, and the city of Nymocinum.—Not far from Paphus is the city of Nymocia, which was once fair, but now laid waste by constant earthquakes and by floods coming suddenly from the mountains. This city is set on the seashore directly facing Tyre and Sydon and Baruch. After the loss of Acon the Templars and the Friars of the Hospital of S. John and other nobles and burghers dwelt here, and many of their palaces and castles are seen there.

Concerning the vineyard of Engadi.—Near Nymocine is another vineyard called the little Engadi, in which grow vines of many different kinds, which a man cannot gird with his arms. But they are not tall, nor do they produce much fruit.[1]

YIALIA (xxvi)

Two miles east of the village and farther up the river lie the ruins of a church known to the villagers as Monastir, or Agios Cornuto. The church is very ruined, but so far as can now be seen it was a circular building with later additions. It may be possible that the original church was completely roofed over, as both the inside and outside walls have traces of paintings. No legend seems to survive concerning this church, except that it was Latin, which very probably is true. It must have been a building of some importance, and circular churches are very rare and uncommon.

Yialia is a completely Turkish village, one of the prettiest in Cyprus, and consists of houses straggling for a mile and a half up a narrow valley surrounded by orange gardens.

YIALOUSA (iii)

The principal church of the village is dedicated to the Archangel, and consists of a small thirteenth-century building with an eighteenth-century church tacked on to it

[1] *Excerpta Cypria*, p. 19.

at a later date. The apse of the older church is arcaded in the Byzantine manner. Fragments of wall paintings still survive in the older building.

The village contains a number of other churches, but they are without interest.

YIOLOU (xxxv)

The Church of the B.V.M. was built in the early years of the eighteenth century. It contains a much-repainted icon of the Virgin, which dates from the seventeenth century. This icon is said to have been formerly in the Church of Peristerona, but a man of Yiolou dreamt that that church was going to be destroyed by fire. He at once got up and proceeded to Peristerona, and as he reached the church it burst into flames, but he was able to save the icon. This icon has various curative powers, and can also compel rain, but it cannot be taken from the niche in which it stands unless the Virgin herself allows it. On occasions, when the villagers have wished to take it round the fields to bring rain, the icon has been known to become stubbornly obstinate and refuse to be moved from its resting-place, resisting all efforts to lift it.

ZOOPIYI (xlviii)

The Church of Zoodotospygi, or the Life Giving Fountain, is a large nineteenth-century building. It contains a curious icon of the Madonna, probably early fifteenth century; her silver-gilt halo is set with blue enamel medallions of the four Evangelists, not unlike coarse Limoges work.

There is also a church dedicated to St. Marina, built in the eighteenth century and now used as a school. In the interior still remains a wall painting of the saint herself.

BIBLIOGRAPHY

GENERAL DESCRIPTION

DELAPORTE, R., L'Ile de Chypre. Paris, 1898.

HAGGARD, SIR H. RIDER, A Winter Pilgrimage. London: Longmans, 1901.

HOGARTH, D. G., The Nearer East. London: Heinemann, 1902.

LUKE, H. C., The Fringe of the East. London: Macmillan, 1913.

MALLOCK, W. H., In an Enchanted Island. London: Nelson, 1889.

STORRS, SIR RONALD, and O'BRIEN, B. J., The Handbook of Cyprus. London: Christophers, 1930.

HISTORY

BOUSTRON, FLORIO, Chronique (1560). Pub.: de Mas Latrie, Paris, 1884.

COBHAM, C. D., Excerpta Cypria (extracts descriptive and historical, from eighty writers and twelve tongues; also includes his Bibliography in an expanded form, containing 860 entries). Cambridge: Univ. Press, 1908.

GRAZIANI, A. M., The History of the War of Cyprus. Translated by R. Midgley. London, 1687.

HACKETT, J., A History of the Orthodox Church of Cyprus. London: Methuen, 1901.

JEFFERY, G., Cyprus under an English King in the Twelfth Century. Govt. Print. Press, Nicosia, 1926.

LUKE, H. C., Cyprus under the Turks. London: Milford, 1921.

LUSIGNANO, STEFANO, Chorograffia . . . di Cipro. Bologna, 1572 and 1573.

MAKHAIRAS, LEONTIOS, Chronicle of. Edited by R. M. Dawkins. Oxford, 1932.

MARITI, G., Travels in Cyprus in 1769. Translated by C. D. Cobham. Cambridge: Univ. Press, 1909.

MAS LATRIE, L. COMTE DE, Histoire de l'Ile de Chypre sous le Règne des Princes de la Maison de Lusignan. Paris, 1852–61.

ORR, C. W. J., Cyprus under British Rule. London: Scott, 1918.

STORRS, SIR RONALD, A Chronology of Cyprus. Nicosia, 1930.

STUBBS, W., The Medieval Kingdoms of Cyprus and Armenia, three lectures, *vide* Sixteen Lectures on the Study of Mediaeval and Modern History. Oxford: Clarendon Press, 1886.

ANTIQUITIES

CESNOLA, L. P. DI, Cyprus: Its ancient Cities, Tombs and Temples. London: Murray, 1877.

CHAMBERLAYNE, T. J., Lacrymae Nicossienses. Paris, 1894.

ENLART, M.C., L'Art Gothique et la Renaissance en Chypre. Paris, 1899.

HILL, G. F., Catalogue of Coins: Cyprus. British Museum, 1904.

HOGARTH, D. G., Devia Cypria: Archaeological Journey in Cyprus. Oxford: Frowde, 1889.

JEFFERY, G., The Historic Monuments of Cyprus. Nicosia, 1919.

MYRES, J. L., Handbook of the Cesnola Collection of Antiquities from Cyprus. New York, 1914.

ORNITHOLOGY, GEOLOGY, BOTANY, ETC.

BATE, MISS D. M., Field Notes on Birds of Cyprus (*Ibis*, Oct.). London, 1903.

BELLAMY, C. V., and JUKES-BROWN, A., Geology of Cyprus. Plymouth, 1905.

BUCKNILL, I. A., Ornithology of Cyprus (*Ibis*). London, 1900, 1910, 1911, 1913.

HOLMBOE, JAN, Vegetation of Cyprus. Bergen, 1914.

LILFORD, LORD, History of the Birds of Cyprus (*Ibis*, July 1889). London, 1889.

CHRONOLOGY OF CYPRUS

B.C.

4000 NEOLITHIC AGE

BRONZE AGE

Large population distinct from Egypt, Syria, and Cilicia.

3000–1000 (*a*) Copper implements :hand-made pottery : imports unknown.

(*b*) Bronze implements : painted pottery : imports, Egyptian blue glazed beads and cylindrical Asiatic seals.

(*c*) Mycenaean Culture (1500–1200) and industries; wheel-made pottery; gold, ivory, glass, enamels : extended imports : Aegean script.

1450 Conquered by Thothmes III : (Egyptian name of Cyprus Asi).

IRON AGE

710 Seven Cypriote Kings pay homage to Sargon II.

CLASSICAL PERIOD

525 Cyprus conquered by Persians (Cambyses).

392 Evagoras master of Cyprus.

386 Cyprus openly revolts from Persia.

336 Birth at Kition of Zeno, founder of Stoic Philosophy.

PTOLEMAIC

320 Ptolemy I occupies Cyprus with fleet.

ROMAN

58 Cyprus as a detached portion of the Roman province of Cilicia.

B.C.

47 Julius Caesar restores Cyprus to Egypt under Arsinoe and Ptolemy. Marcus Antonius presents Cyprus to Cleopatra.

46 After Actium Augustus Caesar withdraws cession of Cyprus.

A.D.

45 SS. Paul and Barnabas with John Mark land at Salamis: cross to Paphos and convert the Proconsul Sergius Paulus.

50 Visit of Emperor Titus.

115 Insurrection of the Jews under Artemion.

117–137 Construction under Hadrian of Salamis and abolition of human sacrifices thereat.

350 Emperor Constantinus III rebuilds Salamis.

BYZANTINE

395 Partition of Roman Empire: Cyprus under Constantinople.

478 Anthemios, Orthodox archbishop.

646 Death, in Cyprus, of Umm Haram, Nurse of Prophet Mohammed.

647 Moslem Invasion.

958 Basil the Armenian, Byzantine general, retakes Cyprus from the Arabs.

1105 Death, in Cyprus, of Eric, first King of Denmark.

1184–1191 Isaac Komnenos, great-nephew of Emperor Manuel I, and Imperial Governor of Tarsus, Emperor, Katapan, and Despot.

1191 May 6th, Richard I of England takes Amathus.

1191 Sunday, May 12th, feast of SS. Nereus, Achilles and Pancras, Martyrs. King Richard marries Berengaria of Navarre. Armenian Baron Leon or Levon, afterwards King of Armenia, present. Guy de Lusignan, jure uxoris King of Jerusalem, captures for King Richard the Castles of Kyrenia and St. Hilarion. Isaac emerges from Kantara and surrenders to Richard, who hands him to the Hospitallers, by whom he is confined in the Castle of Margat, near Tripoli (dies 1194). King Richard sells Cyprus to Knights Templar for 100,000 byzants (£300,000).

A.D.

1192 Insurrection against the Templars, who restore their purchase to Cœur de Lion.

LUSIGNAN

1192 King Richard transfers Cyprus thus retroceded to Guy de Lusignan, younger son of Hugh VIII, Count de la Marche.

1193 Guy de Lusignan takes possession of his Kingdom of Cyprus.

1194–1205 Amaury de Lusignan assumes title of King. Crown conferred by German Emperor Frederick.

1195 Order of St. Spiritus established.

1205–1218 Hugh I, marries Alice, daughter of Henry of Champagne, King of Jerusalem.

1218–1253 Henry I, marries (1) in 1229 Alice of Montferrat; (2) 1237, Stephania, sister of Hetum I, King of Armeno-Cilicia; (3) 1250, Piacenza, daughter of Bohemond V of Antioch.

1222 See of Kition abolished by Cardinal Pelagius.

1253–1267 Hugh II a minor. Queen Piacenza regent.

1267–1284 Hugh III of Antioch, marries Isabelle d'Ibelin.

1285–1324 Henry II, marries Constance of Aragon and Sicily.

1300 Famagusta springs up as a first-class fortress city and Mediterranean emporium.

1324–1358 Hugh IV, nephew of Henry II; marries (1) Mary d'Ibelin, (2) Alice d'Ibelin.

1358–1369 Peter I, marries (1) 1342, Echive de Montfort, (2) 1353, Eleanor of Aragon.

1362 Peter I goes to Europe to prepare Crusade and visits England.

1363 Peter I entertained in Vinters' Hall, London, by Sir Henry Picard (Lord Mayor in 1356) with Kings of England, France, Scotland, and Denmark, and the Black Prince.

1367 Peter I is recognized King of Armenia.

1369 Assassination of Peter I (January 17th), buried in St. Dominic, Nicosia.

1369–1382 Peter II, marries Valentine Visconti, 1372.

1369 Final revision of Godfroi de Bouillon's *Assizes for Kingdom of Cyprus* (pub. Venice, 1535).

A.D.

1372 Fracas between the Genoese and Venetians during the coronation ceremonies. Massacre of Genoese in Famagusta. The Genoese depart. Appeals to the Pope for mediation.

1373 Invasion of Cyprus by the Genoese and capture of Famagusta through treachery. The sack of Famagusta destroys its prosperity. Capture of Limassol and Paphos. Capture and pillage of Nicosia.

1382–1398 James I (a prisoner at Genoa), marries Heloise de Brunswick-Grubenhagen.

1396 After the death of Leon, James I is proclaimed King of Armenia in the Church of Saint Sophia in Nicosia. To the Royal Arms of Cyprus is added the lion of Armenia.

1398–1432 Janus, son of James I; marries (1) Louise Visconti, (2) Charlotte de Bourbon.

1424 Mamluk Sultan Barsbai's privateers plunder and burn Limassol.

1426 The Mamluk troops seize Limassol, conquer and capture King Janus at Battle of Chirokitia.

1427 Janus taken in chains to Cairo, ransomed by Venetian and other consuls for 300,000 dinars plus 20,000 tribute and sent back to Cyprus.

1432–1458 John II, son of Charlotte de Bourbon.

1440 John II, marries Medea, daughter of John James Palaeologus, Marquis of Montferrat. Her sudden death.

1441 John II, marries Helena Palaeologus, daughter of the ruler of the Morea. Revival of Orthodox influence. Unsuccessful attempt to recover Famagusta.

1456 Charlotte, daughter of John II, marries John, Prince of Portugal, who dies the same year.

1458–1460 Charlotte, Queen of Cyprus; marries Louis of Savoy (died 1482).

1459 Jacques de Lusignan, Archbishop of Cyprus and bastard of late King, afterward James II, rebels against Queen Charlotte, flies to Inal, Sultan of Egypt, who equips fleet to place James on throne of Cyprus. Queen Charlotte assisted by Savoy and Pope retains throne after second expedition prepared at time of Inal's death.

A.D.

1460–1473 James II.

1468 John Langstrother (an Englishman), Grand Commander of Colossi.

1472 Marriage of James II with Caterina Cornaro by proxy in Venice.

1473 Death of James II under suspicious circumstances. Burial at Famagusta.

Mocenigo, Venetian Admiral, arrives and promises support to Queen Caterina.

1473–1474 James III (posthumous heir). Dies under suspicious circumstances.

1474–1489 Caterina Cornaro Queen.

1481 Visit of Leonardo da Vinci.

1489 Caterina Cornaro cedes Cyprus to the Doge Agostino Barbarigo. Caterina hands over government to Francesco Barbarigo, First Lieutenant-Governor.

VENETIAN

1505 Christophoro Moro (hero of Shakespeare's *Othello*), Lieutenant-Governor of the Island.

1560 Filippo II. Mocenigo (last Latin primate of Cyprus) nominated to See of Nicosia.

1567 Present fortification of Nicosia started under Francesco Barbaro, Proveditore, from design of Sammichele.

1570 The Turks under Lala Mustapha, on September 15th, take Nicosia defended by Dandolo.

Sack of Limassol.

TURKISH

1571 Fall of Famagusta and death of Mark Antony Bragadino.

1572 Expulsion of the Latin Hierarchy and the restoration of the Orthodox prelates.

1630 Henry, Duke of Rohan, offers to buy the Island from the Sultan.

1692 One-third of the inhabitants destroyed by plague.

1720 Cyprus given as dowry to the daughter of the Sultan, who marries the Grand Vizier.

A.D.

1734–1759 Philotheos Orthodox archbishop, who goes to Constantinople and persuades the Turkish authorities to reduce the Capital Tax.

1745 Cyprus taken from the Grand Vizier and given to the Master of the Horse.

1748 Cyprus declared a Colony of the Ottoman Empire and given to the Grand Vizier again.

1799 Revolt of Janizaries in Cyprus. Put down by Sir Sydney Smith, who with General Junot, afterwards Duke of Abrantes, visits the Island while prisoner on H.M.S. *Tigre*.

1821 Trial and execution of Orthodox archbishop, bishops, and two hundred notables for suspected complicity in the revolution of Greece.

1866 General di Cesnola, American consul, discovers ancient treasure of Curium, afterwards sold to Metropolitan Museum, New York.

1868 Subh-i-Ezel, head of the Bab Sect, exiled to Famagusta.

1876 Earliest known bilingual Phoenician and Cypriote "Documents" found in Cyprus, by Duc de Luynes at Dali (Idalion).

BRITISH

1878 (June 4th) Ceded to Great Britain.

(July 12th) Admiral Lord John Hay takes possession.

(July 22nd) Sir Garnet Wolseley gazetted first High Commissioner.

1879 (June) Sir Robert Biddulph, High Commissioner.

1880–1883 Lieutenant (later Captain) H. H. Kitchener, R.E., conducts Survey of the Island.

1885 (August) Sir H. E. Bulwer appointed High Commissioner.

1892 (February) Sir Walter J. Sendall appointed High Commissioner.

1897 Sir W. Haynes Smith appointed High Commissioner.

1898–1899 Dukhobors settled in Cyprus for one year.

A.D.

1904 Sir C. A. King Harman High Commissioner.
Famagusta–Nicosia Railway begun.

1911 (October 12th) Sir Hamilton Gool-Adams High Commissioner.

1915 Cyprus offered to Greece as a condition of the latter's entry into the Great War on the side of Great Britain, and refused.
(January 8th) Sir J. E. Clauson High Commissioner.

1920 (July) Sir Malcolm Stevenson High Commissioner.

1925. Cyprus a Crown Colony.
Title of High Commissioner abolished. Sir Malcolm Stevenson becomes Governor (May 1st).

1926 (December) Sir Ronald Storrs Governor.

1927 Cyprus relieved of "Tribute" (Debt Charge).

1931 Riots. Government House burnt.

1932 Sir Edward Stubbs Governor.

1933 Sir Richmond Palmer Governor.

INDEX

Churches, chapels, and monasteries are indexed under their titles with the name of the place added in an alphabetical sequence : but those of the chief towns will be found indexed under the name of the town.

H

N

R

S

T

www.ingramcontent.com/pod-product-compliance
Lightning Source LLC
LaVergne TN
LVHW050910080826
845145LV00001B/44

* 9 7 8 0 9 5 4 4 5 2 3 9 1 *